Alternative Religions

Edited by:

Nicole Suzanne Ruskell

Academic Publications
Santa Barbara, California

Academic Publications
2022 Cliff Drive, Ste. 153
Santa Barbara, California 93107
USA

ISBN: 0-9639501-6-9

Printed in the United States of America
First Edition

Contents

Introduction

Although new religions have often been the topic of journalistic stories, it is rare that the body of scholars who study them make the news. It was thus somewhat of a surprise when the annual meeting of CESNUR, the premier international association of new religion scholars, was the subject of a feature article—"Oh, Gods!" by Toby Lester—in the February 2002 issue of *The Atlantic Monthly*. In his piece the author observed, among other things, that "The study of new religious movements—NRMs for short—has become a growth industry." In a similar vein, he also noted that "The NRM field is only a few decades old, but already it has made its mark." (p. 38)

The appearance of an article like "Oh, Gods!" is an indicator that the study of NRMs has achieved the status of a recognized academic specialty. This development is rather surprising when one considers that "in 1970 one could count the number of active researchers on new religions on one's hands" (Melton 2004). What accounts for the meteoric growth of this field of study? The short answer is that it arose in response to the cult controversy of the early 1970s, and continued to grow in the wake of a series of headline-grabbing tragedies involving religious groups like the People's Temple and Heavens Gate. The long answer is somewhat more complicated.

As a field of scholarly endeavor, NRM studies had actually emerged several decades earlier in Japan in the wake of the explosion of religious innovation following the second world war. Even the name "new religions" is a direct translation of the expression *shin shukyo* that Japanese sociologists coined to refer to this phenomenon. Although the generation of new religious groups has been an ongoing process in Western countries (not to mention in the world as a whole) for millennia, the study of such groups and movements was the province of pre-existing academic specializations in the West until the Seventies. Thus, to cite a few examples, the Pentecostal movement was studied as part of church history and phenomena like cargo cults were researched by anthropologists.

However, when a wave of non-traditional religiosity exploded out of the declining counterculture in the late 1960s and early 1970s, academics perceived it (correctly or incorrectly) as representing a different phenomenon from prior cycles of religious innovation. Not only did most of these new religions represent radical theological departures from the traditionally-dominant Christian tradition, but—in contrast to movements like Pentecostalism—they also tended to recruit their adherents from the offspring of the middle class. Such characteristics caused these emergent religions to be regarded as categorical departures from the past, and they initially attracted scholars from a wide variety of disciplines. It was at this juncture that NRMs began to develop as a distinct field of scholarship in Western countries. And it should be noted that this development took place shortly *before* the cult controversy had begun to heat up. Two academic anthologies representative of this era are Glock and Bellah's *The New Religious Consciousness* (1976), and Needleman and Baker's *Understanding the New Religions* (1978). As reflected in many of the articles in these collections, the overall focus at the time was to attempt to assess the broader social significance of the newest wave of NRMs.

This academic landscape changed over the course of the Seventies. By the latter part of the decade, it had become clear that new religions were *not* indicative of a broader social transformation—or at least not the kind of transformation observers had anticipated. Also during the

Seventies, issues raised by the cult controversy gradually came to dominate the field. Because social conflict is a bread-and-butter issue for sociology, more and more sociologists were drawn to the study of new religions. By the time of the Jonestown tragedy in 1978, NRMs was a recognized specialization within the sociology of religion.

It took much longer for new religions to achieve recognition as a legitimate specialization from the religious studies academy. This was partially the result of the expansion of religious studies and its own quest for legitimacy within a mostly-secular university system. During the early 1970's—at precisely the same time period when new religions were becoming a public issue—religious studies was busy establishing itself as an academic discipline. As members of a discipline sometimes perceived as marginal, most religion scholars were reluctant to further marginalize themselves by giving serious attention to what at the time seemed a transitory social phenomenon, and as a consequence left the study of new religions to sociologists. Consequently, it was not until a series of major tragedies that took place in the 1990s—specifically, the Branch Davidian debacle, the Solar Temple suicide/murders, the AUM Shinrikyo gas attack and the Heavens Gate suicides—that the field of NRMs was truly embraced by the religious studies establishment.

The Cult Controversy

Although, as has already been indicated, the cult controversy was not responsible for actually initiating the new religions field, the development of this area of study almost immediately became tied to the controversy. From the very beginning, most mainstream academic researchers rejected the popular stereotype of NRMs deceptively recruiting and "brainwashing" their members. Furthermore, almost all of the studies supporting the notion of "cultic mind control" were so obviously biased that mainstream social scientific journals routinely refused to publish them. Beginning in the mid-seventies, mainstream scholars steadily churned out studies directly relevant to this controversy. At present, a collection of academic books devoted to this controversy plus books on new religions containing at least one full chapter addressing the controversy would easily fill several standard library bookcases. This does not include the significant number of relevant articles published in academic journals.

The operative question new religion specialists have asked about mind control is: How does one distinguish cultic brainwashing from other forms of social influence—forms of social influence like advertising, military training, or even the normal socialization routines of public schools? Particularly in the 1970s, anti-cultists were supporting the notion that cult members were trapped in a kind of quasi-hypnotic trance, while others asserted that the ability of cult members to process certain kinds of information had "snapped." (Conway & Siegelman 1979) The problem with these and similar theories was that if cultic influences actually overrode the brain's ability to logically process information, then individuals suffering from cultic influences should perform poorly on I.Q. tests or, at the very least, should manifest pathological symptoms when they took standardized tests of mental health—and when tested, they did not. In point of fact, such empirical studies often indicated that members of NRMs were actually smarter and healthier than the average member of mainstream society. (e.g., Sowards, Walser & Hoyle 1994)

Other kinds of studies also failed to support the view that new religions relied upon non-ordinary forms of social influence to gain and retain members. For example, if NRMs possessed powerful techniques of mind control that effectively overrode a potential convert's free will, then everyone—or at least a large percentage—of attendees at recruiting seminars should be unable to avoid conversion. However, in her important study *The Making of a Moonie* (1984), Eileen Barker found that less than ten percent of the people who visited centers run by the Unification Church—an organization many regard as the evil cult *par excellence*—eventually attended recruitment seminars. Of those who attended such seminars, less than ten percent joined the Church (a net recruitment rate of under one percent). Furthermore, of those who joined, more than half dropped out within the first year of their membership. In another important study, *Radical Departures: Desperate Detours to Growing Up* (1984), psychiatrist Saul Levine found that, out of a sample of over 800 people who had joined controversial religious groups, more than 90% dropped out within two years of membership—not the kind of statistics one would anticipate from groups wielding powerful techniques of mind control.

In the face of these and other empirical studies, researchers asked the further questions of, Given the lack of empirical support, where does the brainwashing notion come from? And, What is the more fundamental conflict that the cult stereotype obfuscates? The general conclusion of sociologists—as analyzed, for example, in David Bromley and Anson Shupe's *Strange Gods: The Great American Cult Scare* (1981)—was that the principal source of the controversy was a parent-child conflict in which parents failed to understand the religious choices of their adult children, and attempted to reassert parental control by marshaling the forces of public opinion against the religious bodies to which their offspring had converted.

This core conflict was then exacerbated by irresponsible mass media that profited by printing and broadcasting exciting stories about weird cults that trapped their members and kept them in psychological bondage with exotic techniques of mind control. Also, once an industry was established that generated profits by "rescuing" entrapped cult members (via the practice of "deprogramming"), special interest groups emerged that had vested interests in promoting the most negative stereotypes of alternative religions. These special interest groups added further fuel to the parent-child conflict by scaring parents with lurid stories of what would happen to their adult child if they failed to have her or him deprogrammed. In this manner, many otherwise reasonable and well-meaning people were recruited into the controversy.

This, essentially, is the picture of the cult controversy that academic researchers pieced together over the last three decades. Because of its vested interest in maintaining the conflict, the anti-cult movement was unresponsive to critical studies and proceeded with business as usual, as if these studies were non-existent. Rather than responding directly to mainstream scholarship, a handful of anti-cultists with academic credentials instead conducted research in their own terms, creating alternative publications that featured pseudo-scientific studies supporting the cult stereotype.

One of the consequences of this situation was that researchers found themselves forced to work in a highly-politicized atmosphere. Articles on controversial religious groups published in specialized academic journals could directly impact people's lives, particularly when cited in legal briefs and judicial decisions. Thus, in contrast to academics who studied things like the mating habits of insects or the spectrum of light generated by distant galaxies, NRM specialists regularly found themselves the subjects of scrutiny and criticism.

Because mainstream New Religion scholars have generally been critical of the cult stereotype (particularly the notion of cult mind control), they have, in turn, been criticized by those interested in perpetuating this stereotype. One counter strategy commonly utilized by such interest groups is to refer to academicians whose research tends to undermine anti-cult ideology as "cult apologists," implying that they are in a conspiracy with–perhaps even covertly accepting money from–malevolent religious groups. The cult apologist accusation is a handy ideological tool because, in the hands of most anti-cultists, it is wielded as a tautology, immune to empirical disconfirmation. In other words, if a cult apologist is defined (usually implicitly) as any researcher producing scholarship critical of the cult stereotype, then anyone whose scholarship is critical of the cult stereotype is *ipso facto* a cult apologist. This strategy allows anti-cultists to reject any scholarship with which they disagree *a priori*, saving them from the awkward necessity of taking it seriously.

Anti-cultists adhering to this rhetorical strategy sometimes make it appear that sinister pseudo-religious organizations regularly seek out scholars to legitimate their group and to attack their critics. One of the more absurd examples of this strategy can be found in the introduction to Michael Newton's *Raising Hell* (1993). Newton takes "liberal" academics to task who criticize the notion of occult crime—referring to them as "cult apologists" (p. 2) as if they were mercenaries on the payroll of some grand underground satanic conspiracy, or, no less implausibly, as if their souls had been purchased by the Prince of Darkness himself.

In point of fact, only a few groups like the Unification Church—which for many years courted academicians, presumably because of its Confucian-derived understanding of the importance of scholars in society—have believed that academicians wielded this kind of power. The leaders of most other new religions have been far less naive about the social influence of scholars. Perhaps the only area where academic researchers have played a significant role in the cult controversy is in the debunking of mind control notions and other aspects of the cult stereotype, making this the one area where academic specialists have entered the fray in support of NRMs. The fact that some of the most prominent scholars in the field have testified against the brainwashing thesis in relevant legislative hearings and legal cases has evoked the ire of anti-cultists, and is the principal evidence for their contention that such academicians are "apologists."

Boundary and Disciplinary Issues

One question I would like to address is why certain categories of new religions are studied and certain others not. Like religious studies more generally, NRM studies is, as Melton points out, "defined by its subject matter rather than methodology" (Melton 2004). As a field significantly shaped by the cult conflict, the core of NRM studies is constituted by analyses of controversial new religions and analyses of the controversy itself. If everything related to these two topics was subtracted from the corpus of new religions scholarship, relatively little would be left. Like the emergent popularity of Islamic studies since the 9-11 attacks, NRM studies rose to prominence as a direct consequence of the public perception of certain religions as potential social threats. Thus, despite the regular expressions of dismay one sometimes overhears at academic conferences (e.g., as recorded by Lester, "I'm so damn sick of the cult–anti-cult debate, I could just puke!" [p. 41]), it is unlikely that this situation will change in the immediate future.

Because of this focus, it is appropriate to ask what this field of study might look like if not for the cult controversy. Certainly one of the major differences would be that existing scholarship would not be clustered around a couple dozen small groups. There have been more than a few major studies of groups such as the Unification Church that have a relatively small presence in Western countries. In contrast, there have been no monographs written about much larger—but less controversial—new religions like Eckankar. A more comprehensive approach that examined the many NRMs not locked in social conflict would likely provide a much different picture of the nature of these movements. Perhaps certain characteristics shared by the majority of new religions might have been warped or even missed as a consequence of focusing on the controversial groups.

Another issue is that NRM studies is in many ways a residual category. Although the designation "new religions" implies that all kinds of emergent religions are part of this field, in practice NRM scholars have tended to avoid studying movements perceived as the "turf" of other scholarly specialities. I have already mentioned that certain Christian new religious movements like Pentecostalism have for the most part been left to church historians, and that third world NRMs like cargo cults have been left to anthropologists. Similarly, although new religions researchers have occasionally examined Black NRMs and Native American NRMs, the tendency has been to leave the study of these movements to scholars of Black religions and scholars of Native American religions. And, finally, certain elite movements like the feminist spirituality movement have, with few exceptions, been left to other specialties, such as scholars of women's religion. Again, the problem with leaving out certain classes of new religions is that it potentially misses or obscures some of the more general traits of NRMs.

One final factor that has shaped the new religions field is that, because of the historical circumstances noted earlier, sociologists of religion were largely free to lay the foundations for the field of contemporary new religions. Sociology, however, views new religions as arising out of social forces; as a discipline, sociology does not consider religious experience as independent motivating factors for the emergence of new religious forms. In recent years, as more and more religious studies academics have become involved in the study of new religions, the tendency has been to build upon these foundations uncritically. Little thought has been given to considering what this phenomenon might look like when viewed in terms of some of the other theoretical perspectives utilized in religious studies—such as perspectives that take religious experiences seriously as powerful, independent motivating factors. It should also be recalled that prior generations of scholars were seemingly *obsessed* with the issue of the beginnings of religion. This interest may have been misplaced, but it seems that the ruminations of our academic ancestors should be explored for potential insights into the process of the generation of new religious forms. On the other hand, perhaps studies of current new religions could throw light on such classic questions.

References:

American Psychiatric Association. *Diagnostic and Statistical Manual of Mental Disorders*. Washington, DC, 4th ed. 1994.

Barker, Eileen. *The Making of a Moonie: Choice or Brainwashing?* Oxford: Blackwell 1984.

Bromley, David G., and Anson D. Shupe. *Strange Gods: The Great American Cult Scare.* Boston: Beacon, 1981.

Conway, Flo, and Jim Siegelman. *Snapping: America's Epidemic of Sudden Personality Change.* New York: Lippencott, 1979.

Glock, Charles Y., and Robert N. Bellah, eds. *The New Religious Consciousness.* Berkeley: University of California Press,1976

Lester, Toby. "Oh, Gods!" *The Atlantic Monthly* 289:2. February 2002.

Levine, Saul. *Radical Departures: Desperate Detours to Growing Up.* New York: Harcourt Brace, Javanovitch, 1984.

Melton, J. Gordon. "An Introduction to New Religions." In James R. Lewis, ed. *The Oxford Handbook of New Religious Movements.* New York: Oxford University Press, 2004.

Needleman, Jacob, and George Baker. *Understanding the New Religions.* New York: Seabury,1978.

Newton, Michael. *Raising Hell: An Encyclopedia of Devil Worship and Satanic Crime.* New York: Avon Books, 1993.

Sowards, Bruce A., Michael J. Walser and Rick H. Hoyle. "Personality and Intelligence Measurement of the Church Universal and Triumphant." In James R. Lewis and J. Gordon Melton, eds. *Church Universal and Triumphant in Scholarly Perspective.* Special Issue of *Syzygy: Journal of Alternative Religion and Culture.* 1994.

Wach, Joachim. *The Comparative Study of Religions.* New York: Columbia University Press, 1958.

New Religion Adherents:
An Overview of Anglophone Census & Survey Data

General estimates of the extent of the New Religions phenomenon vary considerably. The two basic quantitative questions in this area are: How many groups? And, How many people? These questions are not as simple as they might at first appear. A more fundamental question involves classification: Where does one draw the line between alternative and non-alternative religions? What one finds when one actually tries to determine where to draw such a line is that the difference between "mainstream" and "alternative" is a matter of degree rather than a sharply-defined distinction.

The indeterminacy of this dividing line allows anticultists like the late Margaret Singer to assert, without fear of direct contradiction, that as many as twenty million people have been involved in three to five thousand cults in the United States (Singer and Lalich 1995). In contrast, Gordon Melton estimates five to six hundred alternative religions in the United States (Melton 1992). Similarly, Peter Clarke estimates four to five hundred new religions in the United Kingdom (Clarke 1984). The situation is rather different in Japan, where New Religions have been thriving since the end of WWII. Japanese sociologists estimate anywhere from eight hundred to several thousand (Arweck 2000) such groups. And finally, Eileen Barker puts forward a figure of two thousand or more New Religions in the West, and a figure in the lower tens of thousands worldwide (Barker 1999).

An important though neglected source of information bearing on the question of numbers of adherents to alternative religions is national census data. In 2001, the censuses of four English-speaking countries–New Zealand, Australia, Canada and the United Kingdom–collected information on religious membership that included select New Religions. There was also an important religion survey conducted in the United States in the same year, the American Religious Identification Survey (ARIS).

Though a few scholars of New Religions have referred to one or more of these censuses, no one has attempted a general survey. Following an examination of one estimate of world religious adherents, the current article examines census data for the light such data sheds on participation rates in alternative religions. In the final section of the paper, relevant data from the ARIS survey will also be examined.

World Membership in Alternative Religions

An example of how the ambiguity between what is and what is not a New Religion can produce incongruous results can be found in David Barrett and Todd Johnson's "A Statistical Approach to the World's Religious Adherents" (2002). In terms of worldwide membership, these statistics appear to be the best figures available.

Barrett and Johnson divide the world's religions into 19 categories, with three subcategories for Christianity: Christian (Catholic, Protestant, Independent), Muslim, Baha'i, Hindu, Sikh, Jain, Buddhist, Zoroastrian, Jewish, Confucian, Taoist, Chinese Folk Religion, Shinto, Spiritist, Ethnoreligionist, Atheist, Nonreligious, Neoreligionist, and Other. They describe the Neoreligionist (New Religionist) as "twentieth-century new religions, new religious movements, radical new crisis religions, and non-Christian syncretistic mass religions, all founded since 1800 and most since 1945, mostly Asian in origin and membership but increasingly with worldwide followings." The Other category is described as "a handful of smaller religions, quasi-religions, pseudo religions, parareligions, religious or mystic systems, religious and semireligious brotherhoods of numerous varieties." Though I sharply question the designation "pseudo religion," it otherwise appears that most of the religions classified as Other are also New Religions. Finally, they neglect to define the Spiritism category. However, because, according to their statistics, 12,039,000 of the world's 12,334,000 Spiritists are located in Latin America and the Caribbean, it is clear that this category is meant primarily to encompass Afro-Caribbean and Afro-Brazilian New Religions like Santeria and Umbanda.

Out of a total world population of 6,055,049,000 people, Barrett and Johnson find that 102,356,000 are members of New Religions, 12,334,000 are Spiritists and 1,067,000 are in the Other category, meaning about 1.9% of the world population belong to alternative religions. This figure does not sound unreasonable, until one discovers that almost all of the people in New Religions – 100,639,000 members – are Asian. In order to analyze and critique their statistics, it will be useful to lay out all of Barrett and Johnson's relevant figures for the year 2,000, continent by continent:

Table 1

Numbers of Members in New Religions Worldwide

	New Religions	Spiritism	Other	Total Population
Africa	28,400	2,500	65,700	784,445,000
Asia	100,639,000	1,900	62,100	3,682,550,000
Europe	158,000	133,000	236,000	728,887,000
Latin America	622,000	12,039,000	98,000	519,138,000
North America	845,000	151,000	597,000	309,631,000
Australia (& Oceania)	66,500	7,000	9,400	30,393,000

Their figure for Asian New Religions immediately strikes one as suspect. Even after being adjusted for population difference, the data still seems to indicate over ten times as many members of New Religions in Asia as in North America. This is probably the result of using different criteria for these two areas of the world. Barrett and Johnson almost certainly classified certain large groups like Soka Gakkai (Soka Gakkai has nine million members) as New Religions rather than as Buddhists. In contrast, they almost certainly classified the many new Protestant sects that are constantly coming into being in the United States as Christian rather than as New Religions.

Given the large number of New Religions in sub-Sahara Africa, their low figure for African New Religions is clearly off-base. Because African New Religions tend to draw heavily on traditional Ethnoreligions, Christianity, or both, Barrett and Johnson must have classified most of these religious groups as either Ethnoreligious or Christian.

The European figure also seems quite low. Because of the concern over alternative religions in Europe since the first Solar Temple tragedy in 1994, there have been a number of official government surveys, though results have been less satisfactory than one might have hoped. For example, in 1998 the German Parliament's Enquete Commission reported the results of a national survey which indicated that eight to nine million people considered themselves members of non-traditional religious groups. In contrast, the Swedish Government Report of 1998 put forward a national figure of 50,000-60,000 (about 0.15% of the population), exclusive of New Age groups – a considerably lower proportion than the German figure.

As for North America, using only the New Religions figure gives us slightly less than 0.3%. Alternately, adding all of the data from the New Religions, Spiritism and Other categories results in slightly more than 0.5%. As it turns out, the 0.3% - 0.5% range receives support from the national census statistics of other English-speaking countries.

New Zealand National Census Data

A number of countries have begun to include religious affiliation as part of their national censuses. One of the most useful is the 2001 New Zealand census because of the large number of distinct groups enumerated (see Table 2).

The total of 17,436 members represents 0.46% of the 3,737,277 people who responded to the 2001 census, which compares favorably with the 0.3% to 0.5% participation rate for North America derived from the Barrett and Johnson data. This is being cautious. One could also make a reasonable argument for including Vineyard Christian Fellowship (sometimes called a "cult," with 774 members in the census), some of the 1,107 people who self-identified as Taoist, and some of the 4,641 people who the census classified as simply Other Religion. This would bring the participation rate up to 0.5%. However, the New Zealand census allowed people to report more than one affiliation, and as a consequence the census collected 3,841,932 responses from a total of 3,737,277 people, or 104,655 extra responses. Though not all of these extra responses could have been supplied by individuals self-identifying as members of New Religions, it is reasonable to infer that there were enough double or even triple responses by participants in alternative religions to undermine the solidness of the 0.46% figure. So to be cautious, one might want to reduce this percentage to 0.4% or even 0.3%.

There is, however, at least one more consideration to take into account. Though almost all major alternative religions have an outpost in New Zealand, few were explicitly included on the census. In particular, there are numerous Buddhist groups that appeal primarily if not exclusively to Westerners. If one goes to the New Zealand Buddhist Directory (http://www.buddhanet.net/nzealand.htm), one will find groups like Soka Gakkai, Shambhala Center plus a wide variety of Vipassana meditation and Tibetan Buddhist organizations. These groups are usually classified in the alternative religions category in general survey books on New Religions (e.g., Chryssides 1999; Lewis 2001; Ellwood and Partin 1998). Participants in these groups were not distinguished from the other Buddhists constituting the 41,469 Buddhists reported in the 2001 census.

One way of getting a handle on the number of people involved in Western-oriented Buddhist groups (groups usually considered New Religions in the West, despite their lineage) is the ethnic backgrounds of participants. Because the website for the 2001 New Zealand census includes a table correlating ethnicity and religion, this information is readily available. The Ethnic Group and Sex by Religious Affiliation table records that 10,890 New Zealand Buddhists are of European heritage. Assuming that some of these European Buddhists are converts because of marriage and other factors, it is reasonable to infer that at least half – or 5,445 – are involved in Western-oriented Buddhist groups.

Table 2

Alternative Religion Statistics from the 2001 New Zealand Census

Religion	Number of Members
Zen Buddhism*	126
Sukyo Mahikari	111
Tenrikyo	12
Yoga	414
Hare Krishna	363
Animism**	213
Pantheism**	342
Nature and Earth-based Religions	2,961
Wiccan	2,196
Druidism	150
Satanism	891
Other New Age Religion	1,485
Rastafarianism	1,296
Sufi***	195
Scientology	282
Spiritualism	5,853
Liberal Catholic Church	135
Unification Church	153
Christian Science	258
Total	17,436

* Like the Hare Krishna movement, Zen Buddhism is considered a New Religion when Westerners become involved.

** Both the New Zealand and the Australian Census identify Animism and Pantheism as Neo-Pagan religions for statistical purposes (e.g., in Table 3, the 2001 figure for the Nature and Earth Based category represents the sum of the Animism, Pantheism, Nature and Earth-based Religions, Wiccan and Druidism figures in Table 2). The religions of indigenous peoples were represented by other categories.

*** Few contemporary Muslims would self-identify as Sufis, indicating that all or most of the members of the Sufi category are members of one of several Sufi groups appealing primarily to Westerners. Like Western Zen Buddhism, Western Sufi groups are considered New Religions.

Source: Statistics New Zealand

There are also Swedenborgian and Unity School of Christianity churches in New Zealand, the members of which were lumped in with the 192,165 generic Christians recorded in the census. Unfortunately, estimating participation in alternative Christian groups cannot be addressed via ethnicity. Additionally, there are followers of Satya Sai Baba, Maharaji, and a wide variety of other South Asian groups who may have been lumped in with the 38,769 Hindus noted in the census. The census reported 4,329 Ethnic Europeans who self-identified as Hindus. Using the same cautious percentage (50%) we applied to European Buddhists, this would mean 2,114 people involved in Western-oriented Hindu groups. Finally, one wonders what happened to members of other groups like the Raelians, Eckankar, Falun Gong, and Theosophy, all of which have a presence in New Zealand. When all of these organizations are considered, raising the estimated participation rate to 0.5% is quite legitimate.

New Zealand also collected less detailed information about religious membership in censuses prior to 2001. This data reflects a interesting pattern of growth:

Table 3

Growth in Alternative Religions from 1999 to 2001 in New Zealand

	1991	1996	2001
Nature and Earth Based Religions	318	1,722	5,862
Spiritualist	3,333	5,100	5,853
New Age Religions	696	1,839	3,210
Satanism	645	909	894
Scientology	207	219	282
Totals	5,196	9,786	16,062

Source: Statistics New Zealand

As can be seen, the overall pattern reflects a tripling of total numbers in a decade. The fastest growing segment is Paganism ("Nature and Earth Based Religions"). Only Satanism fell off between 1996 and 2001. The decline of the latter may be due, in part, to the uninspired leadership that assumed control of the Church of Satan following the death of Anton LaVey in 1997 (in this regard, refer to Lewis 2002).

Australia National Census Data

The Australian census contains information similar to the New Zealand census. One more category for alternative religious groups is provided, and all of the data from 2001 is arranged into a straightforward comparison with the 1996 census:

Table 4

New Religion Statistics from the 1996-2001 Australian Census

Religion	1996 Members	2001 Members
Animism	727	763
Caodaism	964	819
Christian Science	1,494	1666
Druidism	554	697
Eckankar	829	747
Gnostic Christian	559	723
Liberal Catholic Church	596	498
Nature Religions*	1,734	2225
New Churches (Swedenborgian)	504	427
Paganism	4,353	10,632
Pantheism	835	1085
Rastafarianism	1,023	1066
Religious Science	634	417
Satanism	2,091	1798
Scientology	1,488	2032
Spiritualism	8,140	9279
Sukyo Mahikari	668	513
Tenrikyo	46	60
Theosophy	1,423	1627
Wiccan/Witchcraft	1,849	8755
Total	30,501	45,829

* I infer that "Nature Religions" refers to Neopaganism.

The rise from 30,501 members to 45,829 members represents slightly more than a 50% increase in five years. (Religions in the Neopagan categories experienced the most rapid rate of growth–an average 250% increase.) With respect to number of census respondents in 1996 (17,750,000) and 2001(18.767,000) this represents a rise from 0.17% to 0.24%. This rate of participation is considerably less than New Zealand. Unlike New Zealand, the Australian census seems not to have allowed people to respond to more than one item. Like New Zealand, Australia has an abundance of alternative religion groups that "slipped through the cracks" of the above categories because they were recorded as generic Christians, Buddhists, and Hindus. Unfortunately, an Australian census table correlating religious membership with ethnicity is unavailable without paying a fee, so I was unable to obtain the same kind of figures for Western participation in Asian Religions as I did for New Zealand. We can say that, because of the many New Religions missed by the census, a 0.3% - 0.4% participation rate for 2001 would be a reasonable but still conservative estimate.

One problem with this estimate is that it contrasts so significantly from the corresponding 0.5% estimate for New Zealand. Is there really such a marked difference in participation rates between these two sister countries? In terms of numbers of people responding to their respective national censuses, there were five times as many Australians as New Zealanders in 2001. Of the comparable religions in the two censuses, only Christian Science had more than five times as many members in Australia than in New Zealand. Australian Mahikari and Tenrikyo members were almost five times as numerous as corresponding New Zealand members. But all of the other groups fell well below the one-to-five relationship. In the case of Rastafarianism, there were actually more total members in New Zealand than in Australia. So it seems there is a genuine difference in participation rates between these two countries.

It could be counter-argued that there are probably more alternative religions in Australia than in New Zealand and thus more Australian participants who missed the census net. And it could be further argued that, being a larger country, there are a greater number of religious "species" in Australia that draw away some of the people who would have joined other groups, thus explaining why the one-to-five ratio does not hold for most of the religions found in both censuses. However, even if a greater variety in religious fauna between the two countries is a factor to consider, it seems highly unlikely that it would be enough to account for the comparatively large difference between the two participation rates.

If we restate the data from "down under" as 0.3% - 0.5%, then we have a statistic comparable to the Barrett and Johnson data for North America. Adding together their New Religions, Spiritism, and Other data, Barrett and Johnson's participation rate for Australia and New Zealand works out to 0.34%, which is in the same range.

United Kingdom National Census Data

The United Kingdom also conducted a census in 2001. The census recorded a reasonably good spread of different groups. Regretfully, religious participation was not measured in previous censuses. The figures for the England and Wales part of the census are as follows:

Table 5

New Religion Statistics for England and Wales from the 2001 British Census*

Group	Members
Spiritualist	32404
Pagan	30569
Wicca	7227
Rastafarian	4692
Scientology	1781
Druidism	1657
Pantheism	1603
Satanism	1525
Christian Spiritualist Church	1461
New Age	906
Hare Krishna	640
Christian Scientist	578
Celtic Pagan	508
Eckankar	426
Animism	401
Brahma Kumari	331
Heathen**	278
Raja Yoga	261
Unification Church	252
Vodun	123
Occult	99
Asatru	93
Sant Mat	53
Divine Light mission	21
Santeria	21
Total	87,189

* Source: Census 2001. Crown Copyright 2004. Crown copyright material is reproduced with the permission of the controller of HMSO.

** This is a term of self-reference used by certain Neopagans.

With respect to a population of 52,041,916, a total of 87,189 members represents a participation rate of less than 0.17%. The larger number of categories means that somewhat fewer respondents were absorbed into the statistics for their parent traditions, though these categories are still far from comprehensive. Although a handful of Hindu-related groups are included, Buddhist New Religions are noticeably absent. New Thought groups like Unity and Religious Science are also not represented as separate categories, as well as many other groups that have a presence in Great Britain.

An important factor influencing the outcome of the religion aspect of the census was that someone decided it would be a fine bit of humor to encourage people to write "Jedi Knight" in the religion category. As a consequence, 390,127 people in England and Wales responded that they belonged to the Jedi Knight religion. Although this is quite amusing, I would guess that proportionally more of these self-designated Jedis were involved in some form of alternative spirituality than the general population, though how much more is difficult to determine. Minus the Jedi factor, I estimate that 0.17% would rise to at least 0.2%.

Like the New Zealand census, the UK census provides information on ethnicity and religion. In England and Wales, 0.12% of the 47,520,866 White population is Buddhist and .02% Hindu. Taking these percentages and then dropping the resulting figures by 50% gives 28,512 Western Buddhists and 4,752 Western Hindus. There are also Christian New Religions that have slipped through the census categories. When the minus-the-Jedi consideration is combined with the estimate for the various New Religions found in the Buddhist and Hindu folds, plus a conservative guess for the number of people in Christian New Religions, a cautious estimate would place the participation rate in the UK in the 0.25% - 0.3% range.

Canada National Census Data

Although the religion categories for the 2001 Canadian Census are even less satisfactory than the categories used in the Australian, New Zealand, and British Censuses, they are nonetheless useful for comparative purposes. In a country with a population of 28,000,000, the census recorded 38,000 members of alternative religions, or a participation rate of less than 0.14%.

Similar to the New Zealand and Australian censuses, Buddhist and Hindu groups regarded as New Religions were not separated for statistical purposes. And unlike New Zealand and Australia, even non-traditional Christian groups like Christian Science were apparently collapsed into Christianity. The addition of the classifications "Gnostic" and "New Age" appear to have been for the purpose of including alternative religious groups that did not fall handily into other categories. The New Age as a more general spiritual influence escapes straightforward efforts at measurement, as will be discussed below. I think it would be quite reasonable to estimate much higher participation rates for Canada than indicated by these truncated census figures, more in the 0.25% - 0.3% range at least.

Table 6

New Religion Statistics from the 2001 Canadian Census

Religion	Number of Members
Gnostic	1,165
New Age	1,525
Paganism	21,085
Rastafarian	1,135
Satanism	850
Scientology	1,525
Spiritualist	3,295
Swedenborg	1,015
Unity/New Thought	4,000
Vineyard Christian Fellowship	2,600
Total	38,215

Adapted from: Statistics Canada's Internet Site, http://www12.statcan.ca/english/census01/products/highlight/religion. Extracted April 23, 2004.

Religion Survey Data for the United States

Unfortunately, the U.S. census does not collect religion membership data. However, in 1990, the Graduate Center of the City University of New York conducted a National Survey of Religious Identification (NSRI) via randomly dialed phone numbers (113,723 people were surveyed). Eleven years later, in 2001, the same center carried out the American Religious Identification Survey (ARIS) in the same manner (over 50,000 people responded), though callers probed for more information than the earlier NSRI. Categories were developed post-facto. The results were quite interesting (refer to Table 7).

Although it would have been much more useful had the researchers broken down their data into more subcategories, their results are nevertheless striking. In a period of eleven years, the overall participation rate in alternative religions increased sevenfold. Once again, however, we are plagued by the collapsing of important New Religions into their parent traditions. Had the various Christian alternative religions been separately categorized, the results would likely have been much different.

For the Buddhist and Hindu traditions, we can obtain a rough estimate of participation in New Religions by separating ethnic Buddhists and Hindus from Western converts. Although the NSRI did not record ethnicity, the ARIS did. Out of an estimated 766,000 Hindus, 2% were White. Out of an estimated 1,082,000 Buddhists, 28.5% were White. Taking these percentages and then halving the resulting figures gives 7,660 Euro-American Hindus and 154,185 Euro-American Buddhists. Adding these numbers to the 583,000 figure and dividing the sum by a U.S. population estimate of 207,980,000 gives a participation rate of 0.35%.

Table 7

New Religion Data from NSRI and ARIS

	1990	2001
Scientologist	45,000*	55,000
New Age	20,000	68,000
Eckankar	18,000	26,000
Rastafarian	14,000	11,000
Wicca	8,000	134,000
Druid**		33,000
Santeria**		22,000
Pagan**		140,000
Spiritualist**		116,000
Totals	79,000	583,000

*Numbers have been rounded off to the nearest 1,000. Unlike a census, which attempts to reach the entire population, these figures represent statistical extrapolations.

**The final four categories did not emerge as significant in the 1990 NSRI survey.

Source: B. A. Kosmin and A. Keysar, *Religion in the Marketplace* (Ithaca, NY: Paramount Books, 2004). Adapted table used with permission.

Had all alternative religions—including the Christian, Buddhist and Hindu groups missed by the two surveys—been considered together, the sevenfold growth rate would likely have been less spectacular. Like the Australian and New Zealand census data, the NSRI-ARIS data has been sharply affected by the meteoric growth of Neopaganism (here represented by the Wicca-Druid-Pagan figures) in recent years. Also, if Christian alternative religions had been distinguished so that they could have been included in the final total, the 0.35% participation rate derived from the ARIS data would have been higher. How high this rate would rise if we had more complete data again depends on where one decides to draw the line between what is and what is not an "alternative" religion. If we take a conservative approach, a 0.5% participation rate represents a reasonable estimate. Of course, if we adopted looser criteria for what constitutes a New Religion, much higher estimates would be possible.

Concluding Remarks

Generalizing from the data presented in the prior sections brings us to the conclusion that participation in alternative religions is quite low. In the Anglophone world, the participation rate is 0.3% - 0.5%. And though certain countries might have a lower rate than 0.3%, I would speculate that the participation rate in Western Europe as a whole probably falls into the same range.

The statistical picture of New Religions reflected in this data is that of a small-scale phenomenon involving a fraction of a percent of the population. For religious groups that have formal memberships, this is probably an accurate portrait.

However, informal spiritual trends such as the strand of spirituality referred to as "New Age" often cross taken-for-granted boundaries between religions. For example, in the late nineties, George Gallup and Michael Lindsay found that a surprising number of self-identified born-again Christians in North America held "New-Ageish" beliefs. Out of their sample, 20% believed in reincarnation and 26% believed in astrology. Although these statistics do *not* mean that 20% or more of all Evangelicals are "really" New Agers, they *do* indicate that alternative spirituality has infiltrated society in ways that are missed when the population is measured in terms of mutually exclusive religious categories, and thus slip through the net of surveys and censuses.

References:

Arweck, Elisabeth. 2002. "New Religious Movements." In *Religions in the Modern World,* ed. Linda Woodhead, Paul Fletcher, Jiroko Kawanami, and David Smith, 264-288. London: Routledge.

Australian National Census 96: Religion. http://www.aph.gov.au/library/pubs/rn/1997-98/98n27.htm

Barker, Eileen. 1999. "New Religious Movements: Their Incidence and Significance." In *New Religious Movements: Challenge and Response*, ed. Bryan Wilson and Jamie Cresswell, 15-31. London: Routledge.

Barrett, David B., and Todd M. Johnson. 2002. "A Statistical Approach to the World's Religious Adherents." In *Religions of the World: A Comprehensive Encyclopedia of Beliefs and Practices*, ed. J. Gordon Melton and Martin Baumann, xxvii-xxxviii. Santa Barbara: ABC-Clio.

Chryssides, George D. 1999. *Exploring New Religions.* London: Cassell.

Clarke, Peter B. 1984. "New Paths to Salvation." *Religion Today* 1:1, 1-3.

Canadian National Census 2001. http://ww.statcan.ca.

Ellwood, Robert S., and Harry B. Partin. 1998. *Religious and Spiritual Groups in Modern America.* Essex, UK: Pearson Education, 2nd ed.

Gallup, George, Jr. and D. Michael Lindsay. 1999. *Surveying the Religious Landscape.* Harrisburg, PA: Morehouse.

Kosmin, Barry A., and Ariela Keysar. 2004. *Religion in the Marketplace.* Ithaca, NY: Paramount Books.

Lewis, James R. 2001. *Odd Gods: New Religions and the Cult Controversy.* Amherst, NY: Prometheus Books.

-------------------. 2002. "Diabolical Authority: Anton LaVey, *The Satanic Bible* and the Satanist Tradition."

Marburg Journal of Religious Studies 7:1.

Melton, J. Gordon. 1992. *Encyclopedic Handbook of Cults in America.* 2nd edition. New York: Garland.

Singer, Margaret Thaler, with Janja Lalich. 1995. *Cults in Our Midst: The Hidden Menace in Our Everyday Lives.* San Francisco: Jossey-Bass.

The Prophet Motive:
Religious Experience and the Legitimation of Religion

In this chapter, the contribution of religious experience to the generation of new religious movements will be explored. Such experiences are especially important for legitimating new religions in the minds of their founders. The centrality of religious experiences for understanding the origins of religion has been a major theme in "classic" religious studies methodology (e.g., refer to Wach 1958; Eliade 1954). It is thus surprising that no one has brought these analytic categories to bear on the generation of contemporary new religions.

One of the reasons for this is the discipline of religious studies' own quest for legitimacy, which influenced religious studies academicians to leave the field of new religions to social scientists. Another, related factor is the perception of new religious movements as a trivial phenomenon. Drawing on the audience cult/client cult/cult movements distinction articulated by Stark and Bainbridge (1979), it will be argued that if audience cults and client cults are set aside, many of the remaining movements are serious *religious* movements for which the classic religious studies emphasis on the centrality of religious experience is more relevant. However, as will be discussed below, applying this emphasis to new religions arising within a tradition like Protestant Christianity is problematic.

Experience and the Nature of Religion

In addition to being a source of new religions, religious experiences are also one of the reasons why people join religions. Many alternative religions hold out the possibility of life-transforming experiences—experiences that, to a greater or lesser extent, help one to drop the burden of the past and be reborn into a new and more complete life.

Even many mainstream Protestant denominations–Methodists, Baptists, Presbyterians and the like–once offered the seeker life-transforming experiences in the context of revivals and camp meetings. But as these religious bodies settled down into comfortable accommodation with the surrounding secular society, they lost their intensity. One result of this accommodation was that revivals and camp meetings–and the accompanying intense religious experiences–were relegated to quaint and mildly embarrassing chapters in denominational histories.

Those of us who are happily adjusted to the social-cultural mainstream often have a difficult time understanding intense religiosity. Academics have not been exempt from this tendency. As will be discussed in a later chapter, an earlier generation of sociologists of religion, seemingly obsessed with the issue of conversion to non-mainstream "sect" groups, gave excessive attention to explaining why individuals become involved in such churches.

If, however, rather than dwelling on strange externals, we change our point of focus and attempt to really look at what might attract someone to an alternative religion, such involvement is not difficult to understand. Is the attraction of transformational experiences, for example, really so hard to comprehend? What if we actually could let go of the burden of our past and be reborn as new people? Such transformation may or may not be attainable, but the attractiveness of the possibility is certainly understandable. Many non-mainstream religions–conservative Christian sects included–hold out the promise of such life-changing experiences. Religious experience is, however, only one aspect of the spiritual life, and only one of the factors that attract individuals to deeper religious involvement.

Among the many approaches to religious studies, one of the older, yet still useful scholarly analyses was articulated by the influential historian of religion, Joachim Wach (1944). The core of religion, according to Wach and others, is religious experience. Religious experience, in turn, is expressed in at least three ways:

> In a community (church, ashram, and so on)
> In a doctrine (theology, worldview, and so on)
> In a "cultus" (ritual, gathering, and so on)

The emphasis on–and privileging of–religious experience is central to the approach of such key religious studies theorists as Wach, Rudolf Otto, and Mircea Eliade. This tradition has been heavily criticised over the past decade. Russell T McCutcheon, for example, has caricaturised this approach as "necessitating that the scholar of religion be religious" (1999, 69). He has also attacked the notion that religious experience is *sui generis* (1997). Evaluating the merits of McCutcheon's critique would go beyond the scope of this thesis. For the purpose of the present analysis, it will be assumed that one need not be religious—nor need one defend the notion of religious experience as *sui generis*—in order to utilise this theoretical approach.

From the perspective of Wach's analysis, the fundamental constituents of religion are first, spiritual experience, second, community, third, doctrine/idea system and fourth, gatherings/rituals. In terms of this schema, the issue of legitimation is focused in the experiential and doctrinal aspects of a religion. Direct religious experience is, in a certain sense, self-legitimating: It opens the door to a sacred realm and leaves experiencers transformed. Nevertheless, such encounters do not take place in a vacuum. Those who enter into the presence of the Sacred might check their cultural baggage at the door (although this point is debatable), but they reclaim that baggage immediately after the flight is over.

Although experiences and ideas are intimately bound up with one another, it is nevertheless analytically useful to separate them and to note that religious experiences and religious ideology mutually impact one another. On the one hand, the experiences one has and how one interprets the significance of such experiences are determined by a person's cultural and personal background. On the other hand, a profound encounter with the Sacred can compel one to rethink and reshape her or his religious ideology. This mutual dependence extends to the issue of legitimacy: Religious experiences tend to legitimate a person's religious views, whereas a person's religious background provides the intellectual resources for interpreting her or his encounter with the Sacred and seeing it as a legitimate experience.

Although the sources of religions are diverse, the discipline of religious studies has traditionally given religious experience pride of place as the matrix out of which religions emerge. The Sacred breaks into mundane reality in the form of a hierophany (an appearance of the sacred; the older, theological term is "theophany"—an appearance of god), and, as a consequence, the new prophet goes out and founds a religion: Buddha experiences enlightenment and subsequently forms

Buddhism; Mohammed encounters the Archangel Gabriel and subsequently forms Islam; Guru Nanak has a vision of God and subsequently forms Sikhism; etc. (The most well-known theorist in this regard is Mircea Eliade, who described this pattern in a number of different volumes—for example, Eliade 1954; Eliade 1959.)

There are, nevertheless, many problematic aspects of this scenario as a paradigm for the beginning of *all* new religions, particularly for understanding the emergence of new sects and new denominational bodies. For example, the impulse behind the formation of many new organisations is often rooted in internal political disputes and personality clashes. New *organisations* that do not differ substantially from their parent traditions represent a somewhat different phenomenon, in that they do not actually constitute new *religions*. More problematic are the new groups that emerge out of substantial doctrinal disagreements. While such conflicts rarely generate completely new religious *traditions*, the sects thus formed *are* technically new *religions*. And although a doctrinal dispute can have its roots in a deep religious experience, frequently this is not the case.

This category of exceptions was never addressed in discussions of the classic religious studies approach to the origins of religion. In the West, this method for generating new religious sects is especially—though certainly not exclusively—evident in the many new groups formed within the Protestant tradition. Thus the failure to take this pattern into account may have been at least partially the result of the older division of labour between history of religions and church history, which tacitly reserved Christianity as the exclusive "turf" of church historians.

Ever since Martin Luther articulated the doctrine of *sola scriptura* ("scripture only") as the sole principle of religious authority, variant interpretations of the Bible have been central to the legitimation of new Christian groups. Furthermore, as will be noted in the present and in future chapters, creative reinterpretations of traditional scriptures have also played a key role as a legitimation strategy in some non-traditional religions. Even when new prophets reject key components of the Christian tradition, in the western cultural milieu the words of the Bible continue to bear such an aura of authority that religious innovators feel compelled to integrate them into their new spiritual syntheses in some manner.

The Prophet Motive

Almost all religions with an historically-specifiable point of origin are initially founded by a single person. In this regard, new religions are much like new businesses: new businesses are almost always the manifestation of the vision and work of a single entrepreneur. In contrast, few if any successful businesses are the outgrowth of a committee. And there are other ways in which the model of an economic entrepreneur is an appropriate lens through which to view religious prophets.

In an insightful article published over two decades ago, sociologists of religion Rodney Stark and William Bainbridge presented several paradigms for understanding the birth of religions, including one they termed the "entrepreneurial model" (Bainbridge and Stark, 1979). In certain important ways, the authors suggest, the founding prophets of new religious movements are like individuals who start new companies: Relying on their experience with prior employment in a certain line of business, entrepreneurs strike out on their own with a similar business, improving or otherwise modifying the new company in some way so as to be competitive with their former employer and with other, similar companies. In a parallel fashion, new prophets have usually been active participants in other religions. As a consequence, their new spiritual syntheses inevitably bear resemblances to their original religions.

The entrepreneurial model is useful as long as one does not equate the *prophet* motive with the *profit* motive. Though a significant motivation for the leading figures of so-called "audience cults" or "client cults" (Bainbridge and Stark 1980) may be the income derived from their activities, too much self-sacrifice is required to found most other kinds of religious bodies for economic benefits to be the primary driving force.

A less obvious problem with the entrepreneurial metaphor is that a prophet does not typically sit down in her or his drawing room and consciously develop a blueprint for a new religion in the same way an entrepreneur might develop a business plan for a new company. Instead, founders of many new religions begin prophetic careers in response to hierophanies—direct encounters with the sacred. These encounters with other realms contain the seeds of new insights that in some way challenge or supersede the doctrines and practices of their "parent" religions. The new revelations are typically experienced as originating from a higher, divine authority, rather than from the personal creativity of the prophets. Such religious experiences subsequently become primary points of reference for the articulation and legitimation of new religious forms.

Although there has been a proliferation of studies on contemporary new religions within the past few decades, comparatively few religious studies scholars have chosen to focus on the process by which religious innovators arrive at their new spiritual syntheses. This state of affairs is surprising, given that the origin of religion has traditionally been a core concern of religious studies as an academic discipline. Hence it seems that religious studies scholars have consciously or unconsciously capitulated to the popular perception of new religions as not *really* religious. At the very least, it appears that contemporary new religions have been judged as not originating out of the same depth of religious consciousness as more traditional religions like Buddhism and Islam.

The present situation has come about for a number of different reasons. In the first place, during the late 1960s and early 1970s–at precisely the same time period when some of the more exotic new religions were becoming prominent–religious studies was busy establishing itself in the university system as an academic discipline. In the United States, the threshold event opening the door for religious studies departments in state universities was a 1963 Supreme Court decision, *Abington Township School District vs Schempp*. Although the Court ruled that public schools could not engage in Bible reading, prayer or other devotional practices, the justices went out of their way to note that the non-devotional "teaching about" rather than the "teaching of" religion was completely consistent with secular education. An unforeseen consequence of this decision was the "promotion of religious studies in institutions of higher education" (Wiebe 1999, 107). Not coincidently, the very next year the primary professional organisation for the teaching of religious studies in the United States, the National Association of Biblical Instructors, changed its name to the American Academy of Religion. However, stripped of the "devotional, ethical, and cultural purposes that religious studies founders believed to be essential to their academic work...religious studies could not produce a set of compelling intellectual reasons for its place in the university" (Hart 1999, 202-203). Thus, despite the fact that by 1979 the American Council of Learned Societies had admitted the AAR as a member, acceptance of religious studies as a legitimate discipline within the university came slowly.

As members of a discipline generally perceived as marginal, most religion scholars were reluctant to further marginalize themselves by giving serious attention to what at the time seemed a transitory social phenomenon. One indication of the reluctance of the religious studies academy to deal seriously with NRMs is that the first meeting of what became the New Religious Movements Group within the AAR did not take place until 1982, despite that fact that public controversy over new religions had been raging for at least ten years prior. It was not, in fact, until a series of major tragedies that took place in the 1990s—specifically, the Branch Davidian debacle, the Solar Temple suicide/murders, the AUM Shinrikyo gas attack and the Heavens Gate suicides—that the field of NRMs was truly embraced by the religious studies establishment.

As a consequence of this situation, the study of new religions was left to sociologists until relatively recently. Sociologists of religion were thus largely free to lay the foundations for the field of contemporary new religions. During the 1970s, issues raised by the cult controversy dominated social perceptions of new religions. And because social conflict is a basic issue for sociology, more and more sociologists were drawn to the study of new religions. By the time of the Jonestown tragedy in 1978—and in sharp contrast to the situation with religious studies—NRMs was already a recognised specialisation within the sociology of religion.

Sociology, however, views new religions as arising out of social forces—as a discipline, sociology does not consider religious experiences as independent motivating factors for the emergence of new religious forms. In recent years, as more and more religion academics have become involved in the study of new religions, the tendency has been to build upon these foundations uncritically. Little thought has been given to considering what this phenomenon might look like when viewed in terms of some of the unique theoretical perspectives utilised in religious studies—perspectives that, as mentioned earlier in this chapter, take religious experiences seriously as powerful, independent motivating factors (Wach, 1958, 36).

In the second place, many of the phenomena encountered in the metaphysical/occult/new age subculture–the breeding ground for the majority of groups contemporary new religions scholars study–are the conscious fabrications of their founders, transparently designed to have the broadest possible appeal in what some have referred to as the "spiritual marketplace". The entrepreneurial model is most appropriate for such popular writer-lecturers as Deepak Chopra and Lynn Andrews, and for certain therapy-oriented movements such as est. Because of the relatively high profile of such figures and movements, it is relatively easy to infer that every religious leader in this subculture is cut from the same fabric. For this reason, scholars working in the field are predisposed to view newly emergent religions as less legitimate than more traditional religions, and this usually unconscious value-judgment influences them to approach such religions with less sensitivity than they might approach more established religious bodies: The implicit assumption seems to be, why should anyone seriously attempt to grapple with the religious consciousness of the founders of such superficial systems of spiritual teachings?

The corrective to this misperception can be found in yet another Stark and Bainbridge article, "Of Churches, Sects and Cults" (Stark and Bainbridge, 1979). In this piece, the authors distinguish between quasi-religious phenomena represented by the informal followings attracted to figures like Andrews and Chopra ("audience cults"), to movements like est ("client cults"), and more formal groups that embody characteristics of *religion* proper ("cult movements"). When observers take this distinction into account, they find that many contemporary new *religions* exhibit traits of more traditional religious bodies. It should thus be possible to understand such religions in terms of interpretive perspectives developed in the context of the study of established religions.

The present chapter undertakes such a project via the concrete example of the formation of the Church of the Movement of Spiritual Inner Awareness (MSIA), one of the many new religions to emerge out of the metaphysical-occult subculture of the early 1970s (Lewis, 1998). It will be demonstrated that, in common with other religious traditions and in contrast to the more secular motivations underlying audience cults and client cults, MSIA grows out of the religious experiences of its founder. As part of this analysis, I will further demonstrate that the common characterisation of MSIA as being little more than a reworked spin-off of Eckankar falls far short of offering an adequate portrayal of this diverse religious movement. The main body of the discussion will be preceded by a brief overview of MSIA, Eckankar and the Sant Mat tradition.

MSIA, Eckankar and the Sant Mat Tradition

Similar to western Gnosticism, the North Indian Sant Mat tradition teaches that the cosmos is a multi-level emanation in which human souls are trapped, and that the spiritual aspirant needs a series of words or names keyed to each of the lower levels in order to move through them and reach the divine source. A sound current (a "river" of vibration; alternately pictured as a ray of light) from the higher levels–an emanation from the high God her/him/itself–flows down through all of the lower levels. A living guru imparts five secret names (the simram) to the aspirant at the time of initiation. Contemplating the sound current and the inner light (the visual aspect of the divine sound) with the Master's guidance allows the individual to follow the sound back to the source from which it emanated (the Supreme Being), resulting in spiritual liberation. Those who follow the system must live according to a code of behaviour that includes vegetarianism, abstinence from alcohol, and high moral character. Two and a half hours per day are to be set aside for meditation.

In contrast to the Sant Mat lineage, Eckankar is a new religious movement founded by Paul Twitchell in California in 1965. Twitchell was a spiritual seeker who was involved in a variety of different alternative religions–including Ruhani Satsang, a Sant Mat group–before starting Eckankar. He asserted that in 1956 he experienced God-realisation when he was initiated by a group of spiritual masters, the Order of the Vairagi Masters. Twitchell and his organisation gained widespread attention following the publication of Twitchell's biography, *In My Soul I Am Free* (1968), written by the prominent metaphysical author Brad Steiger. Building on contemporaneous popular interest in astral projection, Eckankar's early teachings emphasised "soul travel", a practice portrayed as a blend of astral projection and sound current meditation. Critics have often accused Twitchell of plagiarising and then reworking Sant Mat teachings so as to disguise their true origins.

The Movement of Spiritual Inner Awareness is a new religion founded by John-Roger Hinkins, generally referred to as "J-R" (Following MSIA convention, I will regularly refer to Hinkins as John-Roger.) In 1963, while undergoing surgery for a kidney stone, he fell into a nine-day coma. Upon awakening, he found himself aware of a new spiritual personality–"John"–who had superseded or merged with his old personality. After the operation, Hinkins began to refer to himself as "John-Roger" in recognition of his transformed self. In 1971, he formally incorporated the Church of the Movement of Spiritual Inner Awareness. In 1988, he passed the spiritual leadership of MSIA on to John Morton.

There are many levels of involvement in MSIA. These include five formal initiations (the first two are done together, making four distinct initiation events), each of which indicates progressively deeper involvement in the spiritual path that is at the core of MSIA's various practices. By way of contrast, Sant Mat groups such as Ruhani Satsang have only one initiation; Eckankar, on the other hand, has ten initiations.

MSIA also teaches that people have multilevel awareness and that 90% of a person's consciousness is in the spiritual levels; only 10% is in the physical world. Because the focus of MSIA is on the 90% level, MSIA members are free to decide how they wish to lead their lives at the 10% level. In practical terms, what this means is that members make their own decisions about such matters as diet, clothing, sexual preference, whom to associate with, and the like.

MSIA, Eckankar and the Metaphysical Subculture

As different immigrant populations have established their religions in the West, the religious ecology of Europe and the United States has become ever more complex, making any attempt at generalisation problematic. With that caveat, we can nevertheless distinguish two major spiritual subcultures that stand out on the current religious landscape: traditionally-dominant Christianity and a strand of alternative spirituality designated variously as metaphysical, metaphysical-occult, new age, etc. Two distinct categories of bookstores that can be found in almost any large urban area are broadly emblematic of these two religious subcultures: Christian bookstores and metaphysical bookstores. There is almost no overlap in either the stock or the clientele of these retail outlets.

Though the diversity of ideas and institutions represented in metaphysical bookstores is far broader than that found in Christian bookstores, there are, nevertheless, broad areas of agreement within the metaphysical subculture that might escape the notice of the casual observer. Many of the specifics of this shared world view arise out of the denominational traditions that came into being in the nineteenth century, particularly Theosophy, Spiritualism and New Thought. Hence, almost all contemporary participants in the metaphysical subculture share beliefs in reincarnation, the ultimate interconnectedness of reality, the existence of other "planes" of reality inhabited by disembodied entities, the power of the mind to influence events, and so forth.

Although they might consciously distance themselves from certain segments of it, both MSIA and Eckankar grow out of this subculture and share its basic assumptions. For this reason, the fact that both share beliefs in reincarnation and other common metaphysical ideas cannot be taken as evidence that either MSIA or Eckankar borrowed these specific ideas from each other. Once we eliminate the commonalities originating from shared roots in the metaphysical subculture, it becomes clear how different the two systems are.

For example, MSIA teaches a christology that sets it apart from both the Sant Mat tradition and Eckankar. Specifically, MSIA gives tremendous spiritual significance to the role of the Christ—a significance that does not correspond within anything in either the Radhasoami lineage or Eckankar. MSIA further claims (1) that Jesus Christ is the head of the Church of the Movement of Spiritual Inner Awareness (Hinkins calls Jesus his "boss"), and (2) that "the Traveler's work through MSIA (Soul Transcendence) is based on Jesus' work." *(Soul Transcendence* 1995, p. 11). Though the organisation does not embrace the label "Christian," like Christianity the Movement views itself as deriving from Christ's teachings rather than from Eckankar or the Sant tradition.

This assertion seems implausible unless one is familiar with the figure of Christ in Theosophy, New Thought and the metaphysical subculture more generally. To anyone so informed, it is obvious that John-Roger has drunk deeply from the well of esoteric Christianity, and that MSIA is saturated with the language and the ideology of this strand of spirituality. In fact, if one deletes the component of MSIA relating to sound current practices and soul travel ideology, what is left looks a lot like a metaphysical church.

This emphasis on Christ stands in sharp contrast to Eckankar, which sees Christianity as a lower path. When one understands that MSIA's primary sources of spiritual nourishment are the "Christian" tradition (broadly understood) and the larger metaphysical subculture, it seems odd that anyone could characterise MSIA as nothing more than an Eckankar or a Sant Mat spin-off.

This misunderstanding appears to have been created primarily by David Christopher Lane, the only scholar to have carried out substantive work on Eckankar and MSIA. Lane's principal treatment of MSIA is contained in his 1984 essay, "The JR Controversy". This piece was later incorporated into his 1994 book, *Exposing Cults*. The essay is highly polemical. After pointing out a number of parallels–such as correspondences between Eckankar's cosmology and MSIA's cosmology–Lane dismisses John-Roger as a spiritual "plagiarist" (Lane, 1994, 109).

It does not require much reflection, however, to perceive the flawed logic in Lane's line of argumentation. In the first place, it is difficult to imagine how one could possibly distinguish religious *plagiarism* from other kinds of transmissions of religious ideas and practices. For the sake of discussion, imagine a minority group in the First Baptist Church that objects to something their church is doing, and decides to go off to found the Second Baptist Church. After about a month, someone from First Baptist goes to spy on Second Baptist, and discovers that the new schism has "plagiarised" almost everything from the original congregation–They use the same Bible (printed by the same publishing company, with changing so much as a single word!), and, Oh my God, they even talk about the same Jesus dying for their sins! As ludicrous as this example may seem, it elucidates a fundamental error in Lane's critique.

In the second place, with respect to the discussion of Eckankar and MSIA, Lane's argument is even more off-base because of the substantial differences between Twitchell's and Hinkins's teachings. MSIA's emphasis on Christ is only the most obvious of these differences. In point of fact, the only area of overlap–excepting the commonalities inherent in the metaphysical subculture–is that both MSIA and Eckankar teach sound current meditation. Even in this area, the widespread presence of sound current traditions in North America–everyone from Kirpal Singh to Guru Maharaji has taught surat shabd yoga–suggests that John-Roger's ideas on this topic may have originated from a source other than Eckankar. On the other hand, Hinkins read Twitchell's writings for a couple of years, making Eckankar the most plausible source for MSIA's sound current teachings.

A spiritual seeker and self-described "metaphysical tramp" during his early adulthood, John-Roger read about and participated in any number of different spiritual groups. He has been particularly forthcoming about his familiarity with Eckankar and Paul Twitchell, and readily admits that there are parallels between MSIA and the Sant Mat tradition. In an email communication to this writer (7/22/98), Hinkins briefly described the period of his life during which he read Eckankar publications and participated in Eckankar events:

> I was reading much information–i.e., Rosicrucians, Readers Digest, World Books, etc.–all around the same time. I went to three or four of Eckankar's conferences, and read some of their books and discourses for around two years and continued with others over a much longer period of time.

Despite this participation, John-Roger was never a formal "student" of Twitchell, in the sense of being an Eckankar initiate. The assertion that Hinkins was a second level initiate–an assertion one sometimes finds in anti-MSIA polemical literature–seems to be based upon a mistaken inference: Eckankar teaches that students engaged in the study of the group's monthly discourses will usually receive their first initiation on the inner levels (for example, in a dream) during their first year or so of study. At the end of two years, students may then request the second initiation, which involves the physical presence of an Eck minister empowered to administer a formal initiation. Hence when John-Roger says he took Eckankar's discourses for two years, "two years" is a spiritually significant cycle of time. An Eckankar insider might easily (though mistakenly) infer that Hinkins had received his second initiation.

Despite his involvement with Eckankar, John-Roger has claimed that his sound current teachings were not derived from that organisation. Instead of Eckankar or Radhasoami, he asserts that MSIA stands in the lineage of Jesus, who, as the Mystical Traveler of his time, initiated his disciples into the sound current. Although no historian of religion would embrace such a position as historical fact, there are, as shall presently be seen, persuasive reasons to take this as a true statement of John-Roger's personal belief about the ultimate source of his own teachings.

As discussed earlier, the founders of most new religious movements differ from founders of new businesses in that they do *not* sit down in their living rooms and consciously draw up the contours of their new religious synthesis in the same way an entrepreneur draws up a business plan. This discussion thus brings us back around to the question of the nature of the prophetic consciousness. The next section will develop this issue with reference to John-Roger Hinkins.

Religious Experience and the Prophetic Consciousness

A useful counterpoint for elucidating the nature of prophetic consciousness is provided by Andrea Grace Diem in her 1995 dissertation, "Shabdism in North America: The Influence of Radhasoami on Guru Movements." Diem prefaces her work with the claim that she is following the "phenomenological method," meaning that she is engaged in a neutral, descriptive exercise. This disclaimer is, however, belied by the great bulk of her analysis of MSIA, Eckankar and other emergent sound current groups, which focuses squarely on the issue of their "dependence" on the Radhasoami tradition. In point of fact, Diem engages in a covert polemic by relying upon a simplistic version of the entrepreneurial model, naively assuming that the *prophet*-motive (especially for all founders of Radhasoami-related movements in the West) is always the *profit*-motive. Even a superficial perusal of her section on MSIA makes it clear that Diem's underlying interest is to have the reader walk away with a negative impression of John-Roger and the Movement of Spiritual Inner Awareness.

Nowhere is this agenda clearer than in the passages where she imputes motivations. For example, after accusing Paul Twitchell of having reduced the daily meditation time characteristic of Sant Mat lineages from two hours to two periods of twenty minutes in order to attract more students, she then notes that, like Sant Mat teachers, John-Roger Hinkins recommends two hours per day. (Diem is technically incorrect on this point: What Hinkins actually says is that fifteen minutes is adequate, but that it may take two hours to quiet the mental chatter before one can have fifteen minutes of "quality time.") This guideline–which, Diem admits, reduces the appeal of MSIA–is presumably part of John-Roger's attempt to add "lustre and authenticity to his fledgling movement" by by-passing Eckankar and linking MSIA to the larger Sant Mat tradition (Diem, 1995, 174).

However, much later in her discussion, Diem characterises MSIA, Eckankar and related groups as organisations that have stripped Sant Mat of its "cultural moorings"–such as "strict ethical guidelines" (245)–in order "to present a streamlined, modern path intertwined with any number of fashionable religious trends which may have caught the eye of the buying public." She then flatly states that "John-Roger of MSIA is a prime example of this type" (247). In other words, according to Diem, John-Roger dropped Sant Mat moral prohibitions against such "sins" as meat-eating and homosexuality in order to increase the appeal of MSIA on the spiritual marketplace.

The problem with this analysis of Hinkins and other founders of modern spiritual groups is that Diem *invariably* portrays calculated decisions as lying behind *every* aspect of MSIA, Eckankar etc. Such a one-sided attribution of motives is based on the unstated assumption that John-Roger and others are self-seeking charlatans. Thus, if Hinkins makes MSIA *more* rigorous by advising movement participants to meditate for two hours per day, it must be because he wants to legitimise his organisation. If, on the other hand, Hinkins makes MSIA *less* rigorous by having no proscriptions against meat-eating and homosexuality, it must be because he wants to increase the appeal of his organisation to the "buying public." One suspects that, had Diem known that John-Roger advised meditating only fifteen minutes per day, she would have portrayed his motivation for setting forth this guideline as wanting to broaden the appeal of MSIA. Alternately, had he proscribed meat-eating and homosexuality, the motive would have been the quest for greater legitimacy.

What about the possibility that, based on his personal religious experiences, Hinkins had concluded that two hours of spiritual exercises per day was the ideal meditation period? Or, isn't it even vaguely possible that he came to the sincere conclusion that meat-eating and homosexuality were not harmful to one's spiritual health? To uniformly attribute self-seeking motives to John-Roger is to carry out a covert polemic—a far cry from the phenomenological approach Diem claims to follow.

An important aspect of the phenomenological method as it is *properly* deployed in religious studies is that religious experiences are taken seriously. Without pronouncing judgement on the ontological status of the spiritual agencies encountered in such experiences, a disciplined effort is made to understand the consciousness of those for whom the encounter with the sacred is ultimately real and meaningful. Theorists as diverse as Joachim Wach, Rudolf Otto, Gerardus van der Leeuw, and Mircea Eliade have gone so far as to make such experiences both the starting point and the living core of religion.

With respect to John-Roger, the turning point in his spiritual life was the near-death experience (NDE) he went through during his kidney stone operation in 1963. (Many modern NDE accounts bear resemblances to a "classic shamanic initiation" [Ellwood, 1992, 64], a significant category of religious experience.) The stage was set for this operation by an earlier automobile accident:

On July the 4th of '63 in Hollywood, California, we were driving down Yucca Street.... We had the green light and as we came across a guy ran the light and hit us. I didn't see him coming, except barely. I was putting the seat belt on, and I'd just put it in to get ready to tighten it down and they hit us. My head went up, and there's a bar across where the window is, and I kind of hit it. It was like, "What happened?" Of course, our car was moving around. And, I got out and I couldn't walk. I was really dizzy. And, phew, I think that put me in the hospital for a week or so....

The car wreck had pulled my kidney loose, and had dislodged or moved a kidney stone. And the kidney stone was [causing] blood to come out.... On December 3rd, my kidney was taken out of my body, opened, and the stone removed.... For nine days, I was, they told me, unconscious. But I would open my eyes and look around and talk to them. My mother was there all the time.... I remember one day opening my eyes, laying on my side.... And she said, "Who are you?" I remember this. And a voice said, "John." And she said, "Okay. Is Roger there?" And he said, "Yeah. Would you like to speak to Roger?" She said, "Yeah." And, it was like–click click–there was Roger....

[Later] I went to see a couple [who] channeled.... They're the ones who came up with the name, "John-Roger." This consciousness came through, and I wanted to know what happened during the surgery.... And so I said, "Who are you? What do you do? Why are we together? What gives?" And it says, "John the Beloved." ...and I said, "Well, if this is John, am I now John or am I Roger? Who am I in here?" And the [couple] said, "You're both." I said, "Yeah, but Roger's my first name, and [now] I have this John." They said, "John-Roger." And it fit. What I was told...was that I was this consciousness before, and am still this consciousness. (John-Roger Interview 1/28/98)

In the wake of his coma, in other words, Hinkins experienced himself as having two distinct consciousnesses, one of which–the new self–he came to view as having been the biblical personage John the Beloved. It appears that John-Roger was told that Roger, the persona he formerly thought himself to be, was either the reincarnation of John, or that the post-operation Roger was so overshadowed by this "supernatural personality" that the two merged into one consciousness.

Given the apparent profundity of this experience in combination with the interpretation he subsequently accepted as the explanation for his expanded sense of self, it is easy to understand why Hinkins should have come to view his ministry as being in Jesus Christ's lineage: As the reincarnation–or, in some other manner, the embodiment–of one of Jesus' chief disciples, it would make perfect sense for him to assert that Jesus was his "boss" and that he based his work on Jesus' work (that is, it would be natural for him to see MSIA as a latter-day extension of Jesus' ministry).

John-Roger's boss is not, however, the Jesus of conventional Christianity, but the metaphysical Jesus–the world avatar who teaches the full course of esoteric wisdom. With these points in mind, it now becomes clear how Hinkins could seriously claim that Jesus Christ initiated his disciples into the sound current: If John-Roger believes that surat shabd yoga is the most advanced "spiritual exercise" on the planet, he would necessarily have to infer that Jesus had taught such techniques to his disciples.

Although this powerful encounter with other realms was the pivotal religious experience of Hinkins's life, it would be eight years before his revelation would lead to the formation of MSIA. In the intervening years, we can infer that he reflected on this experience and others, interpreting and reinterpreting them as he came to conclusions about the nature of spiritual reality. As with all founders of new religions, at least some of the elements of the new synthesis that would become MSIA were drawn from doctrines and practices with which he was already familiar. However–to pick up on our earlier discussion–John-Roger's spiritual experiences were the touchstones around which all other components of MSIA would be organised.

In light of Hinkins's understanding of himself as being–or as having merged his consciousness with–John the Beloved, the claim that he artificially tacked on some Christian components in order to make it appear "more Western" (Diem, 1995, 163) is clearly mistaken. Instead of beginning with the Sant Mat tradition and adding a Western gloss, John-Roger began with a profound experience of being Christian (esoterically understood), and then reflectively integrated the other elements of occult wisdom he had appropriated into a metaphysical Christian base. This is also evident in his attitude toward the Bible which, because appeals to the authority of the Bible are widespread in the metaphysical tradition as well as within the Christian mainstream, merits examination.

Role of the Bible

The Bible is a powerful authority in western societies. For this reason, the metaphysical tradition relies heavily on what is referred to as a *metaphysical interpretation* of scripture, meaning that biblical passages are interpreted symbolically and metaphorically to reveal their true import. In the case of MSIA, Hinkins draws from the biblical record, although his approach to scripture is complex, simultaneously similar and dissimilar to the approach of metaphysical Christianity. Because the focus of his exegesis is a perspective informed by his religious experience, so that it was possible for John-Roger to find biblical passages containing allusions to soul travel.

Also, unlike some metaphysical churches such as Unity that embrace the Bible as the touchstone of their teachings, MSIA's approach is more selective. Readings from scripture play no role in a typical MSIA gathering, and no set of Hinkins's teachings focus specifically on the Bible. At the same time, John-Roger often cites and otherwise refers to the Bible as an authoritative text. Furthermore, MSIA members are encouraged to read and become familiar with scripture. Although the Bible is authoritative, this authority is not exclusive, as reflected in John-Roger's response to the question, Can I find the Christ in Hindu scriptures? "Yes, but it won't be spelled that way" (Tape #1330, "Christmas Eve with John-Roger").

The aspirant is also warned against over-focusing on scripture. In one of his talks, Hinkins asserts that spiritual teachers always advise one to "seek first the Kingdom," because

If you seek first that which is written, and try to maintain that which is written, then you sacrifice the "moving within consciousness" of God (Tape #1329, "The Meditation of the Christ").

Congruent with the teachings of other metaphysical churches (Judah, 1967, 17-18), John-Roger tends toward a non-literal reading of scripture (John-Roger, 1994, 14-15)

The Bible sometimes does not give us specific answers to our questions, but you must understand that the Bible is coded...(ibid., 24-25).

How, then, does one go about decoding scripture? MSIA does not provide explicit guidelines for this task. Instead, the implicit message seems to be that one can unlock the deeper meaning of the Bible only after one has achieved a certain level of enlightenment. Furthermore, even if we had the keys for interpreting scripture, not all of the mysteries would be found there because not all of the "hidden teachings" were encoded in the Bible. Hinkins notes, for instance, that soul travel is only alluded to in scripture:

The work that we do in soul travel--transcending the physical--is alluded to in the Bible, in a few places. Let me give you two of the references. One says, "when you're out of the body, you're with the Lord." It's like, Why would they make a statement like that? It's like, To worship God you must worship God in the spirit (that is, the Soul) (Tape #1507, "What Is the Secret Center?").

The other example John-Roger mentions in this taped discussion is the familiar Pauline epistle relating the experience of a man who was "taken up" to the third heaven.

Given the Bible's state of incompleteness, one might well ask why one should bother reading it at all. Hinkins's answer is that, although the Bible is not necessary for salvation, it points the way, not unlike how a water almanac points the way to water. One can shake and twist a water almanac all day and never get a single drop of water. Similarly, the Bible does not have a magical potency to save anyone. Instead, it points the way to quenching our spiritual thirst:

What is the value of the Book? The value of the Book is it points a direction. The water almanac points a way–a direction–to where water can be found. And [the Bible] points to where the Living Waters can be found. And it points it out very beautifully, very succinctly, and, believe me, I thrill anew each time that I hear it because I've validated it inside of me (Tape #1330, "Christmas Eve with John-Roger").

Finally, John-Roger has periodically made the observation that our present scriptures will eventually be superseded by a new bible or bibles. He has made this assertion in the context of discussions that portray the present period as being the "biblical times" of the future

Realize that you are biblical scripture now being written and that centuries from now, the lives that are being enthroned in the spiritual records at this time will be the "bible" of people who will say, "If I had lived in that time, if I could have partaken of that Christ Consciousness, then I, too, could have been saintly. I, too, could have expressed eternal love" (John-Roger 1994, 43).

From this passage as well as from many of the other statements cited above, one can see that MSIA departs significantly from tradition. At the same time, John-Roger's utilisation of the Bible as an authoritative document contributes to MSIA's legitimacy.

Religious Experience and the Formation of New Religions

To return to our discussion of religious experience, in twentieth century religious studies "religious experience" is an imprecise notion applied to any number of different kinds of experiences. Though theoretically open-ended, the paradigmatic experience in the back of most people's minds whenever they discuss this topic is a major, life-transforming encounter with the Divine–an overwhelming experience of the kind that overtook Paul on the Damascus Road. John-Roger's NDE falls into this category. As indicated by studies of people who have been through close encounters with death, NDEs are major experiences that transform lives. In the case of Hinkins, his NDE transformed him from a metaphysical dilettante into a serious spiritual seeker.

To refer back to our earlier discussion, it is precisely such transformative encounters that theorists of religion have in mind when they discuss religious experience as the source and central point of reference for concrete religious forms. Wach, for example, analysed the other major components of religion as *expressions* of direct experiences of the sacred. In other words, religious experience is *expressed* in first, doctrine (theology, mythology, ideology), second, cultus (ritual, ceremony, gathering), and third, community (church, ashram, et cetera). In Wach's words

Myth and doctrine comprise the articulation in thought of what has been experienced in the confrontation with Ultimate Reality. *Cultus* is the acting out of this confrontation in worship and service. Both give direction to and "center" the community formed by those who are united in a particular religious experience... (Wach, 1958, 121).

This does not mean that Wach viewed religions as coming into being *ex nihilo* out of an encounter with the Divine. Rather, the components of any new religious synthesis are typically drawn from familiar religious forms in the prophet's environment. But it is the founder's religious experience that provides the starting point–as well as the essential core or "template"–for the form this new synthesis takes. The "prophet motive," in other words, is to express, as best as one can, the ramifications of religious experience in new religious forms. Other, ancillary motivations may contribute to the process, but the core motive remains essentially religious.

Taking this perspective seriously, it is easy to see that any simplistic deployment of the entrepreneurial model is misleading: Probably the majority of founders of new religions do *not* create religious forms primarily with an eye to how well they will "sell" on the spiritual marketplace (the *profit* motive). Instead, religious forms typically emerge out of the consciousness of the founder for the purpose of expressing her or his religious experience, and that will best draw other people into a community to share her or his vision (the *prophet* motive). The impulse lying behind the formation of MSIA, for example, has been described as, "I have this experience and other people want to know about it" (John Morton Interview 6/9/98).

In sharp contrast to self-seeking motives implicit in the entrepreneurial metaphor, prophets not infrequently become involved in the founding of new religious communities *against their own conscious will:* Like the biblical Jonah who rebelled against the dictates that arose out of his encounter with the Divine, prophets sometimes actively resist the promptings that direct them to engage in public ministries. From various statements he has made over the years, we can infer that this was the case with John-Roger, who probably would have preferred to remain Roger Hinkins the "metaphysical tramp" rather than take on the responsibility of serving as a spiritual director.

Concluding Remarks

The focus of the present chapter was on the prophetic consciousness of founders of new religions. The thrust of the discussion was to argue that, with the exception of less formally organised audience cults, the principal source of the "prophet motive" is frequently a profound religious experience, and not the narrow self-seeking suggested by facile appropriations of the entrepreneurial model. It was further argued that the founder often experiences the creative impulses arising out of the encounter with the Divine as the ultimate source of her or his new spiritual synthesis. Hence any analysis that explicitly or implicitly portrays the primarily structuring impulses behind new religions as arising from the calculated decisions of the founder *de facto* denigrates religious experience by ignoring its role in the emergence of many new religions.

References:

Bainbridge, William Sims, and Rodney Stark, "Cult Formation: Three Compatible Models," *Sociological Analysis* 40 (1979): 283-295.

Bainbridge, William Sims, and Rodney Stark, "Client and Audience Cults in America," *Sociological Analysis* 41 (1980): 199-214.

Diem, Andrea Grace. "Shabdism in North America: The Influence of Radhasoami on Guru Movements." Ph.D. diss., University of California, Santa Barbara, 1995.

Eck Satsang Discourses. 3rd Series, #3 (n.p., n.d.).

Eliade, Mircea. *The Myth of the Eternal Return, or: Cosmos and History.* New York: Bollingen, 1954.

----------------. *The Sacred and the Profane: The Nature of Religion.* New York: Harcourt Brace, 1959).

Ellwood, Robert. "How New is the New Age?" In *Perspectives on the New Age*, eds. James R. Lewis and J. Gordon Melton. Albany, NY: State University of New York Press, 1992.

Hart, D.G. *The University Gets Religion: Religious Studies in American Higher Education.* Baltimore: Johns Hopkins U. Pr., 1999.

Introvigne, Massimo. Interview with John-Roger and John Morton, 1/28/98.

John-Roger. *The Christ Within & The Disciples of Christ.* Los Angeles: Mandeville, 1994.

----------------. Personal communication to author, 7/22/98.

----------------. Interview, 1/28/98.

----------------. "The Meditation of the Christ." MSIA Audio Tape #1329.

----------------. "Christmas Eve with John-Roger." MSIA Audio Tape #1330.

----------------. "What Is the Secret Center?" MSIA Audio Tape #1507.

Judah, J. Stillson. *The History and Philosophy of the Metaphysical Movements in America.*
        Philadelphia: Westminster Press, 1967.

Lane, David Christopher. *Exposing Cults: When the Skeptical Mind Confronts the Mystical.* New York:
        Garland, 1994.

Lewis, James R. "Did Jesus Die for Our Karma? Christology and Atonement in a Contemporary
        Metaphysical Church," *Journal of the Society for the Study of Metaphysical Religion* 4 (Fall
        1998).

--------------. *Seeking the Light.* Los Angeles: Mandeville, 1998.

McCutcheon, Russell T., Ed. *The Insider/Outsider problem in the Study of Religion: A Reader.* London:
        Cassell, 1999.

----------------. *Manufacturing Religion: The Discourse On Sui Generis Religion and the Politics of
        Nostalgia.* New York: Oxford U. Pr., 1997.

Morton, John. Interview, 6/9/98

Olson, Roger E. "ECKANKAR: From Ancient Science of Soul Travel to New Age Religion." In
        Timothy Miller, ed. *America's Alternative Religions.* Albany: State University of New York
        Press, 1995.

Otto, Rudolf. *The Idea of the Holy.* London: Oxford Univ. Pr., 2nd ed., 1950. 1992.

Saliba, John. Interview with John-Roger and John Morton, 6/9/98.

Soul Transcendence. Los Angeles: Peace Theological Seminary & College of Philosophy, 1995.

Stark, Rodney, and William Sims Bainbridge, "Of Churches, Sects and Cults," *Journal for the Scientific
        Study of Religion* 18 (1979): 117-133.

Steiger, Brad. *In My Soul I Am Free: The Incredible Paul Twitchell Story.* New York, Lancer Books,
        1968.

van der Leeuw, Gerardus. *Religion in Essence and Manifestation I and II.* Glouchester, MA: Peter
        Smith, 1967.

Wiebe, Donald. *The Politics of Religious Studies.* New York: St. Martins Press, 1999.

Wach, Joachim. *Sociology of Religion.* Chicago: University of Chicago Press, 1944.

----------------. *The Comparative Study of Religions.* New York: Columbia University Press, 1958.

Stepping onto the Path:
Joining the Movement of Spiritual Inner Awareness

Like so many other people in the Sixties, I was searching. I found my vocation as an actress when I was quite young. I combined this career with my involvement in the counter-culture. I appeared in Andy Warhol movies and was touted as the world's "First Nude Actress." Suddenly I was the most "in" thing happening. They had me in *Vogue Magazine* and *Harper's Bazaar.* I was on the Merv Griffen Show and the Dick Cavett Show. Being the first nude actress in the country, much less the world, was really quite a happening.

It was sometime in the winter of 1994-95, and I was attending an introductory MSIA seminar, listening to actress Sally Kirkland. Kirkland is a humorous, entertaining speaker, who is especially engaging when talking out of personal experience. That particular evening, she talked about the experiences that had brought her to John-Roger Hinkin's Movement of Spiritual Inner Awareness (MSIA).

The Church of the Movement of Spiritual Inner Awareness is a contemporary religious movement that was founded in 1971. This was a time when Eastern religions were popular in the early New Age subculture. Thus, while the movement participates in the larger metaphysical/new age subculture, MSIA's core spiritual practices lie in Asia, specifically in the 500-year-old Sant Mat tradition of North India. MSIA was founded by John-Roger Hinkins, generally called John-Roger, or, more informally, "J-R." In 1963, while undergoing surgery for a kidney stone, he fell into a nine-day coma. Upon awakening, he found himself aware of a new spiritual personality—"John"—who had superseded or merged with his old personality. After the operation, Hinkins began to refer to himself as "John-Roger," in recognition of his transformed self.

Currently, about 5000+ people study with MSIA (which means, minimally, that they subscribe to a series of monthly lessons called the Soul Awareness Discourses). Somewhat more than half or these are in the United States, and the rest in other countries. MSIA congregations meet for seminars, conferences, classes, retreats, and other kinds of meetings. MSIA's world headquarters is in Los Angeles, California.

The basic world view of MSIA is similar to that of other religious traditions with roots in the South Asian subcontinent—Hinduism, Buddhism, and Sikhism (particularly the latter). In common with these religions, MSIA accepts the notion that the individual soul is caught up in the material world, which is viewed as less desirable than the state of liberation from this realm. Because of reincarnation, the death of the physical body does not free a person from the material world. Only through the practice of certain spiritual techniques, such as the practice of meditation, can individuals liberate themselves from the cycle of death and rebirth.

Central to the teachings of the Sant Mat tradition is the necessity of a living human master who is competent in initiating disciples into the practice and technique of listening to the inner sound and contemplating the inner light (referred to as "spiritual exercises" in MSIA). While the Sant tradition refers to the living human master with such honorifics as "guru," "Satguru," Perfect Master," and so forth, in MSIA the teacher is referred to as the Mystical Traveler. John-Roger is understood to have been the Mystical Traveler until passing the "keys" of the "Traveler consciousness" to John Morton, his spiritual heir, in 1988.

Kirkland's first encounter with John-Roger occurred in 1972, when she was living in southern California. On the fortieth day of a carrot juice fast, she was hospitalized for an inability to void urine. Unable to determine the cause of the problem, her doctors planned a dangerous operation on her spine. Kirkland, however, had other ideas. After convincing them to give her an outpass, she walked out of the hospital:

> I went outside and Warren Beatty was standing there on the street. I know Warren socially, like I know practically everybody socially. Warren says, "Sally, how are you doing?" and he hugs me. And I burst into tears because guess what's in between me and Warren? A big, huge, catheter bag underneath my very flimsy dress.
>
> I burst into tears, and Warren says, "What's the matter? What did I do? What did I say?" I finally exclaimed, "They told me I'll never pee again!" and go running down the street. Finally, when I'm far enough away from Century Hospital, I see this newspaper stand. One of the papers catches my eye because it doesn't look like a normal newspaper. So I look and, by God, there's Satya Sai Baba on the cover, and he's got his arm around this guy. And the guy's name is John Roger.
>
> So suddenly I'm jealous of this guy because he knows Sai Baba—this high, holy person I've been trying to get to come to this country. So the next thing I know, I take a copy of this newspaper—I think it was called *The Movement*—and suddenly I experience this wave of energy. I just got all blissed out of my little head, and I came back to the hospital. I asked them to take off the catheter, and I peed. So that was my introduction to John-Roger.

While the particulars of Kirkland's story are unique, the more general scenario—joining a religious group in the wake of a spiritual experience—is a typical, though certainly not a universal, pattern.

As part of my research on MSIA, I collected demographic data via a short questionnaire. One of the statistics this survey collected was data on how people become involved in MSIA. Most people become involved with a religious group—whether traditional or non-traditional—through family and friendship networks. I was thus not surprised to find the same pattern among MSIA recruits, over half of whom were introduced to the movement by family or friends. (See Table 1.)

These statistics, however, tell us only how members were brought into *contact* with MSIA, and not specifically what *attracted* them to hang around after the initial contact. In Kirkland's case, for example, her first contact was via an initially impersonal encounter with *The Movement* newspaper. It was, however, the spiritual experience (described as a "wave of energy" in the above passage) accompanying her examination of the paper that prompted her to regard John-Roger as more than just another spiritual teacher.

Table 1 - Mode of Recruitment

1st MSIA Contact	Count	Percent
Impersonal/Media	18	3.6
Friends/Relatives	227	55.4
Insight Seminar	142	28.4
Other	49	9.8
No Response	14	2.8
TOTAL	500	100

One of the few open-ended items on the survey form asked respondents to discuss *briefly* how they had become involved in MSIA. Some members provided more detail than others. In one particularly rich account, the respondent met John-Roger during a trip in Egypt and subsequently, while taking a bath, had a remarkable spiritual experience related to J-R:

A ball of light formed over my head. Then the ball exploded and I knew *everything* and saw all my lifetimes with this man (Roger Hinkins). . . . When I stepped out of the bath, the words in my mind were, "THE SAME" - "HE IS THE SAME." I went to dinner and a clairvoyant friend said to me, "Our Spiritual Master is on this trip! I know because I recognize him as the *same* as the one in my heart." I knew who he meant because of what I had just experienced. I've been active in MSIA ever since.

A number of other respondents reported spiritual experiences in the initial stages of their affiliation with MSIA, though in most cases these were less dramatic than this one. By reflecting on such experiences we can understand one reason why people join non-mainstream religions, which is that many alternative religions hold out the possibility of life-transforming experiences—experiences that, to a greater or lesser extent, help one to drop the burden of the past and be reborn into a new and more complete life.

The mainstream Protestant denominations—Methodists, Baptists, and Presbyterians—once offered the seeker life-transforming experiences in the context of revivals and camp meetings. But as these religious bodies settled down into comfortable accommodation with the surrounding (largely secular) society, they lost their intensity. One result of this accommodation was that revivals and camp meetings—and the accompanying intense religious experiences—were relegated to a quaint and mildly embarrassing chapter in denominational histories.

Those of us who are happily adjusted to the social-cultural mainstream often have a difficult time understanding intense religiosity. Academics have not been exempt from this tendency. An earlier generation of sociologists of religion, seemingly obsessed with the issue of conversion to non-mainstream "sect" groups, gave excessive attention to explaining why individuals become involved in such churches.

If, however, rather than dwelling on strange externals, we change our point of focus and attempt to really look at what might actually attract someone to an alternative religion, such involvement is not really difficult to understand. Is the attraction of transformational experiences, for example, really so hard to comprehend? What if we actually could let go of the burden of our past and be reborn as new people? Such transformation may or may not be attainable, but the *attractiveness* of the *possibility* is certainly understandable. Many non-mainstream religions—conservative Christian sects included—hold out the promise of such life-changing experiences. Religious experience is, however, only one aspect of the spiritual life, and only one of the factors that attract individuals to deeper religious involvement.

Among the many approaches to religious studies, one of the older, yet still useful, scholarly analyses was articulated by the influential historian of religion Joachim Wach. The primary core of religion, according to Wach, is religious experience. Religious experience, in turn, is expressed in at least three ways:

> In a community (church, ashram, etc.)
> In a doctrine (theology, worldview, etc.)
> In a "cultus" (ritual, gathering, etc.)

If we reformulate Wach's schema and place religious experience alongside the three "expressions" of such experiences, we get four fundamental constituents of religion. In outline form, these constituents are:

> Spiritual experience
> Community
> Doctrine/idea system
> Gatherings/rituals

Each of these four components shed light on how individuals become involved in non-traditional religions.

As I have already indicated, many MSIA participants become involved in the group in the wake of a spiritual experience. This factor was particularly emphasized in older academic conversion literature. In this body of literature, the suddenness of the experience is stressed. The implicit or explicit paradigm is the Damascus Road experience, in which the apostle Paul was knocked off his horse by a bolt out of the blue, confronted by Jesus, and converted on the spot. Contemporary studies have found, however, that this is the exception rather than the rule. Instead, in most cases, individuals gradually "drift" into a religious group until they cross a barely perceptible line between outsider and insider, undergoing a series of "mini-conversions" en route.

The stepwise progression involved in such conversions was reflected in many of the responses to the MSIA survey. To cite one in which the respondent had a number of spiritual experiences before joining:

> I had an inner experience of the Traveler's voice. I knew the voice to be that of John-Roger as I'd heard it once at a taped seminar in 1974. I'd gone to it [the seminar] because I'd had a mystical experience, believe it or not, when I saw a poster about MSIA. I was very surprised by the experience and *very* reluctant to get involved. I had a powerful inner experience at the first taped seminar I attended and felt scared. I stayed away for about five years until the next inner experience.

Other participants come to a seminar, have no remarkable experiences, but keep coming back because they like the people or the teachings. They may even begin subscribing to Discourses with no particular intention of making MSIA their spiritual home. However, if they continue returning they eventually step across a threshold between "them" and "us," and, before they know it, begin identifying themselves as a participant in the movement. The great majority of respondents did *not* report spiritual experiences as playing a role in their "conversion" to MSIA; e.g.:

> A friend of mine in Santa Barbara and I were searching for a Master in the physical body. She attended an MSIA seminar, then called and told me I might want to check it out. I went to Conference #3 in 1971. After John-Roger's summer traveling I started going to seminars in El Monte, then moved back to Santa Barbara in November. I heard about discourses, and started them in December 1971. There were no great fireworks or revelations, just this quiet inner peace that let me know I was on the right path.

There were also a significant number of people who experienced what might be labelled "minor" spiritual experiences. Thus one survey respondent visited an acquaintance who "said J-R's name and showed me his photo." This person then felt his "heart expand." As a result of this experience, he began regularly attending MSIA seminars. Another respondent was meditating and "saw J-R inside; then I knew MSIA was my path."

Yet others report having dreams that played a role in their becoming involved in MSIA. Several respondents, for example, dreamed about J-R before meeting him:

> I met some ministers from Australia who gave me a *Wealth 101* tape. J-R and John Morton showed up in a dream that evening (I did not know either of them personally). I

recognized J-R, but did not recognize John Morton. Later I saw a photo and realized it was the same person. This intrigued me.

Other respondents described roughly similar experiences; e.g.:

I met some people who worked with John-Roger. I had a dream in which John-Roger appeared (before I knew what he looked like or what he did). I then met J-R in person and the part of me seeking someone with greater awareness recognized a greater awareness in him. I chose to listen to him and check out his teachings.

Moving even further away from the realm of unusual spiritual phenomena, but still within the arena of direct experience, many respondents reported that they initially became interested in MSIA as a result of meeting members who impressed them in some way; e.g.:

I began massage therapy with a woman in 1977 who was, and still is, a minister in the movement (MSIA). Her gifts continually opened my eyes and my heart, although she never proselytized, and only spoke of her faith in response to my questions.

Other respondents described parallel experiences with MSIA participants; e.g.:

While living in New York I met a person who seemed "at peace." This is quite an accomplishment for living in that city. His friends (who I later found were in MSIA as well) also had this peace. I became interested.

Closely related to the phenomenon of becoming involved in MSIA via an exceptionally "together" individual is the pattern of being attracted to the group as a consequence of the strong fellowship among MSIA participants.

More generally, the community dimension of *any* religious group is the key element in initially attracting new members. We live in a society that would have been an alien world to our ancestors. Surrounded by masses of people, we rarely know the names of our closest neighbors. In traditional societies, by way of contrast, everyone in your village knew everyone else, and took care of everyone else: If, for instance, you saw someone have an accident, you didn't call 911; instead you ran over and helped out as best you could. Some churches and most alternative religions recreate this kind of "extended family" type of community among their members.

The family metaphor is particularly apt. In modern society, our families are not the close emotional units they were in traditional societies. A small religious group many times recreates the sense of belonging to a family. If one has never experienced the closeness of a traditional family, it is easy to understand how the sense of belonging to a family unit would be attractive, and even healing.

The sense of having found a very attractive community of people came though in a number of different ways in the MSIA survey. One respondent reported that when he came through the door of MSIA headquarters he "was instantly struck by the loving energy—even before meeting one person." Another person reported being "really impressed by the goodness of these people. There was a certain energy about then that I found to be very loving and kind—they also laughed a lot."

A metaphor that was often deployed when respondents explained why they joined was that they felt "at home" with the movement almost immediately after encountering MSIA; e.g.: "When I discovered MSIA, I felt like I was `home.'" The feeling of *at-home-ness* can, of course, have different shades of meaning, not all of which connote feeling part of a community of people. In other words, one may have a feeling of at-home-ness with the teachings and practices rather than with the community. There were, however, a significant number of respondents whose expression of at-home-ness clearly carried the sense of having found a community of spiritual brothers and sisters. This set of respondents emphasized the experience of feeling accepted and unconditionally loved by MSIA members; e.g.:

> He [an MSIA minister] shared such a spirit of loving and unconditional giving with me, my socks were blown off. That [experience] began my journey on this path, which has brought me a profound sense of relief, as I know I had been looking for something for many years. Coming into MSIA was truly like coming home.

However, as important as the fellowship dimension is for understanding the attractiveness of MSIA, it should be pointed out that some individuals are acutely aware that many participants are with the organization for primarily social purposes. In a few cases, survey respondents explicitly noted that their involvement was based on other factors; e.g.:

> I am "in the movement" because of the inner experiences I have had. I do not utilize any of the classes for social purposes.

Another respondent stated that:

> I chose MSIA . . . because of my own inner experience, not necessarily the John-Roger seminars or discourses or the group connection, but because of what I experienced as an individual consciousness.

While most discourse subscribers participate in MSIA events, one can be a member in good standing entirely through the mail without ever seeing another MSIA person (except during initiations). Thus as powerful of a factor as fellowship is in understanding the involvement of many participants, it can be overstressed.

Another important factor is the teachings and the general worldview of MSIA. In a traditional society, beliefs about the ultimate nature of the universe are largely taken for granted.

It contemporary society, by way of contrast, nothing can be taken for granted except death and taxes. We are taught to be "nice" by our school system, but this moral teaching is not grounded in an ultimate source of value. We are also instructed in the basic skills necessary to operate in society, but public school teachers are quiet about the greater questions of death, purpose, and the meaning of life.

We may place a positive or a negative evaluation on this relativistic education, but we have to acknowledge that our culture's ambiguous approach to socialization departs radically from the socialization strategies of earlier societies. The results of this ambiguity may be liberating to some, but to others it is confusing. Without some kind of ultimate grounding, this is necessarily the case. While ethical teachings within various movements vary widely, they generally share the trait of grounding morality in the Divinity. Once one has stable criteria for what is good and true, this clarity and stability can then free one to go about the business of working, loving, and living life without debilitating anxieties about transcendent meaning and value. As one respondent to the MSIA survey wrote, "I have a solid foundation inside to draw on."

Only a relative handful of survey respondents emphasized what we might call the "intellectual" dimension of MSIA teachings as the primary factor in their initial attraction to the movement. One respondent in this category wrote that:

> I was very impressed with MSIA's philosophy. It was the most advanced, profound religion I had ever been exposed to.

Another respondent praised the teachings as the "highest" on the planet, though in the same breath was careful not to depreciate other teachings:

> The Mystical Traveler's teaching is, in my opinion, the highest teaching available on the planet today. This is not meant to imply that all the other teachings it has been my privilege to encounter are not also great teachings, or that the mystery teachings of the past in India and Egypt were not of the highest, but only to state that at the present time, *this is it!*

More often than not, when respondents mentioned MSIA's teachings it was in terms of the *resonance* between themselves and the teachings, rather than to remark on their philosophical profundity; e.g.:

> I found in MSIA teachings [what] I already believed in yet could find no one else that put it in words and print—I found my truth.

The impression that, for most participants, the attraction to MSIA is predominately non-discursive is reinforced by the fact that few people became involved in the movement as a direct result of reading one of the best-selling books that John-Roger co-authored with Peter

McWilliams. In my survey of 500 current and former members, only two mentioned books in the Life 101 series as being primary factors in prompting their participation in the movement.

Part of the issue here is that a significant percentage of MSIA's basic teachings are not unique to John-Roger, so that no great leap is required to make the transition from some other group in the New Age/metaphysical spectrum to MSIA. Sally Kirkland, for example, came to MSIA already convinced of the basic ideas shared by the Hindu yoga tradition and Sant Mat—particularly the notions of reincarnation, karma, and the idea that the ultimate goal of life was to escape the cycle of death and rebirth. Where her conversion occurred was accepting the notion that MSIA was the best path to achieve liberation.

The pattern of her experience was not unusual. It is infrequently the case that people without a prior disposition become deeply involved in an intensive religious group. If they do, they rarely remain for any length of time. In a benchmark study by the eminent British sociologist Eileen Barker, evidence is presented which supports the assertion that people who remain affiliated with the Unification Church for more than a few years were already grappling with some of the issues addressed by Unification theology long before they encountered this movement. This finding can be extrapolated to other religious groups.

People join alternate religions for the same sorts of reasons one would join any other religion, namely fellowship, a satisfying belief system, and so forth. When these needs are no longer being fulfilled in an acceptable manner, people leave, much as one would leave an unsatisfying marriage. The great majority of people who responded to the questionnaire had been seeking an appropriate spiritual path for many years before encountering MSIA. The following excerpt from one of the surveys is not atypical:

> Before MSIA, I was interested in meditation and yoga at a Kundalini Ashram. I lived there for approximately six months, and then spent a short time with Stephen Gaskin's "The Farm" group. I also studied with Guru Maharaji and went to India. I spent a month there. I also directed a choir with a metaphysical group originating in France.

Within the metaphysical/New Age subculture, this kink of sequential experimentation with one religious group after another is not untypical. Sociologists of religion have even coined a phrase for this pattern—the "conversion career"—meaning that the overall pattern of such individuals' spiritual lives is switching from one group to another.

However, the problem with this phrase as well as with the whole project of examining spiritual experimentation in the New Age subculture through the perspective of prior research on conversion in traditional religions is that "conversion" implies a rejection of one's earlier religious group as *false* while simultaneously embracing one's new faith as *true*. This is based on a marked tendency within traditional religions to emphasize the sharp transition from a non-enlightened or non-saved state to enlightenment or salvation. In contrast, contemporary occult/metaphysical spirituality emphasizes gradual growth, expansion of consciousness, and learning across time, including growth across many different lifetimes.

This gradual spiritual expansion constitutes a kind of evolution of the soul, and the metaphor of spiritual *evolution* is often expressed in the literature of this subculture. As a result, one's earlier involvements are not viewed as dead ends on the path to enlightenment, but, rather, as stepping stones, appropriate for the stage one was in at the time. Thus another MSIA seeker, in her contribution to an early (1974) compilation entitled *Across the Golden Bridge*, described her pre-MSIA journey in the following words:

> I studied Unity, Physiciana, Seekers of Truth, and became a 4th degree initiate, and then studied Divine Truth and Divine Science for three or four years. I was a doctor and licensed in the New Thought Movement, and a licensed minister in the Spiritualist Church, and also in Practical Christianity. From each of these groups I gained a deeper understanding, but something was missing.

As reflected in this passage, this person's experiences of other groups are viewed as *incomplete* rather than as *false*—as partial truths that led up to, and prepared the way for, her "conversion" to MSIA. This passage also reflects the dominant metaphor used to describe the process of spiritual evolution: *Learning.*

The tendency to utilize educational discourse and learning metaphors to embody essentially religious meanings is pervasive within the New Age/metaphysical subculture. For example, in the introduction to John-Roger's *The Way Out Book*, J-R talks about life experience being the "teacher" that prepares us to "graduate" from the cycle of death and rebirth. In addition, the dominant "ceremonies" in this subculture are workshops, lectures, seminars, and classes rather than worship ceremonies. These educational settings reflect a view of the human condition that sees spiritual development as a gradual learning process, rather than as the kind of abrupt "conversion experience" that occurs in the midst of traditional Protestant revivals. (For this reason, one should carefully note that MSIA classes, seminars, lectures, and workshops are *religious* activities, structurally comparable to Christian worship services, revivals, and prayer meetings.)

For many participants, the pattern of sampling one teaching after another does not stop after they join MSIA. John-Roger's teachings are tolerant and open-ended—an openness one member described as a lack of "religious walls." Furthermore, J-R is careful not to denounce other religious groups as false. As a consequence, members feel free to experiment with non-MSIA spiritual techniques and paths. In the words of one respondent:

> MSIA is the only set of teachings I have found to satisfactorily answer all life questions, and also feels right to participate. I have continued to sample other spiritual paths as a check that I'm still on the right path for me. I use a scientific approach to verify the correctness of my choice of spiritual association.

In a couple of cases, respondents expressed dissatisfaction with the movement, indicating that they were ready to drop their MSIA affiliation as soon as something else more attractive came along.

Not unsurprisingly, even people who had left MSIA tended to view their membership period positively, as a *learning* experience. In addition to current participants, questionnaires were also sent to people who had formerly been active in the group. Out of the 53 people who responded, most felt they benefitted in one way or another from their participation in the movement. This feeling of having benefitted from involvement was explicitly measured by an item on the questionnaire that asked respondents if their MSIA involvement had helped or hurt them:

How has your involvement in MSIA influenced your life, for better or for worse?

Responses to this questionnaire item are tabulated below, in Table 7 - Better/Worse for the Experience.

Table 2 - Better/Worse for the Experience

	Count	Percent
Better	38	71.1
Worse	4	7.8
Mixed	3	5.7
Neither	6	11.3
N/R	2	3.8

With almost three-fourths of the sample willing to assert unambiguously that they feel they are better off for having participated in MSIA, it is easy to see how so few ex-members felt a need to castigate the movement, the teachings, or the founder. This situation is perfectly understandable if we realize that most of the people who have defected from MSIA still consider themselves "on the path," in the larger sense, and continue to participate in some form of metaphysical/New Age spirituality. Such people thus regard their membership period as part of their larger quest, and, as a consequence, positively value the time and energy they invested in MSIA.

The pattern of responses to another questionnaire item that assessed the value of the membership period reinforces this interpretation. This item asked respondents to imaginatively place themselves back in time at the point where they initially became involved in MSIA:

If you could be transported back to the time you began your involvement with MSIA, you would probably
       1. Do it all over again with few or no changes

2. Do it all over again with many changes
3. Not get so deeply involved
4. Not get involved at all

Responses to this questionnaire item are tabulated below, in Table 3 - Would You Do It All Over Again?

Table 3 - Would You Do It All Over Again?

	Count	Percent
1	32	60.4
2	5	9.4
3	5	9.4
4	7	13.2
N/R	4	7.5

Here once again we have an exaggerated pattern of response. In this particular case, the great majority of the sample (more than three-fifths) assert that, if they had their membership period to do over again, they would "do it all over again with few or no changes."

The ex-member survey form also contained an open-ended item that asked respondents how their involvement in MSIA had influenced their lives, for better or for worse. Parallel to responses from current members indicating that their earlier affiliations had prepared them for MSIA, ex-members tended to view MSIA as a prior stage in their development; e.g., to cite from one questionnaire: "I view MSIA as a preparatory phase for what I am doing now." Also, as we might have anticipated, some former participants couched their responses in terms of what they had *learned;* e.g.:

> One of the most useful things I learned was about karma—that our soul is here to learn and experience things that we incarnate onto this planet to do. It has helped me not to be judgmental of other people and myself.

Another way in "conversion" carries connotations inappropriate for interpreting organizations like MSIA is that such movements are not *conversionist* in the traditional sense. A general belief in the New Age/metaphysical subculture is that, in J-R's words, "not one soul will be lost." In other words, in sharp contrast to Christianity and certain other traditional faiths, no one is going to be damned to hell for eternity. If not a single soul will be lost, there is, as a consequence, no burning need to immediately bring everyone into the fold.

If anything, MSIA's spiritual atmosphere seems to be permeated by an *anti*-conversionist ethic. I received the impression that if anyone were to attempt to collar strangers and bring them to MSIA events, he or she would be censured by other members, or, at the very least, perceived as not embodying the spirit of the movement. This anti-conversionist ethic was reflected in the MSIA questionnaire in a number of ways. For instance, at least a dozen survey respondents reported that, far from experiencing proselytization, they had to twist their contact person's arm before the person revealed his or her religious affiliation.

Furthermore, MSIA's anti-conversionist ethic was frequently cited as a significant (though never the primary) factor in attracting people to the movement. This "conversion aversion" was described by several survey respondents as "non-inflictive"; e.g.:

> I have appreciated the community of MSIA and feel comfortable around the people and the non-inflictive approach.

MSIA's non-inflictive approach flows out of its open-minded acceptance of human diversity. In the words of one respondent:

> One of the key concepts which touched me deeply was hearing J-R say one evening that, "There are as many roads (paths) to God as there are beings on this planet."

With the notion of human diversity at the core of the movement's teachings, it follows that MSIA can be the appropriate path for only a certain number of people. Thus, as I have heard many participants articulate in a variety of ways, the individuals who the movement is meant to attract will find their way to the teachings. When these people stumble across MSIA, they will recognize that they have found their spiritual "home," and will eventually join the movement.

On the other hand, people for whom there is no pre-existing resonance with MSIA should not be persuaded to participate, no matter how universal and wholesome one might feel the movement to be. In most cases, such people will affiliate only briefly, and then leave. This being the case, How can one proselytize?

This aspect of the teachings leads to an ambivalence about movement growth. Participants are generally happy and want to share their happiness, but at the same time do not want to "inflict" their beliefs on other. This has led to, among other things, a movement-wide *ambivalence* about growth. In the 1970s MSIA expanded rapidly until it had grown to about five thousand members. At that point growth in total numbers stopped. Over the years people have come and gone, while the overall membership figure has remained about the same.

In terms of this non-expansion, MSIA presents a profile of being similar to a traditional community in the Hindu tradition centered around a guru and his intimate disciples. Normally, this kind of a movement does not attempt to grow beyond a close community of teacher and students. Using this model as a lens through which to view MSIA, it is not surprising that the group has essentially the same number of members as it did twenty years ago. This pattern sharply contrasts with the media portrayal of MSIA as an aggressively expansionist organization out to convert as many members as possible.

Before shifting away from the theme of open-minded acceptance, it should be noted that a number of respondents called attention to MSIA's acceptance of homosexuality as a factor in their involvement. Several stressed that, "There were no judgments from J-R concerning my homosexual orientation." While the organization is composed predominantly of heterosexuals, I noted a significant number of homosexuals (at least in the Los Angeles area) who are accepted on an equal footing with other participants.

As I bring this discussion to a close, I should note a number of other factors influencing certain respondents' recruitment into MSIA. One of these was that at least three survey respondents were adult children of MSIA members. Given complete freedom to become involved or to stay away from the organization, these individuals chose to join the fold; e.g.:

> My parents became involved when I was two. They have always encouraged me to explore other religions, however, which I have done. It wasn't until recently that I decided MSIA was for me.

I could not determine if this pattern was typical or atypical of individuals raised in the movement.

Another factor for some members was that John-Roger had been one of their High School teachers; e.g.:

> I have known about MSIA since high school, when John-Roger (then Mr. Roger Hinkins) was my English teacher. About two years ago I was reminded of MSIA by a series of what I call significant events, so I decided to check it out.

Only a relative handful of currently active participants had J-R as their High School teacher.

Finally, more than a few respondents indicated that one of the factors which attracted them to MSIA was the organization's *Christian* emphasis. This initially surprised me, as the movement departs markedly from traditional Christianity. Theologically, MSIA's christology is comparable to the christology found in many metaphysical/New Age religions. In these traditions, Jesus is demoted from his status as the third face of the godhead, and becomes, instead, a master medium or master teacher. From MSIA's particular perspective, Jesus was the physical anchor for the Mystical Traveler Consciousness.

While christology is not at the core of MSIA's teaching, members nevertheless regard themselves as "followers of the Christ." And while John-Roger feels free to draw upon all traditions, he often draws upon the teachings and example of Jesus. A number of survey respondents found this tendency comforting; e.g.:

> What I was taught as a child, within a traditional Protestant setup, has "come alive." Jesus, the Christ, and his teachings mean so much to me, and MSIA has helped me in the journey.

For at least a dozen respondents, a major factor attracting them to MSIA was its "Christian" emphasis.

References:

About MSIA: The Movement of Spiritual Inner Awareness. MSIA Brochure. Los Angeles: The Church of the Movement of Spiritual Inner Awareness, n.d.

Beck, Sanderson and Mark T. Holmes, eds. *Across the Golden Bridge.* Los Angeles: Golden Age Education Publications, 1974.

Hinkins, John-Roger. *The Way Out Book.* Los Angeles, California: Baraka Press, 1986; rpt of 1980.

Lewis, James R. "The Cult Stereotype as a Resource in Social Conflicts: A Case Study of the Movement of Spiritual Inner Awareness." *Syzygy: Journal of Alternative Religion and Culture,* 3:1-2. 1994.

Lewis, James R. and J. Gordon Melton, eds. *Perspectives on the New Age.* Albany: State University of New York Press, 1992.

Melton, J. Gordon. *Encyclopedia of American Religion.* Detroit: Gale Research, 4th ed., 1993.

Singh, Kirpal. *The Crown of Life: A Study in Yoga.* Delhi: Ruhani Satsang, 1971.

Soul Transcendence, Introduction to the Movement of Spiritual Inner Awareness. MSIA Brochure. Los Angeles: The Church of the Movement of Spiritual Inner Awareness, 1995.

Zonta, Michela (and James R. Lewis). "A Demographic Profile of the Movement of Spiritual Inner Awareness." *Syzygy: Journal of Alternative Religion and Culture,* 4:1-2. 1995.

In the Lens of Jonestown
Suicide and the Branch Davidians

I do not think the United States government is responsible for the fact that a bunch of religious fanatics decided to kill themselves.

> — Bill Clinton (cited in Kopel and Blackman 1997:204)

On February 27, 1993, Sharon Wheeler, a secretary working for the Bureau of Alcohol, Tobacco, and Firearms in Dallas, called various news media, some from as far away as Oklahoma: Would they be interested in reporting a weapons raid against a local "cult"? (She later denied being this specific; rather, she claimed, she had just informed them that "something big" was going to happen.) The ATF initially denied contacting the media, but this was just clumsy prevarication. Uncovered by the congressional committee investigating the Waco fiasco, Wheeler's phone call was but one manifestation of the increasingly ghoulish pact between media and law enforcement: You give me free publicity; I'll give you newsworthy violence. Even the codeword for initiating the raid, "Showtime,"[1] implies that the raid was staged as a PR stunt (Grigg 2003). This ill-considered bid for the media spotlight, sanctioned and initiated by senior ATF officials, set the stage for the tragic fiasco at the Mt. Carmel headquarters of the Branch Davidian Seventh-day Adventists.

The next day, the Davidians learned of the raid at least 45 minutes—some sources say two hours—beforehand. When news of the tip-off became public, the ATF immediately fingered the media as the responsible party. If this attribution is correct, it means the agency, which contacted the press the preceding day, has only itself to blame for the deaths of its agents (Wessinger 2000:62). There are, however, additional factors at work that had clued the community into the fact that they were under surveillance well before February 28. In particular, the Davidians were wise to the undercover informant, Agent Robert Rodriguez, who lived in a run-down shack near Mt. Carmel, but who also wore new clothing and drove a late model automobile (Reavis 1998:67). On the morning of the attack, Koresh told Rodriguez he knew they were coming. Before the agent bolted from the community that Sunday morning, Koresh shock his hand and said, using the words Jesus spoke to Judas, "What thou doest, do quickly" (Tabor 1994:17). The agent then drove rapidly down the driveway to the undercover house just across the road and immediately phoned Charles Sarabyn, the raid commander: "Chuck, they know. They know. They know we're coming!" (Willman and Bunting 1995). In light of this information, Rodriguez assumed the raid would be called off. However, not wishing to disappoint the reporters who had gathered to see the show, Sarabyn asked the agent if he had seen any weapons or if the Davidians appeared to be mobilizing. When Rodriguez replied, "They were praying" (Grigg 2003), the raid commander decided to proceed with the assault anyway.

The many ATF agents clad in body armor and gun gear who were suspiciously milling around in motel lobbies throughout Waco earlier Sunday morning might also have contributed to the community's foreknowledge of the raid (Oliver 1993:75). This situation prompted Col. Charlie Beckwith, retired founder of the U.S. Army's elite Delta Force, to remark that, "The ATF might just as well run a flag up telling everyone something was about to happen" (1994:69). Beckwith's analysis of the ATF attack, originally published in the July issue of *Soldier of Fortune* magazine, also called attention to the "gross error of judgement" involved in the selection of the time for the assault: "Successful assault operations are conducted during the hours of darkness or a few minutes before first light" (ibid.:70). One can only surmise the agency selected full daylight because of their overriding concern that the raid be recorded by TV cameramen.[2] There were at least eleven reporters on the scene prior to the arrival of the assault team. Given this gross neglect of basic security matters, it is no surprise the Davidians found out ahead of time.

One of the Branch Davidians I interviewed, Stan Sylvia, had been with Koresh for over ten years. An important piece of the puzzle I learned from Sylvia was that, contrary to the NBC docudrama, "Ambush at Waco," community members were *not* systematically trained to use weapons—Sylvia had fired a gun a total of twice in the ten years he was with David Koresh. Most of the guns at the community, which constituted the inventory for member Paul Fatta's gunshow business, were kept boxed and never fired (Wessinger 2000:62). The ATF knew all of this, which probably explains why they felt safe going ahead and attacking Mt. Carmel even after they knew they had lost the element of surprise. Some of the Davidians, however, took guns from Fatta's stock (he was at a gun show on the morning of the raid) after the community had been tipped off, and prepared to fight off attackers.

Ninety-one heavily-armed ATF agents drove up to Mt. Carmel—almost as many agents as community members. They were hidden in cattle trailers, but the Davidians knew who their visitors were. The agency claimed Davidians fired first. However, given ATF's track record of spinning out one self-serving falsehood after another, as well as Koresh's prior history of peaceful cooperation with law enforcement officials, the Davidian prophet's assertion that he just opened the door and was shot at seems more believable than the agency account. To a religious group nourished on apocalyptic images from the book of Revelation, the assault must have seemed like the first skirmish in Armageddon. While it is difficult to verify every particular, the following account, pieced together from diverse sources, represents a fairly accurate description of what occurred that fateful Sunday morning.

Showdown at the Waco Corral

Hearts were pounding in tense expectancy when three National Guard helicopters swooped over the ridgeline and converged on Mt. Carmel. There was an exchange of gunfire, during which at least some of the community's casualties were incurred. Shortly afterwards, two trucks pulling canvas-covered livestock trailers rushed up the driveway and stopped in front of the building, positioning themselves between the reporters who had gathered in the front lawn and Mt. Carmel.

Hoping to avoid violence, David Koresh, unarmed, opened the front door, and began shouting, "Go away! There are women and children here! Let's talk!" According to some accounts, this gesture of appeasement was answered by a bullet, fired by Agent Steve Willis, who had been assigned to "take out" Koresh. Willis, seated on the passenger side of an ATF vehicle, fired at the Davidian prophet with a suppressed (silenced) nine millimeter H & K machine gun in such a way that the press would not see his act of aggression (Vinzant 1994, p. 49). At the same time, ATF agents in dark blue uniforms jumped out of the cattle trailers, tossing concussion grenades and screaming "Come out!" A lead agent shouted "It's showtime!" as he jumped from the trailer (Wessinger 2000:61). Willis initially missed Koresh, who slammed the door and dove for cover as a fusillade of bullets crashed through the door. Koresh was eventually hit twice, in the wrist and in the abdomen. The Davidians who had armed themselves began shooting back, taking particular aim at Willis, who was the first agent to die.

The firefight then began in earnest. Hundreds of bullets filled the air, crashing through the buildings and vehicles, and throwing up geysers of dirt as they furiously buried themselves in the soft Texas earth. It happened quickly, like the crashing of a tidal wave over a sleepy costal village. Peter Gent, who had been scrapping rust off of the community water tower—the ATF subsequently dubbed it a "watchtower"—died as he turned his head to see what the commotion was all about. Jaydean Wendell, an ex-policewoman and mother of four, died when a bullet struck her on the top of the head. Winston Blake, who was sitting on the edge of his bed eating a late breakfast of french toast, was gunned down by unseen assailants firing wildly into the thin wooden walls of Mt. Carmel. The children, screaming in fear, hid themselves under the beds and any available cover as the undirected fusillade of bullets whizzed through the air.

The Davidians quickly called 911 for help. The details of this conversation reveal a community startled by the violence of the assault. At one point Koresh, speaking to the Waco police, shouted in anguish, "You killed some of my children!" "There is a bunch of us dead and a bunch of you guys dead now—that's your fault!" At other points in the conversation, Koresh made assertions like, "We told you we wanted to talk!" "Now we are willing and we've been willing all this time to sit down with anybody!" These assertions align well with the attitude of cooperation the Davidians had displayed in the past, and sharply call into question the necessity for a dramatic, quasimilitary assault.

Despite public statements to the contrary, agents fired blindly into walls and windows, a shooting style pejoratively referred to as "spray and pray" in law enforcement circles. The attack plan failed to foresee the possibility that the assault team crossing the roof from south to north would be in the line of gunfire from agents firing from behind vehicles located on the front (west) side of the building complex. Also, helicopter gunfire was misdirected so that it went completely through the building and impacted among agents on the ground. The failure to take this crossfire situation into account was compounded by the special bullets utilized by agents, the 9mm Cyclone. This bullet, available only to law enforcement, is a hollow steel cylinder designed to slice through body armor like a "flying cookie cutter," in the words of one writer. To increase its power to pierce through armor and other obstacles, the powder in the shell propels the bullet to exceedingly high velocities (Kopel and Blackman 1997:107-108). These deep penetration bullets could only have increased the possibility of agents shooting each other as they assaulted different parts of the complex. Thus, despite heated ATF denials, it is probable that some—perhaps even the majority—of agency casualties were sustained as a result of "friendly fire" (Wessinger 2000:67).

Outside the building complex, a bullet shattered the windshield of one of the press vehicles. Another flattened a tire. KWTX cameraman Dan Mulloney later told the *Dallas Morning News*, "The first five minutes was just a job. Then we started seeing people get hit and we heard bullets hitting around us. I figured I was going to get shot. I started thinking of my kids . . . ." KWTX reporter John McLemore related that "People were being hit. You could hear people screaming with the agony." One agent shouted at McLemore: "Hey! TV man! Call for an ambulance!" He got up and rushed some yards across open ground, leaping into his jeep and grabbing his radio as a round impacted against the door. Other bullets made sickening metallic sounds as they slammed into the side of his vehicle. "I got scared," he recalled (Pate 1993a).

Two ATF casualties occurred when a team of agents went for upper rooms believed to contain an armory and Koresh's bedroom. Video footage from this dramatic episode—showing an agent on the roof dodging bullets fired through an adjacent wall—appeared on the TV news the same day. This clip was shown over and over again in subsequent weeks, not unlike the video footage of Rodney King's beating that was aired every time the King case was mentioned on TV. Three agents were wounded and two killed in this tragically botched phase of the operation. Had the raid truly been a surprise, they would have effectively prevented the Davidians from arming themselves. Without a backup plan, however, the agents charged blindly forward with this phase of the attack. Agents Todd McKeehan and Conway LeBleu were shot and killed. Other agents on the roof were wounded and escaped. (Reavis 1998:151-155).

Soon after the failed raid, rumors—based in part on news video footage—circulated to the effect that the exchange of gunfire did not begin until after LeBleu slipped on a ladder, accidently shot himself in the foot, and started yelling "I'm hit! I'm hit!" (Kopel and Blackman 1997:103). His pistol had discharged while still in the holster. Despite this wound, he continued to carry out his assigned part of the raid, eventually meeting death with Agent McKeehan. Though this self-inflicted wound may not have actually initiated the fire fight, the image of a flawed, unprofessional raid beginning with an agent shooting himself in the foot has a certain strange appeal, which may explain why the story was repeated over and over again in the media.

Toward the end of the raid, a lone Davidian repeatedly called for "peace" as he appeared in a lower story doorway. Each time, he was answered with a hail of gunfire. The ATF did not see fit to end the assault until they were out of ammunition. Only at that point did they call for a cease fire, which the community readily granted. The Davidians further allowed the ATF to remove wounded agents, even assisting then with this task. These acts of reasonableness and kindness, coming from a community that had been violently and undeservedly assaulted, were quickly forgotten. Both the agency and the media, motivated by different but convergent agendas, proceeded immediately to demonize the Davidians as evil fanatics.

Though the ATF repeatedly asserted they had been practicing the assault for months, at least some of the agents involved were not briefed until the preceding day, and were never told they would be facing high power, assault-type weapons. Incredibly, the ATF did not even bring a doctor to treat wounded agents—a standard practice of more professional agencies like the FBI. These inept, keystone cop antics of the ATF are difficult to understand unless we suppose that agency officials simply assumed the Davidians would give up at the first sign of a superior force—a fatal assumption that would have been immediately rejected by anyone who knew anything about survivalist religious groups. The stupidity of the attack was exceeded only by the stupidity of the explanation ATF spokespersons offered for the attack's failure: "We had an excellent plan and we practiced it for months. Everything would have been fine, except we were outgunned" (Richardson 1994:181).

What? If ATF was serving a search warrant to a heavily-armed "cult" believed to have automatic weapons and perhaps even hand grenades, Why were they surprised by the Davidians' powerful gunfire? Especially after they lost the element of surprise, Why did ATF agents charge in with guns blazing? If Mt. Carmel was such a dangerous place, Why didn't they just lay siege to it from the very beginning rather than sacrificing the lives of their agents? The reason given to the public was that, in the words of one ATF official, "Either they were going to come out and attack the citizens of Waco or do a Jonestown, which was why an operation was staged that placed our agents between a rock and a hard place. Our information was that was how bad its was" (cited in Lewis 2000:100).

The perception that Mt. Carmel was another Jonestown waiting to happen is interesting from a number of different points of view. John R. Hall (2002; Hall et al. 2000; 1995) has argued that the ATF sincerely believed they were dealing with a suicide cult, which helps explain a number of aspects of the attack that are otherwise difficult to interpret. This initial attribution of being suicidal was later reinforced by the FBI who, following the deadly second attack, claimed the Branch Davidians had committed mass suicide—an explanation conveniently absolving them of any blame for the resulting deaths (Palmer 1994; Lewis 1994b; Bradford 1994).

After surveying the Davidians, the Adventist tradition out of which they emerged, and Koresh's interpretation of scripture, this chapter will focus on the "suicide cult" perception and how it helped shape the Davidian tragedy of 1993. Also, current theorists have stressed the important role hostile external forces play in the precipitation of most new religion-related violence. This line of thinking—which seems to have originated from careful reflection on the Jonestown murder-suicides—received considerable impetus from the Branch Davidians, who were for the most part victims rather than perpetrators of violence.[3] It will thus be useful to explore in some detail the "exogenous" factors (Robbins 2002:58) that set the Mt. Carmel tragedy in motion.

Meeting the Lord in the Air[4]

The Adventist tradition from which the Davidians ultimately derive originated with the evangelism of the Baptist layman William Miller. After an intensive study of the Bible, he became convinced he was living near the end of his age and that he had to tell the world about it. After Baptists gave him a license to preach in September 1833, Miller dedicated ten years of his life to preaching and teaching his message of the imminent return of Jesus. Central to Miller's belief was the conviction, based on his study of the books of Daniel and Revelation, that he had deciphered the chronology pinpointing the end of the age. His view, sustained by several figures, was that 1843 was the year of the "cleansing of the sanctuary," which he derived from Daniel 8:14 and which he interpreted to mean the Second Coming (Miller 1842).

As the movement expanded, the Millerites, as they were called, became targets of ridicule. One of the more colorful bits of folklore about the Millerites was that they dressed themselves in white "ascension robes" (Ehrlich 1994) in preparation for the Second Coming. The idea seems to have been that they would thus be wearing appropriately heavenly attire when they rose to meet Jesus in the air (I Thessalonians 4:17). It was even said that some Millerites sat on their rooftops on the appointed day to avoid bumping their heads against their ceilings as they floated upwards during the rapture.

Miller gave himself a wide margin of error, predicting that the end would come sometime between March 21st, 1843 and March 21st, 1844. Although a large comet as well as other spectacular phenomena appeared in the sky in late February, the Second Coming did not occur. Soon new adjustments in Miller's chronology were made by Samuel S. Snow, who looked to October 22, 1844, as the real date of return. But once again nothing happened, and a "Great Disappointment" resulted that left the movement in chaos. Miller soon retired from active leadership in the movement, while believers organized themselves into a number of new denominational bodies. Some groups of followers decided to return to the original source of revelation and seek a new date for the endtime. Few of these groups lasted beyond their projected new dates.

One Millerite, Ellen G. White, developed the interpretation that Miller was not wrong about the *occurrence* of the eschatologically significant event, but that he was wrong about the *nature* of the event. Jesus did not return to earth in 1844, but he did begin the cleansing of the *heavenly* sanctuary (Hebrews 8:1-2). By 1863, White and others had brought together the network of remaining Adventists sufficiently to organize the Seventh Day Adventist Church. Many Adventist beliefs were taken over from the Baptist roots of the early members. Other beliefs and practices, such as the Sabbatarian (observing Saturday as the Sabbath) teachings of the Old Testament were accepted, as were many of the dietary regulations. Members were forbidden to use tobacco or alcohol. The Seventh-Day Adventist Church also came to teach that White was a prophet, which provides a background for understanding Koresh's later assumption of a prophetic mantle.

The Davidian Seventh-day Adventists—originally known as the Shepherd's Rod—were a small Adventist splinter group founded by Victor T. Houteff. Houteff was a Bulgarian immigrant who converted to Seventh-Day Adventism. He served as assistant Sabbath day superintendent and began developing his own ideas about religion. He eventually felt a spiritual calling that led him to claim a prophetic role (Pitts 1995:21). In 1930, he started publishing tracts under the title *Shepherd's Rod* (from Micah 6:9 "Hear ye the rod"). Houteff saw himself as an Adventist reformer, but this view was not shared by the leaders of the General Conference Seventh-day Adventists, who disfellowshipped him in 1930.

Seeking a new site for his ministry, Houteff moved to Texas (Pitts 2002:265). In 1935, he established a community near Waco he that named Mt. Carmel. Their principal activity was the production of tracts. Originally designated the Shepherd's Rod, the group adopted the name Davidian Seventh-Day Adventists in 1942 as a way of helping members establish conscientious objector status during the second world war (the new designation identified them more closely with their parent body, which the government already recognized as pacificist).

When Houteff died in 1955, his wife Florence succeeded him. Although Houteff fully expected the Advent to take place soon—the logo he created for his church was a clock with its hands set near 11:00, indicating humanity was in its last hour (Pitts 1995:25)—he never set a date. Florence Houteff, despite strong internal opposition from Davidian leaders, prophesied that on April 22, 1959, the Kingdom of God would be established. Davidians believed only God's chosen faithful would avoid being destroyed. Many members believed Victor Houteff would be resurrected to assume leadership. In the wake of the prophecy, group membership swelled to 1,500. Between 500 and 1,000 believers sold their homes and possessions and moved to Waco in 1959 in anticipation of the End. When Florence Houteff's prophecy failed, there was widespread disillusionment among members. The faithful began to scatter and some started splinter groups. Many of Florence Houteff's former followers joined the Branch Seventh-Day Adventists. Three years later she announced that her teachings contained errors, dissolved her church, and sold most of the Mt. Carmel property.

The Branch SDA had formed earlier as one of several splinters that broke with the main body of Davidian SDAs following Victor Houteff's death. The name comes from Benjamin Roden's warning to "get off the dead Rod and move onto a living Branch" (Linedecker 1993:57). This faction had never accepted Florence Houteff as a prophet. Like both Victor and Florence, Benjamin Roden and later his wife Lois assumed a prophetic role that made them more than simply leaders of a new denomination. In addition to claiming prophetic status, the Rodens also legitimated their authority by identifying themselves as successors of a lineage that went back through Victor Houteff to Ellen White and William Miller (Bromley and Silver 1995a).

Florence Houteff's failed prophecy presented Benjamin Roden with an opportunity to lead the church—a role he had sought earlier following Victor Houteff's passing. Within a short time, the 57-year-old Roden won over most of the remaining Davidians and, after a period of litigation, managed to acquire control over what remained of Mt. Carmel's property. Roden saw his mission as creating a Christlike moral character in the ranks of the membership. In fact, he taught that the Second Coming would occur soon after members had attained sufficient moral rectitude. In 1970, Benjamin Roden announced that he had a vision which his followers came to view as the beginning of the "rule of God on earth" (ibid.:51). He also enhanced his prophetic status by placing himself in King David's lineage. He granted the power to name his successor to the chairman of the executive council, a position Roden himself held, and he installed his son George Roden as second in command and heir apparent.

Benjamin Roden's wife Lois began having spiritual visions in 1977. Central to her revelations was the discovery that the Holy Spirit was female. She also taught that God is female as well as male, and that the new messiah would be a woman. She started a magazine, *SHEkinah*, to promulgate her views (Pitts 1995:36). Not long after her vision, she undertook a study of the scriptures and acquired ministerial credentials. On October 22, 1978, Benjamin Roden died. Lois quickly laid claim to leadership. However, half of Mt. Carmel's members left as a result of political infighting and Lois's new theological doctrines. George Roden initiated an effort to regain what he believed to be his rightful place as leader. He unsuccessfully appealed to Mt. Carmel residents and the courts. The conflict between George and his mother quickly escalated until Lois Roden finally took out a court order that barred her son from Mt. Carmel.

"Mine Iniquities are More Than the Hairs of Mine Head"

The same year Florence Houteff's prophecy failed, Vernon Howell—who would later change his name to David Koresh—was born to a young single mother in Houston, Texas. He lived with his grandmother during the first five years of his life until his mother married. Continuous academic problems created by a learning disability troubled his early school years. Howell dropped out of high school in 1974 before completing the tenth grade. His passions as a teenager were playing guitar and studying the Bible. He memorized long sections of the New Testament, preaching to anyone who would listen. In the years that followed, he held a succession of short-term jobs, often as a carpenter.

In 1979, Howell began participating in study sessions at a Seventh-Day Adventist Church in Tyler, Texas, that his mother attended. There were a succession of incidents in which he announced that God intended him to marry the pastor's daughter, continually preached his own version of SDA theology to other church members, and took over the pulpit to propound his theological views. He was eventually disfellowshipped (Linedecker 1993:84).

Howell learned of the Branch Davidians from an SDA friend and began working as a handyman at Mt. Carmel in 1981. He became a favorite of 67-year-old Lois Roden. Rumors began circulating that Roden and Howell's close relationship was not platonic. The relationship raised Howell's status within the group and Lois Roden acquired an ally. Lois tried to head off an emerging power struggle between Howell and her son by designating Howell as her successor. She arranged for Davidian members to come and listen to his teachings. Howell attracted young adults in part because of his own youth (prior Davidian leaders had been much older), and because of his musical interests and talent. Attracting younger people was something the Rodens had been unable to do. Converts point to Howell's biblical knowledge more than any other single factor explaining their attraction to the Branch Davidians.

In 1984 Howell created a family alliance by marrying 14-year-old Rachael Jones, whose father Perry Jones was one of the most senior and respected members of the Davidian community. Jones had been an early and loyal follower of the Rodens, and had served as a journalist for *SHEkinah* (Bromley and Silver 1995a:53). Over the next five years the couple gave birth to a son, Cyrus, and a daughter, Star.

George Roden organized and won an election for the presidency of the Branch Davidians in 1985, after which he evicted Howell and his followers from Mt. Carmel, and renamed the community Rodenville. Howell and a couple dozen followers, half of whom were children, moved to the Texas community of Palestine, about 100 miles from Waco. They constructed crude structures and led a primitive, marginal lifestyle.

In 1986 Lois Roden died. By this time, only two or three dozen residents remained at Mt. Carmel and Howell had won the loyalty of most of the community. The Branch Davidians' financial position had deteriorated to the point where they were unable to pay property taxes. The 1979 injunction Lois Roden had taken out against George remained in effect, so the Howell faction started proceedings to have George Roden found in contempt of court and evict him from Mt. Carmel. In retaliation, George Roden filed a series of legal motions and suits against Howell that were filled with so many profanities that Roden was threatened with contempt citations.

George Roden also tried to trump Howell in the spiritual arena by challenging him to a "resurrection contest." He dug up the casket of Anna Hughes, who had died 20 years earlier at Mt. Carmel, and proposed that the two of them compete to raise her from the dead. Howell lodged a complaint with the sheriff's office, but was told nothing could be done without evidence. So on the evening of November 3, 1987, he and some others went to Mt. Carmel to take a photograph of the woman's remains that could be used as evidence to prosecute Roden. This led to a gun battle in which Roden received a minor wound. Howell and his group were tried for attempted murder, but charges were eventually dismissed (Bromley and Silver 1995b:153). Roden, on the other hand, got into trouble for his violation of Lois Roden's restraining order and for filing suits containing profanity.

After murdering another man in 1989, he was committed to the Big Spring State Hospital mental facility in west Texas. (Wagner-Pacifici 2000:35)

Howell and his followers quickly re-occupied Mt. Carmel. They found and removed an illegal methamphetamine laboratory and a large quantity of pornography. Shortly thereafter, Howell convinced a well-to-do Branch Davidian family to pay back taxes on the property. The group also undertook a major cleanup and reconstruction project that expanded their living quarters.

The membership of the group had been severely depleted as a consequence of the infighting that had plagued Davidians since 1960. Under Howell's leadership, they began to recruit both nationally and internationally, traveling to Hawaii, Canada, England, Israel and Australia. Efforts at street recruiting were unsuccessful, so the recruitment campaigns targeted current or former Seventh-Day Adventists. Branch Davidians were willing to disrupt SDA church services to gain a hearing for their message. Those who converted were usually disfellowshipped from the SDA. The recruitment campaigns yielded several dozen converts and created an international, interracial community of about 100 at Mt. Carmel.

By 1993 more than one-third of the population at Ranch Apocalypse were children as a consequence of the demographics of the adult population, which were in the 20-45 year old range. Asians, Hispanics, and Blacks constituted 50% of the community. Though mostly American, members were also British, Australian, Canadian, Jamaican and Filipino. Some men worked in manufacturing plants and a number of women were nurses. Those who held outside jobs contributed their income, while the elderly contributed their Social Security payments and food stamps. Well-to-do members donated money and sometimes property. Members attempted to be as self-sufficient as possible, growing their own food and even making some of their own clothing.[5] The community also had an automobile repair/renovation enterprise that grew out of the prophet's automotive skills. Member Paul Fatta operated a weapons business that purchased guns and gun-related commodities and resold them at gun shows (Bromley and Silver 1995:55). It was this latter business, which represented such a radical departure from the pacifist tradition of the SDA, that made them a target for the ATF.

On a typical day, community residents rose at 6 a.m. and took their breakfasts in the shared dining room. Members then went off to work at outside jobs or engaged in activities at Mt. Carmel such as building, gardening and child rearing. At times children were educated in local schools; at others they were home-schooled. Following dinner there were regular Bible study periods that could last well into the night. Morning and afternoon study sessions were sometimes held as well. Devotional activity was at the center of community life. Living conditions were primitive. The buildings had no central heating or air conditioning, and little indoor plumbing. Members pumped water from a well at Mt. Carmel and daily removed waste from the buildings.

"The Bible was Written for Our Time"

In 1990 Howell legally adopted the name David Koresh. "Koresh" is Hebrew for Cyrus, the Persian king who conquered the Babylonians and restored the Jewish people to Palestine. The Jews regard Cyrus as a messiah. In the Hebrew scriptures, messiahs are individuals anointed to carry out a mission assigned to them by God, which means there have been many "messiahs," not just the final Messiah who Christians identify as Jesus. As Ben Roden had done earlier, Koresh also asserted spiritual descendent from King David, from whose lineage the messiah was prophesied to come (Romans 1:3; Acts 2:30).

The Branch Davidians retained a Biblical base for their teachings, but the Bible was interpreted through the revelations of the living prophet. Congruent with the Adventist tradition, they observed a Saturday Sabbath and eschewed meat, alcohol, and tobacco. They rejected ostentatious dress and grooming, birthday celebrations and television viewing. Koresh taught that Christ died only for those who lived prior to his crucifixion. Koresh's mission was to permit the salvation of all subsequent generations. In contrast to Christ, who was sinless and therefore an impossible role model, Koresh was a "sinful messiah" (a self-designation derived from Psalms 40:12, where the messianic figure in the text declares, "mine iniquities . . . are more than the hairs of mine head"). And in contrast to Ben Roden's moralizing, Koresh taught that human sinfulness does not prevent humans from attaining salvation. He also prophesied that Armageddon would begin in the United States with an attack on the Branch Davidians, even renaming Mt. Carmel "Ranch Apocalypse." The Davidians subsequently adopted survivalist practices, such as stockpiling food, fuel, weapons, and ammunition. When the attack finally did materialize, it confirmed the Davidian leader's prophetic powers in the minds of his followers (Gallagher 2000:100).

The messianic figure in Psalms 45 who took many wives ("Kings' daughters"), the biblical patriarchs Abraham and Jacob, and King David all provide models for polygamy. In 1987, Koresh began making young, unmarried Davidian females his "spiritual wives." In most cases, he received the blessings of the parents either before or after the relationship commenced. For example, Koresh obtained permission from Bruce and Lisa Gent to initiate an intimate relationship with their daughter Nicole who was nineteen at the time. He eventually extended this practice to include potentially every woman in the community, including married women. Koresh announced his controversial "New Light" teaching in 1989. He asserted that, as the messiah, he was the perfect husband of every female follower. The men were taught to observe celibacy. The new teaching effectively annulled the spousal sexual exclusivity of all Davidian marriages. Some members felt unable to go along with his demands in this area and left the group.

A central aspect of his mission became fathering a new lineage of God's children. Mentioned in Pslams 45:17—in the same chapter that discusses the polygamous messiah—these children would ultimately rule the world ("thy children, whom thou mayest make princes in all the earth"). During the early days of the siege, twenty-one children were released from Mt. Carmel. When FBI negotiators asked why the other children had not been similarly released, Koresh responded, "We're dealing with my children now, and my children are different than the other children." When pressed on this point a few days latter, he clarified by unambiguously identifying them as his biological children, even making a videotape in which he introduced each of his twelve offspring (Tabor and Gallagher 1995:66 & 73). All of these children later died in the fire.

Though Koresh's assumption of a prophetic mantle may seem a radical departure from traditional Christianity, is not strange for the Adventist tradition out of which the Branch SDA and the Davidian SDA spring—a tradition that recognizes living prophets. In his role as prophet, Houteff had stressed that truth was revealed progressively (Pitts 1995:23). Thus the theological innovations introduced by later leaders—such as Lois Roden's revelation about the feminine nature of the holy spirit—were recognized as legitimate because God was continually revealing new truths through His prophets. The mainstream SDA Church teaches that William Miller and Ellen White were prophets. The Branch Davidians accepted Miller and White, and added Victor Houteff (skipping Florence Houteff as a false prophet), Ben Roden, Lois Roden, and David Koresh. The Davidians also embraced certain earlier non-SDA Protestant reformers as progressively shedding "New Light" on the faith, specifically: Luther, Knox, Wesley and Campbell.[6] It is in this context of ongoing revelation that one should understand Koresh's theological and lifestyle innovations.

Koresh, however, understood himself as being more than a prophet in the Seventh Day Adventist sense. While living in Israel in 1985, a voice came to him that revealed the complex levels of interrelated and intertwined meanings in scripture—"insights and understanding were given to him, day by day, poured like a flood in his ear" (Tabor 1995:268). He also apparently felt he had ascended to heaven where he was shown mysteries, an experience he may have understood in terms of the Jewish *merkabah* mystics who his earthly mentor, Lois Roden, had studied (Tabor and Gallagher 1995:61 & 230n15). Koresh saw himself as having received the final, definitive revelation that unlocked the mysteries of the Bible and the mysteries of all prior prophets; in his words, "It's true that what I teach is the true interpretation of the Bible. It's so true that people for the first time in their life can understand the complexity of scripture. That's my work and that's my mission" (cited in Gallagher 2000:85).

He identified himself as the message delivered by the Seventh Angel in Revelation 11:15. In other words, he was the seventh and final messenger who was to appear shortly before the Second Coming—not Christ Himself (contrary to stories widely but incorrectly reported during the siege). Furthermore, Koresh saw himself mentioned throughout the Bible in many different places, especially as God's mysterious servant in Isaiah 40-55, as the messiah figure in Psalms 40 and 45, and in various sections of the books of Daniel and Revelation. In the Davidian prophet's mind, all of these passages referred to the same individual. And when he preached, Koresh would often take his followers through these sections, repeating over and over again that Jesus could not have been this mysterious figure because Jesus did not fulfil any of the prophecies associated with that figure (Tabor 1995:270). Instead, the Bible was, in Koresh's words, "written for our time" (cited in Gallagher 2000:86), and the Davidian prophet saw himself as the individual referred to in all of these passages.

Perhaps most importantly, he claimed to be the Lamb mentioned in Revelation (5:6 and following) who was to open the Seven Seals—another messianic figure the Church has traditionally identified with Jesus. For the Davidian Prophet, Revelation was the most important book in the Bible. He saw the rest of the Bible through the lens of Revelation, and interpreted Revelation through other biblical books. Especially important were certain chapters from the book of Psalms, which he interpreted to be the enigmatic "key of David" mentioned in Revelation 3:7. In a live radio interview conducted shortly after the ATF raid, Koresh told his audience that "We are now in the fifth seal" (cited in Tabor 1995:265). He also asserted that Psalm 2 (in which nations conspire against the Lord in vain), and perhaps Psalm 89 (in which King David's enemies breach his walls and lay waste to his strongholds), would shortly to be fulfilled. Had Federal agents taken Koresh's religious discourse seriously (clearly they never did [Ammerman 1995]), they might have had a better sense of the frightening potential of the situation they were facing. The fifth seal is described in Revelation 6:9-11:

And when he had opened the fifth seal, I saw under the altar the souls of them that were slain for the word of God, and for the testimony which they held: And they cried with a loud voice, saying, How long, O Lord, holy and true, dost thou not judge and avenge our blood on them that dwell on the earth? And white robes were given unto every one of them; and it was said unto them, that they should rest yet for a little season, until their fellow servants also and their brethren, that should be killed as they were, should be fulfilled.

Koresh was reading the Bible like a script that told him what was going to happen next, and that also gave him instructions on what to do. The "souls of those who had been slaughtered" referred to the six community residents who had died during the ATF raid. They were being told to "wait a little season." However, they were also being told that they were "soon to be killed." Two biblical scholars particularly interested in apocalypticism, Phillip Arnold and James Tabor, contacted the FBI and tried to convey to them the seriousness of the situation. They especially feared that the Davidians might—believing they should follow out the next step in the script God had provided—provoke a violent denouement in order to push the situation along to the sixth seal, the Day of Judgement (Tabor 1994:15-17).

Arnold and Tabor spent many hours speaking with Livingston Fagan, a Branch Davidian Koresh had sent out to negotiate, but who had been thrown into jail. These conversations helped them piece together the Davidian prophet's biblical self-understanding, particularly with reference to the fifth seal. Despite Koresh's outward confidence, it was clear that he was confused. Although the endtime scenario in Revelation called for the events described in Revelation 6:9-11 to take place, he had previously anticipated all of this happening in another time and place. And, despite the seeming applicability of these particular verses, many other things did not seem to match (Tabor 1995:272-273).

As analyzed by Tabor and others, the dynamics of interpreting contemporary events in terms of the biblical text involve three principal factors:

1. The text of the Bible, which is fixed.
2. The interpreter, who attempts to understand and apply the text to events.
3. The fluid context in which the individual or group finds itself. (Ibid.:270)

Although the Bible acts as a roadmap that cannot be changed, there is a high degree of flexibility in applying the text to actual events. The interpreter is always interpreting. The two scholars thus felt they might be able to intervene in Koresh's interpretive world and offer an alternative scenario.

After receiving a token response from the FBI, Arnold and Tabor arranged to speak on a radio program they knew the Davidians listened to in order to put forward an alternative interpretation of Revelation—one in which the remaining members of the community did not have to die. Specifically, they discussed the "little book" that is the subject of Chapter Ten of Revelation. Arnold and Tabor knew Koresh regarded himself as the figure in that text who receives a book containing the "mystery of God" as "declared to his servants the prophets" (10:7). This figure is initially told not to write anything down (10:4). But after being given the "little book," he is then commanded, "Thou must prophesy again before many peoples, and nations, and tongues, and kings" (10:11).

On April 14, two weeks after the radio program and five days before the FBI attack, Koresh declared the waiting period over. God had commanded him to write a book unveiling the meaning of the Seven Seals (referred to as "the seven thunders" in Revelation 10:4). The letter he released through his lawyer Dick DeGuerin read:

I am presently being permitted to document in structured form the decoded messages of the seven seals. Upon the completion of this task, I will be freed of my "waiting period." I hope to finish this as soon as possible and stand before man and answer any and all questions regarding my activities . . . . I have been praying for so long for this opportunity to put the Seals in written form. Speaking the truth seems to have very little effect on man. I have been shown that as soon as I am given over to the hands of man, I will be made a spectacle of and people will not be concerned about the truth of God, but just the bizarrity of me in the flesh. I want the people of this generation to be saved. I am working night and day to complete my final work of writing out these seals. I thank my Father, He has finally granted me this chance to do this. It will bring new light and hope for many and they won't have to deal with me the person. . . . As soon as I can see that people like Jim Tabor and Phil Arnold have a copy, I will come out and then you can do your thing with this beast (cited in Tabor 1994:19).

Arnold, Tabor, and DeGuerin were convinced Koresh would be true to his word and come out peaceably after he had finished his exposition of the seven seals. Unfortunately, the FBI, tired of what they derisively referred to as "Bible babble," were equally certain this was just one more delaying tactic and went ahead with the assault.

On the evening of April 19, following the fiery holocaust, Jeffrey Jamar, the FBI agent in command at Mt. Carmel, asserted on the *Larry King Show* and *Nightline* that, through the agency's classified surveillance techniques, the FBI had "incontrovertible evidence" that Koresh not only had not started working on his manuscript, but that he never intended to do so. This confident claim was, however, either based on misinformation or an audacious lie. The Davidian prophet had, in fact, finished his exegesis of the first seal. One of the few survivors of the attack, Ruth Riddle, had typed up the first chapter of Koresh's hand-written manuscript on April 18. On the day of the fire, she escaped with a computer disk in her jacket containing a record of this manuscript.[7]

"Another Jonestown"

The first assault by agents of the Bureau of Alcohol, Tobacco, and Firearms was the end result of the differing but convergent agendas of the ATF and hostile former Davidians. Both of these groups drew heavily on the evocative power of the cult stereotype to legitimate (Lewis 2003:198-213) their respective agendas. As analyzed by John R. Hall, "After Jonestown, 'mass suicide' became a term of general cultural currency, a touchstone for describing the stark danger posed by cults" (2002:151-152). Davidian apostates led by Marc Breault raised the specter of Mt. Carmel becoming a potential

Jonestown over a year before the raid (Breault and King 1993:11-12). When the ATF became involved, they uncritically adopted the perspective of disaffected former members.

Had it not been for these outside forces, it is highly unlikely the community would ever have been engulfed in violence. The Branch Davidians were infrequently a problem to their immediate neighbors or to the residents of Waco. The only incident of note was the 1987 shoot-out with George Roden. In the wake of this incident, the local sheriff, Jack Harwell, had phoned Koresh and informed him that charges were pending from the shoot-out and that he would have to be placed under arrest and give up his weapons. Koresh promised the sheriff full cooperation. Two law officers were then dispatched to Mt. Carmel where they arrested him and seven associates, and confiscated their weapons. (ATF officials could have learned some lessons in etiquette, not to mention proper law enforcement procedure, from the McLennan County Sheriff's department.) The Davidians were eventually acquitted on charges of attempted murder.

The prosecutor in the case, then District Attorney Vic Feazell, recalled that the Davidians had cooperated completely with law enforcement officials, and condemned the ATF assault on Mt. Carmel as totally unnecessary: "We treated them like human beings, rather than storm-trooping the place. They were extremely polite." Feazell further condemned the ATF raid as "a vulgar display of power on the part of the feds . . . . If they'd called and talked to them, the Davidians would've given them what they wanted." Within a few days after the ATF raid, he offered to help mediate the crisis. In words that seem prophetic in retrospect, Feazell expressed his doubts about the final outcome of the siege:

> The feds are preparing to kill them. That way they can bury their mistakes. And they won't have attorneys looking over what they did later at a trial. I'd represent these boys for free if they'd surrender without bloodshed. But I'm afraid I'm going to wake up and see headlines that say they all died. It's sad for the Davidians. And it's sad for our government (cited in Bragg 1993:7A).

Given the Davidians' history, which reflects an obvious desire on the part of the community to cooperate with authorities, locals felt no fear of the Branch Davidians. Rather than arising from local concerns, the intrusion of federal agents was the product of forces operating outside the socio-political ecosystem of McLennan County.

The individual perhaps most responsible for initiating the Davidian tragedy was Marc Breault of Melbourne, Australia. Portrayed by the media as a former member crusading to make the world aware of Koresh's atrocities, surviving Davidians paint a very different picture. Breault, it seems, had been a convert to the Branch Davidians who fancied himself a prophet (Reavis 1998:41), and started his own group (Tabor and Gallagher 1995:83). (He later claimed he had formed his own group for the sole purpose of rescuing people from Koresh's clutches.) The problem, however, was that, to Breault's chagrin, the Davidians failed to be convinced he had "out-propheted" Koresh, and, as a consequence, he attracted few followers. This disappointment led Breault to undertake a concerted campaign to bring down his rival.

Breault sent innumerable letters to various U.S. government agencies alleging everything from child sacrifice to the accusation that the Branch Davidians were a violent, apocalyptic cult ready either to massacre every citizen of Waco or to re-enact Jonestown at the drop of a hat. Finding himself brushed aside on the absurd charge of child sacrifice, he soon moderated his allegations to sex with underage females—an accusation that, while still sensational, was easier for authorities to swallow. As for the horrific charge of massacring the citizenry of Waco, this was soon moderated to simpler charges of illegally modifying weapons to fire in full-automatic mode and manufacturing live grenades. His accusations in combination with the accusations of other disgruntled ex-members of the group were the driving force behind Child Protective Service investigations of the Mt. Carmel children—investigations that always exonerated the Davidians. Breault's allegations, minus child sacrifice, were reprinted in the March 15, 1993, issue of *People* magazine and, later, in his and Martin King's potboiler, *Inside the Cult* (1993). Breault's prolonged efforts to invoke the repressive power of the government finally paid off when the ATF accepted his accusations about Koresh illegally modifying firearms.

As part of Fatta's gun show business, the Davidians had purchased empty grenade casings. These were cut in half, mounted on frames, and sold as a novelty item. The Bureau of Alcohol, Tobacco and Firearms initially turned its attention to the community in May 1992 after a UPS driver making deliveries to Mt. Carmel saw some of the grenade casings and reported it to authorities (Kopel and Blackman 1997:49). Possessing empty grenades is not illegal, but the UPS driver was either unaware of this or assumed he had seen live grenades. The ATF assigned Davy Aguilera to investigate, and he subsequently met with Waco Assistant U.S. Attorney Bill Johnston and Gene Barber of the sheriff's office. Both Johnston and Barber had met with Geoffrey Hossack, a private investigator working for Breault and the other Davidian apostates, two years earlier. They were thus familiar with Breault's accusations, and passed them along to Aguilera. It was at this juncture that the ATF began to become entwined in the "webs of discourse that had been spun by Koresh's opponents" (Hall 2002:159).

The ATF, however, was not a disinterested player in the Waco drama. Before the Mt. Carmel assault, the ATF had been investigated for discriminating against minorities in its hiring and promotion practices. The agency had also been accused of turning a blind eye to sexual harassment within its ranks. As discussed at length in the first chapter of Kopel and Blackman's *No More Wacos*, the prospect of overcoming this tarnished image seems to have been a major impetus behind conducting a high-profile raid of the Branch Davidian community. It is also apparent in retrospect that ATF began searching for such a high-profile operation soon after it became clear that Bill Clinton would become the next president of the United States. Clinton had been broadcasting a strong anti-gun message, and certain ATF officials perceived an opportunity to expand the scope, powers, and above all the funding of their agency within the new president's anti-gun agenda. The Waco attack, if this suggestion is correct, was designed to attract positive attention to the ATF in a highly publicized raid. The raid seems to have been planned with an eye to the Senate Appropriations Subcommittee on Treasury, Postal Service, and General Government slated to meet in early March (Kopel and Blackman 1997:47-48).

By October 1992, Aguilera was told to start drawing up an affidavit for search and arrest warrants. However, on November 2, ATF headquarters reported back to Aguilera that the evidence he had provided was insufficient justification for a search warrant. The agency then decided to establish direct contact with Davidian apostates and unhappy relatives of current members. In order not to compromise the secrecy of their investigation, they "limited themselves to interviewing committed opponents of Koresh" (Hall 2002:160). This self-limitation seems to have guaranteed that the ATF would come to perceive the Branch Davidians as a potential Jonestown. Recounting interviews with Breault and other hostile apostates, a U.S. Treasury Department report noted that, "Several former cult members, most forcefully Breault, noted the distinct possibility that Koresh might respond to a siege by leading his followers in a mass suicide" (1993:46). In an ATF interview recounted in *Inside the Cult*, Breault also responded to a question about Koresh allowing women and children to leave Mt. Carmel by asserting: "No way. He would use them as hostages. Vernon always said that if the authorities ever came to take the children, they wouldn't take them alive" (1993:305-306). Breault's perspective was adopted and repeated to Treasury officials—officials who wanted to call off the raid—by Stephen Higgens, then-director of the ATF. Higgens explained that a forceful entry was necessary "because BATF feared that Koresh and his followers might destroy evidence or commit mass suicide if given the opportunity" (U.S. Department of Treasury 1993:53, B126). The most aggressive approach was chosen, and, despite statements to the contrary, the ATF never intended to try peaceably to serve a search warrant (Tabor and Gallagher 1995:2).

The extent to which ATF discourse about mass suicide at Mt. Carmel reflected genuine concern versus the extent to which such discourse was simply rhetoric meant to legitimate "dynamic entry" is difficult to determine. On the one hand, staging a dramatic raid immediately prior to the Senate Subcommittee hearing in combination with the agency's shameless courting of media attention indicate self-serving factors were the primary factors at work in the Waco tragedy. On the other hand, Hall's argument that the specter of mass suicide can explain a number of oddities about the assault, including why the ATF never contemplated siege as a fallback option, is also convincing (2002:165). Probably the fear that Mt. Carmel might become another Jonestown was a genuine but secondary influence.

Other, less direct factors at work in the Waco standoff were the media and the anticult movement. The notion that most "cults" are mass suicides waiting to happen is a standard component of anticult discourse, one that undoubtedly influenced the expectations of the ATF and later the FBI. The negative stereotype of alternative religions was also significantly responsible for shaping the attitudes of FBI negotiators, who seem never to have taken Koresh's religious views seriously; "The power of the term 'cult'. . . render[ed] "all other attempts at understanding unnecessary" (Ammerman 1995:295, n2). This view of the Branch Davidians dominated the interpretation of events in new media coverage of the standoff.

Exorcising the Demons

Less than a week after the ATF attack on the Branch Davidian community, the Rev. Mike Evans, who in 1986 had published a popular book about the end of the world, pronounced that David Koresh was demon-possessed. The Waco confrontation had already begun to settle into the routine of an uneventful standoff, and the media was searching around for colorful news—hence the decision to feature a story on the Texas evangelist. "Satan is alive and well on planet earth," claimed Evans in the words of a popular book title. "The spirit that is in Koresh and his followers needs to be exorcised."

He generously offered his services to the authorities: "If it would save innocent lives, I would be willing to go in there one on one with him and cast that demon out." While he said that he "would prefer going in there and laying hands on him and rebuking the demons in him," Brother Evans also noted that the next best thing to a personal exorcism would be to repeat a prayer through a loudspeaker, "rebuking the demon spirits in Koresh and commanding them to come out in the name of Jesus. Turn it up so loud that Koresh will not have a moment of rest 24 hours a day."

Perhaps taking their cue from pastor Evans, it was not long afterwards that the FBI initiated an harassment campaign against Mt. Carmel. However, rather than attempting to exorcise Koresh, the FBI seemed intent on feeding his demons. Instead of prayers, authorities broadcast, among other sound tracks, Nancy Sinatra music (admittedly pretty bad, but for *real* harassment they should have tried Barry Manilow), the sound of a dentist's drill (talk about cruel and unusual punishment), and the cries of rabbits being tortured to death. (One wonders what kind of tape library stocks rabbit murder sounds—Or were the fuzzy cottontails slain at the behest of the FBI and custom-taped for the occasion?) It is difficult to understand what this audio assault and the accompanying light show could have accomplished, except to increase the level of paranoia among the Davidians.

While Rev. Evans had recommended casting out demons, and while the FBI tried to provoke Koresh's inner devils, the media took a somewhat different approach and proceeded to demonize the Davidian leader. In addition to the usual generic accusations about evil "cult" leaders and the ad nauseam comparisons with Jim Jones, reporters searched far and wide for dirt about David Koresh and dutifully repeated every slanderous remark, however disreputable the source. Clearly the intention was to appeal to readers/viewers with sensationalism rather than to produce a balanced picture of the Branch Davidians.

More generally, the journalistic penchant for sensationalism has been a decisive factor in promoting the cult stereotype to the larger society.[8] The mass media are not, of course, motivated primarily by the quest for truth, although some reporters have more integrity than others. Instead, the mainstream media is driven by market forces and by the necessity of competing with other newspapers, other TV news shows, and so forth.

This is not to say that reporters necessarily lie or fabricate their stories. Rather, in the case of New Religious Movements (NRMs), news people tend to accentuate those facets of these groups that seem to be strange, exploitative, dangerous, totalitarian, sensational, and the like because such portrayals titillate consumers of news. This kind of reporting contributes to the perpetuation of the cult stereotype. In the words of British sociologist James Beckford,

Journalists need no other reason for writing about any particular NRM except that it is counted as a cult. This categorization is sufficient to justify a story, especially if the story illustrates many of the other components which conventionally make up the "cult" category. This puts pressure on journalists to find more and more evidence which conforms with the categorical image of cults and therefore confirms the idea that a NRM is newsworthy to the extent that it does match the category. It is no part of conventional journalistic practice to look for stories about NRMs which do *not* conform to the category of cult (Becford 1994:146).

Another important factor is the marked tendency of the mass media to report on a phenomenon only when it results in conflicts and problems. To again cite from Beckford:

NRMs are only newsworthy when a problem occurs. Scandals, atrocities, spectacular failures, "tug-of-love" stories, defections, exposés, outrageous conduct—these are the main criteria of NRMs' newsworthiness. . . . And, of course, the unspectacular, non-sensational NRMs are permanently invisible in journalists' accounts (ibid.:144-145).

The different media vary somewhat in their tendency to produce imbalanced reports. TV tabloids such as *20/20* and *Dateline* that have to compete with prime time TV programming tend to be the most imbalanced. Rather than attempting to produce programs that examine the complex ramifications of issues, news shows usually present melodramas in which people in white hats are shown locked in conflict with other people in black hats. On the opposite extreme are the major newspapers, such as the *Los Angeles Times* and the *Washington Post*, that tend to do the best job of presenting balanced articles on controversial subjects. Such "balance," however, usually only means finding the space for opposing views. The journalist appears to be objective when her or his story is two-sided rather than one-sided. The news magazines such as *Time* and *Newsweek* tend to fall somewhere in between, although on the "cult" issue they have generally been as bad if not worse than the worst of the TV tabloids.

On a personal note, in the wake of the initial assault on the Davidian Compound, I spent an entire week answering phone calls from reporters. As an academic specialist with a non-hysterical view of alternative religions, my perspective ran against the grain of the story most journalists wanted to compose. I was sometimes cited in newspaper accounts that aimed to include opposing views. However, the TV news show and mass circulation news magazine reporters with whom I spoke never cited me once, despite many long hours of interviews. Among radio stations, only the BBC aired my interview. I was sometimes cited in newspapers, though often in "two-sided" articles in which my views were contrasted with "cult experts" who were allowed to "refute" my points. What I learned from this exercise was that the mass media excludes perspectives that fly in the face of prevailing public opinion. And when unpopular views are permitted to be expressed, they appear in a context where they are challenged by voices that express the dominant view.

The Mt. Carmel standoff also instructively demonstrates the point that the anticult movement is simultaneously powerful and impotent. There were only a couple of *direct* connections between law enforcement authorities and the anticult movement. The testimony of deprogrammed former Davidians was used to support the contention that Koresh had to be served a search warrant (reports of deprogrammees about their former religious group are notoriously suspect). Also, Rick Ross, a deprogrammer, was consulted by the ATF prior to the attack. Before the blood had even dried in the Mt. Carmel killing fields, Ross was busy promoting himself to the media on the basis of his advisor role to the ATF. Ross's only credentials, however, were that he was a deprogrammer who had deprogrammed several Branch Davidians. In common with almost all deprogrammers, he had no professional training in counseling. And as someone who made his living kidnapping cult members for money, Ross clearly had a vested interest in portraying non-traditional religions in the worst possible light. It is easy to see how ATF's distorted impressions of the Branch Davidians might have been influenced by information received from this individual.

However, beyond the consultation with Rose, which was probably minimal, the anticult movement exercised relatively little real direct power in Waco. Where it was most influential was in helping to construct and reinforce negative stereotypes about non-traditional religions in the mass media. The three-decade-long interaction between the anticult movement and the media has been partially responsible for the widespread view that all non-traditional religions are dangerous organizations—this despite the fact that comparatively few such groups constitute a genuine threat, either to themselves or to society. The general atmosphere of distrust toward minority religions contributed significantly to public support for the ATF assault on Mt. Carmel, and probably even explains why the ATF picked a group like the Davidians for their dramatic, public raid.

What all this means for the Waco situation was that the Branch Davidians lost their chance for a fair hearing as soon as the label "cult" was applied. After that, it was only a matter of time before the media completely demonized Koresh and his followers. And after this demonization had been successfully carried out, the entire community—men, women, and children—could be consigned to the flames with little more than a peep of protest from the American public, a public that overwhelmingly approved (more than 80%) of the FBI's tragic final assault on Mt. Carmel.

"A Bunch of Religious Fanatics Decided to Kill Themselves"

On April 19, 1993, the day of the final tragedy, the FBI's workday began somewhat prior to the gas attack. As reported by a nurse interviewed on two different radio programs—one in Laporte and the other in Waco—the FBI dropped by the local hospital at 5:00 a.m. Monday morning to find out how the facility was equipped to handle burn victims (Kelly 1995:366). This incident indicates the FBI fully *expected* Mt. Carmel to catch fire, and stands in sharp contrast to the agency's *apparent* lack of preparedness for the final fiery holocaust. The nurse's radio interview is, however, only the most glaring item of information in a rather lengthy laundry list of suspicious events and situations—bits of information that, while insignificant in isolation, together indicate that the Mt. Carmel fire was intentionally set by the FBI rather than on the order of a suicidal cult leader.

Consider, for example, that, tactically, the best times for tear gas attacks are days on which the wind is still, allowing the gas to hang in the air around its target rather than being blown away. Instead of waiting for such conditions, the Feds chose to move on a day when the wind was blowing at a brisk thirty miles per hour. On top of that, they called the Davidians at 5:50 a.m. and informed them *ahead of time* that the FBI was about to mount a gas attack (Linedecker 1993:230-231). It doesn't take a genius to figure out that the people inside the community would respond by opening up the windows and doors, so as to allow the wind simply to blow the gas through the building and out the other end. This would have created a wind-tunnel effect—an effect *amplified* by the large, gaping holes the tanks created as they ripped into the building and inserted gas. Clearly these were *poor* conditions for a tear gas attack, but *ideal* for setting fire to a wood frame structure.

The potential for Mt. Carmel to go up in flames should have been readily apparent. Electricity had been cut off on March 12, compelling the community to use gasoline-powered generators, propane, and kerosene lamps. The building itself was a crudely built firetrap, constructed from plywood, both used and new lumber, and tacked together with tar paper. Bales of hay had been pushed against windows to help stop bullets.

On April 26, a team of arson investigators led by Paul Gray, assistant chief investigator for the Houston Fire Department who insisted his group of experts was independent of any federal law enforcement agency, issued their report. Gray and his team concluded the blaze must have been initiated by people inside the building in two or more different locations at about the same time. (Defending the scenario of several simultaneous starting points was an important point in eliminating the possibility that one of the tanks tipped over a lamp that set the building on fire—the Davidian version of the story.) However, other authoritative sources assert that flames broke out at different points *within 50 to 120 seconds* of each other—not exactly "simultaneous" when we take into consideration a thirty mile per hour wind in a firetrap that burnt to the ground in less than forty-five minutes.

Suspicions began to be raised on April 28 when *CBS News* correspondent Sarah Hughes broadcast the information that the "independent" arson team had close ties with the FBI. It was also discovered that the wife of arson team leader Paul Gray was an employee of the ATF. Gray responded indignantly to these revelations with the assertion that to "even suggest that any information we may be getting from the FBI is somehow tainted is absolutely ridiculous." However, on *Nightline* that same evening, lawyer Jack Zimmermann posed the question, "Why in the world did they bring in, as chief of this investigating team looking into the fire, a fellow who had been on an ATF joint task force for eight to ten years, out of the Houston office of the ATF, the office that planned and executed the raid?"[9]

In a situation already reeking with the stench of dissimulation and cover-up, choosing an individual with close personal ties to the very agencies he was hired to exonerate could only have the opposite effect of increasing rather than decreasing widely-held suspicions. As if to *further* confirm critics' suspicions, the burned-out remains of Mt. Carmel—along with any remaining evidence—were bulldozed on May 12. This action, which assured that no *truly* independent arson investigator would ever be able to sift through the charred remains and construct an alternative scenario, was justified on the pretext of safety and health concerns—filling holes, burying trash, and so on (Kopel and Blackman 1997:227).[10]

The government's interpretation assumes that, like Jonestown, the Davidians had actually planned a mass suicide. Given this assumption, it is plausible they set fire to Mt. Carmel rather than surrender to government forces. Otherwise, the contention that Koresh's followers torched their own community is implausible. Prior to the initial ATF attack, the only sources for the view that Mt. Carmel was another Jonestown were Mark Breault, other hostile ex-members, and self-appointed "cult experts" like Rick Ross (Kopel and Blackman:142-143)[11]—none reliable sources of information.

There is far more evidence to support the alternative contention, namely that the Davidians were not suicidal, and that Koresh and his followers were planning on living into the future.

From as authoritative a source as William Sessions, then-director of the FBI, we learn that the agency had concluded before the April 19 assault that Koresh was *not* suicidal: "[E]very single analysis made of his writing, of what he had said, of what he had said to his lawyers, of what the behavioral science people said, what the psychologists thought, the psycholinguist thought, what the psychiatrists believed, was that this man was not suicidal, that he would not take his life" (U.S. House of Representatives 1993:124).

On April 29, Dr. Murray Miron, a psycholinguistics professor consulted by the FBI, informed newsman Tom Brokaw that, with respect to the letters authored by Koresh that he had been asked to analyze, "All of his communications were future oriented. He claimed to be working on a manuscript. He was talking about the publication rights to that manuscript through his lawyer. He was intent upon furthering his cause."[12] Koresh even went so far as to retain literary attorney Ken Burrows to handle his story. He also requested another attorney to prepare a will that would protect Davidian property rights, as well as establish a trust for his children to safeguard any future income from books or movies.

Beyond Koresh himself, there are many indications that the other Davidians were not suicidal. For example, despite claims by the FBI that the community had not tried to save its children during the final fire, a May 14 report issued by the Associated Press revealed that "most of the children were found huddled in the concrete bunker, enveloped in the protective embraces of their mothers" (cited in Lee 1995), in what had clearly been an attempt to protect the children from the flames. These and many other particulars that could be cited indicate the Davidians were not suicidal.

Yet other kinds of questions are raised by the FBI's choice of tear gas. The gas used in the attack—a white, crystalline powder called CS (O-chlorobenzylidene malonitrile)—causes nausea, disorientation, dizziness, shortness of breath, tightness in the chest, burning of the skin, intense tearing, coughing, and vomiting. If dispersed in a flammable medium—as it was at Waco—it is also quite flammable. It is so inhumane that in January 1993, shortly before the ATF attack on Mt. Carmel, the United States and 130 other nations signed the Chemical Weapons Convention agreement banning CS gas. This treaty did not, however, cover internal uses, such as quelling domestic disturbances.

On April 23, 1993, Benjamin C. Garrett, director of the Chemical and Biological Arms Control Institute in Alexandria, Virginia, was quoted in the *Washington Times* as saying that CS gas would have had the greatest impact on the children at Mt. Carmel. "The reaction would have intensified for the children," Garrett said, because "the smaller you are, the sooner you would feel response" (cited in Lee 1993). According to the FBI, the anticipated scenario was that mothers, in an effort to protect their children, would leave the building with their offspring after the gas had thoroughly saturated it. White House spokesman George Stephanopoulos, speaking at a news conference, was unwilling (or unable) to account for why such a deadly form of tear gas—one that temporarily blinds and disables people—was selected over other possibilities.

Given the deadly choice of tear gas, the question of how the fires started on the plains of east Texas that fateful day becomes all the more intriguing. All of the survivors, despite FBI claims to the contrary, denied that Davidians had started the fire. Instead, they asserted the tanks had knocked over lanterns, which probably set the blaze. The Davidians were, however, more generous to the FBI than the evidence indicates. As we have already noted, it seems the FBI took steps to guarantee flames would spread quickly, and could not be stopped once started. A dry, windy day was chosen for the assault—a day that, as pointed out earlier, would have been terrible for a tear gas attack, but perfect for incinerating a building.

Despite the obvious risk of a fire, fire trucks were nowhere near the scene when the assault began. When smoke began to appear, the FBI waited at least ten minutes before calling 911 to request fire fighters from Waco be dispatched. The McLennan County Sheriff's Department relayed the request to the fire station:

> Dispatcher: "Sheriff's office dispatch."
> Fireman: "Yes."
> Dispatcher: "Is this Hawthorne?"
> Fireman: "Yeah, it is."
> Dispatcher: "They've got a fire at the compound."
> Fireman: "Tell me!"
> Dispatcher: "Are y'all en route?"
> Fireman: "No, we're looking at it. Just waitin' for you to call."
> Dispatcher: "Okay, take off then." (Pate 1993b)

Clearly, stopping the fire was not a high priority on anyone's list. When fire trucks finally arrived, they were held at the checkpoint *under FBI order* for another sixteen minutes—more than enough time to guarantee Mt. Carmel would be reduced to a pile of embers before a drop of water touched the flames. The FBI's explanation? In the words of Jeff Jamar, FBI officer in charge of the siege, "The reason the fire trucks were not allowed to go in immediately was the fireman's safety. It's that simple. There were people there with automatic weapons ready to fire" (cited in Lewis 1994b:119). How individuals dying in the inferno could have posed a risk to firemen was not explained.

What does all of this indicate? Given the FBI's visit to the local hospital early that morning to enquire about burn facilities, given the conditions that were less than ideal for a tear gas attack, given the inadequate preparations for the possibility of a fire, et cetera, et cetera, it is impossible to avoid the conclusion that the agency *planned* to torch Mt. Carmel from the very beginning. In the years following the tragedy, a wide variety of observers pointedly raised doubts about the government's claim that the Davidians had committed mass suicide (e.g., Bradford 1994; Kopel and Blackman 1997; Lewis 1994b; Palmer 1994; Reavis 1998; Tabor and Gallagher 1995; Wright 1995). However, after over six years of denial, it finally came out that the FBI had misled everyone—government and public alike—about the use of "incendiary devices" on the final day of the assault (Wright 2002:102; also refer to Handcock 1999). The FBI had even withheld parts of relevant documents from public scrutiny that had authorized the use of pyrotechnic military rounds (Kellman 1999). Whether intentionally or unintentionally, these rounds were almost certainly the proximate cause of the fire. Clearly the FBI believed so, or the agency would not have gone to such lengths to hid the evidence.

Although the perpetrators of the Waco tragedy will likely never be brought to justice, these revelations definitively demolish the Branch Davidians' undeserved reputation as a suicide cult. And if there is a lesson here, it is that we should hesitate before unreflectively accusing other non-traditional religious groups of being potential Jonestowns.

Endnotes

1. "Showtime" was the codeword for *beginning* the raid. The raid itself was codenamed "Operation Trojan Horse," which referred to the fact that the agents arrived hidden in cattle trailers.

2. Special Information Officers were also assigned to the operation. Their duties included overseeing the videotaping of all phases of the raid—even the ground troops carried cameras—and making copies of these productions. The plan had been to pass them out to television outlets in the wake of the raid (Daniels 1999:134; Reavis 1998:32-33), though this plan was canceled because of the raid's abysmal failure.

3. Even Robert Jay Lifton, who no one can accuse of being a "cult apologist," has characterized the Davidians as "an armed but not violent" religious sect (Lifton 1999:329).

4. The account in this section and the next section is based on a number of sources: Bergman 1995; Bromley and Silver 1995a; Linedecker 1993; Pitts 1994; Pitts 1995; Pitts 2002; Reavis 1998; Tabor and Gallagher 1995; Wessinger 2000.

5. It should be noted that the goal of self-sufficiency was inherited from Victor Houteff (Pitts 1995:26-27), rather than one of Koresh's innovations.

6. The situation is not unlike that of the Church of Jesus Christ of Latter-day Saints—popularly known as Mormons—who recognize the President of the Church as a living prophet, empowered to reveal new truths.

7. This brief exposition has appeared in a number of places, including as an appendix in Tabor and Gallagher 1995.

8. There are a number of illuminating analyses of how the media played into the Mt. Carmel tragedy. See, for example, the treatments in Richardson 1995, Shupe and Hadden 1995, and Chapter Six of Tabor and Gallagher (1995).

9. Also refer to Zimmerman's more extended remarks, as well as remarks by Dick DeGuerin, who was Koresh's lawyer during the siege, cited in Kopel and Blackman (1997:226-227).

10. As anyone who has studied Branch Davidian fiasco in any detail knows, there were so many unusual aspects of the case that it is impossible to avoid the impression of a systematic cover-up. To take another particularly gruesome example, "there were thirty Davidian corpses stored in the Tarrant County medical examiner's refrigeration unit that somehow was turned off. All the corpses deteriorated, making additional examination impossible" (Wessinger 2000:67).

11. A book on the Waco tragedy for which Ross wrote the foreword spends an entire chapter drawing out he "parallels" between Koresh and Jim Jones (Madigan 1993:59-75).

12. Also refer to Miron's remarks cited in Tabor and Gallagher (1995:169).

References

Ammerman, Nancy T. 1995. "Waco, Federal Law Enforcement, and Scholars of Religion." In *Armageddon in Waco: Critical Perspectives on the Branch Davidian Conflict.*, ed. Stuart A. Wright, 282-296. Chicago: University of Chicago Press.

Becford, James A. 1994. "The Media and New Religious Movements." In *From the Ashes: Making Sense of Waco,* ed. James R. Lewis, 143-148. Lanham, Maryland: Rowman and Littlefield.

Beckwith, Charlie. 1994. "What Went Wrong in Waco? Poor Planning, Bad Tactics Result in Botched Raid." In *From the Ashes: Making Sense of Waco,* ed. James R. Lewis, 67-70. Lanham, Maryland: Rowman and Littlefield. Originally published in *Soldier of Fortune* magazine, July 1993.

Bergman, Jerry. 1995. "The Adventist and Jehovah's Witness Branch of Protestantism." In *America's Alternative Religions*, ed. Timothy Miller, 33-46. Albany: State University of New York Press.

Bradford, R.W. 1994. "Who Started the Fires?: Mass Murder, American Style." In *From the Ashes: Making Sense of Waco,* ed. James R. Lewis, 111-114. Lanham, Maryland: Rowman and Littlefield.

Bragg, Roy. 1993. ""Ex-Prosecutor Laments Agents' 'Storm Trooper' Tactics." *Huston Chronicle* March 2, p. 7A.

Breault, Marc, and Martin King. 1993. *Inside the Cult: A Member's Chilling, Exclusive Account of Madness and Depravity in David Koresh's Compound.* New York: Penguin Signet.

Bromley, David G., and Edward D. Silver. 1995a. "The Davidian Tradition: From Patronal Clan to Prophetic Movement." In *Armageddon in Waco: Critical Perspectives on the Branch Davidian Conflict.*, ed. Stuart A. Wright, 43-72. Chicago: University of Chicago Press.

--. 1995b. "The Branch Davidians: A Social Profile and Organizational History." In *America's Alternative Religions*, ed. Timothy Miller, 149-158. Albany: State University of New York Press.

Daniels, Ted. 1999. *A Doomsday Reader: Prophets, Predictors, and Hucksters of Salvation.* New York: New York University Press.

Ehrlich, James. 1994 [1975]. "Ascension Robes and Other Millerite Fables: The Millerites in American Literature. *Journal of Adventist Education* (October/November), 18-22. [This article originally appeared in *Adventist Heritage* (Summer).]

Gallagher, Eugene V. 2000. "'Theology is Life and Death: David Koresh on Violence, Persecution, and the Millennium." In *Millennialism, Persecution, and Violence: Historical Cases,* ed. Catherine Wessinger, 82-100. Syracuse, New York: Syracuse University Press.

Grigg, William Norman. 2003. "Waco Revisited." *The New American* 19:4 (February 24).

Hall, John R. 1995. "Public Narratives and the Apocalyptic Sect: From Jonestown to Mt. Carmel." In *Armageddon in Waco: Critical Perspectives on the Branch Davidian Conflict.*, ed. Stuart A. Wright, 205-235. Chicago: University of Chicago Press.

--------------. 2002. "Mass Suicide and the Branch Davidians." In *Cults, Religion and Violence*, ed. David G. Bromley and J. Gordon Melton, 149-169. New York: Cambridge University Press.

Hall, John R., with Philip D. Schuyler and Sylvaine Trinh. 2000. *Apocalypse Observed: Religious*

Movements and Violence in North America, Europe, and Japan. London: Routledge.

Handcock, Lee. 1999. "Waco: FBI to acknowledge use of pyrotechnic devices—New account on Branch Davidian fire expected." *The Dallas Morning News.* August 25.

Kellman, Laurie. 1999. "FBI Aware Early of Waco Tear Gas." Associated Press, September 11. http://www.cesnur.org/testi/waco10.htm This article can also be found at http://www.rickross.com/reference/waco/waco54/.html

Kelly, Dean M. 1995. "The Implosion of Mt. Carmel: Is It All Over Yet?" In *Armageddon in Waco: Critical Perspectives on the Branch Davidian Conflict.*, ed. Stuart A. Wright, 359-378. Chicago: University of Chicago Press.

Kopel, David B., and Paul H. Blackman. 1997. *No More Wacos: What's Wrong with Federal Law Enforcement and How to Fix It.* Amherst, New York: Prometheus Books.

Lee, Robert W. 1995. "Waco Whitewash." *The New American.* http://reformed-theology.org/html/issue09/waco-whitewash.htm

------------------. 1993. "Truth and Cover-up." *The New American* 9:12. June 14. http://www.thenewamerican.com/focus/waco/vo09no12_waco.htm

Lewis, James R. 1994a. "Showdown at the Waco Coral: ATF Cowboys Shoot Themselves in the Foot." In *From the Ashes: Making Sense of Waco,* ed. James R. Lewis, 87-94. Lanham, Maryland: Rowman and Littlefield.

----------------. 1994b. "Fanning the Flames of Suspicion: The Case Against Mass Suicide at Waco." In *From the Ashes: Making Sense of Waco,* ed. James R. Lewis, 115-120. Lanham, Maryland: Rowman and Littlefield.

----------------. 2000. *Doomsday Prophecies: A Complete Guide to the End of the World.* Amherst, New York: Prometheus Books.

----------------. 2003. *Legitimating New Religions.* New Brunswick: Rutgers University Press.

Linedecker, Clifford L. 1993. *Massacre at Waco, Texas: The Shocking True Story of Cult Leader David Koresh and the Branch Davidians.* New York: St. Martin's Paperbacks.

Lifton, Robert Jay. 1999. *Destroying the World to Save it: Aum Shinrikyo, Apocalyptic Violence, and the New Global Terrorism.* New York: Henry Holt and Co.

Madigan, Tim. 1993. *See No Evil: Blind Devotion and Bloodshed in David Koresh's Holy War.* Fort Worth, Texas: The Summit Group.

Miller, William. 1842. *Letter to Joshua V. Himes, On the Cleansing of the Sanctuary.* Boston: Published by Joshua V. Himes. [14-page pamphlet]

Oliver, Moorman, Jr. 1994. "Killed by Semantics: Or Was It a Keystone Kop Kaleidoscope Kaper? In *From the Ashes: Making Sense of Waco,* ed. James R. Lewis, 71-86. Lanham, Maryland: Rowman and Littlefield.

Palmer, Susan J. 1994. "Excavating Waco" In *From the Ashes: Making Sense of Waco,* ed. James R. Lewis, 99-110. Lanham, Maryland: Rowman and Littlefield.

Pate, James L. 1993a. "Gun Gestapo's Day of Infamy." *Soldier of Fortune* magazine (June).

----------------. 1993b. "Waco Standoff Ends in Disaster." *Soldier of Fortune* magazine (July).

Pitts, William L. 1994. "The Davidian Tradition." In *From the Ashes: Making Sense of Waco,* ed. James R. Lewis, 33-39. Lanham, Maryland: Rowman and Littlefield.

------------------. 1995. "Davidians and Branch Davidians: 1929-1987." In *Armageddon in Waco: Critical Perspectives on the Branch Davidian Conflict.*, ed. Stuart A. Wright, 20-42. Chicago: University of Chicago Press.

-----------------. 2002. "Davidian Seventh-Day Adventists." In *The Encyclopedia of Cults, Sects and New Religions*, ed. James R. Lewis, 265-268. Amherst, New York: Prometheus Books.

Reavis, Dick J. 1998 [1995]. *The Ashes of Waco: An Investigation.* Syracuse: Syracuse University Press [originally published by Simon & Schuster].

Richardson, James T. 1994. "Lessons from Waco: Will We Ever Learn?" In *From the Ashes: Making Sense of Waco,* ed. James R. Lewis, 181-184. Lanham, Maryland: Rowman and Littlefield.

-----------------------, 1995. "Manufacturing Consent about Koresh: A Structural Analysis of the Role of Media in the Waco Tragedy." In *Armageddon in Waco: Critical Perspectives on the Branch Davidian Conflict.*, ed. Stuart A. Wright, 153-176. Chicago: University of Chicago Press.

Robbins, Thomas. 2002. "Sources of Volatility in Religious Movements." In *Cults, Religion and Violence,* ed. David G. Bromley and J. Gordon Melton, 57-79. New York: Cambridge University Press.

Shupe, Anson, and Jeffrey K. Hadden. 1995. "Cops, News Copy, and Public Opinion." In *Armageddon in Waco: Critical Perspectives on the Branch Davidian Conflict.*, ed. Stuart A. Wright, 177-202. Chicago: University of Chicago Press.

Tabor. James D. 1994. "The Waco Tragedy: An Autobiographical Account of One Attempt to Avert Disaster." In *From the Ashes: Making Sense of Waco,* ed. James R. Lewis, 13-21. Lanham, Maryland: Rowman and Littlefield.

-------------------. 1995. "Religious Discourse and Failed Negotiations: The Dynamics of Biblical Apocalypticism at Waco." In *Armageddon in Waco: Critical Perspectives on the Branch Davidian Conflict.*, ed. Stuart A. Wright, 263-281. Chicago: University of Chicago Press.

Tabor, James D., and Eugene D. Gallagher. 1995. *Why Waco? Cults and the Battle for Religious Freedom in America.* Berkeley: University of California Press.

U.S. Department of the Treasury. 1993. *Report of the Department of the Treasury on the Bureau of Alcohol, Tobacco, and Firearms Investigation of Vernon Wayne Howell, Also Known as David Koresh.* Washington, DC: U.S. Government Printing Office.

U.S. House of Representatives. 1993. *Events Surrounding the Branch Davidian Cult Standoff in Waco, Texas.* Hearing before the Committee on the Judiciary, U.S. House of Representatives, 103rd Cong., 1st Sess. April 28.

Vinzant, Carol. 1994. "ATF-Troop." *Spy* (March).

Wagner-Pacifici, Robin. 2000. *Theorizing the Standoff: Contingency in Action.* Cambridge, UK: Cambridge University Press.

Wessinger, Catherine. 2000a. *How the Millennium Comes Violently: From Jonestown to Heaven's Gate.* Chappaqua, NY: Seven Bridges Press.

Willman, David, and Glenn F. Bunting. 1995. "Agent Disputes Boss on Waco Raid Warning." *Los Angeles Times* (July 25). http://www.waco93.com/latimes7_25_95.htm

Wright, Stuart A. 2002. "Public Agency Involvement in Government-Religious Movement Confrontations." In *Cults, Religion and Violence*, ed. David G. Bromley and J. Gordon Melton, 102-122. New York: Cambridge University Press.

-------------------. 1995. *Armageddon in Waco: Critical Perspectives on the Branch Davidian Conflict.* Chicago: University of Chicago Press.

Graduating to the Next Level:
Heaven's Gate and New Age Ideology

> Earthlings will awaken to...the lake seething and the great destruction of tall buildings.... The scenes of that day will be as mad...the event will begin at dawn and end swiftly as a passing cloud.... When the resurrected have been taken up...it will be as a great burst of light.... In the midst of this it is to be recorded that a great wave rushes into the mountains.... The slopes of the side to the east will be the beginning of a new civilization upon which will be the new order, in light....

In this prophecy one finds many familiar apocalyptic elements, from the theme of universal destruction to the post-apocalypse vision of a dawning new order. One can well imagine that these words spilled unbidden from the trembling lips of an ecstatic, Middle Eastern prophet. Alternately, perhaps they were uttered by a fiery preacher in harsh, dramatic tones from the pulpit of some backwoods church.

Instead, however, this prediction was one of the central transmissions of Space Brother Sananda (aka Jesus) to Marian Keech, a middle-aged, middle class suburbanite who transcribed them via the medium of automatic writing in the comfort of her own living room. In other messages, Sananda assured Mrs. Keech that she and a select group of followers would be taken up by a flying saucer in a kind of *technological rapture* before the destruction commenced on December 21, 1954. Needless to say, neither the rapture nor the predicted apocalypse occurred–a dramatic non-event, the significance of which was captured in the title of the first and only study of the group, *When Prophecy Fails* (Festinger et al. 1956). The scenario predicted in Ms. Keech's prophecy is eerily similar to that of Heaven's Gate.

On March 26, 1997, the bodies of 39 men and women were found in a well-appointed mansion outside San Diego, victims of a mass suicide. Messages left by the group indicate that they believed they were stepping out of their "physical containers" in order to ascend to a UFO that was arriving in the wake of the Hale-Bopp comet. They also asserted that this comet, or parts of it, would subsequently crash into the earth and cause widespread destruction. In a taped message, their leader further noted that our calendars were off–that the year 1997 was really the year 2000, as if everyone was in agreement that the world would end precisely two millennia after the time of Jesus. (Thomas 1997)

Heaven's Gate–formerly known as Human Individual Metamorphosis (HIM)–originally made headlines in September 1975 when, following a public lecture in Waldport, Oregon, over thirty people vanished overnight. This disappearance became the occasion for a media event. For the next several months, reporters generated story after story about brainwashed cult groupies abandoning their everyday lives to follow the strange couple who alternately referred to themselves as "Bo and Peep," "the Two," "Do and Ti," and other bizarre names.

Bo (Marshall Herff Applewhite) and Peep (Bonnie Lu Nettles) met in 1972, and founded one of the most unusual flying saucer religions ever to emerge out of the occult-metaphysical-New Age subculture. Preaching an unusual synthesis of occult spirituality and UFO soteriology, they began recruiting in New Age circles in the spring of 1975. Followers were required to abandon friends and family, detach themselves completely from human emotions as well as material possessions, and focus exclusively on perfecting themselves in preparation for a physical transition (kind of a "beaming up") to the next kingdom (in the form of a flying saucer)–a metamorphosis that would be facilitated by ufonauts.

Bo and Peep were surprisingly effective at recruiting people to their strange gospel, though their activities did not attract much attention until the Waldport, Oregon, meeting. Six weeks later, the group was infiltrated by University of Montana sociologist Robert Balch and a research assistant, David Taylor. Balch and Taylor presented themselves as interested seekers, and became pseudo-followers in order to clandestinely conduct field research. As they would later report in subsequent papers, the great majority of the people who became involved with Bo and Peep were either marginal individuals living on the fringes of society or people who had been deeply involved with occult spirituality for some time before their affiliation with the Two. (Balch 1995)

However, as useful as this particular insight into the Two's recruits might be, our minds still recoil in incomprehension at the transparent absurdity of Bo and Peep's teachings–How could any sane human being buy into such silliness? And how could a "prophet" who looked like Micky Mouse and sounded like Mr. Rogers lead a group of over three dozen people to their deaths? Mind control notions that portray "cultists" as suffering from damaged powers of reasoning are little more than expressions of social disapproval that substitute disparaging labels for real understanding, and hence are barren of insight. Given that Heavens Gate chose to exit as a group, perhaps a sociological approach would yield more insight than a psychological/psychiatric approach.

Issues of power and obedience were at the very core of the classic sociologist Max Weber's thinking about the legitimation of authority. Weber proposed a tripartite schema of traditional, rational-legal, and charismatic legitimations of authority. The dynamics (in the sense of upsetting rather than reinforcing established authority structures) of this schema were largely confined to the factor of charisma, a form of legitimation Weber viewed as particularly–though not exclusively–characteristic of new religious movements.

The discussion of the strategies power elites deploy to maintain their position has consumed a small lake of scholarly ink, not to mention a small forest of trees that sacrificed their lives to the paper industry. In sharp contrast, the analysis of the legitimation strategies deployed by new religions has not moved forward substantially since Weber. While other, more recent researchers have touched on the subject in passing, no one has published a single article (much less a book) focused on this issue–despite the fact that legitimacy is a core issue for emergent religious movements. The rudimentary state of this topic means that any attempt to extend Weber's discussion in this arena must necessarily be preliminary and exploratory.

Weber's work on the legitimation of authority provides a useful starting point for understanding the legitimation strategies deployed by new religions, but it should immediately be noted that his analysis is also inadequate. For example, in contrast to what one might anticipate from the discussion of charismatic authority in Weber's *Economy and Society* (1968), one often finds new religions appealing to tradition–though the explicit nature of such appeals means that they constitute a variation from what Weber had in mind by the traditional legitimation of authority (which he viewed as largely implicit). Also, when nascent movements attempt to justify a new idea, practice or social arrangement by attributing it to the authority of tradition, it is usually through a reinterpretation of the past that they are able to portray themselves as the true embodiment of tradition. Such modifications of his schema indicate that Weber did not have the last word on this issue. In fact, upon closer examination one finds that contemporary new religions rely upon a wide range of different legitimation strategies.

Charisma–which, in Weber's use of the term, includes direct revelations from divinity as well as the leader's ability to provide both mundane and supernatural benefits to followers– may be the keystone in a new movement's attractiveness, but charismatic leaders typically appeal to a variety of other sources of legitimacy. For instance, as I have already mentioned, founders of new religions often appeal to the authority of tradition. Many modern movements also appeal to the authority of reason and science. Yet another strategy is to appeal to an ancient wisdom or to a primordial religiosity that antedates current religions.

In the case of Heavens Gate, Applewhite and Nettles appealed to a wide variety sources– particularly to a number of facets of New Age ideology, but also to certain aspects of the Christian tradition–to legitimate their authority and their unusual religious vision. This mix of sources is evident in their claim to be Jesus (Applewhite) and God the Father (Nettles) returned, while simultaneously asserting that they were extraterrestrial "walk-ins" (a New Age notion). A number of observers have emphasized Heavens Gate's Christian component, to the point of characterizing the Two's teaching as "space-age neo-Christian." (Hall 2000, p. 178) However, though I do not want to downplay the Christian component of their ideological synthesis, it seems clear that the Christian elements were grafted onto a basically New Age matrix. The simple fact that Heavens Gate attracted seekers from the New Age subculture rather than from the Christian subculture–that "New Agers" rather than Christians could entertain the Two's ideology as a viable, appealing teaching–underscores this point.

In the midst of a society in which the belief system propagated by the Two seems absurd, it is also appropriate to ask how they legitimated their unusual world view to followers. And finally, after Nettles had passed away from cancer, which elements of their belief system was Applewhite able to draw upon to legitimate a group suicide? In view of the dramatic end of Heaven's Gate, it might well repay our efforts if we examined the larger spiritual subculture within which such a teachings might sound plausible rather than absurd. Though not all aspects of Applewhite's theological synthesis were drawn from New Age thinking, most components of the group's overarching worldview were characteristically New Age, as shall be demonstrated.

Ascended Masters and UFOs

Since at least the 19th century, the industrialized West has been home to a strand of alternative religiosity that has been variously referred to as "occult," "metaphysical," or, more recently, as "New Age." This non-traditional spiritual subculture has given birth to a variety of distinct organizations and churches, from the various Theosophical organizations and New Thought churches to spiritualist denominations and less formally organized "light centers." (Melton *et al.* 1990)

Despite the existence of formal organizational structures, the core of this ambiguous subculture is constituted by a largely unaffiliated population of "seekers" who drift promiscuously from one spiritual group to another, never committing themselves to any single vision of truth. One result of the general weakness of doctrinally-oriented organizations is that this subculture can be infiltrated by almost any interesting new idea not overtly antagonistic to the basic tenets of New Age ideology. (Lewis 1992)

As an unusually fascinating form of rejected knowledge that mainstream scientists tend to classify as paranormal, UFOs have always attracted considerable interest within the occult/metaphysical/New Age subculture. Almost from the beginning, however, this subculture transformed flying saucers and their presumed extraterrestrial pilots into spiritual beings who had come to earth to help us along the spiritual path. To accomplish the transformation of E.T.s into wise, esoteric beings, "ufonauts" were assimilated into earlier models of spiritual sages, particularly the so-called Ascended Masters.

The concept of Ascended Masters or the Great White Brotherhood was codified within Theosophy by Helena Petrovna Blavatsky in the 1880s, and from there has been derived by various religious groups that descend from the Theosophical Society. Many people in the New Age movement believe that such Masters guide the spiritual progress of humanity. The equation of Ascended Masters with ufonauts seems to have developed out of an earlier idea, which was that at least some of the Masters were from other planets in our solar system, such as Venus.

In contrast to the modern UFO era which began with Kenneth Arnold's sightings on June 24, 1947, the Theosophical claim of extraterrestrial contact goes back to the late nineteenth century. A useful, somewhat later example of such contact claims can be found in the story of the "I AM" Activity. The "I AM" Religious Activity is a popularized form of Theosophy, reformulated to appeal to a broader audience than earlier Theosophical organizations. The founder of the movement was Guy Ballard, who had long been interested in occultism and had studied Theosophical teachings.

Ballard was engaged in mining exploration and promotion. In 1930, while he was working near Mt. Shasta–a giant volcanic cone in northern California where strange occult events had been said to occur–he had his first substantive contact with another world. While hiking in the woods around the mountain, Ballard reports that he encountered a hiker who introduced himself as the Ascended Master Saint Germain. The Compte de Saint Germain was one of the most famous occultists of modern times. Ballard was, he related, chosen as a messenger to restore the truths of re-embodiment to humankind. Saint Germain imparted information about karma, the inner reality of the divine–which he referred to as the "Mighty I AM Presence"–occult world history, and the creative power of thought.

One New Year's Eve, the Master and Ballard joined a gathering inside a cavern in Royal Teton Mountain. The individuals at this assembly played host to twelve Venusians who appeared in their midst in a dazzling display of light, not unlike a Star Trek beam-in. These Venusian "Lords of the Flame" played harp and violin music, and showed the gathered terrestrials scenes of advanced technological achievements from their home world on a great mirror. These events from the early Thirties were reported in Ballard's *Unveiled Mysteries*, which was published a dozen years before Kenneth Arnold's celebrated encounter. (Melton 1994)

The first noteworthy prophet to emerge in the wake of post-war flying saucer sightings was George Adamski. In the early 1940s he became intrigued with Unidentified Flying Objects, long before they were much discussed by the public. Adamski reported that on November 20, 1952, he experienced telepathic contact with a humanoid Venusian, and the following month reported another contact in which a hieroglyphic message was given. These encounters were reported in *Flying Saucers Have Landed* (1953), one of the most popular flying saucer books ever written. Adamski gained a broad following and was a much sought-after lecturer.

As we can see from Ballard's report of the Royal Teton gathering, religious and other revelations from Venusians were nothing new. Adamski was thus not an innovator in this regard. Rather, Adamski's contribution was to connect the earlier notion of receiving information from extraterrestrials with the emergent interest in flying saucers. The Ballard example of "Venusian masters" also allows us to see that the human imagination has a predisposition to respond to flying saucers–viewed as alien spacecraft–in religious terms. (Lewis 2000)

Even much "secular" thinking about UFOs embodies quasi-religious themes, such as the crypto-religious notion that the world is on the verge of destruction and that ufonauts are somehow going to rescue humanity–either by forcibly preventing a nuclear Armageddon or by taking select members of the human race to another planet to preserve the species. The psychologist Carl Jung was referring to the latter portrayal of ufonauts when he called them "technological angels." The idea of positive, helpful extraterrestrials has been a common theme of much science fiction, from *Superman* (who, it will be remembered, was from another planet) to the friendly alien of Steven Spielberg's *E.T.*

Jung postulated a drive towards self-realization and self-integration which he referred to as the individuation process. The goal of this process is represented by the Self archetype, an archetype characterized by wholeness and completeness. One of the concrete manifestations of this archetype is as a circle symbol, and it was various forms of the circle that Jung referred to as Mandalas. According to Jung, mandala symbols emerge in dreams when the individual is seeking harmony and wholeness–seeking which frequently occurs during periods of crisis and insecurity. Jung interpreted the phenomenon of flying saucers–which often appear in the form of circular disks–as Mandala symbols, reflecting the human mind's desire for stability in a confused world. From a depth psychological point of view, it is thus no coincidence that the chariots of the gods should manifest in the form of a flying *saucer*. (Jung 1956; Jung 1978)

But if UFOs are the chariots of the gods, then why don't the Space Brothers just land and communicate their ideas to humanity in person? The same question has sometimes been asked with respect to the Great White Brotherhood. One of the salient characteristics of the Ascended Masters was that they preferred to communicate their occult teachings through the medium of telepathic messages sent to select individuals. These chosen vessels then relayed the Masters' messages to the larger public, either vocally in a form of mediumship that would later be called "channeling" or in written form via a process usually referred to as automatic writing. Because the Ascended Masters are the primary model for the Space Brothers, it comes as no surprise that later-day UFO prophets should employ the same methods for communicating the wisdom of the ufonauts to the larger public.

George King, founder of the Aetherius Society, proposed that these Masters were actually extraterrestrials who were members of a "space command" managing the affairs of the solar system. (Saliba 1998) This concept has been built upon by other channelers and groups, such as Michael and Aurora El-Legion, who channel the "Ashtar Command." It was from this tradition that Applewhite and Nettles took the basic idea of spiritually advanced ufonauts. And it is easy to connect the Two directly to the Theosophical tradition: before meeting Applewhite, Nettles had belonged to the Theosophical Society and had attended New Age channeling sessions at which extraterrestrial beings may have been channeled.

The Journey of Bo and Peep

In addition to teaching that ufonauts were spiritually advanced beings, Applewhite and Nettles also taught that aliens had come to pick up spiritual evolved human beings who would join the ranks of flying saucer crews. Only a select few members of humanity would be chosen to advance to this transhuman state. The rest would be left to wallow in the spiritually poisoned atmosphere of a corrupt world. Applewhite would later teach that after the elect had been picked up by the space brothers, the planet would be engulfed in cataclysmic destruction. When, in 1993, under the name of Total Overcomers Anonymous, the group ran an advertisement in *USA Today*, their portrayal of the post-rapture world was far more apocalyptic than Applewhite and Nettles had taught in the seventies:

> The Earth's present "civilization" is about to be recycled–"spaded under." Its inhabitants are refusing to evolve. The "weeds" have taken over the garden and disturbed its usefulness beyond repair. (Cited in Balch 1995, p. 163)

For followers of the Two, the focus of day-to-day existence was to follow a disciplined regime referred to as the overcoming process or, simply, the process. The goal of this process was to overcome human weaknesses–a goal not dissimilar to the goal of certain spiritual practices followed by more mainstream monastic communities. For Applewhite, however, it appears that stamping out one's sexuality was the core issue. Furthermore, it is clear that his focus on sexual issues was tied to the problems he had experienced in the past as a direct result of his own sexuality.

Despite the outward success of Applewhite's early academic and musical career, he had been deeply troubled. Married and the father of two children, he secretly carried on a double life as a homosexual. Guilty and confused, he is said to have longed for a platonic relationship within which he could develop his full potential without being troubled by his sexual urges. He eventually divorced his wife and, in 1970, was terminated by St. Thomas University. Devastated, Applewhite became bitter and depressed.

He met Nettles at a hospital where he was seeking help for his sexual and psychological problems. Nettles and Applewhite quickly became inseparable. For a short while they together operated a metaphysical center. After the center folded, they continued holding classes in a house they called *Knowplace*. In 1973 they began traveling in search of a higher purpose. They eventually camped out in an isolated spot near the Oregon coast and, after six weeks, came to the realization that they were the two witnesses prophesied in Revelation 11.

In the spring of 1975 they recruited their first followers, beginning with a metaphysical teacher named Clarence Klug and 23 of his students. As the first step in the transformational process taught by the Two, their followers abandoned everything that tied them to their everyday lives, including their jobs, families, and most of their possessions except for cars and camping supplies (necessary for leading a quasi-nomadic lifestyle). Mirroring their own process, the Two placed males and females together in non-sexual partnerships in which each was instructed to assist their partner in the overcoming process. They also attempted to tune in to the next level, again reflecting the process that Applewhite and Nettles had experienced during their six week retreat.

The group developed quietly until the media interest that was evoked in the wake of the Waldport, Oregon meeting put them in the spotlight. This new attention awakened fears that Bo and Peep might be assassinated before they could fulfill their mission. They subsequently canceled a planned meeting in Chicago, and split the group into a number of autonomous "families" consisting of a dozen or more individuals. These families were then sent on their way, traveling, camping out, begging food, and occasionally recruiting new members. Many of the faithful fell away during this period. Around the end of 1975 or the beginning of 1976, the Two re-emerged, gathered together the remnants of their following, and eventually began a new round of recruiting activities.

In the face of strong ridicule, however, Nettles abruptly announced that "the doors to the next level are closed," and their missionary activity ceased. The harvest had ended, with less than a hundred individuals engaged in the process. Another change was the subsequent announcement that the *Demonstration* had been canceled because their followers had not been making rapid enough progress in the overcoming process. Rather than focusing on the time when they would be taken up by the saucers, they must concentrate on their own development.

To this end, the Two developed more practices and disciplines to help their followers overcome their human weaknesses. For example, in one exercise known as "tomb time," followers would go for days without saying anything except "yes," "no," or "I don't know" (other communications took place via written notes). Followers also began to wear uniform clothing.

The semi-nomadic period ended within a few years when two followers inherited a total of approximately $300,000. They then rented houses, initially in Denver and later in the Dallas-Fort Worth area. Each house, which they called a "craft," had the windows covered to prevent neighbors from watching their activities. Followers adhered to a strict routine. Immersed in the intensity of their structured lifestyle, the teachings of the Two became more and more real to members.

Experiences that seemed to disconfirm the Heavens Gate world view were addressed by attributing them to the machinations of evil aliens, who were referred to as "Luciferians" by the Two. For this aspect of their teaching, Applewhite and Nettles adopted a strategy deployed within certain ultra-conservative Christian groups, which dismisses any challenge to their theology as motivated by demons. However, their vision of a world under assault by evil aliens who keep human beings bound to continuous reincarnations on the earth plane through delusion and through the distraction of physical pleasures is more clearly related to certain strands of traditional gnosticism than Christian demonology--though it should immediately be added that Bo and Peep's group did not otherwise exhibit enough relevant traits to be classified as a gnostic group. (Hall 2000, p. 177)

The group's strict segregation from society was suddenly altered in 1983 when many followers visited their families on Mother's Day. However, these members dropped out of contact as soon as they left. It was during these visits that they communicated to their families that they were learning computer technology. Another change took place in 1985 when Nettles died of cancer. The group surfaced again in 1994 when, thinking the lift-off would begin in a year or two, they held another series of public meetings. It was as part of this new cycle of missionary activity that the *USA Today* ad appeared.

Details about how the group came to attach apocalyptic significance to the Hale-Bopp Comet are tantalizingly scanty. For whatever reason, someone outside the group had come to the conclusion that a giant UFO was coming to earth, "hidden" in the wake of Hale-Bopp. When Heaven's Gate heard this information, Applewhite took it as an indication that the long awaited pick-up of his group by aliens was finally about to take place. The decision that the time had come to make their final exit could not have been made more than a few weeks before the mass suicide. Applewhite had rethought his theology after his beloved partner died because, in order to be reunited with Nettles, her spirit would have to acquire a new body aboard the spacecraft. The death of Nettles seems to have been the decisive influence leading him to later adopt the view that the group would ascend together spiritually rather than physically. (Wessinger 2000, pp. 237- 239)

Applewhite may have chosen the option of a group suicide because there seemed to be no other viable solution to the problem of what followers would do after he passed away. This quandary relates Heavens Gate to one of the more well-known themes in Weber's analysis of religion, namely that the death of the founder of a religion represents a crisis typically addressed via the routinization of the prophet's charisma–by which Weber meant the transmission and regularization of her or his charisma in the form of new institutions. Heavens Gate, however, was never large enough to prompt the Two to consider setting up anything like an institution. And the teaching that the Space Brothers would pick them up within their lifetime effectively prevented Applewhite from considering the option of appointing a successor. (Wessinger 2000, p. 244) So in the end, getting older, and failing in health (Perkins and Jackson 1997, p. 81), Applewhite–having already decided some years before that they would make their exit via a group suicide–seems to have been predisposed to interpret any indication that the Space Brothers were coming as a sign it was time to leave. Hence, the rumor that a large UFO was approaching earth in the wake of Hale-Bopp–a rumor widely repeated among UFO buffs on the internet and discussed in such popular forums as the Art Bell radio show (Perkins and Jackson 1997, pp. 76-79)–provided Applewhite with the sign he was waiting for to set in motion the final solution to his quandary.

Graduating to the Next Level

The idea that the group might depart via suicide had emerged in Applewhite's thinking only within the prior few years. The Two's earlier idea–an idea that had set Heaven's Gate apart from everyone else–was that a group of individuals selected to move to the next level would bodily ascend to the saucers in a kind of "technological rapture." Applewhite and Nettles had originally taught that the goal of the process they were teaching their followers was to prepare them to be physically taken aboard the spacecraft where they would enter a cocoon-like state, eventually being reborn in a transformed physical body.

Christianity's view of resurrection reflects the influence of the cultures in which it originated and spread during its first centuries in the Mediterranean basin. The idea of resurrection, which was originally formulated within Zoroastrianism, was introduced in Christianity from Judaism. This idea developed in tandem with an apocalyptic vision of history that entailed the end of the world as we know it, and which would result in the defeat of death and evil. (Lewis 1994)

The notion of resurrection is also central to Chapter 11 of the Book of Revelation, the biblical passage Applewhite and Nettles came to view as describing their particular ministry. This chapter recounts the story of two prophets who will be slain. Then, three and a half days later, they will be resurrected and taken up in a cloud:

> At the end of the three days and a half the breath of life from God came into them; and they stood up on their feet to the terror of all who saw it. Then a loud voice was heard speaking to them from heaven, which said, "Come up here!" And they went up to heaven in a cloud, in full view of their enemies. At that same moment there was a violent earthquake.... (Rev 11:11-13)

In the early phase of their movement, Applewhite and Nettles prophesied that they would soon be assassinated. Using the above passage as a script for future events, they further predicted that they would be resurrected three and a half days later and taken up into a flying saucer. The Two asserted that this event would prove the truth of their teachings. As for their followers, they taught that Heaven was the literal, physical heavens, and those few people chosen to depart with the Two would, after their physical transformation, become crew members aboard UFOs.

While the basic teachings seem to have remained constant, the details of their ideology were flexible enough to undergo modification over time. For example, in the early days,

Applewhite and Nettles told their followers that they were extraterrestrial beings. However, after the notion of walk-ins became popular within the New Age subculture, the Two changed their tune and began describing themselves as extraterrestrial walk-ins.

A walk-in is an entity who occupies a body that has been vacated by its original soul. An *extraterrestrial* walk-in is a walk-in who is supposedly from another planet. The walk-in situation is somewhat similar to possession, although in possession the original soul is merely overshadowed–rather than completely supplanted–by the possessing entity. The contemporary notion of walk-ins was popularized by Ruth Montgomery, who developed the walk-in notion in her 1979 book, *Strangers Among Us*. According to Montgomery, walk-ins are usually highly evolved souls here to help humanity. In order to avoid the delay of incarnating as a baby, and thus having to spend two decades maturing to adulthood, they contact living people who, because of the frustrating circumstances of life or for some other reason, no longer desire to remain in the body. Discarnate entities find such people, persuade them to hand over their bodies, and then begin lives as walk-ins.

The walk-in concept seems to be related to certain traditional South Asian tales about aging yoga masters taking over the bodies of young people who die prematurely. Another possible source for the contemporary walk-in notion is the well-known (in theosophical circles) teaching that Jesus and Christ were separate souls. According to this teaching, Jesus prepared his physical body to receive Christ and, at a certain point in his career, vacated his body and allowed Christ to take it over and preach to the world. An underlying notion here is that Christ was such a highly evolved soul that it would have been difficult if not impossible for him to have incarnated as a baby–and, even if he could have done so, it would have been a waste of precious time for such a highly developed soul to have to go through childhood.

Ruth Montgomery, more than any other single person, is responsible for popularizing the contemporary notion of walk-ins. She describes the phenomenon rather dramatically:

> There are Walk-ins on this planet. Tens of thousands of them. Enlightened beings, who, after successfully completing numerous incarnations, have attained sufficient awareness of the meaning of life that they can forego the time-consuming process of birth and childhood, returning directly into adult bodies. A Walk-in is a high-minded entity who is permitted to take over the body of another human being who wishes to depart.... The motivation of a Walk-in is humanitarian. He returns to physical being in order to help others help themselves, planting seed-concepts that will grow and flourish for the benefit of mankind. (1979, 11-12)

In 1983 Montgomery published another book, *Threshold to Tomorrow*, containing case histories of seventeen walk-ins. According to Montgomery, history is full of walk-ins, including such famous historical figures as Moses, Jesus, Muhammad, Christopher Columbus, Abraham Lincoln, Mary Baker Eddy, Gandhi, George Washington, Benjamin Franklin, Thomas Jefferson, Alexander Hamilton, and James Madison. In fact, it seems that Montgomery would identify almost everyone manifesting exceptional creativity and leadership as a walk-in. In her words, "Some of the world's greatest spiritual and political leaders, scientists, and philosophers in ages past are said to have been Walk-ins." (p. 12)

In a later book, *Aliens Among Us* (1985), Montgomery developed the notion of extra-terrestrial walk-ins—the idea that souls from other planets have come to earth to take over the bodies of human beings. This notion dovetailed nicely with popular interest in UFOs, which had already been incorporated into New Age spirituality. Following Montgomery, the New Age movement came to view extraterrestrial walk-ins as part of the larger community of advanced souls that had come to earth to help humanity through a period of transition and crisis. It is easy to see how this basic notion fit into the Two's ideology, explaining away their human personal histories as the histories of the souls who formerly occupied the bodies of Applewhite and Nettles.

It should be noted that the walk-in idea—a notion implying a radical disjunction between soul and body—also provided Applewhite with an essential ideological component in his rethinking of the ascension scenario, and ultimately legitimating their radical departure. In other words, after the death of Nettles, Applewhite had to come to grips with the fact that—under the physical ascension scenario which had been a cornerstone of their teachings for almost two decades—his spiritual partner would miss the chance to escape the planet with the rest of the group. This option was, however, unimaginable to Applewhite. Hence, by the time of the suicides, Applewhite had reconceptualized the ascension as an event in which Heaven's Gate members would let go of their physical containers and ascend *spiritually* to the waiting saucers. Once on board, they would then consciously "walk-into" a new physical body and join the crew of the Next Level spacecraft. This scenario is related in one of the group's Internet statements:

> Their final separation is the willful separation from their human body, when they have changed enough to identify as the spirit/mind/soul—ready to put on a biological body belonging to the Kingdom of Heaven. (This entering into their "glorified" or heavenly body takes place aboard a Next Level spacecraft, above the Earth's surface.) (Heaven's Gate 1996)

Presumably, these new physical bodies would be supplied to Heaven's Gate members out of some sort of "cloning bank" kept aboard the spaceships.

Ancient Astronauts and Earth Changes

Another notion the Two picked up from the metaphysical subculture of their day was the ancient astronaut hypothesis. The expression "ancient astronauts" is used to refer to various forms of the concept that ufonauts visited our planet in the distant past. The basic idea that many, if not all of the powerful sky gods of traditional religions were really extraterrestrial visitors intervening in human history had been around for many decades. However, it was not until a book about *The Chariots of the Gods* authored by Erich van Däniken in 1970 that this notion was popularized. While later writers such as Zecharia Sitchin (1976; 1995) have developed this view with greater sophistication, none have been as influential as van Däniken.

This view, which seems to call into question the validity of religion, has been adopted by large segments of the New Age culture in a way that is not seen as contradicting metaphysical spirituality. Instead, believers view the "Space Brothers" as working in cooperation with spiritual forces to stimulate the spiritual evolution of this planet. One aspect of the ancient astronaut hypothesis is the idea that the contemporary human race is the offspring of a union between aliens and native terrestrials. Some even believe that a distorted record of this event can be found in a few enigmatic verses in the book of Genesis about the sons of God copulating with the daughters of men. This union produced an intermediate species referred to in Genesis as the "Nephilim." In a different version of the same idea, ancient ufonauts stimulated the evolution of our ape-like forebears to produce present-day humanity. Our space "fathers" have subsequently been watching over us, and will, according to some New Age notions, return to mingle with their distant offspring during the imminent New Age. (Lewis and Oliver, 1995)

Applewhite and Nettles taught a slightly modified version of the ancient astronaut hypothesis: aliens planted the seeds of current humanity millions of years ago, and have come to reap the harvest of their work in the form of spiritually-evolved individuals who will join the ranks of flying saucer crews. Only a select few members of humanity will be chosen to advance to this transhuman state. The rest will be left to wallow in the spiritually poisoned atmosphere of a corrupt world.

Applewhite would later teach that after the elect had been picked up by the Space Brothers, the planet would be engulfed in cataclysmic destruction. Though Applewhite's apocalyptic teachings might at first appear to be derived entirely from his Biblical background, his decidedly "this-worldly" vision of our planet's end suggests that his ideology was decisively influenced by the New Age subculture and by the more recent discussion of colliding asteroids found in contemporary popular culture. (Thomas 1997)

Particularly in the teachings of New Age channels, one often finds the theme of apocalyptic "earth changes" that were supposed to have taken place around the end of the last millennium. This notion appears to have originally been introduced into the metaphysical subculture via the teachings of Edgar Cayce, as published by his son Hugh Lynn Cayce. (e.g. 1980) Furthermore, these upheavals in the Earth's crust are often thought of as coming about as a direct result of a planetary "pole shift," a subsidiary notion that was popularized by Ruth Montgomery. (1985) (Though in sharp contrast to Applewhite, New Age thinkers postulate that these dramatic earth changes will herald a terrestrial Golden Age.) The idea that global destruction would come about as the result of a wandering asteroid is a more recent notion that has been discussed in popular magazine articles and television specials only within the last half-dozen years or so.

Because these notions about walk-ins and earth changes would have been familiar to the seekers Bo and Peep attracted to Heavens Gate, there would have been no need to legitimate or even explain them to new recruits. As hard as it may be for most non-new agers to grasp, such ideas were not only familiar, they were also plausible to members of the New Age subculture. The same observation applies to most of the other key beliefs of the Two's ideological synthesis, such as the notion that the earth is a schoolroom for spiritual development.

Our Terrestrial Classroom

Another theme Applewhite and Nettles absorbed from the metaphysical subculture was the view that the spiritual life is a series of learning experiences culminating–in the case of Heaven's Gate–in a "graduation" to the next evolutionary kingdom. Members of the group thought of themselves as "students," their fellows as "classmates," and Applewhite as their "tutor." (Heaven's Gate 1996) These educational metaphors would have been particularly comfortable and natural for a man who had been a popular university teacher during the first part of his adult life.

Like other religious and cultural systems, the world view of the contemporary New Age movement is held together by a shared set of symbols and metaphors–shared images of life reflected in the discourse of participants as a set of commonly used terms. For example, due partly to a vision of metaphysical unity inherited from Theosophy and from Asian religious philosophy–but also due to this subculture's reaction against the perceived fragmentation and alienation of mainstream society–the New Age movement emphasizes the values of unity and relatedness. These values find expression in such common terms as "holistic," "oneness," "wholeness," and "community." This spiritual subculture also values growth and dynamism–an evaluation expressed in discourse about "evolution," "transformation," "process," and so forth.

The image of education is related to the growth metaphor (e.g., one of our linguistic conventions is that education allows a person to "grow"). If we examine the metaphysical subculture through the lens of the education theme, we discover that, in contrast to many other religious movements, the dominant New Age "ceremonies" are workshops, lectures and classes rather than worship ceremonies. Even large New Age gatherings such as the While Life Expo resemble academic conferences more than they resemble camp meetings. (Lewis 1997)

It is also interesting to note the extent to which educational metaphors inform New Age thought. In terms of the way the Western metaphysical tradition has interpreted the ongoing process of reincarnation, spiritual growth and even life itself are learning experiences. To cite some of examples of this, Katar, a New Age medium, channels such messages as, "Here on Earth, you *are* your teacher, your books, your lessons and the classroom as well as the student." (Clark 1988, p. 7) This message is amplified by J.L. Simmons, a sociologist, who, in his *The Emerging New Age*, describes life on the physical plane as the "Earth School," (1990, p. 91) and asserts that "we are here to learn...and will continue to return until we 'do the course' and 'graduate.'" (p. 73)

Similar images are reflected in an essay on "The Role of the Esoteric in Planetary Culture," where David Spangler argues that spiritual wisdom is esoteric "only because so few people expend the time, the energy, the effort, the openness and the love to gain it, just as only a few are willing to invest what is required to become a nuclear physicist or a neurosurgeon." (Spangler 1977, pp. 193-194) It would not be going too far to assert that, in the New Age vision of things, the image of the whole of human life–particularly when that life is directed toward spiritual goals–can be summed up as a learning experience:

> Each of us has an Inner Teacher, a part of ourselves which knows exactly what we need to learn, and constantly creates the opportunity for us to learn just that. We have the choice either to cooperate with this part of ourselves or to ignore it. If we decide to cooperate, we can see lessons constantly in front of us; every challenge is a chance to grow and develop. If, on the other hand, we try to ignore this Inner Teacher, we can find ourselves hitting the same problem again and again, because we are not perceiving and responding to the lesson we have created for ourselves. [It] is, however, the daily awareness of and cooperation with spirit [that] pulls humanity upwards on the evolutionary spiral, and the constant invocation and evocation of spirit enables a rapid unfolding of human potential. When the Inner Teacher and the evolutionary force of the Universe are able to work together with our full cooperation, wonders unfold. (Findhorn Foundation 1986)

In these passages, we see not only the decisive role of the education metaphor, but also how this metaphor has itself been reshaped by the spiritual subculture's emphasis on holism and growth. In other words, the kind of education this subculture values is the education of "the whole person," sometimes termed "holistic education," and this form of education is an expression of the "evolutionary force of the Universe" (a parallel to what, in more traditional language, might be called the redemptive activity of the Holy Spirit). Thus, despite the marked tendency to deploy images drawn from the sphere of formal education–a tendency that has created a realm of discourse saturated with metaphors of "classrooms," "graduations," and the like–the metaphysical subculture's sense of the educational process has tended to be more informal (more or less equivalent to learning in the general sense), as well as more continuous–a process from which there may be periodic graduations, but from which there is never a *final* graduation after which the learning process ceases. Even for Heaven's Gate members, graduation from the earth plane represented entering a new sphere of never-ending personal evolution–The Evolutionary Kingdom Level Above Human.

Though some aspects of this view of the spiritual life as a learning experience are based on tradition (e.g., the Pythagorean "school"), the widespread appeal of this image of spirituality is a more or less direct result of the manner in which modern society's emphasis on education informs our consciousness. The various social, economic, and historical forces that have led to the increased stress on education in the contemporary world are too complex to develop here. Obvious factors are such things as the increasing complexity of technology and of the socio-economic system. Less obvious factors are such considerations as the need to delay the entry of new workers into the economy. But whatever the forces at work in the larger society, by the time the babyboom generation began attending college in the 1960s, formal educational institutions had come to assume their present role as major socializing forces in Western societies. Being a college graduate and achieving higher, particularly professional degrees became associated with increased prestige and the potential for increased levels of income. In other words, to a greater extent than previously, education and educational accomplishments had become symbols of wealth and status.

Because the generation from which the majority of participants in the spiritual subculture have been recruited is the babyboom generation, the majority of participants in that subculture have been socialized to place a high value on education. Babyboomers, however, also tend to have been participants in the counterculture of the Sixties, which means that they come from a generation that was highly critical of traditional, formal education.

Though some members of that generation revolted against the educational establishment by denying the value of education altogether, other college students of the time reacted against what they saw as an irrelevant education by setting up alternative educational structures such as the so-called "free schools." These educational enterprises, which could offer students nothing in terms of degrees or certifications, were viable, at least for a time, because they offered courses on subjects people found intrinsically interesting–including such metaphysical topics as yoga, meditation, and so forth. The free school movement, in combination with the adult education programs that emerged in the Seventies, provided the paradigms for the independent, metaphysical educational programs that would eventually emerge.

As is evident from even the most casual perusal of the group's writings, Heaven's Gate was dominated by the educational imagery found in the contemporaneous New Age subculture. As has already been noted, Applewhite viewed himself as a teacher, his followers were students, their spiritual process was likened to an educational process (in their "metamorphic classroom"), and their goal was referred to as a graduation. In the group's writings published on the Internet, they discussed how their "Teachers" on the Next Level had an "extremely detailed lesson plan" designed for their personal growth. Then, toward the end, they received signals that their "classroom time was over" and that they were ready to graduate to the next level. (Jwnody 1996)

The same basic images can be found in the teachings of innumerable contemporary spiritual teachers. For example, John-Roger, the founder of the Movement of Spiritual Inner Awareness (MSIA), asserts that:

> The earth has been designated as the classroom where you learn lessons. [Y]ou're...in a continual learning process, which will bring forth that which is for your highest good. When you have finished your lessons, you graduate to other levels of consciousness. (John-Roger 1980)

This is not, of course, to imply that MSIA is another potential Heaven's Gate, but rather that the basic images at work in Applewhite's teachings were derived more or less directly out of the same metaphysical subculture that shaped MSIA and certain other emergent religions.

Thus, with the exceptions of (1) suicide being the means by which the transition to the next evolutionary sphere is to take place and (2) the next sphere being a literal, physical realm (a spacecraft), the basic concepts informing Heavens Gate's thought world would have been recognizable to any serious metaphysical seeker. However, even the notion of a physical spaceship being a quasi-heavenly realm is already implicit in the marked tendency of the New Age movement to portray ufonauts as spiritual beings (a tendency already noted in earlier sections). Furthermore, the widely accepted walk-in notion provides a readily understandable mechanism by which such a transition could be accomplished.

Death in the New Age

This leaves only suicide as the one anomalous component of Applewhite's synthesis. We should note, however, that there are many phases of the New Age movement that portray death–if not suicide–in a positive light. For example, the basic metaphysical/New Age afterlife notion is reincarnation, though this process is regarded somewhat differently by the New Age than by the Asian religions from which the notion is derived. Whereas in a tradition like Buddhism reincarnation is viewed negatively, as a process that brings one back into the world to suffer, in the metaphysical subculture reincarnation is viewed as part of an extended education program stretched across many lifetimes, and is thus part of a positive process. In the same vein, the interest many participants in occult-metaphysical spirituality have displayed in learning about their past lifetimes in the hope of discovering that they had been some famous or otherwise exalted personality would be anathema to a traditional Buddhist.

The New Age movement is also home to advocates of conscious dying. The expression "conscious dying" refers to an approach to dying in which death is regarded as a means of liberation of one's own consciousness–in other words, as a means of achieving enlightenment. This approach, ultimately inspired by Tibetan Buddhism, was popularized in the New Age subculture through the work of Baba Ram Das and Stephen Levine. In line with the New Age emphasis on spiritual-unfoldment-as-education, dying thus acquires a positive valence as part of the larger learning process. (Bednaroski 1989)

Finally, it is within the metaphysical subculture that one finds the most interest in the near death experience. The expression near death experience (NDE), sometimes also called the "pseudo-death" experience, refers to the seemingly supernatural experiences often encountered by individuals who have suffered apparent death, and have been restored to life. The principal impetus for modern studies on NDEs was the publication in 1975 of the book *Life After Life*, by psychiatrist Raymond A. Moody, which followed earlier researches on this topic by other physicians such as Elizabeth Kubler-Ross and Russell Noyes.

Moody's work describes the results of more than eleven years of inquiry into near death experiences and is based on a sample of about 150 cases. He outlines nine elements that seem to occur generally (but not universally) in the NDE experiences:

    1. Hearing a buzzing or ringing noise, while having a sense of being dead. At this initial stage of the NDE, the experiencers are confused and try, unsuccessfully, to communicate with other people at the scene of their death.

    2. Peace and painlessness. While people are dying they may be in intense pain, but, as soon as they leave the body, the pain vanishes and they experience peace.

3. Out-of-body experience. NDEers often have the experience of rising up and floating above their own body surrounded by a medical team, and watching it down below, while feeling very detached and comfortable. They experience the feeling of being in a spiritual body that looks like a sort of living energy field.

4. The tunnel experience. The NDEers then experience being drawn into darkness through a tunnel, at an extremely high speed, or going up a stairway (or some other symbol of crossing a threshold) until they achieve a realm of radiant golden-white light.

5. Rising rapidly into the heavens. Instead of a tunnel, some NDEers report an experience of rising suddenly into the heavens, and seeing the earth and the celestial sphere as if they were astronauts in space.

6. People of light. Once on the other side of the tunnel, or after they have risen into the heavens, NDEers meet people who glow with an inner light. Often they find that friends and relatives who have already died are there to greet them.

7. The Being of light. After connecting with these beings, NDEers meet a powerful, spiritual Being who some have called an angel, God, or Jesus.

8. The life review. This higher Being presents NDEers with a panoramic review of everything they have done. In particular, they experience the effects of every act they have ever done to other people, and come away feeling that love is the most important thing in life.

9. Reluctance to return. The higher Being sometimes says that the NDEer must return to life. In other experiences, the NDEer is given a choice of staying or returning. In either case, NDEers experience a reluctance to return. The people who choose to return do so only because of loved ones they do not wish to leave behind.

The near death experience has attracted extensive public interest because of its seeming support for the notion of life after death. As reflected in the above list of characteristics, it is clear that the overall picture of the dying process to emerge from NDE studies is quite positive, even attractive. Furthermore, with respect to our larger discussion, it should also be noted that trait number five sounds like it could have been (though I actually doubt that it was) the immediate source of Applewhite's idea that his group could die and ascend to a waiting spacecraft.

In this regard, in another one of his books (1989), Moody mentions an ecstatic vision Carl Jung experienced during an apparent NDE. Following a heart attack, Jung found himself a thousand miles above the surface of the earth, on the threshold of entering a floating temple in a giant rock where he would finally discover the answers to all of his questions. In this vision, Jung vividly describes the terrestrial globe, his sense of letting go of everything associated with earthly life, and his sense of anticipation of the glories awaiting him upon his entrance into the temple:

It seemed to me that I was high up in space. Far below I saw the globe of the earth, bathed in a gloriously blue light. I saw the deep blue sea and the continents.... A short distance away I saw in space a tremendous dark block of stone, like a meteorite.... As I approached the steps leading up to the entrance into the rock, a strange thing happened: I had the feeling that everything was being sloughed away; everything I aimed at or wished for or thought, the whole phantasmagoria of earthly existence, fell away.... I had the certainty that I was about to enter an illuminated room and would meet there all those people to whom I belong in reality.... There I would at last understand...what historical nexus I or my life fitted into. (Jung 1965, pp. 289-291)

Finally, Jung notes his profound disappointment when his doctor brings him back to his body before he had a chance to cross the threshold.

Again, with only a little interpretation (e.g., floating rock = spacecraft), the whole experience could be taken as almost a blueprint for what Heaven's Gate members believed would happened after their deaths. This is not, of course, to assert that either NDE research or the writings of Carl Jung encourage people to take their own lives. It is, however, clear that, if taken seriously, reports of near death experiences paint a positive enough portrait of dying to take the sting out of death. Thus, far from being crazy or irrational, even the final dramatic exit of Heaven's Gate becomes understandable in terms of the thought world of the metaphysical subculture from which Applewhite drew his theological synthesis.

Conclusion

A factor in failing to understand movements like Heavens Gate is a mistaken theoretical perspective–derived ultimately from Weber–that portrays the personal charisma of the founder as the "glue" holding together alternate views of reality. Such a perspective misconstrues the role of charisma. In the first place, no matter how charismatic the prophet, his or her message must somehow address the concerns of potential recruits in a satisfactory manner if he or she is to convince more than a handful of close associates. In other words, a new vision has to have more going for it than merely the personality of the revealer.

In the second place, although the prophet's charisma may be necessary in giving life to the vision during the nascent stages of the new movement, the actual adoption of an emergent religion by a group of followers recruits the forces of social consensus to the side of the new revelation–forces that tend to maintain the alternate vision of reality independently of the charisma of the founder. To think of this in terms of the micro-sociology of knowledge (Berger and Luckmann 1966), the plausibility of a particular world view and its accompanying lifestyle is maintained by the ongoing "conversation" that takes place among the members of a particular community. Thus as long as a new religion continues satisfactorily to address the concerns of followers, even things like a failed prophecy or a leader's blatant hypocrisy will not induce a crisis of faith.

Finally, prophets themselves do not rely upon their personal charisma as their sole source of legtimation. Instead, they plant their new visions on the familiar foundations of pre-existing religious ideas, which allows their new teachings to appear plausible to potential recruits. In other words, despite what critics sometimes allege, founders of new religious movements do not invent their religious systems *ex nihilo*. With respect to Heavens Gate–

and although it may seem counter-intuitive to anyone not familiar with the many exotic ideas floating around the New Age subculture–the Two's message was really not all that "weird" to the people who became their followers. Similarly, the notion that death is a potentially positive experience and the notion that one can exit one's body to consciously reemerge in another realm are simply not odd or irrational within religious communities, New Age or otherwise. It was thus a relatively small step for Applewhite to legitimate a group suicide, meaning that the group's dramatic exit was a completely plausible scenario undertaken willingly–not the exceptional act of a mesmeric cult leader pushing his blind sheep over the edge of an abyss.

Bibliography:

Adamski, George and Desmond Leslie. *Flying Saucers Have Landed*. New York: British Book Centre, 1953; London: Werner Laurie, 1953.

Balch, Robert W. "Waiting for the Ships: Disillusionment and the Revitalization of Faith in Bo and Peep's UFO Cult." In James R. Lewis, Ed. *The Gods Have Landed: New Religions From Other Worlds*. Albany, NY: State University of New York Press, 1995.

Bednaroski, Mary Farrell. 1989. *New Religions and the Theological Imagination in America*. Bloomington: Indiana University Press.

Berger, Peter L., and Thomas Luckmann. *The Social Construction of Reality*. Garden City, NY: Anchor Books, 1966.

Cayce, Hugh Lynn. *Earth Changes Update*. Virginia Beach: A.R.E. Press, 1980.

Chryssides, George D. *Exploring New Religions*. London: Cassell, 1999.

Clark [channeled by Katar]. "Back to School--Earth Revisited." *Open Channel: A Journal with Spirit* 2. November-December 1988.

Daniken, Erich von. *Chariots of the Gods?: Unsolved Mysteries of the Past*. New York: Berkley Publishing, 1969.

Festinger, Leon, Henry W. Riecken and Stanley Schachter. *When Prophecy Fails*. Minneapolis: University of Minnesota Press, 1956.

Findhorn Foundation. *Catalog*. Autumn-Winter 1986-87.

Hall, John R. *Apocalypse Observed: Religious Movements and Violence in North America, Europe and Japan*. London: Routledge, 2000.

Heaven's Gate. "Time to Die for God?--The Imminent 'Holy War'--Which Side are You On?" Heaven's Gate Internet Statement. September 24, 1996.

John-Roger. *The Way Out Book*. Los Angeles: Baraka Press, 1980.

Jung, Carl Gustav. *Flying Saucers: A Modern Myth of Things Seen Flying in the Sky*. Princeton, NJ: Princeton University Press, 1978.

----------------. *Memories, Dreams, Reflections*. New York: Vintage, 1965.

----------------. *Symbols of Transformation*. New York: Harper Torchbooks, 1956.

Jwnody. "Overview of Present Mission." Heaven's Gate Internet Statement. April 1996.

King, Godfre Ray (pseudo. of Guy Ballard), *Unveiled Mysteries*. Chicago: St. Germain Press, 1935.

Lewis, James R. "Approaches to the Study of the New Age." In James R. Lewis and J. Gordon Melton. *Perspectives on the New Age*. Albany, NY: State University of New York Press, 1992.

------------. *The Gods Have Landed: New Religions From Other Worlds*. Albany, NY: State University of New York Press, 1995.

------------. *Encyclopedia of Afterlife Beliefs and Phenomena*. Detroit, MI: Gale Research, 1994.

------------. *The Encyclopedic Sourcebook of UFO Religions*. Amherst, NY: Prometheus Books, 2002.

------------. *Seeking the Light: Uncovering the Truth About the Movement for Spiritual Inner Awareness*. Los Angeles: Mandeville Press, 1997.

------------. *UFOs and Popular Culture: An Encyclopedia of Contemporary Myth*. Santa Barbara, CA: ABC-Clio, 2000.

Lewis, James R., and Evelyn Dorothy Oliver. *Angels A to Z*. Detroit: Gale Research, 1995.

Melton, J. Gordon, et al. *New Age Encyclopedia*. Detroit: Gale Research, 1990.

Melton, J. Gordon. "Church Universal and Triumphant: Its Heritage and Thoughtworld." In James R. Lewis and J. Gordon Melton, Eds. *Church Universal and Triumphant in Scholarly Perspective*. Stanford, California: Center for Academic Publication, 1994.

Montgomery, Ruth. *Strangers Among Us: Enlightened Beings from a World to Come*. New York: Coward, McCann & Geoghegan, 1979.

----------------. *Threshold to Tomorrow*. New York: G. P. Putnam's Sons, 1983.

----------------. *Aliens Among Us*. New York: Putnam's. 1985.

Moody, Raymond A. *Life After Life*. New York: Bantam, 1976.

----------------. *The Light Beyond*. New York: Bantam, 1989.

Perkins, Rodney, and Forrest Jackson. *Cosmic Suicide: The Tragedy and Transcendence of Heaven's Gate*. Dallas, TX: Pentaradial Press, 1997.

Saliba, John A. "The Aetherius Society." In James R. Lewis. *UFOs A to Z*. Chicago: Contemporary Books, 1998.

Simmons, J.L. *The Emerging New Age*. Santa Fe, New Mexico: Bear and Co., 1990.

Sitchin, Zecharia. *The Twelfth Planet*. NY: Avon, 1976.

----------------. *Divine Encounters: A Guide to Visions, Angels, and Other Emissaries*. NY: Avon, 1995.

Spangler, David. "The Role of the Esoteric in Planetary Culture." In Michael Katz, William P. Marsh and Gail Gordon Thompson, Eds. *Earth's Answer: Explorations of Planetary Culture at the Lindisfarne Conferences*. New York: Harper & Row, 1977.

Thomas, Evan. "The Next Level." *Newsweek Magazine*. April 7, 1997.

Von Däniken, Erich. *Chariots of the Gods? Unsolved Mysteries of the Past*. New York: G.P. Putnam's Sons, 1970.

Weber, Max. *Basic Concepts in Sociology*. H. P. Secher (trans). New York: Philosophical Library, 1962.

------------. *Economy and Society: An Outline of Interpretive Sociology*. Ed. Guenther Roth and Clau Wittich. Transl. Ephraim Fischoff et al. New York: Bedminster Press, 1968.

Wessinger, Catherine. *How the Millennium comes Violently: From Jonestown to Heaven's Gate*. New York: Seven Bridges, 2000.

The Solar Temple "Transits":
Beyond the Millennialist Hypothesis

> [Various] problems, internal and external, are crucial in understanding the OTS's gradual distortion and disintegration. Di Mambro had gathered around him a group that lent an appearance of reality to the fictions he created. And now this imaginary universe began to come under critical scrutiny. The head of the Solar Temple apparently decided to respond by taking himself and his followers away from the scene altogether.
> — Jean-Francois Mayer, "Our Terrestrial Journey Is Coming to an End."

In October 1994, fifty-three members of the Order of the Solar Temple (Ordre du Temple Solaire, or OTS) in Switzerland and Québec were murdered or committed suicide. On October 4, a fire destroyed Joseph Di Mambro's (the group's leader) villa in Morin Heights, Canada. Police found five charred bodies in the ruins. Three had been stabbed to death before the fire. At 1:00 a.m. on October 5, a fire started in Ferme des Rochettes, near Cheiry, in the Canton of Fribourg, one of the centers of the Solar Temple in Switzerland. Police found twenty-three bodies in a room that had been converted into a temple. Some had been shot; many others were found with their heads inside plastic bags. At 3:00 a.m. the same day, three chalets inhabited by members of the Solar Temple caught fire almost simultaneously at Les Granges sur Salvan, in the Valais Canton. Police found twenty-five bodies, along with the remains of the devices that had initiated the fires as well as the pistol that had shot the people near Cheiry.

For many months prior to this initial spate of murder-suicides, rumors of financial mismanagement had been circulating among Solar Temple members. On September 30, shortly before the group's dramatic final "transit," a three-month-old infant was killed at their Canadian site by driving a wooden stake through its heart. The parents, who were ex-members of the Temple, were also brutally murdered. Surviving members explained that Di Mambro had ordered the killing because the baby was the Anti-Christ. Several days later, Di Mambro and twelve followers convened a ritual Last Supper together. The murders-suicides took place not long after this meeting. Fifteen members of the inner circle—referred to as the "awakened"—took poison. Thirty others—the "immortals"—were shot or smothered to death. Eight others, termed "traitors," were also murdered.

The plan seems to have been for the fire to more or less completely destroy everything in the Swiss centers. This would have compelled investigators to focus on the group's self-interpretation of their actions—a self interpretation embodied in four letters, or "Testaments," that were sent to sixty journalists, scholars, and government officials. However, because the incineration devices at the main center in the Cheiry farmhouse failed to ignite, many documents and other artifacts were left intact. One of the testaments, addressed "To All Those Who Can Still Understand the Voice of Wisdom," issued a call for other Solar Temple sympathizers to follow their example: "[F]rom the Planes where we will work from now on and by a just law of magnetism, we will be in the position of calling back the last Servants capable of hearing this last message . . . may our Love and our Peace accompany you during the terrible tests of the Apocalypse that await you. Know that from where we will be, we will always hold our arms open to receive those who are worthy of joining us." (*Gnosis Magazine* 1995:90)

This invitation to join them in the beyond found a receptive audience. On December 16, 1995, sixteen of the remaining European members disappeared from their homes in France and Switzerland. Four left notes hinting at a second mass suicide. Thirteen adults and three children were later found dead in a remote forest in southeast France. Investigators concluded that at least four of the sixteen did not die willingly. Most had been drugged. Two of the sixteen shot the others, poured gasoline over their bodies, set them on fire, and then shot themselves so they would fall into the flames.

Finally, five additional adult members and three teenage children apparently tried to commit suicide on the spring equinox of March 20, 1997, in Quebec, Canada. The attempt failed due to faulty equipment. The teenage sons and daughter of one of the couples convinced their parents that they wanted to live. They were then allowed to leave, and the adults subsequently succeeded in burning down the house with themselves in it. Four of the bodies were arranged to form a cross. The teens were found drugged and disoriented, but otherwise safe, in a nearby building. A note was found that described the group belief that death on earth leads to a transit to a new planet where their lives would continue.

More than a few serious observers have analyzed the OTS in detail, giving particular attention to the factors that seem to have precipitated the murder-suicides. Especially in studies comparing different alternative religions that have been involved in violence, explanations tend to emphasize these groups' millennialist belief systems—implicitly or explicitly portraying such beliefs as the key to understanding their violence. In this chapter, I will present an overview of the Solar Temple. In the latter part of the chapter I will also argue, among other things, against the primacy of millennialism as an explanatory factor for understanding group suicide.

Neo-Templarism and Esotericism

Di Mambro had sampled a variety of different esoteric groups, including the Ancient and Mystical Order Rosae Crucis (AMORC), which he joined in 1956, and of which he was a member until at least 1968. In the 1960s, he came into contact with several persons who would later play a role in Solar Temple history, including Jacques Breyer who had initiated a "Templar resurgence" in France in 1952. Several groups, including the Order of the Solar Temple, have their roots in Breyer's work.

"Templar" in this context refers to the Knights Templar, the medieval order to which groups in the Neo-Templar tradition ultimately trace their lineage. (This claimed lineage is almost certainly spurious; instead, Neo-Templar groups are esoteric organizations in the theosophical tradition.) A wealthy, powerful order, the Knights Templar had inspired envy among European rulers. As a consequence, in 1307 the Templars were accused (probably falsely) of heresy and arrested en masse. In 1310, fifty-four knights who had recanted earlier confessions were burned alive at the stake. And four years later, the Grand Master of the order and a provincial leader were similarly burned alive. The fires set or attempted by Solar Temple members during all of the murder-suicide incidents seem to have been inspired by the fiery deaths of the original Templars. According to Introvigne (1995:279), the fifty-three OTS deaths also represented an attempt to mimic the fifty-four Templar deaths—an attempt frustrated by the last-minute escape of Theirry Huguenin, a Swiss dentist and ex-member who had "sensed trouble at the Granges sur Salvan and fled" before he could be murdered (Harriss 1997).

Though a secretive organization, the original Knights Templar were almost certainly orthodox Christians. However, their secrecy in combination with the charges of heresy leveled against them in the fourteenth century provided fertile grounds for speculation, allowing later esotericists to construct a hypothesis that the order was secretly an esoteric-magical group. This line of speculation—bolstered by the unlikely claim that the order secretly survived into modern times—underlies contemporary neo-Templarism.

Massimo Introvigne, a scholar of the Western magical milieu (Introvigne 1990), observes that most modern neo-Templar groups trace their origin to the Order of the Temple founded in 1805 by Bernard-Raymond Fabré-Palaprat. "This French physician and Freemason claimed to represent an uninterrupted succession of Templar 'Grand Masters' operating secretly since the suppression of the medieval Order in the fourteenth century" (Introvigne 2000:140). It was this tradition that Breyer revived in the mid-twentieth century. (For anyone interested in understanding the background of the OTS, there is a good summary of neo-Templarism in Introvigne 1995, and a short but illuminating discussion of the magical milieu, its relation to the alternative spiritual subculture, and the immediate precursors to the Solar Temple in the first section of Introvigne 2000).

The Cult Stereotype and "True Lies"

The Solar Temple tragedies played a pivotal role in inflaming the cult controversy in Europe. Although European anticultists had been active for decades, the spectacle of the murder-suicides influenced public opinion to support harsher actions against new religious movements (NRMs). Interestingly, this came at around the same time that the North American anticult movement suffered a severe setback as a consequence of the bankruptcy of the Cult Awareness Network (Melton 1999:229). The Solar Temple incidents were directly responsible for prompting European governments to begin issuing official reports on the dangers posed by nontraditional religions (Introvigne 2004: 207) and, particularly in France and Belgium, a growing campaign to "combat" alternative religions (Hervieu-Léger 2004:49; Palmer 2004:65; Lucas 2004:346). The incidents also helped bolster the North American anticult movement, which supplied consultants for European governments as well as the mind control ideology that became a central element of European reports and subsequent legislation (Shupe et al. 2004: 198).

Mind control ideology and the tendency to lump all nontraditional religions into the same stereotype have been extensively critiqued by the present writer and others (e.g., Lewis 1998; Dawson 1998; Anthony and Robbins 2004), and there is no need to repeat these arguments here. There is, however, an aspect of the cult stereotype that seems to apply with particular force to the Solar Temple and that merits attention in this case, namely the flawed character of the leadership.

One of the standard accusations hurled again nontraditional religions is that founder-leaders are egotistical, self-seeking charlatans who cynically concoct pseudo-religions for the purposes of self-aggrandizement and the exploitation of converts, both financially and sexually. "Cult leaders" are also often portrayed as mentally imbalanced, paranoid, manipulative and rigidly authoritarian

(Dawson 2002:80). This portrayal obviously represents a caricature—so overstated as to be useless for analytical purposes—but even stereotypes sometimes contain an element of truth.

Having interacted with more than a few leaders of nontraditional religions, I have the strong impression that almost all are sincere (though a critic might say they are sincerely deluded), whatever their personal foibles. Despite the personal benefits—so obvious to outsider observers—of being a spiritual leader, the demands of running even a small religious group are simply too burdensome and involve too many personal sacrifices to attract individuals intent on fulfilling purely selfish goals.

However, I also have the impression that some of the leaders of such groups not infrequently act from mixed motives, though they may convince themselves that they are acting from purely noble motives. The polygamous arrangement that David Koresh established at Mt. Carmel among his closest followers (Bradley 1994:166–167) appears to be an example of this mixing of motives. In other words, even assuming that Koresh sincerely believed God commanded him to take additional wives, it is difficult to dismiss the impression that carnal motives (unconscious though they may have been) played a role in shaping this particular revelation.

More problematic for assessing the ethics of NRMs are cases in which leaders consciously utilize deception. For example, a spiritual leader can straightforwardly request that a follower make a hefty donation without invoking divine sanction. Alternately, a leader might feel an inner prompting that he interprets (correctly or incorrectly) as a prompting from a (typically disembodied) spiritual personality to ask the follower to make a sizeable donation—e.g., "Master D.K. tells me that you should immediately donate $5,000." Yet another scenario would be a case in which the leader wants the follower to make a big donation, but feels he needs to invoke divine sanction in order to realize his request. In this case, he might *say* "Master D.K. tells me you should donate $5,000," but in fact the request has nothing to do with any spiritual prompting. Even this, however, need not be entirely cynical.

Perhaps the leader feels (a) his disciple has plenty of money, (b) the group needs the donation to pay this month's bills, and (c) Master D.K. – assuming the leader truly believes in the real existence of Master D.K. on the inner planes – obviously would not want the group to go into debt. Therefore, Master D.K. would certainly approve of the leader's request for a donation. Hence telling the disciple that "Master D.K. has told me you should donate $5,000" is, from the leader's perspective, a mostly true statement. Though I don't have empirical evidence to support this (and it is frankly difficult to imagine how one would collect such evidence) beyond informal impressions from my fieldwork, my sense is that some NRM leaders engage in these kinds of "slippery" inferences on a regular basis.

Another, related phenomenon is what I have elsewhere called the "true lies" pattern (Lewis 2003). Specifically with respect to the legend of Jesus' trip to India, a succession of otherwise honorable men verified the existence of a nonexistent manuscript, *The Life of Saint Issa*, because it expressed (or expressed after some massaging of the text) what they felt were profound truths. Some of the documents created by Gerald Gardner, the founder of modern Wicca, and his associates exemplify the same phenomenon (Lewis 1999: 345–352). In these cases, the motive for dissimulating is to add a degree of legitimacy to the ideas expressed in fabricated documents. Before we judge this legitimation strategy too harshly, we should remember that the history of religion contains innumerable examples of forged scriptures—including documents in the scriptural canons of some of the major world religions.

The true lies pattern may, however, be extended to nontextual examples. In neo-Templarism, for example, different individuals claimed to have secretly met, and to have been initiated by, representatives of the underground Knights Templar. For instance, Jacques Breyer, the founder of the "Templar Renaissance" that ultimately inspired the OTS, claimed to have received such an initiation on June 12, 1952, in the ruins of the Arginy Castle. Raymond Bernard, founder of the Renewed Order of the Temple, made a similar claim about being initiated in the "crypt" of the Abbey of St. Nilus in the 1960s. Thirty years later, Bernard admitted that his account was fictional, though "based upon deeply moving personal mystical experiences" (Introvigne 2000: 142). Again this is a legitimation strategy; in these cases to legitimate the authority of Breyer and Bernard as neo-Templar leaders.

Though we may judge the actions of these men harshly, the purpose behind the claims of Breyer, Bernard, and others is to amplify their authority so they can be in a better position to propagate what they feel are profound truths. In other words, in most cases of this sort, my impression is that such leaders are otherwise sincere. As argued above, the demands of founding and leading a religious community are such as to make the existence of a completely cynical leader unlikely. Nevertheless, a lack of total cynicism does not mean that the founder-leader of a religious group is thereby necessarily *good*.

Joseph Di Mambro

Joseph Di Mambro was born August 19, 1924, in Pont-Saint-Esprit, France. From the age of sixteen, he was apprenticed as a watchmaker and jeweler and seems to have pursued this profession during the first part of his life. Not much is known about this period except that from a young age he was deeply interested in esotericism, as previously noted.

We first catch a glimpse of the unsavory side of his character from a 1972 conviction on charges of fraud "for impersonating a psychologist and passing bad checks" (Hall et al. 2000: 120). John R. Hall and Philip D. Schuyler speculate that a 1979 fire at La Pyramide, an early communal farm founded by Di Mambro near Geneva, was possibly an insurance swindle. Hall and Schuyler seem to imply that the insurance money from the fire enabled Di Mambro to obtain a mansion in Geneva where he started the Golden Way Foundation (ibid.:120). The Golden Way was the immediate predecessor organization to the Solar Temple.

The International Chivalric Order Solar Tradition (Solar Temple) was founded in 1984. Solar Temple groups were organized in Quebec, Canada, as well as in Australia, Switzerland, France, and other countries. The leadership saw themselves as playing a pivotal role on the world stage. Partially as a consequence of this view, they felt that the Solar Temple was being systematically persecuted by the various governments with whom they were having relatively minor problems. A grandiose self-image is not, of course, unique to the OTS; many other small NRMs perceive themselves as being at the fulcrum of world history (Mayer 1999:172). Nevertheless, this attitude does not speak well for the Solar Temple's sense of social reality.

On the one hand, we should note that Di Mambro was realistic enough about his own lack of charisma that he brought Luc Jouret into the OTS to become the public face of his organization.

Intelligent and charismatic, Jouret had been trained as a medical doctor and was an accomplished practitioner of homeopathy. He also lectured on naturopathy and ecological topics and was active in the wider circuit of the French-speaking New Age movement. He spoke in New Age bookstores and to eclectic esoteric groups in France, Switzerland, Belgium, and Canada, recruiting people for the Solar Temple.

On the other hand, Di Mambro was far from humble and claimed to be the reincarnation of Osiris, Akhnaton, Moses, and Cagliostro (Wessinger 2000a:220–221). He identified various OTS members as having been such famous individuals as Bernard de Clairvaux, Joseph of Arimathea, Queen Hapshetphout, and Rama (Palmer 1996:308). (Regarding past-life claims as a widespread strategy for legitimating charismatic authority, refer to Dawson 2002:82-83.) He was also regarded by his followers "as the only one on Earth who had access" to the Masters (Introvigne and Mayer 2002:183). Furthermore, Di Mambro saw the OTS as producing "cosmic children" who would shape the future destiny of the planet. Chief among these was his own daughter Emmanuelle, who was to be the messiah-avatar of the New Age. Di Mambro required that she wear gloves and a helmet to protect her purity, and she could only be touched by family members.

Although it is almost certain that Di Mambro believed most of what he taught about Cosmic Masters and the like, he "pretended (since at least the late 1970s) to represent the 'Mother Lodge' and to receive his orders from mysterious 'Masters'" (Mayer 1999). He was also not above tricking his followers into thinking he had such a close link to these exalted spiritual personages that they would deign to manifest themselves during Temple initiations. These manifestations were accomplished by means of hidden technology: holographic projections of the Ascended Masters, "together with the robes, candles, incense, and music, created a powerful sacred tableau" (Hall et al. 2000: 126):

> Solar Temple ceremonies were held in darkened inner sanctums. "During ceremonies we would hear sounds from the star Sirius, followed by apparitions of chandeliers, swords and so on, leading up to the appearance of the Masters," recounts a former Canadian member. Sometimes the Master held a sword and tapped the floor in a coded message. Or it could be King Arthur's sword, Excalibur, that materialized before the members' ecstatic eyes. Or the slow, hovering appearance of the Holy Grail, the chalice Christ used at the Last Supper. The apparitions were cleverly designed holograms. "Di Mambro would tell us, 'Do you realize that we are the only people on the planet to see these things?'" (Harris 1997)

A *Readers Digest* reporter was able to examine some of the ritual stage props confiscated by the Canadian police in the wake of the initial transits. He reports that "King Arthur's Excalibur was a large, tinny broadsword crudely painted with fluorescent green and red. In a dark room, black light made it appear suspended in midair, blood dripping from its tip. Another sword had a small nine-volt battery taped to its hilt. Electrical wires, masked with black tape, led to a tiny read light at the tip" (ibid.).

The apparitions and gimmicks convinced members Di Mambro really held the special status he claimed. When his son Elie discovered the technological nature of these manifestations in 1990, he began to speak openly of his father's trickery. The Order's chief "special effects" technician, Tony

Dutoit, also initiated rumors about the holograms. But Tony and his wife Nicki Dutoit went further: They not only defied Di Mambro's order that they not have a child, they also provocatively named him Christopher Emmanuel in what seemed to be an implicit challenge to Emmanuelle's messianic status. Enraged both by the Dutoits' disobedience and by their challenge to Emmanuelle, Di Mambro ordered their son executed as the Anti-Christ shortly before the group transit.

This incident provides us with yet another window into Di Mambro's flawed character: an authoritarian leader, he had directed his followers' personal lives in ways that went far beyond the proper bounds of pastoral care. Of particular note was the Temple's practice of "cosmic coupling" that routinely broke up married couples and paired them with other followers, often resulting in pairs with significant age differences. The authorization for these intrusions into the personal lives of members was attributed to the will of the Cosmic Masters, as indicated by Bruno Klaus's announcement to his wife that he was leaving her because: "The Masters have decided. I am going to live with another woman" (cited in Hall et al. 2000:128). Although Di Mambro may have mistakenly imagined that his personal whims were actually spiritual promptings, it is difficult to avoid the impression—especially in the latter days of his career—that he simply asserted all of his decisions were the will of the Masters, whether he believed so or not.

It should finally be noted that Di Mambro was defensive and paranoid—someone who could never accept responsibility for any of the problems the OTS was experiencing during the last few years before the transit. It was, for example, his decision to "uncouple" Bruno Klaus from his wife that produced the Temple's most persistent critic. Rose-Marie Klaus doggedly sought to revenge herself against the OTS, an effort that eventually paid off after two Canadian members were arrested while attempting to buy silenced semiautomatic pistols (illegal in Canada). Although the court handed out only one year of unsupervised probation and a token fine, Klaus made tabloid headlines a few days following the arrests in which she recounted the hidden "horrors" of the OTS (Hall et al. 2000:132).

The news coverage in combination with the gun charges set in motion police investigations that led Di Mambro to conclude the group was a target of an international conspiracy. As his wife wrote at the time, "Our file is the hottest on the planet, the most important of the last ten years, if not of the century." Additionally, she recorded a message on an audiotape in 1994 in which she stated that "We are rejected by the whole world" (cited in Wessinger 2000a: 225). One of the testaments left behind after the transit even asserted that the OTS had been the target of "systematic persecution" by authorities on three continents. (In this regard, refer to the discussion under the section heading "A Persecution Mania" in Mayer 1999.) Di Mambro also bitterly accused Jouret of having brought ruin on the OTS by his bungling. This exaggerated, paranoid attitude plus his blaming of everyone else for the Solar Temple's problems was, unfortunately, typical Di Mambro.

"Suicide Cults"
The Solar Temple murder-suicides are frequently compared with violent incidents involving other alternative religions, particularly the Jonestown murder-suicides (1978), the ATF/FBI raid on the Mt. Carmel community (1993), the Tokyo subway poison gas attack (1995), and the Heaven's Gate suicides (1997). The sensational violence associated with the murder of members of the Movement for the Restoration of the Ten Commandments of God (2000) is often not included in these

comparisons, partly because it took place more recently and partly because it seems to have been a somewhat different phenomenon (for a brief overview, refer to the discussion in the introduction to the present volume).

Two major monographs that appeared in 2000—John R. Hall's et al. *Apocalypse Observed* and Catherine Wessinger's *How the Millennium Comes Violently*—developed analyses of NRM-related violence that included thick descriptions of some of the more controversial groups, including the People's Temple, Branch Davidians, Solar Temple, AUM Shinrikyo, and Heaven's Gate. Many other observers have taken similar approaches (e.g., Robbins and Palmer 1997; Daniels 1999; Wessinger 2000b; Bromley and Melton 2002). As reflected such titles as *How the Millennium Comes Violently* (Wessinger 2000a), *Millennialism, Persecution and Violence* (Wessinger 2000b), *Millennium, Messiahs, and Mayhem* (Robbins and Palmer 1997), and numerous scholarly articles, Millennialism has been central to these discussions—though it should immediately be noted that contemporary analysts of NRMs and violence are generally careful to "eschew single-factor explanations" (Bromley 2004: 154). Other factors usually considered in attempts to construct a general model of NRM-associated violence are high-demand organization (meaning that participants do not have the option of being casual, part-time members), charismatic leadership, isolation from the surrounding society, and the threatening role played by external forces such as hostile apostates and intrusive governmental authorities. (For a comprehensive discussion, refer to Bromley and Melton 2002.)

At the present juncture, the relatively mature state of this body of literature makes it possible to ask different sorts of questions. Specifically, rather than a straightforward comparison of the five principal groups, what if one focused instead on the three groups that imploded in group suicides – People's Temple, Solar Temple, and Heaven's Gate? While it is true that both the People's Temple and the Solar Temple also engaged in acts of murder, it could be argued that these violent acts were aspects of the suicide event. It is thus possible to distinguish such suicide-related murders from the otherwise comparable violence initiated by the leadership of AUM Shinrikyo and other groups. The balance, therefore, of this chapter will examine the three "suicide cults." (Introvigne and Mayer 2002 compare these same three movements in the concluding section of their analysis, though they do not explicitly note group suicide as the principal shared trait.)

It is often more illuminating to "complexify" rather than to simplify certain phenomena, but for my purposes I will focus on distilling the details of these three groups down to a common core of shared traits. Though this approach is open to criticism – and would certainly never do for a comprehensive explanation – it nevertheless bears fruit as an analytical strategy, as we will see.

As a preliminary move, it should be noted that neither Shoko Asahara nor David Koresh seriously contemplated suicide. When authorities finally located Asahara in a secret room at AUM's Mt. Fuji center, they also found him with an abundant stash of money (not unlike Saddam Hussein) that he planned to support himself with into the foreseeable future. And though Koresh seems to have been willing to die a martyr's death, it also appears he was ready to embrace martyrdom only if all other options (or, perhaps more accurately, all other reasonable options within the horizon of his religious ideology) were closed. The fact that during the siege of Mt. Carmel Koresh retained a literary attorney to handle his story (Lewis 1994:117) should be enough to indicate that he envisioned himself living into the post-siege future—not to mention his explicit assertion to FBI negotiators a few days before the final assault that "I never intended to die in here" (cited in Wessinger 2000a:105). (Also refer to Palmer 1994 in this regard.)

Millennialism

To turn our attention to the People's Temple, the Solar Temple, and Heaven's Gate, what happens when we ruthlessly cut away everything except the bare-bones structure shared by the three "suicide cults"? Surprisingly, the first trait to drop out is apocalypticism-millennialism. Though it is quite possible to argue that Jim Jones was apocalyptic and millenarian (e.g., Chidester 1988; Wessinger 2000a), in point of fact he had no theology in the proper sense, much less a developed eschatology. Well before the establishment of Jonestown, he had become little more than a secular socialist in religious garb. Even as people lined up to drink a mixture of cyanide and Kool-Aid during the final drama, Jones exhorted his followers with the assertion that "This is a revolutionary suicide; this is not a self-destructive suicide" (Hall et al. 2000:37), rather than consoling them with visions of the afterlife—though, as Jonathan Z. Smith notes (1982:117), one can also point to portions of the audiotape made during the event that seem to intimate they would be reunited in a post-mortem state. (Also refer to Chidester's [1988:106] application of Lifton's [1968] notion of "revolutionary immortality" to Jonestown.) I am aware that this assertion flies in the face of almost all other scholarly approaches to the Jonestown suicides. The point being made here thus calls for more discussion.

Millennial movements in the proper sense, to cite Norman Cohn's classic study, always picture the millennium as something "that is to be accomplished by, or with the help of, supernatural agencies" (1970:15). Even current definitions of millennialism typically mention such agencies. However, as in the following excerpt from a recently published encyclopedia of NRMs, the People's Temple is included as a example of a millenarian group, despite Jim Jones's nonbelief in divinities of any sort:

> The terms 'millenarianism' and 'millennialism' are usually applied to the study of apocalyptic beliefs. They refer to the expectation of imminent world transformation, collective salvation, and the establishment of a perfect, new world of harmony and justice to be brought about by otherworldly beings acting in accordance with a divine or superhuman plan. . . . Millenarian ideas associated with new religions often include the belief that the transformation of the present world will be cataclysmic; the worldview (referred to variously as catastrophic millennialism, apocalypticism or premillennialism), expresses a pessimistic view of humanity, maintaining that the world is fatally flawed and unredeemable by human effort, and that only a divinely ordained world cataclysm can usher in a millennial age of peace and prosperity. Groups such as the Branch Davidians, Aum Shinrikyo and the People's Temple exemplify catastrophic millenarian views. (Wojcik 2004:388)

One can, of course, redefine religion to encompass secular visions (as Wessinger does via Tillich's notion of "ultimate concern" [2000a:15]), or redefine millennialism to include secular phenomena (as the editors and some of the contributors do in Robbins and Palmer 1997). The problem with such approaches is that as soon as one expands millennialism to include nonreligious phenomena, one can legitimately ask, Why stop with survivalism, feminism, and radical environmentalism (three groups examined in the Robbins and Palmer collection)? Almost any group of people who look forward to a better tomorrow—including educators and mainstream political parties—could conceivably be viewed as millennialist. At this level of generality, however, millennialism becomes almost meaningless as a category of analysis.

We should also note that millennialism in the primary sense described by Norman Cohn involves a salvation that is "terrestrial, in the sense that it is to be realized on this earth and not in some other-worldly heaven" (1970:15). At the time of their dramatic "exits," however, *not one* of the three suicide groups examined here envisioned returning to a paradisal era that would be established on this planet.

With respect to the related notion of apocalypticism, we should note that almost every religion in the larger Judeo-Christian-Islamic tradition has an apocalyptic theology, even the traditional peace churches that forbid members from participating in the military. Thus, contrary to what one might think, having an apocalyptic theology is not, in itself, an indicator of potential violence (Dawson 2002:96). This is because in most apocalyptic scenarios it is God and his angels who fight the final battle, not flesh-and-blood human beings. The human role is spiritual, and the "saved" fight a spiritual war, not a literal, physical war.

In spite of the line of argument I have been pursuing in the preceding paragraphs, I am not necessarily opposed to redefining millennialism to encompass either secular phenomena or extraterrestrial millennia. Rather, my purpose here is simply to call into question the axiomatic assumption of most analysts that millennial ideology is a *core* characteristic of contemporary violent groups, *essential* for understanding their violence. Though we may be hesitant to restrict the scope of millennialism, the issues raised in the present discussion should nevertheless cast doubt on the adequacy of this concept as a primary category for interpreting NRM-related violence—especially if we are able to isolate other, more compelling factors that can explain group suicides without invoking millennialism.

External Provocation and Social Isolation

Shifting our attention from the People's Temple to Heaven's Gate, we encounter another surprise when we subject Marshall Applewhite & company's dramatic exit to the same kind of analysis: namely, pressing external threats, whether real or imagined, are not one of the essential factors necessary for a group suicide (Wright 2002:104). In all four of the other new religions to be engulfed by violence, hostile outsiders were a major factor precipitating each tragedy—though none were quite as dramatic as the military assault on Mt. Carmel. The press criticism and government scrutiny directed against the Solar Temple and the People's Temple were mild by comparison.

In the case of Heaven's Gate, the group suicide was set in motion by the seemingly innocuous speculation of UFO buffs that a large UFO was approaching earth in the wake of the Hale-Bopp comet. It seems that Applewhite had already decided some years prior that he and his followers would make their exit via a group suicide. Thus he was predisposed to interpret any indication that the space brothers were coming as a sign that it was time to leave (Lewis 2003:129). Although "The Two" (as Applewhite and his partner Bonnie Sue Nettles often referred to themselves) had received hostile media coverage in their early years and even feared assassination—at one point they purchased weapons for fear of being attacked (Hall 2000:171)—these were not factors in March 1997 when Applewhite decided they would exit the planet. This is not, of course, to downplay the important role hostile external forces play in the precipitation of most NRM-related violence, only to make the point that this kind of intrusion by the outside world is not essential to all such violence.

To finally shift our attention to the Solar Temple, yet another trait seemingly shared by all of the new religions involved in violence drops out—namely the group's social isolation. It is the social dynamics of the segregated (usually communal) worlds of certain alternative religions that allow extreme actions to be contemplated, whether the internally directed violence of Heaven's Gate or the externally directed violence of AUM Shinrikyo. The Solar Temple, in contrast, was only semi-segregated from the larger society. Although Di Mambro established his early Pyramid group as a communal organization, the Solar Temple tended to be only partially communal. Thus, for instance, when the Temple was establishing a "survival farm" in Canada, only a half dozen members actually lived in the group's headquarters. The rest lived outside the house and took their meals there. Yet other members scattered about Quebec traveled to the house once a month for a meeting that took place on the full moon (Hall et al. 2000:125). Perhaps more importantly, many Solar Temple members were wealthy and socially established—belonging to "the elite of the Francophone west" (Daniels 1999:147)—people who could have been only partially separated from the larger society without arousing suspicion. (In this regard, also refer to the discussion in Introvigne and Mayer 2002:176).

Nevertheless, one could argue that the leader's distance from the voices of all but his closest followers was an essential factor contributing to his radical actions. In fact, Di Mambro tended to stay behind the scenes surrounded by a core of staunch loyalists, even bringing Jouret into the Temple for the purpose of interacting with outsiders. This finally brings us to a core trait of suicide cults, namely a charismatic leader who surrounds himself with absolutely loyal followers and who does not permit any overt disagreement with the group's ideology.

Here the analysis begins to sound rather like a cult stereotype. Focusing on the personality of the leader—usually portrayed, as we have seen, as a warped megalomaniac—is a staple in anticult discussions of NRMs. In contrast, mainstream scholars tend to include an analysis of the leadership as but one factor among others, such as a given group's social dynamics, ideology, and other less personal factors. Of course the leadership must interact with the membership in order to have any kind of organization at all. But, in the NRMs we have been discussing, the leader is clearly the epicenter. And the quest for commonalities among suicide groups has boiled down to commonalities among their leaders. So though I am not unmindful of group dynamics, and would never downplay the importance of "exogenous" factors (Robbins 2002:58; also refer to Robbins and Anthony 1995), for the sake of simplifying this analysis I will focus narrowly on the leadership.

Di Mambro, Jones, and Applewhite

What can we say about Jim Jones, Joseph Di Mambro, and Marshall Applewhite? If we again try to eliminate everything except shared traits, Applewhite undermines the stereotypical image of the cult leader because he neither demanded to live a better lifestyle than his followers nor did he attempt to seduce any of them (even before he was castrated). It also seems that Applewhite did not feel particularly bitter toward the people who left Heaven's Gate. And he apparently did not cultivate a distance between himself and his followers. In all of these particulars, he was quite different from Jones and especially from Di Mambro.

What all of these men *did* share was (1) an intolerance of any perspective other than own, (2) a need for total commitment—if not absolute obedience—from their followers (all three seem to have been "control freaks" to a greater or lesser extent), and (3) a greater or lesser paranoia about external forces threatening them or their group. And while, as we saw with the Solar Temple, it is not essential that the entire group be segregated from the larger society, self-destructive leaders typically surround themselves with loyalists who effectively isolate them from external input. At this point, however, we are faced with the problem of finding what makes these men *different* from other NRM leaders. Although, unlike the three suicide group leaders, David Koresh seems to have regularly interacted with people outside of his community, Shoko Asahara was every bit as isolated from external reality as Di Mambro, Applewhite, and Jones. Furthermore, Asahara demanded total obedience, was extremely intolerant of other views, and was paranoid about real and imagined enemies. Yet Asahara apparently never contemplated suicide.

So where does that leave us? Though we have managed to identify some essential common traits via comparison-contrast, a factor that sets the Solar Temple, the People's Temple, and Heaven's Gate apart from AUM Shinrikyo and the Branch Davidians seems to have eluded us. Discovering this additional factor requires that we shift our focus away from the traits of NRMs frequently discussed in the literature and focus instead on less commonly discussed characteristics. What do Di Mambro, Applewhite, and Jones share that sets them apart from Koresh and Asahara?

Some years ago while researching Heaven's Gate for an analysis of the strategies by which Marshall Applewhite legitimated suicide, I came across several sources that mentioned his health was failing (e.g., Perkins and Jackson 1997:81). Also, in *How the Millennium Comes Violently*, Wessinger points out that Applewhite never considered the option of appointing a successor who could lead the group after his passing, which likely made the group suicide option more attractive (2000a:81). At the time these seemed like minor factors in explaining the Heaven's Gate tragedy, so they are mentioned only briefly in my study of NRM legitimation strategies (Lewis 2003:129).

In the context of the current discussion, however, these become major factors because they are precisely the traits that set the suicide groups apart from the others. In terms of health, Di Mambro was "suffering from kidney failure and incontinence as well as severe diabetes, and he believed he had cancer" (Wessinger 2000a:221). And Jones—either because he was sedating a genuine physical problem or because he had become a self-destructive addict—was gradually destroying himself with excessive prescription tranquilizers (Templer 1998:8). Thomas Robbins emphasized the importance of a charismatic leader's health in a personal communication to Hall when the latter was writing *Apocalypse Observed*, though Hall quickly passes over the subject after mentioning Robbins's communication in the latter part of his book (2000:193). It is easy to understand how Hall, focused as he was on other aspects of NRMs, would have failed to perceive the health of the charismatic leader as a major explanatory factor. In the context of the current discussion, however, the observation that Applewhite, Di Mambro, and Jones were in failing health, whereas Koresh and Asahara were not, makes this factor suddenly stand out as important: If the three suicide leaders all perceived themselves as dying, then the notion of bringing the whole group along on their post-mortem journeys might strike them as attractive.

In addition to their physical deaths, all three men knew that their respective groups had not only stopped growing but were also likely to decline precipitously in the future, particularly after they died. Neither Applewhite (as noted) nor Jones (apparently) had given serious thought to grooming a successor. Di Mambro, on the other hand, seems for many years to have thought his daughter Emmanuelle would inherit his mantle. By twelve years of age, however, she was already rebelling against the script her father had imagined her fulfilling, effectively frustrating whatever desire he might have had for a legacy. By the time of the Transit, he had also come to nurse an exaggerated hatred for the "barbarian, incompetent and aberrant" Jouret (Introvigne and Mayer 2002: 177), an obvious person to take over should Di Mambro pass from the scene.

To summarize the above discussion into a list of traits, we can say that, based on an analysis of the People's Temple, the Solar Temple, and Heaven's Gate, the essential characteristics of a suicide group are:

1. Absolute intolerance of dissenting views
2. Members must be totally committed
3. Exaggerated paranoia about external threats
4. Leader isolates him/herself or the entire group from the nonbelieving world
5. Leader's health is failing—in a major way, not just a transitory sickness
6. There is no successor and no steps are being taken to provide a successor; or, alternately, succession plans have been frustrated
7. The group is either stagnant or declining, with no realistic hopes for future expansion

As noted earlier, there are numerous points of overlap with AUM Shinrikyo and the Branch Davidians. However, despite major areas of overlap, both of these groups lack several essential traits. Specifically, David Koresh did not segregate himself from unbelievers (Dawson 2002:86-87) and was in good health immediately prior to the ATF raid on Mt. Carmel. Koresh had also fathered a number of children he believed would eventually rule the earth—in effect, his successors. Asahara seems to have been in reasonably good health as well, plus he had already indicated to followers that his children would be his spiritual successors (though it should be pointed out that this successorship was rather vague at the time of the subway attack and only clarified later). Finally, though neither AUM in 1995 and nor the Davidians in 1993 were experiencing rapid growth, they were also not stagnant; both could have reasonably anticipated future growth. In other words, the Davidians lacked traits 4, 5, 6, and 7, whereas AUM lacked 5, 6, and 7.

One final point that needs to be addressed before concluding is the problem raised by the suicides of other Solar Temple members in the years following the original transit. As Introvigne and Mayer argue, "After the second and third tragedies of 1995 and 1997, it became even more apparent that Di Mambro's manipulative behavior could not have been the only explanation for the OTS process of self-destruction" (2002:178). There were also several Heaven's Gate members who took their own lives in the years following the mass suicide of that group.

These later suicides could be marshaled to support a position that the role of the leadership is less central for interpreting the original group suicides than I have been arguing here. However, this position would have to ignore the fact that a number of new influences come into play that are more important for understanding the actions of members who survived the initial suicide event. For instance, participants who had been deeply involved in the Solar Temple or Heaven's Gate would have felt a vital part of their lives had been lost in the wake of the departure of the group. They would also have had to endure the ridicule heaped on their religion by the mass media. Finally, in the exit videos left behind by Heaven's Gate and in the Solar Temple testaments, survivors were explicitly invited to follow the group into the beyond—as we noted in the OTS testament cited in the introductory section of this chapter. In other words, surviving members were acting under a new constellation of influences that make their suicides highly problematic as a basis for interpreting the original suicides.

Conclusion

I have focused this chapter on the founder of the OTS because his idiosyncracies provide keys for understanding the Solar Temple's final "transit." Leaders of many religions (not excluding traditional religions) have utilized questionable strategies, such as fabricating documents that claim special authority for the teachings they contain. The Solar Temple's holographic fabrications, however, put Di Mambro in a class by himself. Nevertheless, though he "acted at times like a common swindler . . . he very likely remained convinced of his message and mission until the end" (Mayer 1999). A deeply flawed character, Di Mambro had founded a fatally flawed organization. And while the murder-suicides were probably not inevitable, it seems that the Solar Temple was early set on a collision course that would eventually have led to some kind of unhappy outcome.

The focus on Di Mambro also feeds a broader analysis of the three primary suicide cults examined by contemporary scholars of alternative religions: the People's Temple, the Solar Temple, and Heaven's Gate. The final sections of the chapter argued that the two factors normally given pride of place in discussions of NRM-associated violence, namely millennialism and external provocation, were not as central for understanding suicide groups as previous analysts have suggested. Instead we found that a leader with failing health, in combination with certain other characteristics of intensive religions, are more important factors for predicting which groups are predisposed to suicide.

References:

Anthony, Dick, and Thomas Robbins. 2004. "Conversion and 'Brainwashing' in New Religious Movements." In *The Oxford Handbook of New Religious Movements*, ed. James R. Lewis, 243-297. New York: Oxford University Press.

Bradley, Martha Sontag. 1994. "A More Righteous Seed: A Comparison of Polygamy among the Branch Davidians and the Fundamentalist Mormons." In *From the Ashes: Making Sense of Waco,* ed. James R. Lewis, 165-168. Lanham, Maryland: Rowman and Littlefield.

Bromley, David G. 2004. "Violence and New Religious Movements." In *The Oxford Handbook of New Religious Movements*, ed. James R. Lewis, 143-162. New York: Oxford University Press.

Bromley, David G., and J. Gordon Melton, eds. 2002. *Cults, Religion, and Violence*. New York: Cambridge University Press.

Campiche, Roland. 1995. "Quand les sects affolent: Ordre du Temple Solaire, médias et fin du millénaire." *Entretiens avec Cyril Dépraz*. Geneva: Labor et Fides.

Chidester, David. 1988. *Salvation and Suicide: An Interpretation of Jim Jones, the Peoples Temple, and Jonestown.* Bloomington: Indiana University Press.

Daniels, Ted, ed. 1999. *A Doomsday Reader: Prophets, Predictors, and Hucksters of Salvation.* New York: New York University Press.

Dawson, Lorne L. 2002. "Crises of Charismatic Legitimacy and Violent Behavior in New Religious Movements." In *Cults, Religion and Violence*, ed. David G. Bromley and J. Gordon Melton, 80-101. New York: Cambridge University Press.

--------------------. 1998. *Comprehending Cults: The Sociology of New Religious Movements.* Toronto and New York: Oxford University Press.

Hall, John R., with Philip D. Schuyler and Sylvaine Trinh. 2000. *Apocalypse Observed: Religious Movements and Violence in North America, Europe, and Japan.* London: Routledge.

Harriss, Joseph A. 1997. "Mystery of a Killer Cult." *Readers Digest,* International Edition (December).

Hervieu-Léger, Danièle. 2004. "France's Obsession with the 'Sectarian Threat.'" In *New Religious Movements in the 21st Century: Legal, Political, and Social Challenges in Global Perspective*, ed. Phillip Charles Lucas and Thomas Robbins, 49-59. New York: Routledge.

Introvigne, Massimo. 1990. *Il cappello del mago. I nuovi movimenti magicci dallo spiritismo al santanismo.* Milan: Sugar Co.

--------------------. 1995. "Ordeal by Fire: The Tragedy of the Solar Temple." *Religion* 25, 267-283.

--------------------. 2000. "The Magic of Death: The Suicides of the Solar Temple." In *Millennialism, Persecution, and Violence: Historical Cases*, ed. Catherine Wessinger, 138-157. Syracuse, New York: Syracuse University Press.

--------------------. 2004. "Something Peculiar About France: Anti-Cult Campaigns in Western Europe and French Religious Exceptionalism." In *The Oxford Handbook of New Religious Movements*, ed. James R. Lewis, 206-220. New York: Oxford University Press.

Introvigne, Massimo, and Jean-Francois Mayer. 2002. "Occult Masters and the Temple of Doom: The Fiery End of the Solar Temple." In *Cults, Religion and Violence*, ed. David G. Bromley and J. Gordon Melton, 170-188. New York: Cambridge University Press.

Lewis, James R. 1994. "Fanning the Flames of Suspicion: The Case Against Mass Suicide at Waco." In *From the Ashes: Making Sense of Waco*, ed. James R. Lewis, 115-120. Lanham, Maryland: Rowman and Littlefield.

----------------. 1998. *Cults in America.* Santa Barbara: ABC-Clio.

----------------. 1999. *Witchcraft Today.* Santa Barbara: ABC-Clio.

----------------. 2003. *Legitimating New Religions.* New Brunswick: Rutgers University Press.

Lifton, Robert Jay. 1968. *Revolutionary Immortality: Mao Tse-Tung and the Chinese Cultural Revolution.* New York: Random House.

Lucas, Phillip Charles. 2004. "Conclusion." In *New Religious Movements in the 21st Century: Legal, Political, and Social Challenges in Global Perspective*, ed. Phillip Charles Lucas and Thomas Robbins, 341-357. New York: Routledge.

Mayer, Jean-Francois. 1999. "'Our Terrestrial Journey Is Coming to an End': The Last Voyage of the Solar Temple." In *Nova Religio* 2, no. 2: 172-196.

Mayer, Jean-Francois, and Massimo Introvigne. 2002. "Occult Masters and the Temple of Doom: The Fiery End of the Solar Temple." In *Cults, Religion, and Violence*, ed. David G. Bromley and J. Gordon Melton, 170-188. New York: Cambridge University Press.

Melton, J. Gordon. 1999. "Anti-Cultists in the United States: An Historical Perspective." In *New Religious Movements: Challenge and Response*, ed. Bryan Wilson and Jamie Cresswell, 213-233. London: Routledge.

OTS. 1995. "To All Those Who Can Still Understand the Voice of Wisdom . . . We Address This Last Message." In *Gnosis Magazine*. No. 34. (winter).

Pagels, Elaine. 1989 [1979]. *The Gnostic Gospels.* New York: Vintage.

Palmer, Susan J. 1994. "Excavating Waco" In *From the Ashes: Making Sense of Waco,* ed. James R. Lewis, 99-110. Lanham, Maryland: Rowman and Littlefield.

----------------. 1996. "Purity and Danger in the Solar Temple." In the *Journal of Contemporary Religion* 1, no.3: 303-318.

----------------. 2004. "The *Secte* Response to Religious Discrimination: Subversives, Martyrs, or Freedom Fighters in the French Sect Wars?" In *New Religious Movements in the 21ˢᵗ Century: Legal, Political, and Social Challenges in Global Perspective,* ed. Phillip Charles Lucas and Thomas Robbins, 61-73. New York: Routledge.

Perkins, Rodney, and Forrest Jackson. 1997. *Cosmic Suicide: The Tragedy and Transcendence of Heaven's Gate.* Dallas: Pentaradial Press.

Robbins, Thomas. 2002. "Sources of Volatility in Religious Movements." In *Cults, Religion and Violence,* ed. David G. Bromley and J. Gordon Melton, 57-79. New York: Cambridge University Press.

Robbins, Thomas, and Dick Anthony. 1995. "Sects and Violence: Factors Enhancing the Volatility of Marginal Religious Movements." In *Armageddon in Waco: Critical Perspectives on the Branch Davidian Conflict,* ed. Stuart A. Wright, 236-259. Chicago: University of Chicago Press.

Robbins, Thomas, and Susan J. Palmer, eds. 1997. *Millennium, Messiahs, and Mayhem: Contemporary Apocalyptic Movements.* New York: Routledge.

Smith, Jonathan Z. 1982. *Imagining Religion: From Babylon to Jonestown.* Chicago: University of Chicago Press.

Shupe, Anson, David G. Bromley, and Susan E. Darnell. 2004. "The North American Anti-Cult Movement: Vicissitudes of Success and Failure." In *The Oxford Handbook of New Religious Movements,* ed. James R. Lewis, 184-205. New York: Oxford University Press.

Templer, Robert. 1998. "Jonestown." In *The Richmond Review.* http://www.richmondreview.co.uk/features/temple02.html

Wessinger, Catherine. 2000a. *How the Millennium Comes Violently: From Jonestown to Heaven's Gate.* Chappaqua, NY: Seven Bridges Press.

-----------------------, ed. 2000b. *Millennialism, Persecution and Violence: Historical Cases.* Syracuse, NY: Syracuse University Press.

Wojcik, Daniel. 2004. "Apocalypticism and Millenarianism" In *Encyclopedia of New Religions: New Religious Movements, Sects, and Alternative Spiritualities,* ed. Christopher Partridge, 388-395. Oxford, England: Lion Publishing.

Wright, Stuart A. 2002. "Public Agency Involvement in Government-Religious Movement Confrontations. " In *Cults, Religion and Violence,* ed. David G. Bromley and J. Gordon Melton, 102-122. New York: Cambridge University Press.

The Burning of the Convent:
Antebellum Anti-Catholicism and the American Captivity Tale Tradition

On the evening of July 28, 1834, Edward Cutter, of Charlestown, Massachusetts, was surprised by the sudden appearance of a distressed woman at his doorstep. Clothed, according to some reports, in a nightgown, and somewhat delirious from a combination of stress and high fever, Elizabeth Harrison's closely shorn hair indicated that she was a resident of the nearby Ursuline convent. Harrison was, in fact, a nun of some thirteen years as well as an accomplished music teacher at the convent school where she had undergone a partial break-down as a result of overwork. Cutter took her to a friend's place in nearby Cambridge where, after the delirium passed, she immediately asked, and was subsequently permitted, to return to the convent.

The news of this unusual but otherwise minor incident somehow filtered out into the surrounding Protestant community–a community largely hostile to the Catholic presence. As tends to happen, the story of this event became hopelessly warped and exaggerated into a sensationalistic tale in which pursuing Catholics recaptured an escaping Harrison and compelled her to return to the convent against her will. A somewhat different version of this same story circulated in the form of a newspaper article which contained a less dramatic recapture–Harrison was supposedly tricked into returning rather than being bodily abducted–but which further alleged, among other things, that, subsequent to her return, she had disappeared:

> MYSTERIOUS.– We understand that a great excitement at present exists in Charlestown, in consequence of the mysterious disappearance of a young lady at the Nunnery in that place. The circumstances, as far as we can learn, are as follows: The young lady was sent to the place in question to complete her education, and became so pleased with the place and its inmates, that she was induced to take the black veil. After some time spent in the Nunnery, she became dissatisfied and made her escape from the institution–but was afterwards persuaded to return, being told that if she would continue but three weeks longer, she would be dismissed with honor. At the end of that time, a few days since, her friends called for her, but she was not to be found, and much alarm is excited in consequence.[1]

Within a short period of time, the rumors became quite exaggerated:

> The nuns, it was said, had not only driven an American lady to madness, but had immured her in a dungeon, and, upon her attempting to escape, had, with the connivance of the bishop and priests, actually tortured her to death.[2]

Certain particulars of this rumor seemed to follow the plot of a tale that was being circulated at the same time by another "escaped nun" from the Ursuline convent, and it is reasonable to suppose that the Harrison tale was shaped, to a greater or lesser extent, by the Reed Story. Rebecca Theresa Reed, who had worked at the convent for a few months as a servant, had, for several years, been propagating the story (which was later published as *Six Months in a Convent*[3]) that "she had actually aspired to be a nun, but 'escaped' from the convent after witnessing unspeakable immorality."[4] One of the focal themes of the anti-Catholic literature of the time was the abuse of young females in Catholic nunneries. The imagination out of which this kind of accusation emerged is vividly illustrated in a letter to the editor that was published in the Boston Recorder immediately following the Charlestown incident:

> [M]any, very many, of the most respectable and influential of our citizens, have a deep conviction that Convents have been, are now, and while continued, ever will be, highly injurious to the great interests of the community. They do not believe that a company of unmarried women can be placed, for life, under the sole control of a company of unmarried men; be excluded from the society of others, except so far as their directors are pleased to permit; and every thing which may be said or done, be hidden from inspection and kept an inviolable secret, without great mischief accruing to the persons themselves and to the public.[5]

This Protestant fantasy was to lead to the production of numerous apostate stories (which one might refer to as "Catholic captivity tales") authored by "escaped" nuns. These women were sometimes genuine former residents of nunneries who presented highly embellished accounts of their experiences, or, more often, fake ex-nuns who fabricated their stories from whole cloth. For nuns to escape, however, they first had to be in a state of bondage, and this state required a certain amount of explanation because Catholics did not bodily carry off their "prisoners." The initial "capture" was explained in terms of flattery and in terms of devious indoctrination designed to influence impressionable young ladies to take the veil. In Reed's words,

> My confessor flattered me in my delusion, telling me that the Lord had endowed my soul with His highest gifts, and He had designed me from all eternity to become a great saint.... At the same time he urged me to hasten my entrance into a Convent, because, if I delayed long in the world, God would withdraw from me those heavenly gifts. As a natural consequence of these false teachings, I soon became puffed up with my own self-righteousness, and was led to regard myself as better than others.[6]

Once inside the convent, the means of retaining captives varied from one author to another. In cruder narratives, inmates were physically imprisoned in the institution and controlled by threat of corporal punishment, and especially reluctant nuns were locked up in subterranean dungeons. In more nuanced accounts inmates were controlled by subtler, psychological means, such as fear of hell and the belief that any doubts were inspired by Satan. To cite again from Reed's account,

> [The Bishop] said the Devil would assail me, as he did Saint Teresa, and make me think I ought to go back to the world; and make me offers of worldly pleasures, and promise me happiness. In order to prevent this, I must watch and pray all the time, and banish entirely worldly thoughts from my mind....[7]

The Reed story and the Harrison rumor appeared to reinforce each other as well as to give substance to Protestant fears about what was going on behind the Nunnery's walls. In the midst of this potentially explosive state of affairs, Lyman Beecher came into town and on Sunday, August 10, delivered an impassioned anti-Catholic sermon in three different churches on the same day.[8] Although the oft-repeated charge that Beecher was directly responsible for ensuing events is unlikely,[9] his stormy denunciations of Rome certainly could not have helped the situation.

Around eight o'clock on the following evening, a mob arrived in front of the Ursuline convent and demanded that they be shown the nun whom they supposed was being held there against her will. Rather than attempting to reason with them, the mother superior responded with threats of her own, such as, "the Bishop has twenty thousand Irishmen at his command in Boston, and they will whip you all into the sea!"[10] This unwise response only infuriated the crowd who, after a short delay, began to force their way in. Nuns and schoolgirls fled into the back garden, and eventually escaped through a wall-like back fence with the aid of their neighbor, Mr. Cutter. It is unlikely that the schoolgirls, many of whom were from Protestant homes, would have been hurt by the attackers, but some of the nuns, and particularly the mother superior, might well have come to harm.[11]

The assault on the convent–which appears to have been motivated, at least in part, by a misguided but nevertheless genuine desire to free "imprisoned" inmates[12]–quickly degenerated into a riot. After failing to discover dungeons or engines of torture, the mob began to run through the abandoned nunnery, looting and destroying as they went. The convent was finally torched, and, intoxicated by the boldness of their actions as well as by rum, the mob turned to the looting and destruction of surrounding buildings. The bishop's house and library were put to flame. The mausoleum in the school's garden was broken into, its coffins opened, and the remains of the dead disturbed. The following evening the mob returned and burned down fences, trees, and everything else they could find on the grounds. Only the presence of troops who were guarding Edward Cutter's home kept them from destroying a nearby Catholic church. For the rest of the week, nightfall found club-wielding mobs roaming the streets looking for trouble. The last act of destruction occurred on Friday night when a shack that served as a home to thirty-five Irish laborers was torched.[13]

Although the public's first reactions to the incident were shock and outrage, prevailing anti-Catholic sentiments quickly overcame this initial response.[14] Of the thirteen persons indicted for arson, all were eventually released, acquitted or pardoned. The state was empowered to reimburse victims for loss of property due to civil disorders, but public opinion frustrated every effort of the Ursulines to recover their losses (the nuns themselves eventually moved to Canada). Although immigrant and native-born laborers had scuffled with each other for years,[15] the burning of the Ursuline convent[16] was the first major act of violence in a long series of incidents that were to reach their peak in the Philadelphia riots of 1844. The anti-Catholic crusade did not, however, really die down until after the nation's passions had been redirected into the slavery issue and the Civil War.

The factors that come into play in shaping antebellum anti-Catholicism in general, and the Ursuline incident in particular, are more complex than one might suppose. The most obvious general factors are the antipathy that Protestants felt toward Catholics (an antipathy exacerbated by the Great Revival, a revival that inspired a militant Protestantism) and the waves of Irish immigration that occurred in the early nineteenth century (accompanied by the usual tensions brought on by competition between native-born and immigrant labor).[17]   Another factor was the perceived undesirability in democratic America of an undemocratic institution that owed its allegiance to a foreign power.[18] A less obvious factor was the force of certain themes in anti-Catholic propaganda: The immigration of Irish labor was portrayed as part of a Popish plot to take over America, and this accusation was apparently given much credence.

Another set of factors impinging on this controversy originated from certain internal tensions within the Protestant community–tensions that were displaced by being projected onto minority communities. One of the sources of these internal tensions was rapid social change; industrialization, "urbanization and territorial expansion unsettled the agrarian lifestyle and created social dislocation." Certain marginal groups "appeared as the logical scapegoats for disruptive social trends,"[19] and persecution of such groups seemed to be an integral part of the reaffirmation of traditional norms.[20]

Other disruptive factors within mainstream society that were projected onto minorities were sexual and aggressive urges that were being increasingly repressed in response to both industrialization and the Great Revival. This phenomenon is especially clear in the Protestant obsession with the institution of the Catholic nunnery; Protestant speculations about priestly liberties with the sisterhood were so omnipresent that nunneries were commonly referred to as "Romish Brothels."[21] These speculations were amplified into atrocities by books that portrayed priests as tricking Protestant girls into joining nunneries.[22]

More directly relevant to the Charlestown incident, convent schools were often portrayed as tools for converting non-Catholics–an accusation which the predominance of Protestant students enrolled in the Ursuline school seemed to verify.[23] The immediate factors at work in the Boston area were religious and class conflicts within the Protestant community itself. The Charlestown nunnery was a finishing school for the daughters of the upper class, and Unitarian families made up the bulk of its clients. To orthodox Congregationalists, it must have appeared that two of their most despised opponents were making common cause against them. Hence anti-Unitarian feelings reinforced already strong anti-Catholic feelings. The members of the working class who made up the great majority of the mob were also motivated by a resentment of wealth which the Ursuline school represented. This feeling comes through in an incident recorded near the end of Whitney's account when the returning crowd encountered a carriage-load of refugee students:

> "Saved yer diamonds?" shouted one young man to Penelope.... "I've got something of yours,
> I guess!" bawled out another, holding up his clenched fist to the carriage, which probably
> contained some valuable which he had stolen.[24]

Yet another factor that could be brought to bear in an interpretation of the Charlestown incident is the Anglo-American mob tradition that was mentioned in chapter five. Riots in which crowds freed impressed sailors or prisoners were a part of this tradition as well as riots in which symbols of tyranny–or, as in colonial Pope Day celebrations, symbols of Catholicism–were burned. Both of these strands of the mob tradition are clearly relevant to understanding the present case. We might note in passing, however, that by the Jacksonian era this tradition had begun to lose much of its legitimacy. Whereas in the colonial period, when towns were smaller and more culturally homogeneous, a large crowd might indeed express something like the will of the community, by 1834 cities were far too large and far too diverse for any given mob to express much more than a partisan position,[25] the Charlestown riot being a case in point.

All of these influences are of undoubted importance for understanding the Charlestown incident, but scholarly analyses have usually failed to emphasize the factor that was, over and above everything else we have mentioned, uppermost in the minds of the mob on that fateful August night–the desire to rescue captives.[26] The crowd, it will be recalled, initially demanded only to see the mysterious lady whom they had reason to believe was being held prisoner. Had the nuns responded by bringing forth Elizabeth Harrison, and perhaps even allowing selected members of the mob to search the convent for hidden prisoners, the ensuing destruction might have been circumvented.[27] As it was, the arrogant, angry response of the mother superior seemed to confirm their worst suspicions. In any event, it was only when other options had been exhausted that, after moving away from the convent and after a delay of approximately an hour (as if consulting with each other about putting "phase two" of a prearranged plan into action), the crowd returned and broke into the nunnery.

It is clear that afterwards the mob felt they had freed prisoners, even without having discovered hidden dungeons in the convent.[28] The many fictive re-presentations of this incident, the plots of which are invariably held together by a captivity-rescue scenario, are especially revealing in this regard.[29] Maria Monk's famous *Awful Disclosures,* published a few years after the Charlestown attack, was yet another fictional tale (though one that paraded as non-fiction) that was similarly built around charges of imprisonment.[30] The fact that the Charlestown riot was both preceded and followed by stories dominated by a motif of captivity is neither coincidental nor unimportant.

While no one would discount the importance of either the Harrison rumor or the Reed story as immediate factors leading to the Charlestown incident, most analyses have tended to emphasize the general background of social and economic tensions as crucial factors. This way of proceeding has caused analysts to miss the broad importance of captivity accusations. Protestants were obsessed with the theme of Catholic bondage, particularly imprisonment in nunneries.[31] If we take this obsession as a lens through which to interpret the attack on the convent, we immediately notice aspects of the incident that other interpreters have missed. Easily the most striking finding is the extent to which the "imagination" of the mob reflected the narrative contained in *The Nun.* Louise Whitney had noted in her account that this novel had recently been published and that it was being read and discussed in Boston at the time.[32] Although academic studies occasionally mention that this particular story helped to fuel Protestant fears,[33] no one has called attention to the remarkable extent to which the Ursuline Convent's attackers seemed to be following out its plot.

Set in Sardinia in the years following the French revolution, *The Nun's* convent had the usual underground prison cells in which doubters (i.e., nuns who were leaning toward Protestantism) were imprisoned. Rumors of this state of affairs reached the neighboring town in which the "spirit of revolution and democracy"[34] had taken hold. A bonfire was lit and a mob came to the convent demanding that the mother superior "produce the miserable creature whom you...have incarcerated these many years."[35] The abbess replied that "you are under a deception...there is no such unhappy creature under this roof."[36] Immediately following this denial, the rioters broke in and began destroying the place. In short order, the heroines were rescued and the convent torched.[37]

Although it is unlikely that the working-class people who actually attacked the Ursuline convent were familiar with *The Nun*, the higher-class individuals who were ultimately responsible for inciting the assault likely were.[38] Hence it is not improbable that Martha Sherwood's novel provided at least partial inspiration for the Charlestown incident. However, even if this specific work was not a factor, the more general fantasy in which Sherwood, the Charlestown mob and many other Protestants participated–the fantasy of Catholic captivity–definitely was a factor. This is particularly evident in the fictional retellings of the attack on the Charlestown nunnery: In the majority of these tales, heroes rescue captive maidens from evil Catholics–despite the fact that no empirical prisoner was ever actually discovered in the Urusline convent.[39]

In *The Convent's Doom, A Tale of Charlestown in 1834*, for example, the heroine is a young Protestant woman whose dying father has been tricked into giving guardianship of his underage daughter to a Catholic priest who then incarcerates her in the Ursuline Convent. The principal motivation behind these machinations is financial–the father is wealthy and his daughter is his only heir–although a villainous Jesuit also lusts after the heroine. She is eventually rescued by the mob and by her boyfriend. The author of this narrative did not hesitate to link the Convent's assaulters with the heroes of American History:

> [L]et the night of the eleventh of August, 1834, be a memorable one in the history of Massachusetts. Let a cry go forth which shall frighten priestcraft, and its echo even startle Rome from her slumbers, and all Protestant Europe will know we have not forgotten the lessons of our grandsires.[40]

The heroine in *The Nun of St. Ursula*, on the other hand, was originally a Protestant student at the Ursuline school who is persuaded/tricked into becoming a novice. Although different in many particulars, the primary motivation for converting the heroine is once again financial: She is the only daughter of a rich widow whose inheritance is sought by the Catholics. Also, the convent's confessor is an evil fellow similar to the Jesuit in *The Convent's Doom*. This stereotypically lecherous priest moves about the nunnery through secret passageways and shows up unexpectedly in the sleeping quarters of beautiful nuns and novices:

> One morning when she awoke from her dreamy slumbers she was startled at beholding, in a devotional attitude beside her couch, the figure of Padre Francis, who was mumbling over a Latin prayer.... At length the monk turned his eyes slowly towards her, with a lascivious expression gleaming from them, which caused her to shrink with horror, and to hide her features beneath the covering of her couch.[41]

His ill-disguised lust for the heroine causes her to have second thoughts about taking final vows, and as a consequence the authorities drug her and compel her to go through the ceremony against her will. It is at this critical juncture that her brother and boyfriend burst in and rescue her, just as the mob begins to attack the convent.

In thus portraying the nunnery as a prison, Americans were not being original. Long before the Eighteen-thirties in North America, a standard item of anti-Catholic propaganda had been the accusation that at least certain residents in monasteries and convents were being held there against their will. This portrayal, especially when combined with exaggerated images of the evil Inquisition, appealed powerfully to the Protestant imagination–as witnessed by the deployment of these themes in the Gothic novel.[42] This largely British literary and religious heritage does not, however, fully explain the North American situation. The American "convent tale," as this genre of popular literature has been called, differed from most comparable European tales by being set in the (then) present time period–Gothic novels and historical romances composed in Britain were usually set in the distant past–as well as by the dominance of the captivity theme. In Gothic novels, one often finds multiple imprisonment incidents, but these captivities are usually brief episodes. By way of contrast, the majority of American convent tales frame the various atrocities that make up the core of the story within a larger imprisonment situation.

Not coincidentally, these traits characterized much other popular American fiction in the early nineteenth century. Of particular relevance for the present discussion is the so-called "frontier romance."[43] The dynamic element within a majority of frontier romances (as exemplified in Fenimore Cooper novels, such as *The Last of the Mohicans*[44]) was captivity at the hands of American Indians. While it would be difficult to establish more than a few specific connections, it is not unreasonable to surmise that this body of literature–in addition to the numerous published accounts of actual Indian captivities–significantly influenced the convent tale, giving it a characteristically American emphasis on imprisonment.[45]

One should also note that a majority of Puritan captivity tales–and consequently a number of the later frontier romances–were set in the French and Indian war (the earliest captivities occurred during King Phillip's War), causing Indians and Catholics to become associated with each other in the Puritan mind. Reverend John Williams's *The Redeemed Captive Returning to Zion*, for example, dwells more on his efforts to prevent Canadian Jesuits from converting other English captives to Catholicism than on his initial capture by Indians.[46] The connection between captive-taking Indians and captive-taking Catholics had thus been established long before the advent of a significant Catholic presence on U.S. soil,[47] and this imaginative connection helps to explain the ease with which Protestants accepted the imprisonment rumors circulating in the Boston area in 1834.[48]

Although the Charlestown incident represents a departure from the captivities of the Barbary pirate era and the Indian wars because of the convent's lack of genuine captives, it is still possible to analyze the stories generated by this event in terms of the four narrative levels that we found in the two earlier conflicts. Louise Goddard Whitney, who was a resident student at the time of the attack, composed an account of the incident over forty years later. As an imputed captive, her straightforward description of events in *The Burning of the Convent* comes closest to being an "historically"-motivated account, parallel, in many ways, to the accounts composed by the Hall sisters.

At the level of propaganda, the rumor circulated in the newspaper account (cited at the beginning of the chapter) constitutes a close parallel to the Kentucky handbill that utilized a brief account of Rachel and Sylvia's capture to recruit militiamen. Rebecca Reed's account also falls into this subgenre. Although not actually published until the year following the destruction of the nunnery, it had apparently been circulating in the form of a rumor for two years. It is further clear from the material in the introduction that *Six Months in a Convent* was consciously intended to fuel the ongoing anti-Catholic crusade.

At the level of sensationalistic accounts,[49] the connections are more indirect. The instant success of the Reed narrative (first published in 1835) was probably directly responsible for the appearance of the most popular convent tale of all time–Maria Monk's *Awful Disclosures of the Hotel Dieu Nunnery of Montreal* (first published in 1836, and the best-selling book in American history until *Uncle Tom's Cabin*[50]). Maria Monk, who had run away from a Catholic asylum rather than from a convent, claimed, among other things, that infants born to nuns (a supposedly frequent event because of regular sexual intercourse with priests) were murdered. Monk recounted observing, for example, two infants who, after being baptized,

> were then taken, one after another, by one of the old nuns, in the presence of us all. She pressed her hand upon the mouth and nose of the first so tight that it could not breathe, and in a few minutes, when the hand was removed, it was dead. She then took the other and treated it in the same way. No sound was heard, and both children were corpses. The greatest indifference was shown by all present during this operation; for all, as I well knew, were long accustomed to such scenes. The little bodies were then taken into the cellar, thrown into the pit I have mentioned, and covered with a quantity of lime.[51]

Although authors of anti-Catholic literature were not hesitant to accuse popish priests of sexual assault, these writers had to work with indirect statement rather than with straightforward description. Monk, for instance, asserted that often the priests "were in our beds before us,"[52] and recalled that,

> The youngest girl who ever took the veil of our sisterhood, was only fourteen years of age, and considered very pious. She lived but a short time. I was told that she was ill-treated by the priests, and believed her death was in consequence.[53]

Expressions like "in our beds before us" and "ill-treated" were about as close as one could come to describing sexual atrocities and still expect to sell books to a middle-class Protestant readership.

The tactic of suggesting rape by the torture of partially clothed females is best represented in the illustrations of the Inquisition and of "popish massacres" that appeared in anti-Catholic newspapers.[54] A comparatively subdued example of this general approach can be found in one of Edward Zane Carroll Judson's novels:

> [U]pon that rack lay stretched the fair and half-naked form of Genita, its symmetry convulsing in matchless tortures, the bosom palpitating awfully with the pangs of that earthly wall, and the exquisitely modeled limbs enduring all the pains of dislocation.[55]

An even more subtle "rape-disguised-as-torture" scene can be found in Monk, where a nun is executed for refusing to assist with the murder of infants:

> On the bed the prisoner was laid with her face upward, and then bound with cords, so that she could not move. In an instant another bed was thrown upon her. One of the priests, named Bonin, sprung like a fury first upon it, and stamped upon it, with all his force. He was speedily followed by the nuns, until there were as many upon the bed as could find room, and all did what they could, not only to smother, but to bruise her. Some stood up and jumped upon the poor girl with their feet, some with their knees, and others in different ways seemed to seek how they might best beat the breath out of her body, and mangle it....[56]

Rather than employing the usual tactic of piercing naked flesh with a sharp instrument, in this case the sexual assault theme is worked out by attacking a helpless woman who is tied down in a bed.

The importance of sexual themes in anti-Catholic rhetoric is probably best accounted for by regarding this literature as the only variety of crypto-pornography[57] in which Americans could allow themselves to indulge with a clear conscience. In other words, one could permit oneself to read lurid descriptions of convent life as long as these descriptions alternated with expressions of moral censure, so that the work as a whole appeared to be edifying in effect. It was this type of accusation, where the discontinuity between fact and fiction was most pronounced, that was at the core of many anti-Catholic convent tales.

The more purely literary productions arising out of the Charlestown incident–stories in which a male hero rescued a sexually threatened heroine from the Ursuline convent–have already been mentioned. We should note again, however, that propagandistic atrocity tales that called out for action contain an implicit captivity-rescue motif in that they invited the reader to play hero. In many convent tales this invitation was stated overtly in the form of calls for governmental action. The conclusion of one ex-nun's story, for example, pleaded that

> [T]he Legislature [should] enact laws for the inspection of Convents.... Let the prison doors of the monasteries and Convents be thrown open to their deluded inmates.[58]

In a different idiom, to a somewhat different audience, this call for action invokes the same captivity-rescue pattern that motivated the Charlestown mob: Break open the prison and free the captives.

References:

1 The Mercantile Journal of August 8. Cited in An Account of the Conflagration of the Ursuline Convent (Boston: "Printed for the Publisher," 1834), p. 5. This "Account" is one of several anthologies of contemporary documents that were put together in the wake of the Charlestown incident.
2 P.J. Mahon & J.M. Hayes, Trials and Triumphs of the Catholic Church in America, Vol. II (Chicago: J.S. Hyland & Co., 1907), p. 670. p. 72.

3 Rebecca Theresa Reed, Six Months in a Convent (Boston: Russel, Odiorne & Metcalf, 1835).

4 Michael Schwartz, The Persistent Prejudice: Anti-Catholicism in America (Huntington, Indiana: Our Sunday Visitor, Inc., 1984), p. 42.

5 Cited in An Account of the Conflagration, p. 18. Emphasis in original.

6 Edith O'Gorman, Convent Life Unveiled (London: Lile & Fawcett, circa 1881; orig. publ. in U.S. circa 1871), p. 7. The same sort of accusation is made in Rebecca Theresa Reed, Six Months in a Convent (Boston: Russell, Odiorne & Metcalf, 1835), pp. 55-56.

7 Reed, p. 89.

8 This sermon, a "Plea for the West," which warned Protestants about popery's plot to take over the American West, was later issued as a book. The published form of Beecher's text, which, the author asserts, is only a slightly enlarged version of the original sermon, continually contrasts Protestantism and Catholicism in terms of liberty vs. bondage. For example, "If they [ordinary Catholics] dared to think for themselves, the contrast of protestant independence with their thraldom, would awaken the desire of equal privileges and put an end to an arbitrary clerical dominion over trembling superstitious minds." Lyman Beecher, Plea for the West (Cincinnati: Truman and Smith, 1835), p. 118. Later in the same work he describes Catholicism as a system of "bondage" and "slavery." Ibid., p. 131.

9 "The respectable persons who listened to his sermons would scarcely take an open part in the rioting that took place, no matter what their personal sentiments might have been." Ray Allen Billington, The Protestant Crusade 1800-1860: A Study of the Origins of American Nativism (New York: Macmillan, 1938), footnote #112, p.83. Billington's work is the classic, and as yet unsurpassed, study of antebellum anti-Catholicism.

10 Louise Goddard Whitney, The Burning of the Convent (New York: Arno Pr., 1969; rpt. of 1877). Although Whitney's book is a very useful primary source, she was a young girl at the time of the attack and did not write down her reminiscences until over forty years later. Hence her account of those aspects of the event which she did not actually witness is often faulty. Carmine A. Prioli's otherwise excellent article, "The Ursuline Outrage," American Heritage 33:2 (February/March 1982), pp. 100-105, is flawed by her sometimes uncritical use of Whitney.

11 A nun who was sick at the time did, however, die later–a death that was at least hastened by overexcitement and exposure. The attorney general attempted to portray this as murder. James T. Austin, Argument of James T. Austin, Attorney General of the Commonwealth, before the Supreme Judicial Court in Middlesex, on the Case of John R. Buzzell (Boston: Printed by Ford & Damrell, 1834), p. 8.

12 The genuineness of this motivation is evident in many different places in extant documents; e.g., when the mob initially broke into the nunnery, "The first cry was to discover where the sick nun lay...." (The members of the mob obviously thought that Harrison was still sick.) The Charlestown Convent; Its Destruction by a Mob on the Night of August 11, 1834. (Boston: Patrick Donahoe, 1870). This is another anthology, probably the best, of the Charlestown incident.

13 The attack on the Charlestown convent is a relatively well-known incident that is often mentioned even in general surveys of American religious history; e.g., Sidney E. Ahlstrom, A Religious History of the American People (New Haven: Yale, 1972), pp. 560-561; and Catherine L. Albanese, America: Religions and Religion (Belmont, California: Wadsworth Publ. Co., 1981), pp. 345-346.

14 While some Protestants expressed outrage over the convent burning, for many others the event was an inspiration for renewed anti-Catholic activity. For example, within a week of the Charlestown incident, two new anti-Catholic newspapers began publication: Downfall of Babylon (Philadelphia) and The

American Protestant Vindicator (New York). Thomas T. McAvoy, A History of the Catholic Church in the United States (Notre Dame: University of Notre Dame, 1969), pp. 134-135.

15 In 1833, the year before the attack on the convent, a drunken Irishman killed an Angloamerican in Charlestown. Then, as troops stood by and watched, a mob smashed and burned houses in the Irish section. David H. Bennett, The Party of Fear: From Nativist Movements to the New Right in American History (Chapel Hill: University of North Carolina, 1988), p. 37.

16 The burning of symbols of Catholicism had many precedents. In the early 18th Century, for example, Massachusetts twice sent an expedition to Maine to burn down a Catholic mission to Indians. Reuben Maury, The Wars of the Godly (New York: Robert M. McBride & Co., 1928), p. 25. Also, until the French came to the aid of the American Revolution, burning the Pope in effigy was practiced annually as part of New England's celebration of "Pope Day," the Colonial equivalent of the British Guy Fawkes Day. Andrew F. Young, "English Plebeian Culture and Eighteenth-Century American Radicalism" in Margaret Jacob and James Jacob, eds., The Origins of Anglo-American Radicalism (London: George Allen & Unwin, 1984), p. 198; Paul A. Gilje, The Road to Mobocracy: Popular Disorder in New York City, 1763-1834 (Chapel Hill: University of North Carolina, 1987), pp. 25-30.. The torching of the dwelling of officials of the British Crown and of other symbols of British tyranny during the Revolution is yet another useful precedent, in the sense that such actions were (and still are) remembered as symbolic assaults on foreign tyranny–certainly a relevant model, considering the manner in which Catholicism was regarded in New England in the 1830s.

17 One historian who has emphasized the importance of the Irish immigrants' prior experience with Protestant persecution is John J. Kane in Catholic-Protestant Conflicts in America (Chicago: Regnery, 1955), pp. 37-38. Kane's utilization of the immigration's Irishness as an explanation for conflict is important, despite the overstress that he gives this factor.

18 This is the principal interpretative perspective put forward by Barbara Welter in, "From Maria Monk to Paul Blanshard: A Century of Anti-Catholicism," in Robert N. Bellah & Frederick E. Greenspahn, eds., Uncivil Religion: Interreligious Hostility in America (New York: Crossroad, 1987), pp. 43-71. Beyond the general argument, the speculations and references in Welter's extensive footnotes are well worth a careful reading for individuals interested in the phenomenon of anti-Catholicism in the United States.

19 Schwartz, p. 39.

20 This is the overarching interpretation put forward in David Brion Davis, "Some Themes of Counter-Subversion: An Analysis of Anti-Masonic, Anti-Catholic, and Anti-Mormon Literature," The Mississippi Valley Historical Review 47:2 (September 1960).

21 A. Murray, Awful Disclosures! Downfall of Popery! Death Bed Confession and Renunciation of the Right Rev. Bishop McMurray, Bishop of the St. Mary's Roman Catholic Church, Montreal, Canada (Buffalo, 1845), p. 27, Cited in Ray Allen Billington, The Protestant Crusade 1800-1860: A Study of the Origins of American Nativism (NY: Macmillan, 1938), p. 366.

22 E.g., Justin Jones [Harry Hazel], The Nun of St. Ursula: The Burning of the Convent (Boston: F. Gleason, 1845); Charles W. Frothingham, Six Hours in a Convent:-or-The Stolen Nuns! (Boston: Graves & Weston, 1855).

23 This was, in fact, one of the accusations implicit in the newspaper account of Elizabeth Harrison's tale that has already been referred to: "The young lady was sent to the place in question to complete her education, and became so pleased with the place and its inmates, that she was induced to seclude herself from the world and take the black veil." Cited in An Account of the Conflagration, p. 5. The same accusation was developed in detail in the introduction to Reed's book.

24 Whitney, pp. 139-140.

25 This transformation of mob action from the colonial to the Jacksonian period is the overarching theme of Gilje's The Road to Mobocracy. Although less explicitly stated, the same theme informs Gilje's earlier article, "The Baltimore Riots of 1812 and the Breakdown of the Anglo-American Mob Tradition," Journal of Social History 13:4 (Summer 1980), pp. 547-564. For an understanding of riots in the changed conditions of the early nineteenth century, also refer to David Grimsted, "Rioting in Its Jacksonian setting," American Historical Review 77:2 (April 1972), pp. 361-397.

26 The "captivity" accusation was taken quite seriously, as is evident in the trial records; e.g., the conspirators held off the attack for three weeks to see if the "recaptured" nun would be released by Catholic authorities. In this regard, refer, for example, to The Charlestown Convent, p. 38 & p. 67.

27 E.g., "Mr. Fitch Cutter [relative of Edward]...is still firm in the opinion that had the Lady Superior been less defiant and intractable, and had come forward with Miss Mary John [spiritual name of Harrison] and the children, and appealed to the feelings, the good sense and magnanimity of the assembled miscellaneous crowd, the result would have been entirely different, and the painful and harrowing events of the night would never have been known." The Charlestown Convent, p. 84. In support of Cutter's position, it should be noted that, in spite of the breakdown of the mob tradition by 1834, rioters could still be talked out of destructive actions in many instances. The point is, however, debatable. There are some indications that at least some individuals were intent on destroying the convent, come what may; e.g., refer to the text of a placard cited by Billington, footnote #108, p. 82 and to the warning which Whitney's father had received on the day before the riot. Whitney, p. 54.

28 E.g., in Whitney's account, as the students are returning to Boston on the morning following the attack, a member of the mob from the night before sees them and calls out, "We've spoiled your prison for you." Whitney, p. 140

29 E.g., Charles W. Frothingham, Six Hours in a Convent:-or-The Stolen Nuns! (Graves & Weston, 1855).

30 Maria Monk, Awful Disclosures of the Hotel Dieu Nunnery of Montreal (1836; rpt. New York: Arno, 1977).

31 E.g., in Ann Blaisdell Tracy's motif index in The Gothic Novel, 1790-1830 (Lexington: University Press of Kentucky, 1981) one finds 27 references to "convent as prison" out of a little over 200 novels. By way of contrast, Tracy lists only one reference to "monastery as prison."

32 "While Six Months in a Convent excited the lower classes of Boston and its vicinity against the Charlestown Nunnery, Mrs. Sherwood's Nun, a fascinating tale which appeared at the time, prejudiced more intelligent people, who could not forbear mentally associating the only Convent they knew about with those of which they were reading in her book." Whitney, pp. 21-22.

33 Billington, p. 71.

34 Martha Butt Sherwood, The Nun (Princeton: Moore Baker, 1834), p. 184.

35 Sherwood, p. 196.

36 Sherwood, p. 197.

37 The more general scenario, burning down a convent and rescuing a heroine from a dungeon, is also found in the well-know Gothic novel, Mathew Lewis's The Monk. Originally published in 1795, The Monk was familiar enough to American audiences that one commentator on the Charlestown incident could mention the "Monk Lewis story" with the expectation that her audience would understand the allusion. Caroline Frances Alden, "The Ursuline Convent," Mrs. Hale's Magazine, cited in An Account of the Conflagration, p. 29. Mary Ann Radcliffe, another author of Gothic romances who was widely read in the

United States, also made use of the convent-as-prison theme in A Sicilian Romance and in The Mysteries of Udolpho.

38 Although they are never identified, contemporaneous documents often make assertions such as, "the rioters were ignorant men, acting under the instigation of individuals better educated, and moving in a higher sphere than themselves." The Charlestown Convent, p. 64.

39 There exist at least four fictional retellings of the Charlestown incident, if one includes Mary Magdalen [Norwood Damon], The Chronicles of Mount Benedict: A Tale of the Ursuline Convent (Boston: Printed for the Publisher, 1837), which is a sort of "spoof" on the convent tale genre.

40 Charles W. Frothingham, The Convent's Doom: A Tale of Charlestown in 1834 (Boston: Graves & Weston, 5th ed., 1854), p. 16. This short work sold 40,000 copies during its first week of publication. Jenny Franchot, Roads to Rome: Catholicism in Antebellum America, Diss. Stanford 1986 (Ann Arbor: UMI, 1989), p. 228.

41 Harry Hazel [Justen Jones], The Nun of St. Ursula: The Burning of the Convent (Boston: F. Gleason, 1845), p. 21.

42 Refer, in this regard, to Richard Gaither Walser, "Anti-Catholicism in the Gothic Novel," Masters Thesis, University of North Carolina at Chapel Hill, 1933.

43 For a general discussion of the frontier romance refer to Louise K. Barnett, The Ignoble Savage: American Literary Racism, 1790-1890 (Westport, Connecticut: Greenwood Press, 1975).

44 Like many other frontier romances, The Last of the Mohicans, Cooper's most popular story, was published in the decade prior to the emergence of the American convent tale.

45 This link is clearest in writers like L. Larned who authored a frontier romance, The Sanfords, or Home Scenes (New York: Elan Bliss, 1836), that was published six years before her convent tale appeared, The American Nun; or, the Effects of Romance (Boston: Otis, Broaders, & Co., 1836). A number of other writers of frontier romances also wrote anti-Catholic novels.

46 John Williams, The Redeemed Captive, Returning to Zion [first printed in Boston by Bartholemew Green in 1707] in Alden T. Vaughan & Edward W. Clark, Puritans Among the Indians: Accounts of Captivity and Redemption, 1676-1724 (Cambridge, Massachusetts: Belknap, 1981), pp. 169-226. As Jenny Franchot notes, "The focus of Williams' narrative, as it describes 'myself and so many of my children and friends in popish captivity' is less Indian brutality than missionary seduction. The true threat emanated from the priests who split up Protestant families, luring or coercing the children into the worst captivity of all: conversion to Catholicism." Franchot, p. 162.

47 In the Protestant imagination of the time, mere adherence to Catholicism was itself a kind of captivity; e.g., one of the heroes in The Nun says to one of the rescued nuns, who has not yet fully converted to Protestantism, that "if I have been the happy means of rescuing you from temporal evils,...I might also be the happy means, unworthy as I am, of rescuing you from the deadly spiritual thraldom in which you have hitherto been held." Sherwood, p. 230.

48 Franchot, however, asserts that slavery was the decisive influence on antebellum images of Catholic captivity: "Fear of captivity to Catholicism occurred within (and was generated by) the context of the contemporary captivity of American blacks. As revealed by both popular and elite fiction, the pseudo-issue of Catholic captivity was intimately, if obliquely related to both sides of the slavery issue--to the horror (and fascinating power) of slaveholding and to the menace and victimmage of the enslaved." Franchot, p. 138. While I think Franchot's argument is suggestive, it fails to explain why accusations of Catholic bondage survived the Civil War.

49 In previous chapters I have referred to the motivation behind sensationalistic narratives as pecuniary. Most anti-Catholic tales falling in this category seem to have been motivated by both financial and propagandistic considerations. In the words of Ray Allen Billington, "Authors soon realized that here was an opportunity both to enrich themselves and to strike a further blow at Catholicism." Billington, p. 99.

50 Bennett, p. 42.

51 Maria Monk, Awful Disclosures of the Hotel Dieu Nunnery of Montreal (New York: Hoisington & Trow, 1836), pp. 155-156.

52 Monk, p. 128.

53 Monk, p. 135.

54 Sex and sadism also abounded in a work that competed with Awful Disclosures for public attention, Rosamond Culbertson's Rosamond: A Narrative of Captivity and Sufferings of an American Female under the Popish Priests in the Island of Cuba (New York: Leavitt, Lord, 1836).

55 Edward Zane Carroll Judson [Ned Buntline], The Jesuit's Daughter; A Novel for Americans to Read (New York, 1854), p. 163. Cited in Franchot, p. 140.

56 Monk, pp. 102-103.

57 Schwartz, p. 42 & p. 44.

58 Edith O'Gorman, Convent Life Unveiled (London: Lile & Fawcett, n.d.; this is a British reprint of an American convent tale), p. 131.

The Cult Stereotype as an Ideological Resource[1]

Conflicts over the legitimacy or illegitimacy of religious groups can be understood as an argument over *classification*. The authority of the governmental agencies that could be invoked against alternative religions is not at issue. Rather, opponents of religious innovation assert that new religious movements–almost always referred to as "cults"–are not "real" religions. Instead, "cults" are exploitative criminal organisations parading as pseudo religions that should be repressed. As a consequence of the sharp contrast critics have drawn between cults and genuine religions, the term "cult" has come to *mean* a harmful pseudo religion run by a self-seeking charlatan. The present chapter examines some concrete conflicts involving efforts to delegitimate a specific religious group by attempting to have it *reclassified* as a "cult."

In prior studies of the cult controversy, sociologically-informed observers have tended to focus on the efforts of the anti-cult movement to gain widespread social acceptance for its peculiar perspective on non-traditional religious groups. Because the consensus among mainstream new religions scholars is that the most dramatic claims made by anti-cultists against minority religions are inaccurate (e.g., Barker, 1984; Bromley and Richardson, 1983; Bromley and Shupe, 1981; Melton and Moore, 1982), analysts have focused on uncovering the deeper interests lying behind rhetoric about brainwashing, cultic manipulation, and the like. These discussions of the anti-cult movement and of the "cult" stereotype propagated by anti-cultists, have drawn on theorising about social movements—theorising that has tended to focus on the "macro" dynamics of such movements. This tendency to emphasise what takes place at the broader levels of society has been prompted by, among other factors, a reaction among social scientists against earlier "micro" theorising that gave excessive attention to explaining why individuals become involved in social movements.

One of the issues that gets missed by focussing excessively on either the individual participant or on the broader social dynamics is understanding how particular minority religions are drawn into the "cult wars", as well as how anti-cult ideology is used in specific conflicts involving individuals and groups who, for the most part, have no interest in the wider anti-cult crusade. To understand social dynamics at this level, which lies somewhere between the "macro" level of the larger anti-cult movement and the "micro" level of individual involvement, some adaptation of earlier theorising is called for. The present discussion will undertake to examine some of the specific conflicts through which a particular minority religion—the Church of the Movement of Spiritual Inner Awareness (MSIA), which was also used as a case study in Chapter Two—has been drawn into the cult controversy. After presenting a brief overview of the anti-cult movement, it will be argued that, for most of the people involved in conflicts with MSIA, the cult stereotype is an ideological

---

[1] I have also discussed the anti-cult movement and the social psychology of stereotyping in my "Self-Fulfilling Stereotypes, the Anticult Movement, and the Waco Confrontation," in Stuart A. Wright, ed., *Armageddon at Waco* (Chicago: U. of Chicago Pr., 1995).

resource, useful for legitimating support for their side of the struggle, but representing no deep involvement in the "anti-cult" cause.

The anti-cult movement itself exercises relatively little real direct power. Where it is most influential is in helping to construct and reinforce negative stereotypes about non-traditional religions in the mass media. However, the popularity of the "cult" stereotype indicates that there is a pre-existing disposition to accept such stereotypes in American society. By attending to certain themes in anti-cult discourse, it should be possible to uncover some of the factors behind the receptivity of contemporary society to negative, stereotyped images of minority religions. Relevant social-psychological research also indicates that, once a stereotype has been accepted, it structures our perceptions so that we tend to notice information that conforms to our image of the stereotyped group, and to neglect or forget other kinds of information. What this means for any given confrontation is that, as soon as the label "cult" has been successfully applied (that is, accepted as appropriate by outsiders not directly involved in the conflict), the information that the mass media gather is selectively appropriated so that almost every item of data conforms to the stereotype about "cults", thus effectively marshalling moral support for the person or group locked in conflict with a minority religion.

The Anti-Cult Movement

In the early seventies, opposition to religious innovation was centred around deprogrammers—individuals who forcibly abducted members of non-traditional religions, locked them up in motel rooms, and assaulted their beliefs until they gave up their religious faith (Kelly, 1977; Shupe and Bromley, 1980). Despite claims that deprogramming is a therapeutic intervention that breaks through "cult" members' "hypnotic trance" and forces them to think again (for example, Hassan, 1988; Langone, 1993; Ross and Langone, 1988), it is clear that deprogrammers are little more than vigilantes acting at the behest of parents upset by the religious choices of their adult children (Bromley and Richardson, 1983; Bromley and Shupe, 1981). This negative evaluation of deprogramming is reinforced by the observation that, as a group, deprogrammers are largely uneducated individuals with little or no training in counselling.

Deprogramming, controlled entirely by independent entrepreneurs, could never have developed into a viable profession without the simultaneous development of secular "cult watchdog groups".[2] These organisations, despite vigorous public denials to the contrary, regularly referred concerned parents to deprogrammers. The evidence for this connection is overwhelming. For example, at the national gatherings of the Cult Awareness Network (CAN; formerly the Citizens Freedom Foundation, or CFF), one could always find a host of deprogrammers actively marketing their services to concerned parents in attendance. Deprogrammers, in turn, allegedly kicked back a

---

[2] Secular anti-cult organisations such as the Cult Awareness Network should be clearly distinguished from Evangelical Christian anti-cult groups. The Christian anti-cult movement stands in marked contrast to the secular anti-cult movement by its focus on theological issues. While the religions criticised by Christian anti-cultists may be accused of exploiting and brainwashing their members, the more important accusation is their theological divergence from Evangelical Christianity. The Christian anti-cult movement, unlike the secular anti-cult movement, has also distanced itself from the practice of deprogramming (Melton, 1992).

certain percentage of their "take" to CAN. John Myles Sweeney, former national director of CAN/CFF, described this arrangement.

> Because of the large amount of money they make due to referrals received from CFF members, deprogrammers usually kick back money to the CFF member who gave the referral...The kick backs would either be in cash or would be hidden in the form of a tax-deductible "donation" to the CFF (Sweeney, 1992, 1).

One of the results of the financial alliance between anti-cult groups and deprogrammers was that anti-cult groups acquired a vested interest in promoting the worst possible stereotypes of non-traditional religions. In other words, if one was profiting from referring worried parents to deprogrammers, it made no sense to inform parents that the religion their child had joined was comparatively benign. Instead, the tendency was to paint such religions in the exaggerated colours of fear and fanaticism, creating the anxiety that, unless their child was "rescued" immediately, he or she could end up as a lobotomised robot, suffering from permanent emotional and psychological damage.

Similarly, it made little sense to propagate a balanced view of alternative religions to the press. If one profited from the fear surrounding such groups, then it was natural to take every opportunity to repeat frightening rumours. It was, in fact, the two-decade-long interaction between the anti-cult movement and the media that has been responsible for the widespread view that all "cults" are dangerous organisations—this despite the fact that comparatively few such groups constitute a genuine threat, either to themselves or to society.

However, with the exception of periodic attention from the mass media, the anti-cult movement (at least in North America) was and is relatively powerless. Even the influence that anti-cult spokespersons had in shaping public perceptions of "cults" was not based upon the intrinsic merit of their interpretations. Rather, anti-cultism feed upon—and in turn feed—a public *predisposition* to perceive non-traditional religions in a negative light. We might best understand this predisposition in terms of the social psychology of stereotyping.

Social Functions of the Cult Stereotype

What is a stereotype? Stereotypes are generalisations about other groups of people, but they are a peculiar type of generalisation. "Stereotypes are used to ascribe incorrectly certain characteristics to whole groups of people and then explain or excuse social problems in light of these characteristics" (Rothenberg, 1988, 253). Stereotypes are also usually held rigidly, in that we tend to ignore or to dismiss evidence that flies in the face of our generalisation. Such rigidity indicates that our stereotype "may be relatively fundamental to our conceptual scheme, it may protect our self-esteem, it may help bring about some desirable situation, or it may shield us from facing [some] unpleasant fact" (Andre, 1988, 257). Thus the stereotype of certain races as "lazy" for example, would simultaneously boost the self-esteem of society's dominant racial group as well as blind one to the inequalities of existing social arrangements. It is relatively easy to perceive that most generalisations about "cults" are little more than negative stereotypes, but what are the social forces that make such stereotypes about non-traditional religions peculiarly attractive to contemporary society?

Unless there are groups that are consciously anti-social or criminal like the Mafia or like gangs, the deviations from the norm that a community chooses to perceive as threatening are somewhat arbitrary. The people that our culture have traditionally construed as "deviants" have been racial (for example, Blacks), ethnic (for example, Jews), and sexual (for example, homosexuals) minorities. In recent years, however, it has become socially unacceptable to persecute these traditional groups, at least in the overt manner in which they have been attacked in the past. This leaves few groups of any significant size to persecute. One of the few minorities that liberals have been slow to defend are non-traditional religions. This is due to a number of different factors, including the resistance of traditionally conservative religions to liberal change. The failure of normally open-minded people to protect religious pluralism has allowed contemporary witchhunters to declare open season on "cults".

Groups of people experienced as threatening frequently become screens onto which a society projects its anxieties. If, for example, a culture is troubled by sexual issues (as is often the case), then its enemies are perceived as perverse, sexually deviant, and so on. Racial minorities, who have often been viewed as "loose" and sexually aggressive, have suffered from this projection (e.g., refer to Gilman, 1985). This was also a dominant theme in nineteenth century anti-Catholic and anti-Mormon literature (Lewis, 1989; Miller, 1983). Contemporary "cults," of course, suffer from the same projection.

In his classical formulation of the notion of psychological projection, Freud (1938), who was especially concerned with sex and violence, viewed projection as a defence mechanism against unacceptable inner urges. Thus in a society with strict sexual mores, an individual constantly keeping a lid on his or her desires might perceive rather ordinary dancing, let us say, as sexually suggestive. Becoming enraged at such "loose" behaviour, he might then attempt to lead a movement to have all of the dance halls in town closed down. It should be clear that this hypothetical individual's *inner* struggle is being "projected" outward to provide a script for an *outer* struggle (i.e., internally he is repressing his desires while symbolically battling the same desires in the outer world). The same process is at work in the collective mind of society, perceiving marginal groups as sexually deviant. For instance, the stereotype of the sexually abusive "cult" leader, routinely forcing devotees to satisfy his or her sexual whims, perfectly captures the fantasy of many members of our society who desire to sexually control any person he or she wishes.

The same kind of process occurs with respect to repressed aggressive urges. We live in a society with strict sanctions against overt violence; simultaneously, violence is glorified in the entertainment media. This sets up a cultural contradiction that is projected onto enemies and deviant groups, with the result that minorities are often perceived as violent and belligerent. This accusation is also regularly projected onto non-traditional religions. In particular, the violent actions of a tiny handful of members of alternative religions is mistakenly taken to indicate a widespread tendency among all such groups.

We can generalise beyond Freudian psychology's emphasis on sex and aggression to see that many other cultural anxieties/cultural contradictions are projected onto minority groups. For instance, our society gives us contradictory messages about the relative importance of wealth and material success. On the one hand, we are taught that economic pursuits should be secondary to higher moral, social, and spiritual concerns. On the other hand, we receive many messages from the surrounding society that the single-minded pursuit of wealth is the be-all and end-all of life. This inherent contradiction is typically ignored or overlooked with regard to mainstream religions where gross economic inequities exist within the same community or where religious elites enjoy favoured status and privilege. Instead of being faced directly, this self-contradiction is examined only after it has been projected onto alternative religions, where it constitutes the basis of the stereotype of the money-hungry "cult" leader who demands that her or his followers lead lives of poverty while the leader wallows in riches.

One of the more important cultural contradictions projected onto alternative religions is reflected in the brainwashing/mind control notion that is the core accusation levelled against such groups. Discourse that glorifies American society usually does so in terms of a rhetoric of liberty and freedom. However, while holding liberty as an ideal, we experience a social environment that is often quite restrictive. Most citizens work as employees in highly disciplined jobs where the only real freedom is the freedom to quit. Also, we are daily bombarded by advertising designed to influence our decisions and even to create new needs. Our frustration with these forms of influence and control is easily displaced and projected onto the separated societies of alternative religions, where the seemingly (but often not actually) restricted flow of information offers a distorted reflection of the situation we experience as members of the dominant society.

The components of the "cult" stereotype that have been enumerated above, and others that could be mentioned, explain certain themes in anti-cult discourse, as well as why this stereotype tends to resonate with public opinion. Without this pre-existing disposition to construe non-traditional religions negatively, the anti-cult movement would have little or no social influence. However, even this influence is limited, in the sense that the stereotype the anti-cult movement has helped to shape has taken on a life of its own, independent of organised anti-cultism.

In their role as moral entrepreneurs, anti-cult spokespersons have effectively marketed their negative stereotype of minority religions to the general public. Because of the pre-existing fit between this negative image and the persistent social anxieties outlined in this section, our society has overwhelmingly bought into the stereotype (or purchased the *moral commodity*, to continue the entrepreneurial metaphor). Because of widespread acceptance of the stereotype, the anti-cult movement could disappear tomorrow and anti-cult discourse would still continue to shape public perceptions of minority religions.

Self-Fulfilling Stereotypes

Once a stereotype is in place, a variety of different kinds of studies have shown that it becomes self-fulfilling and self-reinforcing. Thus in a study by Snyder and Uranowitz, for example, students were asked to read a short biography about "Betty K", a fictitious woman. Her life story was constructed so that it would fulfil certain stereotypes of both heterosexuals and lesbians. In Snyder's words, "Betty, we wrote, never had a steady boyfriend in high school, but did go out on dates. And although we gave her a steady boyfriend in college, we specified that he was more of a close friend than anything else" (1988, 266). A week later, they told some of the students that Betty was currently living with her husband, and another group of students that she was living with another woman in a lesbian relationship. When subsequently requested to answer a series of questions about Betty, they found a marked tendency on the part of students to reconstruct her biography so as to conform to stereotypes about either heterosexuality or homosexuality, depending on the information they had received.

> Those who believed that Betty was a lesbian remembered that Betty had never had a steady boyfriend in high school, but tended to neglect the fact that she had gone out on many dates in college. Those who believed that Betty was now a heterosexual, tended to remember that she had formed a steady relationship with a man in college, but tended to ignore the fact that this relationship was more of a friendship than a romance (1988, 266-267).

More directly relevant to the case at hand is an important article by Jeffrey E Pfeifer (1992) reporting the results of a similar study which compared responses to a biography in which a fictitious student, Bill, dropped out of college to enter a Catholic seminary, join the Marines, or join the Moonies. The short biography incorporated elements of indoctrination often attributed to "cults," such as

> While at the facility, Bill is not allowed very much contact with his friends or family and he notices that he is seldom left alone. He also notices that he never seems to be able to talk to the other four people who signed up for the program and that he is continually surrounded by [Moonies, Marines, Priests] who make him feel guilty if he questions any of their actions or beliefs (1992, 535).

When given a choice of describing Bill's indoctrination experience, subjects who thought Bill had joined the Catholic priesthood most often labelled his indoctrination "resocialisation"; those who were told that he had joined the Marines most frequently labelled the process "conversion"; and those who were under the impression that he had become a Moonie applied the label "brainwashing". On various other questions regarding the desirability and fairness of the indoctrination process, subjects who were told that Bill had joined the Moonies consistently evaluated his experience more negatively than subjects who were under the impression that Bill had joined either the Marines or a priestly order.

The implication of this analysis is that minority religions lose their chance for a fair hearing as soon as the label "cult" is successfully applied to them. After that, the news media selectively seek out and present information that fits the stereotype. It is then only a matter of time before the group in question is completely "demonised."

The Cult Stereotype as an Ideological Resource

Though the "cult" stereotype has come to dominate public discourse about minority religions, and though groups like the Unification Church and People's Temple seem to have become integral parts of that stereotype, there is enough ambiguity in the "cult" label to make its application in particular cases a matter of negotiation. Occasions for such negotiation arise in the context of social conflicts. For individuals or groups locked in certain kinds of struggles with members of minority religions, the "cult" stereotype represents a potent ideological resource which—if they are successful in swaying their immediate audience to reclassify a particular religion as a "cult"—marshals opinion against their opponent, potentially tipping the balance of power in their favour.

Situations in which this strategy can work are not restricted to the kinds of conflicts that are picked up by the national news media. For example, the stigma of the "cult" stereotype has been effectively deployed in child custody cases, in which one parent's membership in a minority religion is portrayed as indicative of her or his unworthiness as a parent. For such "limited domain" legal conflicts, however, it is difficult to deploy the stereotype unless there is some larger, earlier conflict that led to press coverage in which the particular minority religion in question was labelled a "cult." Lacking earlier "bad press," the cult label can still sometimes be made to stick on the basis of testimony by disgruntled former members.

For the most part, individuals involved in such relatively limited conflicts do not become full-time anti-cult crusaders. Although they may enter into a relationship with the anti-cult movement, they normally drift away from this involvement within a short time after the termination of their particular struggle. To refer back to the entrepreneurial model, these people are not so much moral entrepreneurs as they are consumers of a moral commodity—they have "purchased" a pre-packaged cult stereotype, and brought it to bear as one tool in the array of resources they have assembled to legitimate their cause. They may, of course, still have to exercise persuasive skills in getting the public or the court to accept the applicability of the stereotype, but otherwise they are not invested in the product per se. If anti-cult rhetoric fails to accomplish their end, but some other tool works in their particular conflict, they are usually quite ready to dispose of the cult stereotype and adopt an entirely different angle of attack.

As a low-intensity group that does not make excessive demands upon either the time or the resources of most participants, MSIA was largely overlooked by the anti-cult movement until the late eighties. In 1988, the *Los Angeles Times* published a highly critical article on MSIA. A similar article then appeared in *People* magazine. Both pieces dwelt on charges by ex-staff members that MSIA's founder, John-Roger Hinkins, had sexually exploited them. Depending significantly upon the testimony of disgruntled ex-staff and drawing heavily on the "cult" stereotype, MSIA was portrayed as an organisation that was created for no other purpose than to serve the financial, sexual, and ego needs of John-Roger Hinkins. After a brief moment in the spotlight, reporters turned their attention to other stories, and MSIA disappeared from the pages of the mass media.

Two events occurred in 1994 that once again brought MSIA to the attention of the media circus. First was Michael Huffington's campaign to become a California senator. Arianna Huffington, Michael Huffington's wife, was a personal friend of John-Roger, as well as a participant in MSIA. When someone in the media discovered this fact, the link became the focus of a number of sensationalistic articles in which all of the earlier accusations against John-Roger and MSIA were dragged out and uncritically repeated. In the same year as the campaign, Peter McWilliams, an ex-MSIA minister who had co-authored a series of popular books with John-Roger, dropped out of the Movement and authored a bitter anti-MSIA book, *LIFE 102: What To Do When Your Guru Sues You*, which attracted moderate media attention. As a result of this publicity, MSIA became a regular staple of anti-cult movement fare, frequently mentioned in any general discussion of the "cult" menace.

This relatively mild background of controversy set the stage for some of the conflicts in which MSIA has been involved. For example, in the mountains overlooking Santa Barbara, California, the Foundation for the Study of the Individual and World Peace (an organisation inspired by John-Roger Hinkins, the founder of MSIA) purchased some property—later named Windermere—for the purpose of building a retreat facility. Bordered on one side by a national forest, their property is also directly adjacent to a semi-rural neighbourhood populated by individuals who moved away from the city for the purpose of enjoying country living. These people view their new neighbour with concern. When they heard about plans to build a facility that, they imagined, would attract large numbers of outsiders from the Los Angeles area who would disturb their peaceful rural setting, they were upset. Eventually they organised the Cielo Preservation Organization (named after the primary road in the area, Camino Cielo) to oppose the construction of the retreat—construction which cannot proceed without approval from the county.

Not long after the negative *LA Times* piece mentioned earlier (Sipchen and Johnston, 1988) appeared, almost everyone in the neighbourhood received a copy. This slanted article immediately became a centrepiece legitimating the neighbours' opposition to the IIWP's retreat plans. By 1994, the *Times* report had been superseded by the considerable publicity Arianna Huffington's MSIA connections were generating in the southern California media. Thus in a 1994 article in the local paper reporting on the conflict between Windermere and the neighbourhood, Huffington and her "cult" connections were brought up and discussed near the beginning of the article:

> His [John-Roger's] teachings drew national attention during this year's California Senate race between incumbent Diane Feinstein and Rep. Michael Huffington because the Montecito congressman's wife, Arianna, had ties to the John-Roger organization, which some critics claim is a cult. Arianna Huffington has said it is not a cult, and described her past connection with MSIA as a casual one (Schultz, 1994, 1B).

Despite the cautious wording of this passage, the net effect of mentioning such accusations was that otherwise uninformed readers concluded that the "cult" label was probably appropriate for MSIA, influencing them to side with the ranch's neighbours.

This labelling enterprise was highly successful in generating anti-IIWP/anti-MSIA sentiment in Santa Barbara county. The point here, however, is that the Cielo Preservation Organization was less concerned about the ranch owners' religious persuasion than about preventing, in the words of a local organiser, hordes of "LA cowboys" from invading the area, thus spoiling their rural privacy. The claim that the Windermere Ranch was populated by weird cultists is what we have referred to as an ideological resource or a moral commodity—simply one among many accusations hurled at the IIWP in an all-out effort to short circuit their retreat plans.

The mention of the Huffingtons in the Santa Barbara paper alludes to an entirely different type of struggle that provides yet another example of the marshalling of the cult stereotype for deployment in a conflict not directly involving the anti-cult movement. The Feinstein-Huffington campaign for the U.S. Senate was a particularly bitter fight, with both camps relying heavily on expensive, negative TV ads. For a number of reasons, however, the media seemed to take more offence at Michael Huffington's bid for Senator than at Diane Feinstein's efforts to defend her seat in Congress. For one thing, and this may have been his biggest "sin" in the eyes of reporters, he consistently refused to be interviewed by what he felt to be a biased liberal media. Instead, Huffington attempted to bypass the news media altogether, appealing directly to voters through television advertisements. Rebuffed by the Huffington camp, the news media responded by characterising Michael Huffington as a wealthy outsider attempting to buy a Senate seat, and, more generally, sought out and reported whatever negative bits of information they could find on this Republican challenger.

When Arianna Huffington's connection with MSIA was discovered, the mass media in southern California immediately jumped on the information. Uncritically repeating accusations from the 1988 *LA Times* piece and from McWilliams's *Life 102*, reporters quickly reclassified Michael Huffington's senatorial bid from an outsider trying to buy his way into the United States Senate, into the machinations of an evil cult leader working behind the scenes through the candidate's wife to gain political influence for himself and his "cult" agenda. This absurd accusation was repeated (though sometimes more subtly and by implication) in a number of articles published in major magazines (e.g., Carlson, 1994). Not a single reporter bothered to look more deeply into John-Roger and MSIA, much less question the appropriateness of the cult stereotype. Instead, as one might have anticipated, reporters' pre-existing disposition to perceive Huffington negatively led them to accept accusations of his "cult connection" without further reflection. It was then almost inevitable that, as prior research into the self-fulfilling nature of stereotypes would have predicted, any new information gathered on MSIA would be filtered through the "cult" image.

The mass media are not, of course, motivated primarily by the quest for truth. Instead, the mainstream news media are driven by market forces and by the necessity of competing with other newspapers, other TV news shows, and so forth. This is not to say that reporters necessarily fabricate their stories from whole cloth. Rather, in the case of minority religions, news people tend to accentuate those facets of such groups that seem to be strange, dangerous, sensational, and the like because such portrayals titillate consumers of news. This kind of reporting contributes to the perpetuation of the "cult" stereotype. However, while the news media are not particularly interested in uncovering the truth about minority religions, neither are they particularly interested in joining with the anti-cult movement to undertake a protracted campaign to destroy minority religions. Ultimately, all the mass media are concerned about is making a profit and, to the extent that the cult image helps them to accomplish this end, the media buy into—and, in turn, propagate—the stereotype as a moral commodity (Lewis, 1994).

The media may have been tipped off to the Huffingtons' MSIA link by Peter McWilliams, a disgruntled former MSIA minister who wrote and published *Life 102: What To Do When Your Guru Sues You* (Sipchen 1995). McWilliams, who had co-authored a series of popular books (the LIFE 101 Series) with John-Roger, left MSIA in early 1994. At the time of his exit, he owed MSIA, employee for hire of John-Roger, hundreds of thousands of dollars in royalties. When McWilliams indicated that he had no intention of honouring his debt, MSIA sued him. McWilliams responded by writing *Life 102* (as he had previously threatened to do unless MSIA dropped pursuit of royalties owed), attempting to avoid his earlier financial commitment by conducting a campaign of defamation against John-Roger and MSIA. As part of this campaign, McWilliams mouthed the standard anti-cult line about self-serving evil gurus brainwashing helpless devotees, asserting that he was manipulated into listing John-Roger as co-author of books that he alone had written (thus relieving himself of responsibility for the royalty debt to the Church founded by his former spiritual teacher). As in the other instances we have examined, McWilliams was not particularly interested in aligning himself with CAN's campaign against all minority religions. Rather, he was deploying the "cult" stereotype as part of an effort to marshal public opinion against MSIA, hoping thereby to tip the balance of power in his favour so that he would not be required to honour his bad debt.

To conclude this overview of MSIA-related conflicts with one final example, it has already been mentioned that the "cult" stereotype has been effectively deployed in some child custody cases. In the words of Michael Homer, an expert in legal cases involving minority religions

> Religious practices and beliefs have also become the subject of child custody cases where nonmembers attempt to highlight nontraditional aspects of a spouse's or ex-spouse's religion to obtain custody of a minor child. Nonmembers seek to show that the religion deviates from social normalcy and, therefore, adversely affects the child's behavior. It is argued that the church's influence is mentally, physically, and emotionally detrimental to the child's well-being. Nonmembers have been successful when the court determines that the practices complained of are not merely religious but are detrimental practices that harm the child. (Homer 1994, pp. 129-130)

In at least one case, a parent's association with MSIA was effectively used against her by the other parent in a dispute involving their mutual offspring. In this particular case, a divorced mother petitioned the court to permit her to relocate in order to take a position in an MSIA-inspired organisation offering human potentials seminars. As his primary strategy for de-legitimating his wife's position, the ex-husband argued that he did not want his son involved in a "cult." To support his contention, he dragged up all of the old rumours about John-Roger and MSIA in an effort to prevent his ex-wife from leaving the state. Perceiving that not only would she have a difficult time winning, but also that her husband might undertake further actions that could result in her son being taken from her, she dropped her petition.

What is especially ironic about this case is that for several decades the father was deeply involved in EST—a human potentials group that has *very* frequently *(far more* frequently than MSIA) been labelled a "cult." As someone whose participation in EST has surely sensitised him to the cult controversy, the ex-husband's utilisation of the stereotype was clearly little more a tactic intended to win support for his side of the case, rather than a reflection of deeply held views about the dangers of sinister "cults." As the mother stated in a telephone interview, she felt that her former spouse was advised to "Shoot her where you think you can hurt her," and that her involvement in a MSIA-related organisation was simply a convenient target.

The chances of this man becoming a full-time anti-cult crusader are practically nil. Here, as in the other instances we have examined, it is clear that the cult stereotype is an ideological resource, deployed without a deep investment in the stereotype per se. This way of understanding the "cult" image's role in particular struggles represents a variation on earlier theorising. As has already been indicated, most recent theorising has focused on the anti-cult movement's campaign to win acceptance of both its ideology and its agenda by the greater society. By shifting the point of focus from this broad level to more particular struggles, we were able to see that, in the context of grass-roots conflicts, the "cult" stereotype becomes a moral commodity—an ideological resource that can easily be set aside if it is not persuasive, or if some other tactic better suits the situation.

Concluding Remarks

As mentioned at the beginning of the present chapter, conflicts over the legitimacy or illegitimacy of religious groups can be understood as an argument over *classification*. In the context of such controversies, the authority of governmental agencies and courts that potentially threaten new religions is taken for granted. What is at issue is whether a particular group is a legitimate religion or a dangerous pseudo-religion, commonly referred to as a "cult." If a given religion is successfully reclassified as a "cult", then this classification is sufficient reason for legitimating its repression. Typically, however, it is only within the context of specific conflicts such as those examined above that the repressive powers of the state are actually invoked against a religious group or the members of that group.

References:

About MSIA: The Movement of Spiritual Inner Awareness. MSIA Brochure. Los Angeles: The Church of the Movement of Spiritual Inner Awareness, n.d.

Andre, Judith. "Stereotypes: Conceptual and Normative Considerations." In Rothenberg, Paula. *Racism and Sexism*. NY: St. Martins, 1988.

Barker, Eileen. *The Making of a Moonie: Choice or Brainwashing?* Oxford: Blackwell 1984.

Bromley, David G. and James T. Richardson, eds. *The Brainwashing/Deprogramming Controversy: Sociological, Psychological, Legal and Historical Perspectives*. New York: Edwin Mellen, 1983.

Bromley, David G. and Anson D. Shupe. *Strange Gods: The Great American Cult Scare*. Boston: Beacon Pr., 1981.

Carlson, Margaret. "Should the Huffingtons Be Stopped?" *Time Magazine* October 3, 1994.

Freud, Sigmund. *The Basic Writings of Sigmund Freud*. Transl. A.A. Brill. New York: Modern Library, 1938.

Gilman, Sander L. *Difference and Pathology: Stereotypes of Sexuality, Race, and Madness*. Ithaca: Cornell Univ. Pr., 1985.

Homer, Michael W. "Freedom of Religion under the First Amendment: Church Universal and Triumphant." James R. Lewis and J. Gordon Melton, eds. *Church Universal and Triumphant in Scholarly Perspective*. Special Issue of *Syzygy: Journal of Alternative Religion and Culture*. 1994.

Hassan, Steven. *Combatting Mind Control*. Rochester, VT: Park Street Press, 1988.

Juergensmeyer, Mark. *Radhasoami Reality*. Princeton: Princeton University Press, 1991.

Kelley, Dean. "Deprogramming and Religious Liberty." *Civil Liberties Review*. 1977.

Langone, Michael D. *Recovery from Cults*. NY: Norton, 1993.

Lewis, James R. "Apostates and the Legitimation of Repression: Some Historical and Empirical Perspectives on the Cult Controversy." *Sociological Analysis* 49:4. 1989

Lewis, James R. "Reconstructing the `Cult' Experience: Post-Involvement Attitudes as a Function of Mode of Exit and Post-Involvement Socialization." *Sociological Analysis* 46:2. 1986.

Lewis, James R., ed. *From the Ashes: Making Sense of Waco.* Lanham, MD: Rowman & Littlefield, 1994.

Lewis, James R. and J. Gordon Melton, eds. *Perspectives on the New Age.* Albany: State University of New York Press, 1992.

Melton, J. Gordon. *Encyclopedia of American Religion.* Detroit, MI: Gale Research, 1993, 4th ed.

Melton, J. Gordon. *Encyclopedic Handbook of Cults in America.* NY: Garland, 1992, 2nd ed.

Melton, J. Gordon, and Robert L. Moore. *The Cult Experience: Responding to the New Religious Pluralism.* New York: Pilgrim Press, 1982.

Miller, Donald E. "Deprogramming in Historicl Perspective." In Bromley, David G. and James T. Richardson, eds. *The Brainwashing/Deprogramming Controversy: Sociological, Psychological, Legal and Historical Perspectives.* New York: Edwin Mellen, 1983.

Pfeifer, Jeffrey E. "The Psychological Framing of Cults: Schematic Representations and Cult Evaluations." *Journal of Applied Social Psychology* 22:7. 1992.

Ross, Catherine, and Michael D. Langone. *Cults: What Parents Should Know.* Weston, MA: American Family Foundation, 1988.

Rothenberg, Paula. "The Prison of Race and Gender: Stereotypes, Ideology, Language, and Social Control." In Rothenberg, Paula. *Racism and Sexism.* NY: St. Martins, 1988.

Schultz, Chuck. "Neighbors Vow War over Peace Retreat." *Santa Barbara News-Press.* December 27, 1994.

Shupe, Anson D., and David G. Bromley. *The New Vigilantes: Deprogrammers, Anti-Cultists, and the New Religions.* Beverly Hills, CA: Sage, 1980.

Singh, Kirpal. *The Crown of Life: A Study in Yoga.* Delhi: Ruhani Satsang, 1971.

Sipchen, Bob, and David Johnston. "John-Roger" (Part I). *Los Angeles Times.* August 14, 1988. "Negativity Shakes the Movement" (Part II). *Los Angeles Times.* August 15, 1988.

Sipchen, Bob. "The Guru and the Gadfly." *Playboy Magazine.* March 1995.

Snyder, Mark. "Self-Fulfilling Stereotypes." In Rothenberg, Paula. *Racism and Sexism.* NY: St. Martins, 1988.

Soul Transcendence, Introduction to the Movement of Spiritual Inner Awareness. MSIA Brochure. Los Angeles: The Church of the Movement of Spiritual Inner Awareness, 1995.

Sweeney, John Myles, Jr. "Declaration of John Myles Sweeney, Jr." Maricopa County, Arizona: Affidavit, March 17, 1992.

Wright, Stuart A. "Post-Involvement Attitudes of Voluntary Defectors from Controversial New Religious Movements." *Journal for the Scientific Study of Religion* 23:2. 1984.

Cult-Bashing in Sheep's Clothing:
Scholarship and the De-Legitimation of Religion

Although traditional ethnocentric analyses of other people's religions have been rejected by present-day academia, older patterns of prejudicial scholarship have tended to persist in the subfield of new religious movements. As a consequence, researchers have articulated judgmental points of view that, in effect, call into question the legitimacy of certain new religions. The present chapter analyses this issue through an examination of select scholarship on a prominent Japanese new religion, Soka Gakkai International.

Analyses of the proper role of religious studies in the university–a key issue in recent discussions of religious studies as a discipline (for example, Wiebe 1999; McCutcheon 2001)–rarely mention new religious movements. The unconscious value judgment here as elsewhere in the academy appears to be that the field is peripheral and therefore able to offer little insight into the broader concerns of religious studies. Perhaps the thorny issues raised by NRM studies are too raw and immediate, and hence get swept under the rug. In contrast to researchers who study the mating habits of earthworms or the chemical composition of meteorites–and even in contrast to colleagues who specialise in less controversial religions–new religion specialists are forced to work in a highly-politicised atmosphere. Articles on controversial religious groups published in specialised academic journals can directly impact people's lives, particularly when they are cited in legal briefs and judicial decisions.

Because mainstream new religion scholars have generally been critical of the cult stereotype (particularly the notion of cult mind control; e.g., Barker, 1984; Bromley and Richardson, 1983; Bromley and Shupe, 1981;Melton and Moore, 1982), they have, in turn, been criticised by those interested in perpetuating this stereotype. One *de*-legitimation strategy commonly utilised by such interest groups is to refer to academicians whose research tends to undermine anti-cult ideology as "cult apologists", implying that they are in a conspiracy with–and perhaps even covertly accept money from–malevolent religious groups. The cult apologist accusation is a handy tool because, in the hands of most anti-cultists, it is wielded as a tautology, immune to empirical disconfirmation. In other words, if a cult apologist is defined (implicitly or explicitly) as any researcher producing scholarship critical of the cult stereotype, then anyone whose scholarship is critical of the cult stereotype is *ipso facto* a cult apologist. This strategy allows anti-cultists to reject any scholarship with which they disagree *a priori*.

Anti-cultists adhering to this rhetorical strategy sometimes make it appear that sinister groups regularly seek out scholars to legitimate them and attack their critics. One of the more absurd examples of this de-legitimation strategy can be found in the introduction to Michael Newton's *Raising Hell* (1993). Newton takes "liberal" academics to task who criticise the notion of occult crime—referring to them as "cult apologists" as if they were somehow on the payroll of the Church of Satan or, no less implausibly, as if their souls had been purchased by the Prince of Darkness himself. (For another example of this same approach, refer to Raschke, 1990).

In point of fact, only a few groups like the Unification Church–which for many years courted academicians, presumably because of its Confucian-derived view of the importance of scholars in society–have believed that academicians wielded this kind of power. The leaders of most other new religions have been less naive about the social influence of scholars. Perhaps the only area where academic researchers have played a significant role in the cult controversy is in the discrediting of mind control notions and other aspects of the cult stereotype, making this the one area where academic specialists have entered the fray in support of new religions. The fact that some of the more prominent scholars in the field have testified against the brainwashing thesis in relevant legislative hearings and legal cases has evoked the ire of anti-cultists, and is the principal evidence for their contention that such academicians have become "apologists".

Of course, the primary target of anti-cultists is not scholars, but intensive religious groups. Implicitly or explicitly, the principal criticism levelled against such groups is that they are not real (that is, not *legitimate*) religions at all, but are instead elaborate con games. This line of analysis was examined in earlier chapters. A significant component of the anti-cult critique has been that intensive religious groups are illegitimate because they reject certain aspects of secular society. Alternately, among conservative Christian anti-cultists–sometimes referred to as "counter-cultists" to distinguish them from secular anti-cultists–this point is replaced by the accusation that new religions are illegitimate because they are doctrinally flawed.

Although the majority of specialists take a neutral approach, some mainstream scholars have levelled similar sorts of criticisms against controversial religious groups. Such evaluative approaches, however, run counter to the dominant consensus of contemporary religious studies. In the later half of the twentieth century, many different academic disciplines undertook critical re-examinations of earlier periods of scholarship, particularly the scholarship that was carried out by colonialist researchers. As one might anticipate, this scholarship was thoroughly (though often subtly) shaped by imperialist ideology and concerns. Such bias is particularly clear in the area of religious scholarship, where earlier writers all-too-often compared the religions of other peoples with Christianity, to the detriment of the former. (In this regard, refer, for example, to Whaling, 1983; Sharpe, 1986).

Reacting to the excesses of the past, contemporary academic disciplines–especially religious studies–engage in a sustained effort to avoid expressing judgmental opinions about the customs and beliefs of others. Instead, the thrust of modern religious scholarship is on *understanding* rather than *judging* religious communities. Even scholars who proffer the most reductionistic kinds of explanations of religions typically refrain from making overt value judgments. This attitude is the current norm for academia. When this norm is violated, we assume that writers are expressing either personal opinion or the attitude of the faith community to which they belong. For example, when a conservative Christian undertakes a polemic against another religion, we all recognise that he or she is engaged in a partisan theological exercise, and *not* doing objective scholarship.

Given this situation, no contemporary, mainstream scholar would seriously consider criticising a traditional religion as wrong or deluded, particularly in an academic publication. However, although this may be taken for granted with respect to traditions that have persisted for centuries, it seems that the point is less obvious with respect to more recent new religions, particularly when such religions have been the subject of public controversy.

For over half a century, one of the most controversial new religions in Japan has been Soka Gakkai. Although this group has matured into a responsible member of society, its ongoing connection with reformist political activity served to keep it in the public eye. Until relatively recently, it also had a high profile as the result of sensationalist and often irresponsible media coverage. Apparently as a direct consequence of the social consensus against this religion, some scholars have felt free to pen harsh critiques of Soka Gakkai–critiques in which the goal of promoting understanding has been eclipsed by efforts to de-legitimate Soka Gakkai by portraying it as deluded, wrong and/or socially dangerous. This body of "scholarship" presents a useful case study for the paradigmatic manner in which it exemplifies inappropriate approaches to the study of religious bodies.

After briefly surveying Soka Gakkai and articulating a humanistic perspective on emergent religions, the present chapter will undertake to analyse a selection of such publications, discussing the various ways in which these writings reveal more about the polemical agendas of the authors than about the phenomena they purport to examine.

Overview of Soka Gakkai International

Soka Gakkai International (SGI) is a Japanese Buddhist group with a comparatively large following in the United States and other western countries. Founded in the 1930s, Soka Gakkai has grown to become Japan's largest and—until the AUM Shinrikyo incident—most controversial new religion. Although classified as a new religion, SGI's roots lie in thirteenth century. (Relatively recent studies of Soka Gakkai in the West include Wilson and Dobbelaere, 1994; Hammond and Machacek, 1999.)

Like most other Japanese Buddhist groups, SGI belongs to the Mahayana school. One characteristic of many Mahayana Buddhist texts is that they extol the merit gained by reading, copying and otherwise propagating that particular scripture. Reading these claims, later generations of Buddhists were led to ask the question, which text is the most potent? This question was the subject of debate in thirteenth century Japan, when the Buddhist reformer Nichiren concluded that the *Saddharmapundarika*–the Lotus of the True Law, better known simply as the Lotus Sutra–was the most important of all Buddhist books. In fact, the Lotus Sutra was so powerful that all one had to do was to chant Namu-myoho-renge-kyo (which can be translated in various ways, including "I bow to the Lotus Sutra") to gain the merit promised in its pages.

Nichiren and his teachings gave rise to a monastic movement, which eventually splintered into different sects. Soka Gakkai began as a movement of lay practitioners attached to the Nichiren Shoshu (Orthodox Nichiren Sect). By the early 1990's, Soka Gakkai had become an independent movement. The founder, Tsunesaburo Makiguchi (1871-1944), was an educator who died in prison during the Second World War. After the war, Josei Toda (1900-1958) took over as president and built Soka Gakkai into a major religion. This period of rapid growth was accompanied by negative media attention. The group matured under the presidency of Daisaku Ikeda, who became the third president of Soka Gakkai after the passing of Toda.

Soka Gakkai also spread to the United States and Europe, where it aroused controversy as a result of its intensive proselytising activities. Although never as controversial as groups like the Hare Krishna Movement or the Unification Church, Soka Gakkai–which in the United States went under the name Nichiren Shoshu of America until after Soka Gakkai broke with Nichiren Shoshu–was not infrequently stereotyped as a brainwashing cult, particularly by anti-cult authors.

Throughout the latter half of the twentieth century, Soka Gakkai was attacked in Japan because of its support of political activity that challenged the ruling coalition. Exploiting the distrust of organised religion that characterised the public reaction to AUM Shinrikyo–the Japanese religious group responsible for the 1995 poison gas attack in the Tokyo subway system–the LDP (the Liberal Democratic Party, which was the dominant party in the ruling coalition) attempted to weaken its principal political rival, which Soka Gakkai supported. In particular, the LDP engaged in a campaign to portray religion in general, and Soka Gakkai in particular, as being incompatible with the principles of democracy. In 1999, however, the LDP underwent a sudden change of opinion, and allied itself with the New Komeito Party, the party supported by Soka Gakkai. Unsurprisingly, the media assault on Soka Gakkai subsequently evaporated.

A Humanistic Attitude Toward New Religions

One generally accepted observation about new religions is that periods of renewed spiritual activity emerge in the wake of disruptive social and economic changes: The established vision of "how things work" no longer seems to apply, and people begin searching for new visions. Our modern world seems particularly prone to social and economic disruptions. More fundamentally, thinkers like Jurgen Habermas have analysed contemporary society and concluded that we are suffering from a broad-ranging "legitimation crisis" that calls into question our very foundations (Habermas, 1975).

Most ordinary citizens do not, however, feel that the modern world has lost its legitimacy. As a consequence, those of us happily adjusted to the social-cultural mainstream often have a difficult time understanding intense religiosity. Academics have not been immune to this tendency. As mentioned in prior chapters, an earlier generation of sociologists of religion, seemingly obsessed with the issue of conversion to non-mainstream "sect" groups, gave excessive attention to explaining why individuals could become involved in such bizarre churches.

If, however, rather than dwelling on strange externals, we change our point of focus and attempt to really look at what might attract someone to an alternative religion, such involvement is not really difficult to understand. We live in a society that would have been an alien world to our ancestors. Surrounded by masses of people, we rarely know the names of our closest neighbours. In traditional societies, by way of contrast, everyone in a particular village knew everyone else, and took care of everyone else. Most alternative religions recreate this kind of community--a community comparable to an extended family.

The family metaphor is particularly appropriate. In modern society, our families are not the close emotional units they were in traditional societies. A small religious group many times recreates the sense of belonging to a family. If one has never experienced the closeness of a traditional family, it is easy to understand how the sense of belonging to such a unit would be attractive, even healing.

Much the same can be said about worldviews. In a traditional society, beliefs about the ultimate nature of the universe are largely taken for granted. In contemporary society, by way of contrast, nothing can be taken for granted except death and taxes. We are taught to be "nice" by the educational system, but this moral teaching is not grounded in an ultimate source of value. We are also instructed in the basic skills necessary to operate in society, but public school teachers are quiet about the greater questions of death, purpose, and the meaning of life.

We may place a positive or a negative evaluation on this relativistic education, but in either case we have to acknowledge that modern culture's ambiguous approach to socialisation departs radically from the socialisation strategies of earlier societies. Our choices are always varying shades of grey, rather than black and white/good and bad. The results of this ambiguity may be liberating to some people, but to others it is confusing. Without some kind of ultimate grounding, this is necessarily the case.

Non-traditional religions are often criticised for offering their followers the "easy" answers that come with black-and-white thinking. However, to many of the people who belong to these religions, the seeming narrowness of such thinking can be a liberating experience: Once one has stable criteria for what is good and true, this clarity and stability can then free one to go about the business of working, loving, and living life without debilitating anxieties about meaning and value. This is not, of course, to advocate a rigid belief system, but rather to point out why such a system is attractive without depreciating adherents as being somehow weak or defective.

To advocate a humanistic approach to new religions may seem to run against the grain of recent discussions that have been sharply critical of any approach to religion not adhering to the ideal of the quest for "objective knowledge" (Wiebe, 1999, xi). In the words of Donald Wiebe

> A study of religion directed toward spiritual liberation of the individual or of the human race as a whole, toward the moral welfare of the human race, or toward any ulterior end than that of knowledge itself, should not find a home in the university... (ibid., xiii).

Wiebe's primary concern is that any and all *religious* agendas be systematically excluded from the discipline of religious studies. With respect to this specific concern, his argument has much merit; this same concern informs some of the criticisms that will be articulated later in this chapter. However, Wiebe's excessive focus on exorcising religion from religious studies has caused him to miss the fact that the contemporary university does *not* "exclude all values from scientific deliberation except the value called 'objective knowledge'" (ibid., xi). Instead, to take a prominent example, academics in all disciplines that conduct direct research on human subjects are compelled to adhere to strict ethical guidelines.

The Belmont Report issued by the United States Department of Health, Education, and Welfare (1979), for instance, articulates three basic ethical principles that researchers should take into account—respect for persons, beneficence and justice. To cite selectively from different sections of this report

1. Respect for Persons - To respect autonomy is to give weight to autonomous persons' considered opinions and choices while refraining from obstructing their actions unless they are clearly detrimental to others. To show lack of respect for an autonomous agent is to repudiate that person's considered judgments...

2. Beneficence - The term "beneficence" is often understood to cover acts of kindness or charity that go beyond strict obligation. In this document, beneficence is understood in a stronger sense, as an obligation. Two general rules have been formulated as complementary expression of beneficent actions in this sense: (1) do not harm and (2) maximise possible benefits and minimise possible harms...

3. Justice - Questions of justice have long been associated with social practices such as punishment, taxation and political representation. Until recently these questions have not generally been associated with scientific research [,however,] it can be seen how conceptions of justice are relevant to research involving human subjects...

Although scholars of religion rarely engage in the types of research directly addressed by these kinds of guidelines, it would be rather odd to argue that the ideals of respect, beneficence and justice should not therefore be extended religious studies. Religion embodies many of the core beliefs and values informing the lives of the majority of the human race. Thus to analyse religion disrespectfully without concern for the possible social impact of one's research–a very real concern for scholars of NRMs, as was noted earlier–is to violate the ethos of the contemporary university. It is with reference to these values that a humanistic approach to new religions can "legitimately" be undertaken within the university environment. We will now turn to a critique of select scholarship.

Secularist Critiques

A 1976 article, "Rise and Decline of Sokagakkai Japan and the United States," by Hideo Hashimoto and William McPherson, examines the slowdown in growth Soka Gakkai was beginning to experience by the 1970s. This is a mixed piece: The authors are clearly interested in documenting and understanding an empirical phenomenon. At the same time, it is evident that they find the group distasteful, as reflected in a number of judgmental statements found at various junctures in their discussion. These statements contribute nothing to the authors' overall analysis, and only serve to make Soka Gakkai members appear defective and Soka Gakkai itself as socially undesirable.

We can capture the flavour of their discourse by isolating a series of adjectives and other characterisations that they apply to the group. In Hashimoto and McPherson's view, Soka Gakkai is: simplistic, a crutch, escapist, one among many religious fads, and willing to "take advantage of the dislocations and inequities of post-war Japan" in order to gain new converts. Taken together, these items of superfluous rhetoric allow us to infer that–whatever their personal faith commitments may or may not be–the authors are judging Soka Gakkai as "bad" in terms of a marked secularist bias, making this a useful piece to examine in terms of how secularist value-judgements interfere with the task of understanding others.

The appropriate question to begin with is, is secularism the appropriate criterion with which to judge the world of a religious community? Further, is it really so evident that secularism's offspring, modern mass society, should be regarded as the paragon of human possibilities, and any other social arrangement defective? To the contrary, for the great majority of people the advent of the modern world has not been an unmixed blessing. In fact, with the exception of the benefits conferred by technology, humanity as a whole was probably happier in traditional, pre-modern societies.

Prior generations of scholars used adaptation to modern, secular society as the standard for judging rationality and mental health because of an implicit evolutionary paradigm that caused them to view contemporary society as an evolutionary stage beyond traditional societies and secularism as a step above religion. It was assumed that traditional society and religion represented an earlier, child-like stage of development and that the secular social order embodied humanity's emergence into mature adulthood. (In this regard, refer to Fabian, 1983). Any movement contrary to the evolutionary current, such as individual's conversion from a secular to a religious worldview, was thus judged as regressive–a retreat from maturity to childhood. As the twenty-first century begins, these assumptions of our "academic ancestors" now strike us as quaint and naive, though their formulations continue to influence us in subtle or in not-so-subtle ways.

As was discussed earlier, new religions partially re-establish the world of traditional communities–arguably the "natural" environment for human beings. What this means for the present discussion is that, far from being symptomatic of social pathology, perhaps the emergence of new religious movements represent a *healthy*—or at least a health-seeking—response to the dislocations and inequities of modern secular society. From this more humanistic perspective, let us re-examine a few items from Hashimoto and McPherson's rhetorical dismissal of Soka Gakkai.

To begin with a citation from the latter part of the "Rise and Decline of Sokagakkai," the authors quote, with apparent disdain, a passage from a Soka Gakkai publication which asserts that religion will "rescue (them) from the complexities of the world" (91). It is clear Hashimoto and McPherson view this assertion as advice to retreat from mature engagement with modernity. However, to people confused by a complex, rapidly changing social environment, forced to make morally ambiguous choices in a world without ultimate meaning, it is not so self-evident that becoming an alienated cog in mass society is the most life-affirming option. Rather, the simplification introduced by conversion to a new religious movement can provide a stable context for individuals to engage in moral self-affirmation—a self-affirmation that might otherwise be stymied by the "complexities of the world."

The authors also stigmatise Soka Gakkai as "escapist." This particular characterisation is interesting because of the manner in which the evaluative freight being carried by the term "escape" can be inverted when viewed from the perspective of a tale found in Soka Gakkai's primary scripture, the Lotus of the True Law. The relevant image is that of a burning house. The lesson of the parable revolves around the dilemma of an adult who must determine a way of helping a group of children *escape* from the house before they are killed in the fire. The burning building, the Lotus Sutra suggests, is like the world—it will destroy you unless you withdraw from it. From this perspective, escape is a positive act that preserves the integrity of the individual from an impossible situation. Perhaps, then, "escaping" into a religion like Soka Gakkai could also be viewed as a positive, life-affirming act.

Escapism is also one of the charges levelled (in a less dismissive way) in H Neill McFarland's *The Rush Hour of the Gods* (1967), one of the first English-language books on Japanese new religions. *Rush Hour* was composed during the latter part of the middle period of Soka Gakkai's institutional life when it was still expanding rapidly and, in the eyes of some observers, appeared on the verge of taking over Japan. During that period, a number of different authors penned books that raised the spectre of a country run by Soka Gakkai (for example, Brannen 1968; Dator 1969). These ranged from hysterical to more balanced treatments, frequently motivated by the desire to warn people that this movement was a political threat, particularly dangerous to the survival of democracy. Most of these works have long since been forgotten.

Rush Hour, however, has continued to be a useful volume because it deals with a number of religions other than Soka Gakkai. *Rush Hour* has also persisted as a standard reference on the subject for lack of more adequate and up-to-date substitutes. Though in many ways McFarland echoes the concerns of other writers from the late 1950s and early 1960s, he also makes a concerted effort to balance his critical remarks with a more humane attempt to understand Soka Gakkai and to understand the world of Soka Gakkai members. Despite this effort, McFarland falls back on certain stereotyped, judgmental characterisations of mass movements and their participants expressed by such analysts as Eric Hoffer.

Hoffer (1951) describes the traits of members of social movements—including religious movements—with such terms and expressions as "a facility for make-believe", "a proneness to hate", "credulity", and so on. These are presented as if they were objective characteristics rather than disparaging value judgments. If one accepts this kind of discourse as normative, any participant in a mass movement must, by definition, be a defective, weak human being. Though personally far less prejudiced, McFarland's dependence on Hoffer as his theoretical touchstone causes him to attribute the success of Soka Gakkai to "its ability to reach a person who feels that he is nobody and to impart to him new hope and purpose by showing him a fellowship and a cause within which he can find both acceptance and refuge" (212). Hence, what the convert is offered is

> Not real freedom but fraternity and uniformity, signifying deliverance from the frustrations of independent, individual existence, are the goals (213).

This kind of rhetoric may have been tolerable when McFarland wrote *Rush Hour*, but is clearly inappropriate to the contemporary academic norm of viewing social movement participants humanely rather than as defective sociopaths.

Elsewhere, and without fully realising the extent of his insight, McFarland notes that what many converts find in Soka Gakkai is a validation for "the rather primitive reliance upon magic and relic worship that is part of their folk-religious heritage" (204). This is essentially the same point–though expressed in a partial and prejudiced manner–that was advanced in the preceding section of this paper, namely that modern new religions represent an attempt to re-establish the traditional world that has been the natural environment of the human species for millennia.

Let us consider finally one more item from Hashimoto and McPherson's rhetorical arsenal, namely the notion that religion is a "crutch". This particular characterisation has often been levelled against religions, and religionists have sometimes heatedly denied the accusation. Let us, however, let go of the connotations of this criticism and instead ask, what does a crutch actually do? Are crutches really so bad? To the contrary, crutches are devices that enable a person who cannot otherwise walk to exercise the power of movement. Correspondingly, many religions portray the human condition as being primarily a state of brokenness. To use the terminology of Buddha's day, human existence is *dukkha*–Pali for "out of joint". Thus the human condition is one of "crippledness", and religion is the *crutch* that allows us to walk through life.

The point being made here is not that religion is good while secularism is bad (or vice versa, for that matter), but, rather, that it is not self-evident that secularism should be the standard by which religion is evaluated. Hence, instead of dismissing religion as defective because it does not live up to secularist criteria of health and well-being, a humanistic methodology–one that tries to *understand* rather than *judge* the religions of others (for example, Muesse, 1999)–should attempt to describe religionists as acting out of reasonable motives rather than from errors of judgment or psychopathology. Though we may still disagree with their religion, the goal should be to avoid portraying others as weird or defective.

Crypto-Theological Critiques

Another kind of critique that academics have levelled against Soka Gakkai is that some aspect of its ideology is wrong or self-contradictory. Ted Solomon's "Soka Gakkai on the Alleged Compatibility between Nichiren Buddhism and Modern Science", for instance, examines Soka Gakkai's claims that Buddhism is scientific and that Buddhist cosmology and metaphysics are compatible with modern physics. These views are expressed in Daisaku Ikeda's writings on science and religion (Ikeda, 1968), as well as in Ikeda's conversations with the late Arnold Toynbee (Ikeda 1977). The goal of Solomon's critique is to demonstrate that Ikeda, the third president of Soka Gakkai, is *wrong*. In other words, not only is Buddhism not scientific, but also Ikeda is mistaken about the parallels to physics.

On the face of it, the thrust of this article may not strike one as being unusual or as outside the pale of academic norms. There is, however, something very peculiar about a scholar–while acting in the role of a mainstream academic–putting forward what is basically a *theological* critique of a religious leader. The highly unusual nature of this approach might be more evident if we changed the context and examined a few comparable examples of this kind of argument.

Yogis sometimes claim, for instance, that the physical body is interpenetrated by a "subtle" energy body or "sheath" (Sanskrit *kosha*) and that the principal structures in this paraphysical body are seven centres (*chakras*) lying along the spine. This subtle anatomy is the basis for certain yoga techniques, and most yogis would assert that the subtle energy sheath is "real" in a literal, non-figurative sense. Imagine, then, if a scholar of religion wrote an article contesting this claim because science is unable to demonstrate the existence of the energy body?

Or, to refer to another example, take the hypothetical situation of someone who has researched Jewish and Christian eschatology–particularly the notion of the resurrection. The same scholar has a background in the biological sciences. What if they authored an academic publication in which they critiqued eschatological notions on the basis that resurrection was scientifically impossible, hence both Jews and Christians are deluded?

In both cases, colleagues would *severely* question the appropriateness of such criticisms. The aim of mainstream religious scholarship is simply *not* to dispute the truth of other people's religious claims, even when participants in a particular religious tradition believe such claims to be true in a literal, scientific sense. Rather, the goal of mainstream academic analyses with respect to religious belief systems is to determine what others believe, why they believe what they do, and what consequences holding such beliefs have for participants.[1]

In the case at hand, it would have been more appropriate for Solomon to have questioned what led Ikeda to explore this topic, and what advantages are gained for Soka Gakkai if he can convincingly demonstrate a strong compatibility between Buddhism and modern science. Instead, Solomon apparently fears that letting Ikeda's argument stand might give Soka Gakkai some actual legitimacy, and so feels compelled to dispute it. Such concerns are, however, *theological*, and hence inappropriate for a mainstream scholar.

One finds similar problems with Christina Naylor's "Nichiren, Imperialism, and the Peace Movement". This article is a strident polemic denouncing Soka Gakkai's involvement in the world peace movement as hypocritical. The primary basis for Naylor's denunciation is the "unpeaceful" sentiments expressed in the writings of Nichiren, the thirteenth century prophet to whom Soka Gakkai looks as the inspiration for their movement. Stripped of the apparatus of scholarly discourse, footnotes and citations, her heavy-handed critique is little more than an overheated warning to her readers that Soka Gakkai is a wolf in sheep's clothing–a message more appropriate for a journalistic venue than for an academic journal.

One wonders what could possibly have motivated Naylor to have invested such passion into her article. Could it be that she is an adherent of some form of Christianity on a crusade against pagans? This seems like a reasonable assumption, given the two biblical allusions she makes in order to contrast the justice and peacefulness of western religion with Nichiren Buddhism

There is no call for justice, mercy, love for enemies and neighbors, honest work, or a simple lifestyle such as we find in Biblical writers (70).

By contrast, the ideal of *shalom*–a just peace in which people's needs are so adequately and fairly met that they dance for joy–has inspired untold number of people motivated by the love of God, to pioneer or cooperate in peace programs (75).

Whether or not Naylor's theological diatribe arises out of a personal faith commitment, her mention of the Bible provides us with a perfect example with which to compare and contrast her analysis of Nichiren. Specifically, one does not have to be a student of scripture to be aware that many biblical books are not exactly blueprints for a society based on peace and love. To the contrary, the God of the Judeo-Christian scriptures is often a violent divinity who hates his enemies to the extent that he either orders his followers to destroy them, or else destroys them directly with his own power.

On the basis of these parts of the Bible, would we be justified in saying that any Jews or Christians participating in the peace movement were therefore insincere and cynical? The answer here is would have to be "Yes" if we subjected Western religions to the same criteria to which Naylor subjects Soka Gakkai. To drive home this point, we can take one of her statements and make

---

[1] To the extent that McCutcheon's scholar-as-culture-critic (2001) would actively challenge the validity of religion–which, to my way of thinking, would resurrect the worst aspect of traditional Comparative Religion in secular guise–I would have to disagree that this should be the role of religious studies.

the appropriate substitutions so that it applies to her own religious tradition. For instance, the last sentence in Naylor's article reads:

> The claim that the inspiration for Soka Gakkai's peace programs comes from Nichiren is hard to justify. (75)

Substituting Christianity for Soka Gakkai and the Bible for Nichiren, we get the following statement

> The claim that the inspiration for Christianity's peace programs comes from the Bible is hard to justify.

With these substitutions, the statement is at least as accurate as–and perhaps more accurate than–the original.

The point here, of course, is neither to criticise Christianity nor to defend Soka Gakkai, but, rather, to demonstrate the inappropriateness of Naylor's critique: We easily recognise the unscholarly nature of such an attack when levelled against a traditional religion, but are blind-sided when the religious group in question is a highly stigmatised organisation like Soka Gakkai. Yet academics must resist allowing themselves to be swayed by popular prejudice and to lower the standards of what passes the test of sound scholarship. In the case at hand, the concerns expressed in "Nichiren, Imperialism, and the Peace Movement" are primarily *theological*, and hence–to agree emphatically with Wiebe (1999) on this point–inappropriate for mainstream scholarship.

Concluding Remarks

We began by noting that, although certain kinds of analyses of religion have been rejected by the academic mainstream, older patterns of prejudicial scholarship have tended to persist in the subfield of new religious movements. Although there is no sound reason for continuing to permit writers to articulate judgmental points of view that call into question the legitimacy of minority religions, popular prejudice against such religions has served to make us "tone-deaf" to a scholar's biases against such groups.

It was also noted that NRM researchers are forced to work in a highly politicised atmosphere. One result is of this situation is that, unlike most other academic specialties, NRM scholarship can have ramifications outside the university for the groups we study. Thus, by producing scholarship that reinforces popular stereotypes, NRM specialists can unwittingly supply ammunition for critics seeking to destroy minority religions by challenging their legitimacy.

The present chapter analysed select scholarship on Soka Gakkai International, an organisation chosen because it has been highly controversial and because a reasonable quantity of articles and books have been composed on the group. It was also argued that the scholar's first goal should always be to articulate a humanly meaningful *understanding* of a given religion—both an understanding of the world of the participants as well as an understanding of what such religions mean for society as a whole.

References:

Barker, Eileen. The Making of a Moonie: Choice or Brainwashing? Oxford: Blackwell 1984.

Brannen, Noah S. Soka Gakkai; Japan's militant Buddhists. Richmond, John Knox Press, 1968.

Bromley, David G., and James T. Richardson, eds. The Brainwashing/Deprogramming Controversy: Sociological, Psychological, Legal and Historical Perspectives. New York: Edwin Mellen, 1983.

Bromley, David G., and Anson D. Shupe. Strange Gods: The Great American Cult Scare. Boston: Beacon, 1981.

Dator, James Allen. *Soka Gakkai: Builders of the Third Civilization: American and Japanese Members.* Seattle, WA: University of Washington Press,1969.

Eliade, Mircea. "History of Religions and a New Humanism." *History of Religions* 1. 1961.

Fabian, Johannes. *Time and the Other: How Anthropology Makes Its Object.* New York: Columbia University Press, 1983.

Habermas, Jurgen. *Legitimation Crisis.* Boston: Beacon Press, 1975 [1973].

Hammond, Phillip E., and David W. Machacek. *Soka Gakkai in America: Accommodation and Conversion.* New York: Oxford University Press, 1999.

Hashimoto, Hideo, and William McPherson. "Rise and Decline of Sokagakkai Japan and the United States." *Review of Religious Research* 17/2 (1976):82-92.

Hoffer, Eric. *The True Believer: Thoughts on the Nature of Mass Movements.* New York: Harper, 1951.

Ikeda, Daisaku. "Science and Religion." *Complete Works of Daisaku Ikeda*, Vol. 1. Tokyo: Seikyo Press, 1968.

--------------. *Dialogue on Life*, 2 Vols. Tokyo: Nichiren Shoshu International Center, 1977.

McCutcheon, Russell T. *Critics Not Caretakers: Redescribing the Public Study of Religion.* State Univ of New York Press, 2001.

McFarland, H. Neill. *The Rush Hour of the Gods: A Study of New Religious Movements in Japan.* New York: Macmillan, 1967.

Melton, J. Gordon, and Robert L. Moore. *The Cult Experience: Responding to the New Religious Pluralism.* New York: Pilgrim Press, 1982.

Muesse, Mark. "Religious Studies and 'Heaven's Gate': Making the Strange Familiar and the Familiar Strange." In Russell T. McCutcheon, Ed. *The Insider/Outsider problem in the Study of Religion: A Reader.* London: Cassell, 1999.

National Commission for the Protection of Human Subjects of Biomedical and Behavioral Research. "The Belmont Report: Ethical Principles and Guidelines for the Protection of Human Subjects of Research." Washington, DC: Department of Health, Education, and Welfare, April 18, 1979. Http://ohrp.osophs.dhhs.gov/hmansubjects/guidance/belmont.htm

Naylor, Christina. Nichiren, Imperialism, and the Peace Movement. *Japanese Journal of Religious Studies* 18/1 (1991):51-78.

Newton, Michael. *Raising Hell: An Encyclopedia of Devil Worship and Satanic Crime.* New York: Avon Books, 1993.

Raschke, Carl A. *Painted Black.* San Francisco: Harper San Francisco, 1990.

Sharpe, Eric J. *Comparative Religion: A History.* La Salle, IL: Open Court, 2nd ed. 1986.

Solomon, Ted J. "Soka Gakkai on the Alleged Compatibility between Nichiren Buddhism and Modern Science." *Japanese Journal of Religious Studies* 7/1 (1980):34-54.

Whaling, Frank. *Contemporary Approaches to the Study of Religion*, vol. 1. Berlin: Mouton, 1983.

Wiebe, Donald. *The Politics of Religious Studies.* New York: St. Martins Press, 1999.

Wilson, Bryan and Karel Dobbelaere. *A Time to Chant: The Soka Gakkai Buddhists in Britain.* Oxford: The Clarendon Press, 1994.

Diabolical Authority:
Anton LaVey, *The Satanic Bible* and the Satanist "Tradition"[1]

> We have a bible. We have a *pro-human* dogma. We have a church. We have a tradition.
> — *From the Church of Satan's official website.*

The status of *The Satanic Bible* as an authoritative scripture–or, perhaps more accurately, as a kind of *quasi-scripture*–within the Satanic subculture was initially brought to my attention during my first face-to-face encounter with Satanists in the Spring of 2000. Via the internet, I had found a small Satanist group in Portage, Wisconsin, which was about an hour south of where I resided at the time. This group, the Temple of Lylyth, distinguishes itself from Anton LaVey's brand of4 Satanism chiefly by its emphasis on feminine nature of the Dark Power. I arranged to meet with them in Portage on a Friday evening in connection with a research project on which I was working at the time.

Over the course of our conversation, the founder and then leader of the group mentioned that on Friday evenings he was usually downtown where a small group of fervent Christians regularly set up what might be called a "preaching station" to spread the Gospel. This young fellow (he was nineteen at the time) would confront them as a practicing Satanist. He always carried a copy of *The Satanic Bible* with him, not just so he could quote some of accusations LaVey leveled against Christianity, but also so he could correct anything these evangelists might say about Satanism by citing an authoritative source. I'm sure this is something of a caricature, but I was left with the impression of dueling religionists, Christians hurling Bible verses at my informant as he matched blow for blow with quotes from *The Satanic Bible*. This experience led me to pay attention whenever other Satanists mentioned *The Satanic Bible*.

The Temple of Lylyth is part of a loose, decentralized Satanic movement that coheres as a distinct religious community largely by virtue of adherence to certain themes in the thought of Anton LaVey, founder of modern Satanism, though few movement participants outside the Church of Satan would regard themselves as "orthodox LaVeyans" (something of an oxymoron). Following the dissolution of the Church of Satan's grotto system in 1975 and before the explosion of the internet in the mid-nineties, the Satanic movement was propagated almost entirely by *The Satanic Bible*, which has continuously been in print as a widely-available, mass market paperback. Rather than being a guide to Devil-worship, LaVey's work advocates a blend of Epicureanism and Ayn Rand's philosophy, flavored with a pinch of ritual magic. Couched in iconoclastic rhetoric, *The Satanic Bible* has always held particular appeal for rebellious adolescents. The title seems to have originally been chosen for its shock value rather than from any pretense to scriptural status.

The present article examines issues of authority within the Satanic movement and among LaVey's successors in the Church of Satan. The basis of this analysis will be Max Weber's discussion of the legitimation of authority. LaVey was a charismatic individual who appealed to the authority of reason and attacked the authority of tradition. However, LaVey, and particularly *The Satanic Bible*, soon became sources of authority for a new Satanic tradition—part of the process Weber referred to as the *routinization of charisma*.

The Legitimation of Authority

Satanists do not consciously regard *The Satanic Bible* in the same way traditional religionists regard their sacred texts. However, in the course of a research project on modern Satanism conducted in 2000-2001, I discovered that *The Satanic Bible* is treated as an authoritative document which effectively *functions* as scripture within the Satanic community. In particular, LaVey's work is quoted to legitimate particular positions as well as to de-legitimate the positions of other Satanists. This legitimation strategy appears to have been unconsciously derived from the Judeo-Christian tradition, which locates the source of religious authority in a sacred text. In other words, being raised in a religious tradition that emphasizes the authority of scripture creates an attitude that can be unconsciously carried over to other, very different kinds of writings.

The classic discussion of the issue of legitimacy is Max Weber's tripartite schema of traditional, rational-legal, and charismatic legitimations of authority. The dynamics (in the sense of upsetting rather than reinforcing established authority structures) of this schema are largely confined to the factor of charisma, a form of legitimation Weber viewed as particularly—though not exclusively—characteristic of new religious movements.

Weber's work on the legitimation of authority provides a useful starting point for understanding the legitimation strategies deployed by contemporary new religions, but it should immediately be noted that his analysis is also inadequate. For example, in contrast to what one might anticipate from the discussion of charismatic authority in Weber's *Economy and Society*, one often finds new religions appealing to tradition—though the explicit nature of such appeals means that they constitute a variation from what Weber had in mind by the traditional legitimation of authority (which he viewed as more implicit than explicit). Also, when nascent movements attempt to justify a new idea, practice or social arrangement by attributing it to the authority of tradition, it is usually through a reinterpretation of the past that they are able to portray themselves as the true embodiment of tradition. Such variations on what one might anticipate from his schema indicate that Weber did not have the last word on this issue.

Charisma—which, in Weber's use of the term, includes everything from direct revelations from divinity to the leader's ability to provide both mundane and supernatural benefits to followers—may be the keystone in a new movement's initial attractiveness, but charismatic leaders typically appeal to a variety of other sources of legitimacy. For instance, many modern movements appeal to the authority of reason as embodied in natural science.[2] This is because the general populace of industrialized countries tend to give science and science's child, technology, a level of respect and prestige enjoyed by few other social institutions—to the point where, as a number of observers have pointed out, science has come to be viewed quasi-religiously. Thus any religion that claims its approach is in some way *scientific* draws on the prestige and perceived legitimacy of natural science. Religions such as Christian Science, Science of Mind, and Scientology claim just that.

There is, however, a distinct difference between popular notions of science and science proper. Average citizens' views of science are significantly influenced by their experience of technology. Hence, in most people's minds, an important goal of science appears to be the solution of practical problems. This aspect of our cultural view of science shaped the various religious sects that incorporated "science" into their names. In sharp contrast to traditional religions, which emphasize salvation in the afterlife, the emphasis in these religions is on the improvement of this life. Groups within the Metaphysical (Christian Science-New Thought) tradition, for example, usually claim to have discovered spiritual "laws" which, if properly understood and applied, transform and improve the lives of ordinary individuals, much as technology has transformed society.

The notion of spiritual laws is taken directly from the "laws" of classical physics. The eighteenth and nineteenth century mind was enamored of Newton's formulation of the mathematical order in the natural world. A significant aspect of his system of physics was expressed in the laws of gravity. Following Newton's lead, later scientists similarly expressed their discoveries in terms of the same legislative metaphor—e.g., the "law" of evolution.

This legislative rhetoric was carried over into Metaphysical religions, particularly New Thought. Groups in the Metaphysical tradition view themselves as investigating the mind or spirit in a practical, experimental way. The self-perception of the early New Thought movement as "science" is expressed in Lesson One of Ernest Holmes' 1926 classic, *Science of Mind,* in the following way:

> Science is knowledge of facts built around some proven principle. All that we know about any science is that certain things happen under certain conditions. Take electricity as an example; we know that there is such a thing as electricity; we have never seen it, but we know that it exists because we can use it; we know that it operates in a certain way and we have discovered the way it works. From this knowledge we go ahead and deduce certain facts about electricity; and, applying them to the general principle, we receive definite results. ...
>
> The discovery of a law is generally made more or less by accident, or by some one who, after careful thought and observation, has come to the conclusion that such a principle must exist. As soon as a law is discovered experiments are made with it, certain facts are proved to be true, and in this way a science is gradually formulated; for any science consists of the number of known facts about any given principle.... This is true of the Science of Mind. No one has ever seen Mind or Spirit, but who could possibly doubt their existence? Nothing is more self- evident.... (Holmes, p. 38)

Modern Satanism is in some ways in continuity with, and in other ways a departure from, this particular line of development. Although Satanism also appeals to science, its focus is not on developing a pragmatic science of the mind. Rather, when LaVey founded the Church of Satan, he grounded Satanism's legitimacy on a view of human nature shaped by a secularist appropriation of modern science. Unlike Christian Science, Scientology and other groups that claimed to model their approach to spirituality after the *methods* of science, LaVey's strategy was to base Satanism's "anti-Theology" in the secularist *world view* derived from natural science.[3] This world view provided LaVey with an atheistic underpinning for his attacks on Christianity and other forms of supernatural spirituality. At the same time, LaVey went beyond contemporary secularism by suggesting the reality of mysterious, "occult" forces–forces he claimed were not supernatural, but were, rather, natural forces that would eventually be discovered by science. In his notion of mysterious forces that could be manipulated by the will of the magician, LaVey was really not so far from the mentalistic technology of Christian Science, Scientology, etc.

The human nature to which LaVey appealed was humanity's animal nature, viewed through the lens of Darwinism. The human being in this view is little more than an animal with no ultimate morality other than law of the jungle and no purpose other than the survival of the fittest. In terms of Weber's schema, we would say that LaVey's appeal to human nature (meaning, for LaVey, the Darwinist vision of human nature) was a rational legitimation of authority. In other words, LaVey claimed that Satanism was a legitimate religion because it was rational. As a corollary, traditional religion was irrational (unscientific) and therefore illegitimate.

While LaVey was a charismatic individual, and while this charisma was undoubtedly crucial for the successful birth of the Church of Satan, in the present discussion I am less interested in analyzing the initial emergence of religious Satanism than in the transformations that have taken place in the post-charismatic phase of the Satanic movement. Weber was also interested in the this kind of transition, which he discussed in terms of the routinization of charisma. By this Weber meant that, because personal charisma tends to be unstable, charismatic authority must eventually move toward dissolution, legal-rational authority or traditional authority.

With respect to modern Satanism, the waning of LaVey's charismatic authority, particularly after he dismantled the Church of Satan (CoS) as a functioning church in 1975, led to a number of interesting—though somewhat paradoxical—developments. In addition to numerous splinter groups, a decentralized, anarchistic movement emerged that was shaped by the central themes in LaVey's thought, particularly as expressed in *The Satanic Bible*. This book became a doctrinal touchstone of the movement, though independent Satanists felt free to selectively appropriate ideas from *The Satanic Bible* and to mix them with ideas and practices drawn from other sources. LaVey's book became, in a sense, a kind of quasi-scripture, which is a form of what Weber meant by traditional authority (despite the fact that it seems odd to refer to a religion less than forty years old as a "tradition"!). However, many independent Satanists also adhered to LaVey's program of the authority of rationality, feeling free to criticize and even to reject aspects of the LaVeyan tradition. Thus the Satanic movement's legitimacy is based on a dual appeal to independent rational authority and to the authority of the LaVeyan tradition.

In contrast, the remnants of LaVey's church—which is still technically the largest single Satanist group in terms of formal membership—quickly solidified into a doctrinally-rigid organization focused on maintaining the purity of LaVeyan Satanism. This was partly in response to the challenge presented by non-CoS Satanists. In the ongoing argument over legitimacy, LaVey's successors have come to place excessive stress on their role as bearers of his legacy, even asserting that only CoS members are "real" Satanists and characterizing Satanists outside the fold as "pseudo" Satanists. In terms of Weber's analysis, one would say that CoS's legitimation strategy has narrowed to focus almost exclusively on CoS's claim to traditional authority.

Anton LaVey and Modern Religious Satanism

To comprehend religious Satanism, one must first understand that Satan has become an ambivalent symbol within the modern world. Part of the reason for the attractiveness of LaVeyan Satanism is its ability to hold together a number of diverse meanings found in this symbol. In the Western cultural tradition, the Devil represents much more than absolute evil. By default, the Prince of Darkness has come to embody some very attractive attributes. For example, because traditional Christianity has been so anti-sensual, Satan became associated with sex. The Christian tradition has also condemned pride, vengefulness and avarice, and, when allied with the status quo, has promoted conformity and obedience. The three former traits and the antithesis of the latter two traits thus became diabolical characteristics. LaVeyan Satanism celebrates such "vices" as virtues, and identifies them as the core of what Satanism is really all about.

LaVey founded the Church of Satan in 1966, the first organized church in modern times devoted to Satan. As a consequence, Anton LaVey has sometimes been referred to as the "St. Paul of Satanism." LaVey has two biographies, one historical and one legendary. This dichotomy has only become apparent in recent years. His real life was far more prosaic than the story he fabricated for the benefit of the media. LaVey effectively promoted his carefully crafted pseudo-biography through conversations with his disciples, media interviews, and two biographies by associates that he appears to have dictated—*The Devil's Avenger* (1974) by Burton Wolfe and *Secret Life of a Satanist* (1990) by Blanche Barton. LaVey's fictional biography was clearly meant to legitimate his self-appointed role as the "Black Pope" by portraying him as an extraordinary individual.

According to the official biography, he was born Howard Anton Szandor LaVey in Chicago, Illinois. His parents, Joseph and Augusta LaVey, moved to San Francisco while LaVey was still an infant. He was introduced to the occult by his Transylvanian gypsy grandmother. As a teenager he pursued various avenues of occult studies, as well as hypnotism and music. He also played an oboe in the San Francisco Ballet Orchestra. He dropped out of high school at 17 to join the Clyde Beatty Circus and worked as a calliope player and big cat trainer, later learning stage magic as well. While an organist in a burlesque theater, he had an affair with the young Marilyn Monroe shortly before she became famous.

He married in 1950 and about that time took a job as a police photographer, but in 1955 returned to organ playing. Until he formed the Church of Satan in 1966, he was the city of San Francisco's official organist. He divorced in 1960 in order to marry Diane Hegarty. He purchased his house—eventually becoming the Church of Satan headquarters, later dubbed the "Black House"—after he found out it had been the former brothel of the madam Mammy Pleasant.

Drawing on his circus and occult backgrounds, he began to conduct "midnight magic seminars" at his house. This proved popular enough for him to found the Church of Satan in 1966. The basis for his rituals were Nazi rituals recorded on top-secret films he had seen as a teenager. LaVey's showmanship encouraged significant media coverage of such events as the first Satanic wedding and the first Satanic funeral, worship with a nude woman as an the altar, and a cameo appearance as the Devil in the movie "Rosemary's Baby." LaVey made much of being a close friend of Sammy Davis, Jr. and of having had an affair with Jayne Mansfield, two celebrity members of the Church of Satan. At its peak, he claimed that the Church had hundreds of thousands of members. LaVey passed away in 1997.

LaVey's historical biography overlaps his legendary biography at several points. He was born in Chicago and his family did move to San Francisco. He did make his living as a musician and, of course, he actually did found the Church of Satan and died in 1997. He had several marriages. Almost everything else, however, seems to have been a fabrication.

LaVey's self-created legend was not seriously challenged until a 1991 interview in *Rolling Stone* magazine, entitled "Sympathy for the Devil." The author of that article, Lawerence Wright, did a little investigative footwork and discovered that: LaVey was born Howard Stanton Levey to Gertrude and Mike Levey; there never was a "San Francisco Ballet Orchestra"; no one by the name Levey or LaVey worked as a musician or cat trainer for the Beatty Circus during the period he claimed to have been an employee; neither he nor Monroe ever worked for the Mayan "burlesque" theater; he never worked for the San Francisco Police Department; and there was no such thing as an official San Francisco city organist. These discoveries led Wright to remark toward the end of his article:

> Later, as I began to take apart the literary creation he had made of his life, I would realize that "Anton LaVey" was itself his supreme creation, his ultimate satanic object, a sort of android composed of all the elements his mysterious creator had chosen from the universe of dark possibilities. (Wright 1992)

These findings were considerably amplified in "Anton LaVey: Legend and Reality," a 9-page "fact sheet" compiled a little more than three months after LaVey's passing by his estranged daughter Zeena LaVey Schreck and her husband Nikolas Schreck (1998). In addition to repeating the points made by Wright, the fact sheet dismissed most of Anton LaVey's other claims, such as his claims to have had a Gypsy grandmother, seen films of secret German rituals, purchased the "Black House" (it was given to him by his parents, who had lived there, and had never been a brothel), appeared in "Rosemary's Baby," had affairs with Monroe and Mansfield, and so forth.

The current leadership of the Church of Satan has disputed some of these challenges to LaVey's official biography. Their strategy has been to vigorously dispute undocumented challenges while ignoring LaVey's documented fabrications. As one might anticipate, splinter groups from CoS as well as other independent Satanists have seized upon these revelations to challenge the Church leadership's implicit claims to be the only authentic Satanist religious body.

Thinly disguised claims to exclusive legitimacy are peppered throughout CoS documents, such as in some of Blanche Barton's remarks in her "Sycophants Unite!" essay (composed prior to LaVey's death) posted on the CoS official website:

> We're lucky to have a leader like Anton LaVey. He has ensured that his philosophy will not die with him; it has been and will continue to be codified, expanded and applied in new areas *by his organization*. (emphasis in original)

The scope and significance of this dispute is reflected in the *many* attacks on non-CoS Satanists found on the Church of Satan website, particularly in the "Satanic Bunco Sheet," "Sycophants Unite!," "The Myth of the 'Satanic Community,'" "Pretenders to the Throne," and "Recognizing Pseudo-Satanists." Even a superficial perusal of these documents makes it clear that CoS is *obsessed* with shoring up its own legitimacy by attacking the heretics, especially those who criticize LaVey. For example, the unnamed author of the "Satanic Bunco Sheet" blasts non-CoS Satanists for "LaVey-baiting," and then goes on to assert that such pseudo-Satanists deal with LaVey and the Church of Satan by playing "the Christian game of handing out laurels with one hand while stabbing their progenitor in the back with the other. ...they must somehow convince you that the author of *The Satanic Bible* wasn't practicing pure Satanism [and] that his Church has gone awry in the hands of his successors...."

The Church of Satan began generating splinter groups as early as 1973 when the Church of Satanic Brotherhood was formed by group leaders in Michigan, Ohio, and Florida. This Church lasted only until 1974, when one of the founders announced his conversion to Christianity in a dramatic incident staged for the press in St. Petersburg. Other members of the Church of Satan in Kentucky and Indiana left to form the Ordo Templi Satanis, also short lived. As more schisms occurred, LaVey decided to disband the remaining grottos, the local units of the Church of Satan, which left the Church as little more than a paper organization generating a meager income for LaVey through sales of memberships. There are many presently-existing groups which derive directly or indirectly from the Church of Satan, the most important of which is the Temple of Set. The conflict (mostly on the internet) between the original Church of Satan and new Satanist groups accelerated after LaVey's death.

In addition to attacking non-CoS Satanists as illegitimate, LaVey's organizational successors have also sought to legitimate their positions by appealing to the authority of LaVey and his writings. These kinds of appeals are rather ironic, given the Black Pope's rejection of traditional religious authority. As indicated earlier, LaVey himself did not attempt to legitimate his new religion with appeals to tradition or to the supernatural. Rather, he grounded Satanism's legitimacy on a view of human nature shaped by a secularist appropriation of modern science.

Genesis of *The Satanic Bible*

The most significant single document for the Satanic "tradition" is *The Satanic Bible*. The idea for this volume came not from LaVey, but from an Avon Books editor named Peter Mayer. As a direct result of the success of the popular film "Rosemary's Baby" and the subsequent increase of popular interest in Satanism and the occult, Mayer decided that "the time was right for a 'Satanic bible'" and he approached LaVey about authoring it. (Aquino 1999, p. 52)

LaVey and his wife took the material they had on hand, wove it together and expanded on these writings to form what became the core of *The Satanic Bible*. This pre-existing material consisted of:

* A short, mimeographed paper that they had been distributing as an "introduction to Satanism."

* The so-called "rainbow sheets," which were "an assortment of polemical essays" the LaVeys had been mimeographing on colored paper. (Ibid., p. 52)

* A handout describing and containing instructions for the conduct of ritual magic.

The LaVeys then ran into a problem, which was that, even after expanding upon all of their available material, they were still *substantially* short of having a manuscript of sufficient length to satisfy their publisher. So, either because the deadline was coming up quickly or because LaVey just didn't want to write anything else at the time (Aquino describes their situation in terms of the former), LaVey tacked materials written by other authors onto the beginning and end of his manuscript.

Without acknowledging his sources, he took sections of "an obscure, turn-of-the-century political tract," *Might is Right* by New Zealander Arthur Desmond (writing under the pseudonym Ragnar Redbeard), added in a few sentences of his own, and incorporated it as a prologue. He also added the Enochian Keys ("a series of Elizabethan magical incantations") as they had been modified by Aleister Crowley, and "further altered them by replacing their Heavenly references with diabolical ones." Traditional occultists immediately recognized LaVey's source for the Keys, but it was not until 1987 that the source of LaVey's prologue was discovered. (Ibid., p. 65)

It should also be mentioned that, in circles critical of CoS, one often comes across the accusation that LaVey's "Nine Satanic Statements," one of the Church's central doctrinal statements, is an unacknowledged "paraphrase...of passages from Ayn Rand's *Atlas Shrugged*" (Schreck and Schreck 1998), specifically a paraphrase of the character John Galt's lengthy speech in the latter part of Rand's novel. However, when one actually examines these parallels (which are conveniently laid out in Appendix 11 of Aquino's *The Church of Satan*), one finds that this is a caricature of LaVey's indebtedness to Rand. For example, the first Satanic Statement is:

Satan represents indulgence, instead of abstinence!

The Rand passage presented as the source of this statement is:

A doctrine that gives you, as an ideal, the role of a sacrificial animal seeking slaughter on the altars of others, is giving you death as your standard. By the grace of reality and the nature of life, man—every man—is an end in himself. He exists for his own sake, and the achievement of his own happiness is his highest moral purpose.

This passage is rather more lengthy than LaVey's supposed "paraphrase." The second Satanic Statement is as brief as the first Statement:

Satan represents vital existence, instead of spiritual pipe dreams!

The Rand passage said to correspond with this Statement, though shorter than the first, is similarly distant in style and content from LaVey:

My morality, the morality of reason, is contained in a single axiom: existence exists—and in a single choice: to live. The rest proceeds from these.

And there is a similar disparity in the other "parallels" between the Satanic Statements and Rand. Thus, even if it is true that LaVey was looking at *Atlas Shrugged* when he composed the Nine Satanic Statements, it would be more proper to say that he was *inspired* by Rand rather than to assert that he *paraphrased* her work.

I should finally note in this regard that the title of the appendix (which originally appeared as an article by George C. Smith in 1987) in which the LaVey/Rand connection is delineated, "The Hidden Source of the Satanic Philosophy," similarly implies that Rand's philosophy was the *un*acknowledged core of LaVey's thought. This is, however, incorrect; LaVey himself explicitly acknowledged that his religion was "just Ayn Rand's philosophy with ceremony and ritual added" (cited in Ellis, p. 180). (Refer also to the "Satanism and Objectivism" essay on the Church of Satan website where this connection is examined at length.)

Despite the book's diverse source material and piecemeal assembly, it nevertheless coheres as a succinct—and, apparently, quite attractive—statement of Satanic thought and practice. As Aquino observes, "the *Satanic Bible* was somehow 'more than the sum of its parts.' Its argument was an argument of common sense, assembled in part from pre-existing concepts, but the excellence of the book lay in its integration of these into a code of life meaningful to the average individual—not just to occultists and/or academic-level philosophers." (Aquino 1999, p. 52)

One measure of *The Satanic Bible*'s appeal is that it has continuously been in print since it first appeared in 1970, and has been translated into a number of other languages. I have been unable to obtain recent figures, but in his 1991 book, *In Pursuit of Satan*, Robert Hicks mentions a sales figure of 618,000 copies (p. 351). There were also a number of illegal foreign language editions. These include a Spanish translation published in Mexico in the 70s, a Danish translation in the 80s, and a Russian translation in the late 90s. Legal editions include Czech and Swedish translations in the mid 90s and a 1999 German edition. The French translation has been completed but not yet printed. Also, the rights for a Greek translation were purchased, but the book does not seem to have appeared.[4]

The Role of *The Satanic Bible* in Modern Satanism

Although religious Satanism is interesting, academics have almost entirely ignored it. (The relevant academic literature consists of a handful of articles–e.g., Alfred 1976; Harvey 1995–and passing mentions in studies of the ritual abuse scare.) The principal reason for the lack of attention appears to be that Satanism is perceived as a trivial phenomenon rather than as a serious religion. The tendency seems to be to regard Satanists as immature adolescents who have adopted a diabolical veneer as a way of acting out their rebellion against parents and society. Does the phenomenon of adolescent rebellion, however, exhaust the significance of religious Satanism? Are most Satanists, in other words, just angry teenagers who adopt diabolical trappings to express their alienation, only to renounce the Prince of Darkness as soon as they mature into adults? While many youthful Satanists undoubtedly fit this profile, I came to feel that this was, at best, only a partial picture. Instead, I reasoned, there must be a core of committed Satanists who–for whatever reasons they initially become involved–had come to appropriate Satanism as something more than adolescent rebellion.

In order to test this hypothesis–and also because so little had been written on contemporary Satanism–I decided to collect some basic demographic data. To this end, I constructed a simple questionnaire that could be answered in 5 or 10 minutes. I began sending out questionnaires in early August 2000. By the end of February 2001 I had received 140 responses, which I felt was adequate to use as the basis for constructing a preliminary profile.[5]

When I sought feedback on preliminary write-ups of my findings from informants, a few voiced objections to the central role I assigned LaVey and his best-known work, *The Satanic Bible,* in the formation of modern Satanic religion. I was, furthermore, encouraged to shift my emphasis to the work of earlier literary figures ultimately responsible for fashioning the positive image of the Devil that LaVey later adopted for his Church of Satan. My survey findings, however, consistently indicated the centrality of LaVey to modern Satanism. This finding was a surprise, as I had initially assumed that contemporary Satanism had moved well beyond LaVey. I was thus led to conclude that–despite his dependence on prior thinkers–LaVey was directly responsible for the genesis of Satanism as a serious religious (as opposed to a purely literary) movement. Furthermore, however one might criticize and depreciate it, *The Satanic Bible* is still the single most influential document shaping the contemporary Satanic movement. As one of my informants noted, "I do not think Satanists can get away from LaVey, although some seem to take a real issue with him or try to downplay his importance. He wrote the book that codified Satanism into a religion, and for that he should be considered the central figure of the religion."

I do not intend to review all of my survey findings here (they are the subject of Lewis 2001), but I do want to note that I was startled to find that the average respondent had been a Satanist for seven to eight years. I also found that over two-thirds of the sample had been involved in at least one other religion beyond the tradition in which they were raised–usually Neopaganism or some other magical group. Both of these statistics indicate a level of seriousness I had not anticipated.

Because most respondents became involved during their teens, I inferred that many had initially become Satanists as an expression of teenage rebelliousness. It was clear, however, that their involvement did not end after they left home. Rather, they went on to appropriate Satanism as a serious religious option. The fact that the great majority of Satanists have looked into other religions shows that this was not an unconsidered choice, undertaken solely as a reaction against established religions. Also, though a reaction against Christianity may well have been a factor for some, too many respondents indicated that their religious upbringing was superficial, nominal or non-existent for this factor to explain why most people become Satanists.

Before I began collecting questionnaire data, I had received the impression from perusing the internet that contemporary Satanism had developed in different directions from the specific formulation developed by Anton LaVey in the 1960's. In particular, at the time it appeared to me that many contemporary Satanists had moved to a position of regarding Satan as a conscious being. I was thus surprised to discover that LaVey's humanistic approach–which rejects the real existence of personal spiritual beings, diabolical or otherwise–was the dominant form of Satanism professed by respondents.

At least part of the reason for this state of affairs appears to be the pervasive influence of Anton LaVey's *Satanic Bible*. A full 20% of respondents explicitly noted *The Satanic Bible* as the single most important factor attracting them to Satanism. For instance, in response to a questionnaire item asking how they became involved, a number of people simply wrote, "I read the *Satanic Bible*." It is also likely that this book played a major role in the "conversion" of other Satanists in my sample. One respondent elaborated by noting that she had been a Satanist in her "heart first, but I couldn't put a name to it; then I found the *The Satanic Bible*."

Similar stories attributing their infernal "conversions" to *The Satanic Bible* can be found in other sources. The popular book *Lucifer Rising*, for instance, recounts the story of how Martin Lamers, founder of the CoS-affiliated Kerk van Satan (Holland), was initially inspired by his discovery of LaVey's volume. (Baddeley 1999, p. 104) However, not everyone who is converted to Satanism via *The Satanic Bible* feels prompted to join the Church of Satan. *Lucifer Rising* also notes that "the Church of Satanic Liberation was established in January 1986 after its founder, Paul Douglas Valentine, was inspired by reading *The Satanic Bible*." (p. 153) Other stories of conversions directly inspired by *The Satanic Bible* can be found in Michael Aquino's *The Church of Satan* (e.g., the conversion of Robert DeCecco, who would later become a Master of the Temple, p. 69; and Lilith Sinclair, who would eventually become a Priestess and Aquino's wife, p. 82).

To return to the survey, LaVey's influential publication was also referred to a number of times in response to other questionnaire items. For example, one person noted that, "because I agree with and practice the majority of the beliefs set forth in *The Satanic Bible* and other works of Dr. LaVey, I VERY MUCH consider myself just as valid a Satanist as any 'official' priest." Another respondent wrote, "Satan is merely a word, a representative concept that encompasses all that the *Satanic Bible* teaches." And yet another individual stated: "To me, Satan is the personification of mankind's carnal nature. More information can be found in *The Satanic Bible* by Anton Szandor LaVey."

My strong impression was that *The Satanic Bible* was a doctrinal touchstone for most participants in this movement, despite the fact that the great majority of my sample were not formal members of Anton LaVey's Church of Satan. (One respondent, noting that he was not a member of any organization, wrote, "[It's] just me and my *Satanic Bible*.") And whatever LaVey had in mind when he (or his publisher) entitled this publication, in certain ways *The Satanic Bible* has truly come to play the role of a "bible" for many members of this decentralized, anti-authoritarian subculture.

In a follow-up questionnaire, respondents were explicitly asked how they regarded *The Satanic Bible*, and to what extent their personal philosophies aligned with the ideas expressed in its pages. Most stated that their view of the world aligned significantly with *The Satanic Bible*. One Satanist said that *The Satanic Bible* was about the realities of human nature, so that there was "nothing [in *The Satanic Bible*] that I didn't already know or believe myself prior to reading it." Only one respondent completely rejected the LaVeyan tradition. Two respondents asserted that they regarded *The Satanic Bible* as just another "self-help book." Some respondents diminished (without disparaging) *The Satanic Bible* as an "introductory text" or "primer" of Satanism. Most hastened to add that they did not regard it as "dogma."

One can acquire a sense of how *The Satanic Bible* is regarded as a doctrinal touchstone by perusing the official website of the Church of Satan (http://www.churchofsatan.com). For example, the "Satanism FAQ" section of the "Church of Satan Information Pack" states that "critically reading *The Satanic Bible* by Anton Szandor LaVey is tantamount to understanding at least the basics of Satanism." Similarly, the Church's "Church of Satan Youth Communique" asserts that "LaVey wrote *The Satanic Bible* so that people could pick up a copy, read it, and know everything they need to know about Satanism and how to put it to work in their own lives."

In addition to these general assertions, one can find other essays on the Church of Satan (CoS) website in which authoritative tenets are cited from *The Satanic Bible*, as when the "Satanic Bunco

Sheet" notes that "*The Satanic Bible* advises to 'question all things'...." or when, in an essay entitled "Satanism Needs an Enema!", an individual writing under the pseudonym Nemo introduces a series of citations from *The Satanic Bible* to support a point he is arguing with the words, "Other quotes from LaVey's own pen in *The Satanic Bible* reiterate this theme." The clear implication of this statement is that because these quotations come from "LaVey's own pen in *The Satanic Bible*," they are authoritative; thus, there can be no further discussion of the issue. Toward the end of the same essay, Nemo also asserts that,

> We have a bible. We have a *pro-human* dogma. We have a church. We have a tradition. We have ceremonies and rituals. We have a High Priestess.

In other words, with respect to the theme I am pursuing here, Nemo is asserting that CoS has an authoritative scripture, dogma and tradition which support his argument. And it is obvious that Nemo regards his appeal to CoS *tradition* as stronger than direct appeals to science or common sense, which were the touchstones of LaVey's philosophy.

Finally, I found it interesting that one of the accusations leveled against non-CoS Satanists in Nemo's "Recognizing Pseudo-Satanism" essay was that in such groups, "The words of *The Satanic Bible* become twisted and distorted until they no longer have useful meaning!" Furthermore, in his "Satanism Needs an Enema!" essay, the same writer exclaims,

> I am calling for a closing of the ranks and a throwing out of the heretics. I am asking for the Purge! I am asking for a *reverse* Inquisition.

Both of these sets of passages–the first quoting *The Satanic Bible* to make a point and the second accusing heretical breakaways of warping *The Satanic Bible's* meaning (even going so far as to call for an "Inquisition" against heretics within the ranks!)–exemplify all-too-familiar patterns found in the theological conflicts of traditional religions like Christianity.

Quoting *The Satanic Bible* to legitimate a point of argument is not, however, confined to representatives of the Church of Satan. The so called "Xloptuny Curse" is an interesting example of how some of the "heretics" have turned the message of LaVey's writings to their own purposes. A short essay on "The Xloptuny Curse," written by Joe Necchi, was posted on the official website of the First Church of Satan in the summer of 2000. (The First Church of Satan–FCoS–is a newer Satanist organization founded by a former member of CoS whose brand of Satanism is very close to *The Satanic Bible*.) The text discusses the circumstances of a seemingly effective suicide curse that was leveled by Lord Egan, founder/leader of the FCoS, against Xloptuny (John C. Davis), an internet pugilist and member of the CoS. Less than a year before Davis blew his brains out, Egan had cursed Davis, specifying in a public, online communication that he would die by shooting himself.

The passage I would like to focus on for my present purposes is where Necchi remarks,

> What is interesting, however, is the way in which some have predictably tried to rationalize Xloptuny's suicide as a Yukio Mishima-inspired act of heroism. Ironically, those trying so hard

to canonize Mr. Davis thusly now have decided to conveniently ignore the book they are always waving about like a black flag at most other times: *The Satanic Bible*. In this sense, we see that many Satanists really behave exactly like Christians: they follow the precepts of their religion when it's easy to do so, when it suits them, but are quick to abandon them when it really counts.

Page 94 of *The Satanic Bible* specifically states: "Self-sacrifice is not encouraged by the Satanic religion. Therefore, unless death comes as an indulgence because of extreme circumstances which make the termination of life a welcome relief from an unendurable earthly existence, suicide is frowned upon by the Satanic religion." There is little ambiguity in this passage. As there is no reason to believe that Xloptuny was in "extreme circumstances which make the termination of life a welcome relief"; he died as a traitor to the Church whose cause he so often trumpeted, the defense of which he used as a rationale for his often black and bilious attacks on his enemies. Apparently "the great Dr. Anton LaVey's" words meant little or nothing to John C. Davis when he arrived at the moment of truth.

Here again we see *The Satanic Bible* being quoted as an authoritative document in a manner similar to the way sacred texts are quoted in comparable conflicts within other religious traditions. In other words, "The Xloptuny Curse" is yet another example of how *The Satanic Bible* functions as a quasi-scripture within the Satanic community.

Almost all Satanists would deny that *The Satanic Bible* is an "inspired" document in anything like the sense in which the Christian Bible is regarded as an inspired book. Interestingly, however, there are a few individuals–most notably Michael Aquino, a former CoS leader and founder of the Temple of Set–who *would* regard this book as inspired. For example, in the relevant chapter in his history of the Church of Satan, Aquino asserts that:

> The *Satanic Bible* [clothes] itself in the supernatural authority of the Prince of Darkness and his demons. Less this element, the *Satanic Bible* would be merely a social tract by Anton LaVey–not High Priest of Satan, but just one more 1960s'-counterculture-cynic atop a soapbox.
>
> The substance of the *Satanic Bible* therefore turns upon Anton LaVey's sincerity in believing himself to be the vehicle through which the entity known as Satan explains the mysteries of mankind's existential predicament. To the extent that he did, the *Satanic Bible* deserves the dignity of its title. ...
>
> Despite the haphazard nature of its assembly, ... we may therefore consider the *Satanic Bible* in its totality not as argumentative, but as inspired writing. Thus it assumes an importance by its very **existence**, not just by its content. (Aquino 1999, p. 53)

Although Aquino's position would be rejected by most other professing Satanists, something approaching this position seems to be unconsciously informing their attitude toward *The Satanic Bible*.

Conclusion

Anton LaVey's primary legitimation strategy was to appeal to the authority of science, specifically to the secularist world view derived from natural science and to an animalistic image of the human being derived from the Darwinian theory of evolution. In light of his radically secularist legitimation strategy, it is ironic that his organizational successors have subsequently attempted to legitimate their positions by appealing to LaVey as if he had actually been some kind of "Black Pope," and to *The Satanic Bible* as if it was truly a diabolically-revealed scripture. It seems that being raised in a religious tradition that locates the source of authority in religious figures and sacred texts creates an unconscious predisposition that can be carried over to other kinds of persons and books–even in the unlikely context of contemporary Satanism.

Outside the institutional bounds of the Church of Satan, modern Satanism became a loose, decentralized movement that coheres as a distinct religious community largely by virtue of participants' adherence to certain themes in the published words of Anton LaVey, particularly in *The Satanic Bible*. Despite this volume's patchwork quality and haphazard genesis, it came to play an authoritative, quasi-scriptural role within the larger Satanic movement. Unlike members of the Church of Satan, however, non-CoS Satanists felt free to criticize and even to reject aspects of the LaVeyan tradition by appealing to the authority of rationality—a criterion of legitimacy LaVey himself put forward as the very basis of Satanism. And in terms of this criterion, non-CoS Satanism is thus closer to the spirit of LaVey's philosophy than the contemporary Church of Satan.

Notes:

1. A special word of thanks to Satanists who provided me with thoughtful feedback on earlier drafts of this paper, particularly feedback from several members of the Obsidian Enlightenment and the Temple of Lylyth. One comment of particular note was that the social organization (or, perhaps more appropriately, *dis*organization) of modern Satanism cannot accurately be characterized as a "movement," "community" or "subculture." I have nevertheless used these terms throughout for lack of more adequate terminology. Another comment was that "conversion" is not appropriate in the context of Satanism. Again, however, I left this term in the article for lack of a better word. Finally, I was informed that Satanists prefer to refer to their community as the *Satanic* community (movement, subculture, etc.) rather than the *Satanist* community; I have tried to adhere to this convention throughout the present article.

2. "New Religious Movements...articulate themselves, often with a popular fluency, in the discourses of the natural sciences and seek to justify their beliefs by means of para- or pseudoscientific investigation or argument." (Sentes and Palmer 2000)

3. Although the Raelian Movement is very different from Satanism, this particular UFO religion similarly appeals to the world view of secular science for its legitimacy and, like Satanism, attacks other religions as unreasonable because of their lack of a scientific basis. (Chryssides 2000; Sentes and Palmer 2000)

4. Information on foreign language editions courtesy Peter H. Gilmore, High Priest of the Church of Satan.

5. 110 (almost 80%) of my respondents were North American. Because European Satanism is a somewhat different phenomenon, one should be therefore be cautious about making inferences to European Satanism based on my survey findings.

Bibliography:

Aquino, Michael A. The Church of Satan. 4th ed. Self-published, 1999.

Baddeley, Gavin. *Lucifer Rising: Sin, Devil Worship and Rock'n'Roll.* London: Plexus, 1999.

Barton, Blanche. *The Secret Life of a Satanist: The Authorized Biography of Anton LaVey.* Los Angeles, CA: Feral House, 1990.

Chryssides, George D. "Is God a Space Alien? The Cosmology of the Raelian Church." *Culture and Cosmos* 4:1 Spring/Summer 2000.

----------------. "Sycophants Unite!" http://www.churchofsatan.com/home.html

"The Church of Satan Information Pack" http://www.churchofsatan.com/Pages/cosinfopack.pdf

"Church of Satan Youth Communique" http://www.churchofsatan.com/home.html

Ellis, Bill. *Raising the Devil: Satanism, New Religions, and the Media.* Lexington, KY: The University Press of Kentucky, 2000.

Flowers, Stephen E., *Lords of the Left Hand Path.* Smithville, Texas: Runa-Raven Press, 1997.

Holmes, Ernest. *The Science of Mind.* New York: Dodd, Mead, and Company, [1926]1944.

LaVey, Anton Szandor. *The Satanic Bible.* New York: Avon, 1969

Lewis, James R. "Who Serves Satan? A Demographic and Ideological Profile." *Marburg Journal of Religious Studies* 6:2. 2001.

Moody, Edward J. "Magical Therapy: An Anthropological Investigation of Contemporary Satanism." In Irving I. Zaretsky and Mark P. Leone, eds. *Religious Movements in Contemporary America.* Princeton, NJ: Princeton University Press, 1974.

Moynihan, Michael and Didrik Soderlind. *Lords of Chaos: The Bloody Rise of the Satanic Metal Underground.* Venice, CA: Feral House, 1998.

Necchi, Joe. "The Xloptuny Curse." http://www.churchof satan.org/xloptuny.html.

Nemo. "Recognizing Pseudo-Satanism" http://www.churchofsatan.com/home.html

-------------. "Satanism and Objectivism." http://www.churchofsatan.com/Pages/SatObj.html

-------------. "Satanism Needs an Enema!" http://www.churchofsatan.com/home.html

Petersen, Jesper Aagard. "Binary Satanism: Being Dark and Secretive in a Prismatic Digital World." Unpublished paper.

Rand, Ayn. *Atlas Shrugged.* New York: Random House, 1957.

Redbeard, Ragnar. *Might is Right; or, The Survival of the Fittest.* London: W.J. Robbins, 5th ed.1910. [Rpt. of 1896]

Richardson, James, Joel Best and David G. Bromley. *The Satanism Scare.* NY: Aldine de Gruyter, 1991.

"Satanic Bunco Sheet." http://www.churchofsatan.com/home.html

Schreck, Zeena, and Nikolas Schreck. "Anton LaVey: Legend and Reality." 1998. http://www.churchofsatan.org/aslv.html

Sentes, Bryan, and Susan Palmer. "Presumed Immanent: the Raelians, UFO Religions, and the Postmodern Condition." *Novo Religio*

Smith, George C. "The Hidden Source of the Satanic Philosophy." Originally published in *The Scroll of Set,* June 1987. Reprinted as Appendix 11 in Aquino 1999.

Trull, D. "Fortean Slips: Death of a Devil's Advocate."

Weber, Max. *Basic Concepts in Sociology.* H. P. Secher (trans). New York: Philosophical Library, 1962.

Wolfe, Burton H. *The Devil's Avenger: A Biography of Anton Szandor LaVey.* New York: Pyramid Books, 1974.

Wright, Lawrence. "Sympathy for the Devil." *Rolling Stone* September 5, 1991.

The Satanic Bible and the "Satanic Panic"

He leafed through a copy of Anton LaVey's *Satanic Bible*. It was in paperback and came highly recommended.... If what this book said was true, if what this book promised could be realized, then nothing was impossible.... The devil had the answers for life on earth. The devil was the one to contact, the one who would do things for human beings who wanted to achieve. (St. Clair 1987, pp. 50-51)

Say You Love Satan is a "true crimes" potboiler about Ricky Kasso, a troubled teenager who stabbed another teen to death in 1984. In common with other books in this genre, the author creates a lively narrative by embellishing the facts. The above excerpt, however, describes thoughts Kasso simply could not have had; *The Satanic Bible* says absolutely nothing about the power of a literal Prince of Darkness. Instead, LaVey's "bible" advocates a thoroughgoing atheism. For LaVey as for most other religious Satanists, the Devil is merely a symbol of the human being's "true" animal self.

Mistakenly reading traditional folklore about Satan into *The Satanic Bible* became quite common during the Ritual Abuse scare of the Eighties and Nineties. Earlier Christian critics, such as Morris Cerullo in his *The Back Side of Satan*, had presented LaVey's ideas reasonably accurately. But the hysteria of the Satanic Ritual Abuse scare changed all the rules. By the time Carl Raschke's *Painted Black* appeared in 1990, even an academically-trained observer like Raschke was not above quoting *The Satanic Bible* out of context:

In his *Satanic Bible*...LaVey himself offers justification, if not with specific intention, for homicide. The "blood of the freshly slaughtered victim" in the satanic sacrifice, he says, serves to "throw the energy" into an "atmosphere of the magical working." The power of the magician is thus increased. (Raschke 1990, p. 117)

Raschke then goes on to observe that the "same idea...was fundamental" to the individuals directing the Matamoros murders, implying that LaVey and Matamoros group were operating within the same ideological framework. Disingenuously, Raschke neglects to mention that, in the very passage he is quoting from *The Satanic Bible*, LaVey is *not* discussing "satanic sacrifice." Rather, LaVey is describing ritual blood sacrifice *in order to mock it*. On the page immediately following the one selectively cited by Raschke, LaVey goes on to assert that,

The inhibitive and asinine absurdity in the need to kill an innocent living creature at the high-point of a ritual, as practiced by erstwhile "wizards," is obviously their "lesser of the evils" when a discharge of energy is called for. These poor conscience-stricken fools, who have been calling themselves witches and warlocks, would sooner chop the head off a goat or chicken in an attempt to harness its death agony, than have the "blasphemous" bravery to masturbate in full view of the Jehovah whom they claim to deny! ... ONE GOOD ORGASM WOULD PROBABLY KILL THEM! (LaVey 1969, p. 88)

However, Raschke does more than quote LaVey out of context. In other sections of *Painted Black*, he discusses an interview with "Eddie," the pseudonym of a young shopping mall clerk who was somehow able to convince Raschke that he was a sinister Satanic cultist. Among other interesting items of information, Eddie informed the gullible investigator that LaVey was the "head of the satanic movement"—implying that, in addition to being head of the Church of Satan, LaVey was also the leader of a much vaster Satanic underground.

Later in the same book, Raschke exhibits similar credulity when he asks, in a flourish of overheated rhetoric,

Did LaVey create the "new establishment"? With his own furry and clawed hands did he perform confirmation ceremonies for tomorrow's streetside child molesters, cannibals, and heavy-metal mental perverts? A young man...who had been raised since a tender age as an acolyte in the local parish of the Church of Satan before turning to Christianity, said with a straight face, "LaVey knows all, sees all. You can't do anything in the religion without LaVey's authority." (Raschke 1990, p 218)

That a serious writer could repeat such claims "with a straight face" is rather shocking. Raschke is obviously grasping at straws.

There is, however, a very good reason why self-appointed crusaders against the Dark Forces feel compelled to portray Anton LaVey and *The Satanic Bible* as the epicenter of an international Satanic conspiracy—namely, there is no tangible evidence of a grand conspiracy of Satanic cults plotting to take over the world. Thus, despite the fact that LaVey is completely inadequate for the job, he is one of the few readily available anchors for paranoid fantasies about a sinister Satanic underground. As a consequence, LaVey and *The Satanic Bible* are mentioned over and over again by modern witch hunters—though often, as illustrated in the above examples, notions are attributed to him and to his writings that have no relationship with empirical reality.

The notion of an international Satanist conspiracy became prominent during the Satanic Ritual Abuse scare. This scare—often referred to as the "Satanic Panic"—peaked in the late 1980s and early 1990s. During these years, significant segments of the law enforcement community and numerous therapists believed in the existence of a vast, underground network of evil Satanic cults sacrificing and abusing children. Less responsible members of the mass media avidly promoted the idea as an easy way of selling copy and increasing ratings.

The claims of Ritual Abuse advocates were so wildly sensationalistic that it was unnecessary to exaggerate them for mass media consumption. By the peak of the panic in 1992, Evangelical authors Bob and Gretchen Passantino's summary of these claims read like promotional copy for a new horror movie:

A young teenage girl, impregnated during a satanic ritual, is forcibly delivered of her nearly term baby, forced to ritually kill the child and then to cannibalize its heart as cult members watch. Another girl, a small child, is sealed inside the cavity of a disemboweled animal and "rebirthed" by her cultic captors during a ceremony. A preschool class is systematically sexually, emotionally, and physically abused by part of a nationwide, nearly invincible network of satanic pedophiles and pornographers. A young girl is thrown into an electrified cage with wolves and ritually tortured to deliberately produce a "wolf personality," part of her multiple personality disorder. (Passantino and Passantino 1992)

The scare began a sharp decline after 1992. By the mid-nineties professional and public opinion had shifted, and soon the real existence of Satanic Ritual Abuse had been rejected by almost everyone except certain groups of conservative Christians.

What happened? What factors conspired to make these intrinsically implausible claims plausible to the public and to large numbers of otherwise responsible professionals during the Panic?

Because the basic notions underlying Satanic Ritual Abuse derive from Christianity, many analysts have pinned the blame for the Satanic Panic on conservative Christians. Thus a 1989 report, *Satanism in America*, conducted under the auspices of the ultra-secularist Committee for the Scientific Examination of Religion, concluded, in part, that:

It is now abundantly clear that a small minority of ultra-right-wing fundamentalist and evangelicals, believing in both the reality of Satan as a personality and that the Tribulation is at hand, are responsible for the misinterpretation, the dissemination and in some instances the outright fabrication of "facts" to support what is essentially a religious doctrine. These people are not researchers in pursuit of truth, but crusaders against the Antichrist whom they believe a priori is living now among us. We submit that people so deeply committed to this religious view can hardly be counted upon to render skeptical and well-reasoned critiques about the dangers of Satanism or occultism in American society. (Carlson et al. 1989)

Though partially accurate, the authors of this report ignore the important roles that a number of other factors and parties played in the creation, promotion and dissemination of Ritual Abuse ideology.

The folklore that provided the foundation for the Satanic Panic dates back to the Middle Ages. During this period, it was generally believed that a vast, secret network of Devil-worshipers existed who periodically gathered together to celebrate the Black Mass—a blasphemous parody of the Catholic Mass thought to be the central rite of Satanism. In the Catholic Church, a "Black Mass" is a requiem mass at which the priest is dressed in black vestments. As commonly used, however, this expression refers to a rite that was traditionally thought to be the central ritual of Satanism. However, like Satanism more generally, it is unlikely that such rituals were anything more than literary inventions of Church authorities. Though there was much variability in the details of traditional folklore, Anton LaVey's account of the Black Mass in *The Satanic Bible* is a generally accurate description of this Medieval fantasy:

> The popular concept of the black mass is thus: a defrocked priest stands before an altar consisting of a nude woman, her legs spread-eagled and vagina thrust open, each of her outstretched fists grasping a black candle made from the fat of unbaptized babies, and a chalice containing the urine of a prostitute (or blood) reposing on her belly. An inverted cross hangs above the altar, and triangular hosts of ergot-laden bread or black-stained turnip are methodically blessed as the priest dutifully slips them in and out of the altar-lady's labia. Then, we are told, an invocation to Satan and various demons is followed by an array of prayers and psalms chanted backwards or interspersed with obscenities . . . all performed within the confines of a "protective" pentagram drawn on the floor. If the Devil appears he is invariably in the form of a rather eager man wearing the head of a black goat upon his shoulders. Then follows a potpourri of flagellation, prayer-book burning, cunnilingus, fellatio, and general hindquarters kissing—all done to a background of ribald recitations from the Holy Bible, and audible expectorations on the cross! If a baby can be slaughtered during the ritual, so much the better; for as everyone knows, this is the favorite sport of the Satanist! (LaVey 1969, p. 99)

As with other components of diabolical mythology, the belief in the real existence of Black Masses was widespread in the Middle Ages. LaVey, the founder of modern Satanism, drew on a few elements of this literary Satanism—such as black candles and the use of a naked woman for an altar—to create his own version of the Black Mass. However, unlike the imaginary Black Masses of Medieval folklore, LaVey was more concerned with using the Black Mass for psychodrama than for magic. He also noted that if the purpose of the original was to shock one's contemporaries by blaspheming what was holy, then a true modern Black Mass "would consist of the blaspheming of such 'sacred' topics as Eastern mysticism, psychiatry, the psychedelic movement, ultra-liberalism, etc." (all popular topics at the time LaVey founded the Church of Satan in the late Sixties).

The Black Sabbath described in such contemporary accounts as the one found in Evangelical author Rebecca Brown's *He Came to Set the Captives Free* incorporates two components central to the Medieval conception of Black Masses, namely the presence of the Devil and copulation between humans and demons:

> Satan appeared in human form as usual, dressed completely in shining white. But his eyes glowed red as a flame and he threw his head back and gave a howl and a scream and a hideous laugh of victory as the high priest drove a long spike through the man's head, pinning it to the cross, killing him. The crowd went crazy, screaming and shouting and dancing in crazed ecstasy at the "victory." They loudly proclaimed all victory and power and honor to their father Satan. Satan vanished shortly after that to go on to the next Black Sabbath sacrifice. At his departure the meeting turned into a sex orgy. Human with human, and demon with human. (Brown 1986)

Brown's book claimed to present a true account of the life of "Elaine," a former Satanic high priestess. Both the author, a conservative Christian medical doctor, and the pseudonymous Elaine were taken seriously enough to be featured on a Geraldo Rivera special in 1988.

Witches—who had become equated with Satanists by the late Middle Ages—were also thought to delight in the murder of children. Thus in a "confession" reproduced in the *Malleus Maleficarum*, a well-known 15th century witchhunter's manual, an accused witch is quoted as saying that,

> [W]ith our spells we kill them in their cradles or even when they are sleeping by their parents' side, in such a way that they afterwards are thought to have been overlain or to have died some other natural death. Then we secretly take them from their graves, and cook them in a cauldron, until the whole flesh comes away from the bones to make a soup which may easily be drunk. (Kramer Sprenger 1970 [1486])

Medieval churchmen believed that Witches—almost invariably women—slipped out of their homes at night and gathered at prearranged spots in forests, mountains, caves or some other remote area, often by flying, to celebrate Sabbats. These gatherings were originally referred to as "synagogues." Both terms reflect an association between Jews and the Devil in the minds of traditional Christians. Although the Witches' Sabbat was not originally the same as a Black Mass, these two infernal meetings were viewed similarly and eventually became interchangeable. The basic structure of the Sabbat is reflected in the forced confession of an elderly woman who asserted that she had been attending such meetings since she was sixteen:

> [W]omen came riding on sticks. The demon presided, in the form of a cat, whom they all adored. He taught them all manner of crimes and gave them an ointment, with which she had killed more than 100 men and infants; also a powder with which to raise tempests. They feasted on all sorts of dainties and then coupled, demons serving the women who had no men. Finally they flew away on their sticks. (Cited in Lea 1957)

There were numerous variations on this scenario. Satan himself was usually thought of as presiding over the assembly seated on a throne. In addition to adopting the form of the cat, he could also show up as a goat, crow, toad or even as a human being. Participants divested themselves of their clothing and kissed the Devil on his posterior—the origin of the familiar expression "brown nosing." The core of the meeting often involved the sacrifice of a human being. Babies were usually cooked and eaten. New witches signed a pact, renounced Christianity, trampled on a cross, and were marked by Satan's claw.

It is easy to perceive the parallels between these items of Medieval folklore and contemporary Satanic Ritual Abuse folklore. The parallels are obvious because the Satanic Panic witchhunters deliberately drew the details for their fantasies from traditional folklore about the Devil. For example, the Devil's Mark or Witch's Mark was a mark supposedly made by Satan on the bodies of his new initiates. According to different accounts, this was inscribed on the Devil's followers by the Prince of Darkness himself, who scratched them with his claw, branded them with an infernal hot iron, or licked them. This item of medieval superstition was resurrected and presented as fact in *Michelle Remembers*, the popular 1980 book credited with setting the Ritual Abuse scare in motion. In one ritual Michelle claimed to remember, Satan commanded that marks be made upon one of his initiates in doggerel verse:

Make marks on her body so all who see
Will know that she belongs to me.
The marks will heal but not the heart;
It's been forever torn apart. (Smith and Padzer 1980, p. 257)

Michelle Remembers also contained a number of pictures of Michelle's rashes, identified as marks made by the Prince of Darkness himself. One photo caption read:

Michelle experienced "body memories" of her ordeal. Whenever she relived the moments when Satan had his burning tail wrapped around her neck, a sharply defined rash appeared in the shape of the spade-like tip of his tail.

When I passed Michelle Smith's book around in a seminar at the University of Wisconsin, one of my students remarked that the rash in the photo "looked more like a hickey" than the tip of Satan's tail. Given the B-movie quality of the events described in *Michelle Remembers,* it is incredible that the book was ever taken seriously.

The resurrection of Medieval notions about diabolical conspiracies had actually begun somewhat earlier, during the counter-culture period of the Sixties. During that decade, traditional, conservative Christians became concerned about what they perceived as the breakdown of tradition and an accompanying rise of Satanism. Phenomena like the popular movie "Rosemary's Baby" and the formation of Anton LaVey's Church of Satan appeared to provide concrete evidence for the growth of the Prince of Darkness's earthly kingdom. Although LaVey was clear that Satan was no more than an iconoclastic symbol for a basically secular philosophy promoting self-seeking individualism, many Christians assumed that LaVey actually worshiped the fallen angel Lucifer.

Outside of institutional Christianity, Hollywood has been the most influential source of information about Satan and his minions. A threshold period for diabolically-inspired movies was the late Sixties through the mid-Seventies. Those years saw the release of three influential films that have been sometimes described as "Satanic Blockbusters"—*Rosemary's Baby* (1968), *The Exorcist* (1973) and *The Omen* (1976). During the same period, Hammer Studios also produced a number of relevant B-movies. These films uniformly featured a Satanic conspiracy, with the sole exception of *The Exorcist.*

Though modern religious Satanists such as LaVey disliked *The Exorcist,* they were positive about horror movies like *Rosemary's Baby* and *The Omen.* In an interview in Gavin Baddeley's *Lucifer Rising,* LaVey, who claimed to have been a technical advisor for the latter two films, claimed that *Rosemary's Baby* "did for Satanism what *Birth of a Nation* did for the Ku Klux Klan; our membership soared after its release."

What LaVey failed to realize, however, was that the pervasive horror movie theme of Satanic conspiracies—whether the Satanists ended up being portrayed negatively, positively, or some shade of gray—helped shape the Satanic conspiracy theories that became so influential during the Ritual

Abuse scare. As Andrew Tudor, the author of *Monsters and Mad Scientists*, observes, the period of the late Sixties and early Seventies "is dominated by a growing concern with Satanic cults and conspiracies." Similarly, Baddeley notes that the movies of the 1970s "established Satanic cultists as stock movie monsters." Thus while other factors set the scare in motion, it was Hollywood that plowed the ground of cultural awareness in which the seed of the Satanic Ritual Abuse idea was to take root and grow.

Another contributor to the stereotype of Satanic cults was the Manson Family, which had several tenuous connections with organized Satanism. By identifying Charlie Manson as a Satanist, Ritual Abuse believers were able to point to a "real" Satanic group involved in ritualistic murder.

Charles Willie Manson was the leader of a small group of people—the media later dubbed it the "Manson Family"—convicted of a series of highly-publicized murders committed in southern California in the late Sixties. The court determined that, though he did not kill anyone himself, his followers committed crimes at his behest. The Manson Family's most publicized murders occurred at actress Sharon Tate Polanski's home on August 9, 1969. These killings, the so-called Tate Homicides or Tate Murders, took the lives of five adults and Sharon Polanski's unborn child. The trial held the record for the longest running trial with a sequestered jury in California legal history until the O.J. Simpson trial.

Manson did not teach Satanism in any recognizable sense, and his group certainly was not a "Satanic cult." But there were enough direct and indirect connections between the Manson Family and Satanism to enable less careful observers to categorize the group as Satanic. The most prominent feature connecting Manson with Satanism was that his follows would sometimes refer to Manson as "Satan." However, at other times they would also call Manson "God." This dichotomy might have been due to Manson's brief participation in the Process Church of the Final Judgment, an unusual movement for which the reconciliation of good and evil was a central tenet.

Other connections were indirect. Prominent Family member Susan Atkins was associated with organized Satanism at a couple of points in her life. She was, for example, a topless dancer for a nightclub act, Witches' Workshop, organized by LaVey. She was also said to have been a member of the Temple of Set, a Church of Satan schism.

Even more indirect was that Sharon Tate Polanski's husband, Roman Polanski, directed *Rosemary's Baby* (1968)—the most prominent Devil-related horror movie of the sixties. The fact that it had been a box office hit the year before the murders fueled media commentary that brought together the film and the murders—despite the lack of any real link between them. LaVey's claim that he had personally appeared as Satan in the movie provided yet another thin connection.

The Manson Family's vague association with Satanism was revived in the eighties and nineties as part of the Satanic Panic. The Family was one of the few criminal groups that seemed to provide concrete evidence for the claim that "real" Satanic cults existed. Manson's priority of place would hold sway until the Matamoros murders. Although the Matamoros group did not worship the Devil either, it contained more elements that could be interpreted to fit the Satanic cult stereotype than the Manson Family.

In 1989, police discovered that a series of murders had been carried out by a Mexican drug-smuggling gang headquartered in Matamoros, Mexico, just across the border from Brownsville, Texas. Though many of the murders were directly related to the day-to-day violence of the drug-running business, some of the victims were killed in the belief that sacrificing them would provide the gang with magical protection. After the mutilated body of University of Texas student Mark Kilroy and bodies of members of rival gangs were found buried on the grounds of a Mexican ranch, the news media immediately proceeded to sensationalize the story by describing the drug ring as a Satanic cult.

A number of AP wires, for instance, bore such titles as "Satanic Cult People Questioned" and "Satanic Ring Member Arrested." A story in *Time* magazine referred to the group as a "voodoo-practicing cult of drug smugglers" whose rituals were intended to "win satanic protection." Many more examples of news reports in this vein could cited. Mexican authorities apparently courted Anglo-American reporters anxious to seize upon any titillating detail. Gary Cartwright, reporting for the *Texas Monthly*, noted that the comandante "made no attempt to seal off the crime scene. During almost any hour of the day journalists could be found stomping about the ranch...looking for something—anything—that no one else had found."

The twisted spiritual beliefs of the Matamoros group were based on Palo Mayombe, an Afro-Cuban religio-magical system frequently, though erroneously, equated with the better known Santeria. This necromantic sect utilizes human remains in its rites, but practitioners purchase such remains from medical supply houses or (in extreme cases) rob graves rather than murder living human beings. The Palo practices that formed the basis of the Matamoros group's magic rituals had been supplied by Adolfo Constanzo, a 26-year-old Cuban-American from Miami hired by a drug-smuggling family to provide them with supernatural aid. Before being hired by the Hernandez family, Constanzo had developed a reputation as being a sorcerer in Mexico City.

The Palo connection was especially clear from the characteristic cauldrons found at the Matamoros ranch. Reporters dwelled on the human remains in the cauldrons as indicating that the group practiced cannibalism, an assertion reflecting complete ignorance about Palo. Instead of going to the trouble of gathering accurate information, reporters instead drew their attribution of cannibalism from the popular fantasy about Satanic cults sacrificing and eating human beings.

The notion that human sacrifice could provide practitioners with magical power and protection was supplied by Sara Aldrete, one of the group's core followers. This young woman was repeatedly referred to as a "witch" or as Constanzo's "high priestess." Such labels had the net effect of shoring up otherwise dubious parallels between the Matamoros group and the Satanic cult stereotype. Aldrete had been an honor student at Texas Southmost College in Brownsville, where she studied the anthropology of religion. She had also become fascinated with the film *The Believers*, which features a Santeria-like cult composed of rich urbanites who sacrifice human beings to gain supernatural power. Members of Constanzo's group were shown the film over and over again to indoctrinate them into the necessity of committing ritual murder.

Building on news media stories about Matamoros, advocates of Satanic conspiracy theories immediately appropriated the murders as providing concrete evidence for the real existence of a secretive Satanic network plotting to take over the world—despite the fact that the only parallel between the Matamoros group and popular stereotypes of Satanism was human sacrifice. Blinded by their ideology, some diabolical conspiracy buffs even expressed surprise that certain components of the stereotype were missing. For example, one observer asserted that, "Where there's drugs involved, often you will find Satanism. What is odd is that the bodies were not cremated." This comment alludes to a familiar item of Satanic Ritual Abuse lore, namely that Satanists cremate the remains of sacrificed victims as a way of destroying evidence.

In an insightful analysis included as part of his ground-breaking book, *In Pursuit of Satan,* Robert Hicks laid out three reasons why the Matamoros incident appealed to what he called "cult cops":

First, the nine-month spree of murder included the abduction of innocents, a theme which figures significantly in some cult-seminar claims and also in rumors, urban legends, and subversion myths.

Second, cult cops cite Matamoros as indirect proof of the international satanic conspiracy, because the case proves that people like us, fairly well educated with middle-class upbringings, can form secret loyalties that involve murder.

Third, cult cops have taken Matamoros as *satanic* because the newspapers have used the term. If newspapers use it, and Texas Attorney General Mattox uses it as an opportunity to advise Texans against the Satanist forces who left behind the Matamoros bodies on their march to world subversion, then why should cult cops not reap the same rewards of frightened audiences? (Hicks 1990)

Prior to Matamoros, the closest groups to documentable homicidal cults were the Manson Family and Jim Jones's Peoples Temple. But there were problems with using these groups as examples of Satanic cults. Specifically, the Jones group was, even at the time of the mass suicide in Guyana, a member of the Disciples of Christ, a mainline Christian denomination. And the Manson Family, as I already noted, was not a Satanist group in any meaningful sense of the term. Thus while the Matamoros group did not actually worship the Devil, it contained more components than any previous group that could be interpreted to fit the Satanic cult stereotype—hence its immediate adoption as a primary example by believers in Satanic Ritual Abuse.

All of these factors contributed to the emergence of a significant anti-Satanist literature within the conservative Christian subculture. The first important book containing the confessions of an alleged ex-Satanist was Mike Warnke's 1972 *The Satan Seller,* which went on to sell millions of copies. Warnke claimed that he had been a Satanic high priest and that he had attended secret strategy meeting with, among others, Anton LaVey and Charles Manson. As noted by Evangelical authors Bob and Gretchen Passantino,

The *Satan Seller*'s two chief contributions to the development of Christian sensationalism concerning satanism were, first, widespread conspiracy theories; and, second, the incorporation of the earlier trend to use unsubstantiated personal experience stories as "proof" of one's assertions regarding the occult. (Passantino and Passantino 1992)

It is interesting to observe that the first edition of *The Satan Seller*, which was published well before the Satanic Panic of the eighties, failed to mention child abduction, child sacrifice, or child pornography rings—all of which would become central themes in the Satanic cult stereotype of the following decade. In fact, when the ritual abuse scare first broke, Warnke initially admitted on Christian television that he was unaware of child sacrifices. However, after this aspect of the Satanic conspiracy became dominant in the public's mind, he changed his tune and began to claim that "Devil cults" yearly sacrificed some two million children to the Prince of Darkness.

Though Warnke's book would eventually inspire many imitators, the threshold book for the Satanic Panic was *Michelle Remembers*. This work, purporting to present a true story based on the recovered memories of Michelle Smith, provided the remaining components of Ritual Abuse ideology, namely the key concept of Satanic Ritual Abuse, plus a paradigm for recovering repressed memories of such abuse through what would become known as Recovered Memory Therapy.

Michelle Remembers described extreme physical and sexual abuse supposedly subjected upon Smith when she was a child. The horror story she told from her psychiatrist's couch struck such a cord that the Vatican investigated her claims and Hollywood offered her a movie contract. Dedicated to His Satanic Majesty from the age of five by her own mother, Smith claimed to have witnessed murder, extreme debauchery, the mutilation of animals, and the sacrifice of babies. She was forced to eat worms and drink blood. As noted by Bruce A. Robinson of the Ontario Consultants for Religious Tolerance:

> She described the perpetrators as Satanists who believed that the pain inflicted upon their victims increased their magical powers. The group also allegedly engaged in human sacrifice and cannibalism. *Michelle Remembers* was the model for a number of copy-cat books. There were no documented cases of Satanic Ritual Abuse survivors prior to 1980. However, many such cases suddenly appeared in the wake of the success of *Michelle Remembers*. Emergent court cases uncovered abuse situations precisely like (or almost identical to) Michelle's. Subsequent investigations, such as the one conducted by the authors of *Satan's Silence*, revealed that the book was a hoax. The rituals described by the co-author Dr. Lawrence Pazder appear to have been loosely based on his studies of indigenous African religions. (Robinson 2001, p. 636)

Pazder, who coined the expression "Ritual Abuse," took the highly irregular step of leaving his wife to marry his patient. Reciprocating, Smith left her husband to marry her therapist. Given the strict ethical guidelines regulating patient-therapist relationships, this behavior in itself should have called into question the credibility of *Michelle Remembers*.

Concerned that a network of secret Satanists really existed, law enforcement officials began to take charges of Satanic Ritual Abuse seriously in the 1980's. It quickly became evident, however, that there was no hard evidence. Often investigators went to extreme lengths and great expense to recover physical evidence. For instance, in the Paul Ingram ritual abuse case, Mark Papworth, the forensic archeologist assigned to the case thoroughly took apart several sites:

They brought one of their big pieces of equipment out there with a blade and they indicated an area that had been indicated to them by the witnesses against Paul Ingram as an area in which burials had taken place, burials specifically of the remnants of victims of ritual sacrifice, and animals that had been sacrificed and of course the recurrent theme of babies that had been sacrificed. And they buried them out back they said, out back of the house and in the field near by. So I proceeded under the assumption that the only way to do it was to clear a sizable area.... So we took the pasture out back and literally took the top off of it. (Papworth 1996)

Expanding the quest for physical evidence even further, the county directed Papworth to seek out evidence at additional locations where the "victims" claimed they had witnessed sacrificial victims being buried. After an extensive search, the only item he was able to find was a cattle bone. Papworth was taken aback by the response he received to his final report from police investigators:

I said, "There's no evidence. None at all. Zero." And he said to me, "If you were the devil would you leave any evidence?" and I... my hair stood on end and I realized at that point there was no talking to him beyond that and I excused myself. (Papworth 1996)

The only evidence was in the recovered memories of numerous survivors. Retrospectively, it is now clear that these were false memories resulting from improper interview techniques which, in effect, implanted memories of imagined events by suggestion and leading questions.

Another factor at the time was the increasing concern over abused children as an important public issue. Many Ritual Abuse cases were pursued on the basis of the testimony of children. Therapists had been influenced by the then-prevalent line of thinking that children's claims of sexual abuse must be believed at face value, and that the same children were to be disbelieved if they later took back their claims. This approach would later be abandoned after researchers demonstrated that children could be prompted to recount imagined incidents as if they were true in the face of constant questioning. But at the time of the Satanic Ritual Abuse scare, such methods were still regarded as not only acceptable, but as state-of-the-art. Thus counselors and child protection officials pumped children full of leading questions reflecting Ritual Abuse ideology, and, not coincidentally, ended up finding evidence for the existence of Ritual Abuse in children's responses. These dynamics are well exemplified in the McMartin Pre-School Case, which became a paradigm for many subsequent cases.

McMartin was the first high-profile case involving charges of Satanic Ritual Abuse at a day care center. In the wake of an initial spate of publicity surrounding McMartin Pre-School in the early 1980s, a rash of Ritual Abuse cases emerged at other day care centers until it became a national phenomenon. By the beginning of the 1990's, over a hundred investigations of day care cases had taken place on the basis of Satanic Ritual Abuse-type accusations, despite the fact that most of what was alleged to have taken place in these day care centers sounded more like excerpts from a badly written horror novel than real crimes. As summarized in Hicks' *In Pursuit of Satan:*

An inventory of abusive acts and odd elements in day-care cases nationwide, beginning with and including the McMartin case, reads like the special effects in a collective nightmare: the appearance of strange men and women with only one arm, some limping and some with tattooed bodies; Devil worship; secret subterranean tunnels; burned or cooked and eaten babies; murdered and mutilated babies; ceremonies and other activities held in basements; physical abuse, including beatings, slapping, and assaults, particularly during naptime or in the restroom; mock marriages; nude photography; molesters of different races; Christmas-tree lights; children handcuffed or tied with rope; various objects ranging from screwdrivers to crayons inserted in rectums or vaginas; drowned people or animals; clandestine visits to cemeteries, homes, and mortuaries; oral sex on virtually anyone and even on animals; drug-taking; blood drunk or used in ceremonies; pornographic films; burial of children; transportation out of day-care centers in vans or airplanes to go to secret sites; urination and defecation; strangers appearing to molest children; and so on. (Hicks 1990)

In addition to being the most famous case of its type, the McMartin case also has the dubious distinction of being the most expensive, costing over $15,000,000.

Virginia McMartin and her daughter Peggy Buckey owned the McMartin preschool in Manhattan Beach, California. Ray Buckey, the son of Peggy Buckey, also worked there as a part-time aide. The case began on August 12, 1983, when a mentally-disturbed woman accused Ray Buckey of molesting her son, a student at the McMartin school. The accuser was later diagnosed as suffering from paranoid schizophrenia and died from liver problems caused by alcoholism before the trial ever began. This parent's allegations were bizarre from the very beginning. For example, she asserted that the preschool staff had "jabbed scissors into [the boy's] eyes, and staples in his ears, nipples and tongue" and that her son had been compelled to drink blood taken from a baby that he had witnessed Peggy Buckey sacrifice. Even more shocking than her allegations, however, was that the police took them seriously.

Upon investigation, no physical evidence was found, nor did other children confirm the initial accusations. Police also searched the school and scrutinized Ray Buckey. They seized Peggy Buckey's graduation outfit—later described as a "satanic robe"—and Ray Buckey's collection of *Playboy* magazines—later used to support the contention that he was a child molester. Lacking any real evidence, Manhattan Beach police then took the unwise step of issuing a "confidential" letter to about 200 parents with children enrolled in the McMartin school. The letter stated, in part, that:

> Our investigation indicates that possible criminal acts include oral sex, fondling of genitals, buttock or chest areas and sodomy, possibly committed under the pretense of "taking the child's temperature." Also, photos may have been taken of the children without their clothing. Any information from your child regarding having ever observed Ray Buckey to leave a classroom alone with a child during any nap period, or if they have ever observed Ray Buckey tie up a child, is important. (Cited in Hicks 1990, p. 189)

This letter set in motion a panic that would eventually culminate in a trial. Also, when a local TV station got wind of what was happening, during their reporting they speculated that the school might be connected with the pornography and sex business in nearby Los Angeles.

Preschool children did not begin disclosing stories of abuse until after they had been interviewed by the Children's Institute International. By the Spring of 1994, the Institute had reported that some 360 children had been sexually abused. These interviews, which were videotaped, not only reflect a great deal of prompting and suggestive questioning, but also a seeming demand that children provide the "right" answers. For example, at one point in a session, an interviewer admonishes,

> I don't want to hear any more "No's." No, no. Detective Dog and we are going to figure this out. Every little boy and girl in the whole school got touched like that...and some of them were hurt. And some were afraid to tell. (Cited in Hicks 1990, p. 190)

The attitude reflected in this style of questioning—requiring that children confirm conclusions authorities had reached beforehand—would set the tone for the many later Satanic Ritual Abuse cases. With such an *a priori* approach to information gathering, it was easy to develop charges and proceed to a trial. The owners of the school and four teachers were charged initially, but eventually charges were dropped against everyone except Ray and Peggy Buckey.

The case turned a corner after one of the prosecutors became convinced of the innocence of the Buckeys, particularly after watching the interview videos. In many of these videos, it was clear that interviewers would often browbeat children into confirming Ritual Abuse accusations; for example:

> "You're not being a very bright boy. Your friends have come in and told us they were touched. Don't you want to be as smart as them?" (Cited in Hicks 1990, p. 193)

After resigning from the case, the prosecutor disclosed material previously withheld from the trial, such as claims by the original accuser that people had flown through windows. killed lions and had sexual encounters with giraffes. Although the trial continued to wind on, it was only a matter of time before the accused were acquitted.

After the acquittal, suits were filed by some of the former defendants against the city, the county, the Children's Institute International and an ABC TV station. Despite the merits of their grievances, these cases never went anywhere because state law granted immunity from prosecution to workers involved in child protective services.

At various points throughout the case, groups of parents became directly involved in the investigation. They combed the schoolyard for remains of sacrificed animals and infants, and for signs of the underground tunnels or underground rooms the children had described as sites of abuse. During one such search, parents found a turtle shell. This appeared significant at the time because Ray Buckey had supposedly executed a sea turtle with a knife to illustrate what would happen to them if they told. However, a professional examination of the shell found that the sand inside was not from the vicinity, indicating it had been planted, likely by one of the parents anxious to supply hard evidence for the case. Investigators also conducted archeological excavations of the schoolyard to discover evidence of underground rooms and tunnels. These investigations revealed nothing unusual. Though the case is closed, the McMartin school tunnels issue has been kept alive to this day by believers in Satanic Ritual Abuse—especially certain groups of conservative Christians—who continue to believe that the tunnels were real but that the evidence was ignored or covered up.

As already noted, therapists and others supporting the notion of widespread Ritual Abuse by secretive Satanic cults came to rely heavily on Recovered Memory Therapy for providing them with their best evidence for a Satanic conspiracy. To explain why the supposed victims had forgotten their abuse, therapists proposed a diagnosis of Multiple Personality Disorder (a.k.a. Dissociative Identity Disorder). The disorder had, according to this school of thought, been artificially induced by cult "programming" so that victims could be forced to participate in dark rituals without later informing authorities. In other words, like the schizoid state that was the goal of CIA mind control programs like MK-Ultra, one or more dissociated sub-personalities could be induced in subjects. Theoretically, subjects would be unaware of these sub-personalities so that, should agents be caught and interrogated, they could not reveal their true missions. The idea was that an alternate sub-personality, which was programmed to follow the dictates of the programmer, could be triggered by certain key words or other cues implanted in the agent by post-hypnotic suggestion.

For believers in Satanic Ritual Abuse, the MK-Ultra scenario seemed to explain why women who claimed to have been "breeders" for babies sacrificed by Satanic cults could have performed this function while apparently leading ordinary, even innocuous lifestyles. This exotic theory was invoked by Satanic Ritual Abuse advocates despite the fact that the CIA was apparently never successful in inducing such states in its experimental subjects. The mind control hypothesis also explained how the victims could have forgotten the abuse that Recovered Memory Therapy supposedly recovered. While on the one hand Ritual Abuse advocates relied upon MK-Ultra-type notions, on the other hand they drew from popular stereotypes about "cult" brainwashing/mind control. For example, the Los Angeles County Task Force on Ritual Abuse described Satanic cult brainwashing as:

> Mind control is the cornerstone of ritual abuse, the key element in the subjugation and silencing of its victims. Victims of ritual abuse are subjected to a rigorously applied system of mind control designed to rob them of their sense of free will and to impose upon them the will of the cult and its leaders. (Los Angeles County 1989)

This characterization portrays Satanic programming less as a form of CIA mind control and more as a subcategory of the kind of brainwashing the popular press attributes to Moonies, Hare Krishnas and the like.

Although understood as a variant on cult mind control, Satanic mind control was originally invoked for a completely different reason: Cult mind control explained why someone's adult child could join a nutty religious group. On the other hand, Satan programming, as we have noted, explained how a hypothetical network of Satanic cult groups could manage to control both their victims and their members so no one would spill the beans about their existence. It also provided a theoretical background for understanding how Recovered Memory Therapy (RMT) worked and why it was necessary. An important factor contributing to the demise of the Ritual Abuse as a public issue was the rejection of Recovered Memory Therapy as bad science. It eventually became clear to the relevant professions that the "memories" of Ritual Abuse recovered by Recovered Memory Therapy were false memories, unintentionally implanted by therapists with a predisposition to believe in the existence of such abuse.

The Ritual Abuse movement adopted both the stereotype of sinister cults and the mind control notion from the anti-cult movement. The anti-cult movement, for its part, climbed on board the Ritual Abuse bandwagon to expand its own scope of activities. As public concern over Satanism grew, anti-cult groups received so many inquiries about Satanism and clandestine Satanic cults that they developed information packets to sell to callers. Composed largely of xeroxed newspaper and popular magazine articles, such packets simply repeated popular stereotypes. Entering into the arena of public concern about Satanism also gave anti-cultists a new forum within which to promote their perspective on cults and mind control.

Another important player in the Satanic Panic was the mass media. Because of its sensationalism, Satanism and Ritual Abuse have been the topic of numerous talk shows, including episodes of Oprah Winfrey, Sally Jesse Raphael, Phil Donahue, and Geraldo Rivera. Of these programs, Rivera has likely been the most influential on the Ritual Abuse topic. Rivera's most significant program was the television special "Devil Worship: Exposing Satan's Underground," broadcast by NBC on October 25, 1988. Aired for two hours during prime time, this special was designed to fit in with the Halloween season programming. It has been said that this special was watched by more people than any previous television documentary.

In her 1987 book *Prepare for War,* one of Rivera's guests on this important program listed numerous potential "doorways" to demon possession and Satanism, such as fortune tellers, horoscopes, fraternity oaths, vegetarianism, yoga, self-hypnosis, acupuncture, biofeedback, fantasy role-playing games like Dungeons and Dragons, adultery, homosexuality, judo, and karate. She also described rock music as "a carefully masterminded plan by none other than Satan himself." Rivera was careful to confine his questions to this particular "Satanism expert" so as not to elicit comments on these surrealistic aspects of the Satanic threat.

Finally, organized "religious" Satanism, particularly as expressed in LaVey's popular *The Satanic Bible*, came to play an important role in the Satanic Ritual Abuse scare. As noted, the problem confronting Ritual Abuse activists was that the conspiracy of Satanic cults torturing innocent victims had no correlation with the world outside their paranoid fantasies. Hicks observes in his *In Pursuit of Satan* that "Cult cops [were thus forced to] grasp firmly the only tangible evil they can find for public vilification at cult-crime seminars: published, easily available books." Consequently, symbols and artifacts associated with the Church of Satan—usually viewed as an "above ground" front group for "underground" Satanism—were scrutinized for clues to the hidden world of ritual abusers. As a result, *The Satanic Bible* frequently came up for examination in forums for disseminating the Ritual Abuse gospel, such as at occult crime law enforcement conferences. The social dangers of its philosophy of personal indulgence were particularly emphasized at such gatherings.

Despite the fact that LaVey explicitly rejected unlawful activity— especially blood sacrifice—in *The Satanic Bible,* the discovery of a copy of this widely-available mass market paperback at a crime scene was often sufficient evidence for investigators to label the crime *Satanic.* (In contrast, the similar presence of a Christian Bible at a crime scene never led police to label a crime *Christian.*) Perhaps the most significant case of this kind was that of Stanley Dean Baker. Arrested in 1970 after a traffic violation, he confessed, "I have a problem. I'm a cannibal." Police found a human finger in one of Baker's pockets and a copy of *The Satanic Bible* in the other. Baker subsequently regaled authorities and fellow prisoners with tales of his participation in a blood-drinking cult in Wyoming. He later blamed his criminal activities on the influence of drugs, not the Devil.

The other outstanding case of this type was Richard Ramirez, better known as the Night Stalker. A burglar, rapist and sadistic serial murderer who terrorized the Los Angeles area in the mid-eighties, he was captured by civilians on August 31, 1985. A self-identified Satanist, Ramirez had actually read *The Satanic Bible*. His "calling card" was the inverted pentagram traditionally associated with Satanism, which he left drawn on a wall, or, in one case, carved into the body of a victim. In 1983, he even made a special trip to San Francisco to meet LaVey face-to-face. LaVey later commented, "I thought Richard was very nice–very shy. I liked him."

His trial was a media feeding frenzy. Ramirez complied by flashing a pentagram he had drawn in the palm of his hand, shouting "Hail Satan!" and holding up his fingers alongside his head in imitation of devil's horns. Parts of the statement he made during his sentencing even seemed to echo some of the themes of *The Satanic Bible*:

> I am beyond good and evil.... Lucifer dwells in all of us.... I don't believe in the hypocritical, moralistic dogma of this so-called civilized society. I need not look beyond this courtroom to see all the liars, the haters, the killers, the crooks, the paranoid cowards.... Hypocrites one and all. We are all expendable for a cause. No one knows that better than those who kill for policy, clandestinely or openly, as do the governments of the world which kill in the name of God and country.... (Cited in Carlo 1996)

Unlike other cases of so-called occult crime in which the link to the diabolical is tenuous, the Night Stalker forces one to directly confront the assumption that Satanism somehow causes individuals to commit crimes. It takes very little reflection, however, to realize that, as with similar charges leveled at Heavy Metal Music and Role-playing Games like Dungeons & Dragons, Satanic ideology is not an independent motivating factor that somehow transforms otherwise nice people into criminals. Responses to incidents of supposed occult crime such as "We couldn't come up with any other motive for the killing except devil worship"—a police lieutenant's remark cited in Michael Newton's *Raising Hell*—are simply emotional reactions to crimes that always have more mundane explanations. (Newton's sensationalistic book on "Satanic crime" contains at least a dozen cases of crimes in which *The Satanic Bible* supposedly played a role.) Instead of committing crimes because the Devil made them do it, these individuals are simply criminals who adopt selected aspects of Satanic ideology as a way of justifying anti-social acts. This kind of self-justification is clearly reflected in Ramirez's remarks.

References to *The Satanic Bible* in police seminars in combination with the apparent evidence of a connection between *The Satanic Bible* and crime in a few cases like Baker and Ramirez contributed to a number of unfortunate miscarriages of justice, such as the conviction of a young man in the Robin Hood Hills murders.

On May 5, 1993, near West Memphis, Arkansas, three eight-year-old boys were tied up, abused, murdered and mutilated. This crime was quickly perceived in terms of Ritual Abuse. One of the aspects of the case that causes it stand out from others is that it took place after the heyday of the Satanic Panic had passed. By 1993, police departments across the country had become increasingly skeptical of the notion of a covert, international network of Satanic cults that abducted, abused, and murdered children in their diabolical rituals. Most law enforcement agencies had concluded that Satanic Ritual Abuse was a non-existent hoax. Belief in Ritual Abuse nevertheless persisted among certain segments of the conservative Christian subculture, including some policemen.

A juvenile probation officer at the Robin Hood Hills crime scene hypothesized that the boys had been murdered in a Satanic ritual. He believed that the one person in the area who might be capable of the crime was a young man whose case he had followed for years, Damien Echols. From that point onwards, police focused on proving that Echols was the high priest of a Satanic cult. If this could be demonstrated to the satisfaction of a jury, it would be easy to convict Echols of the crimes, despite the lack of hard evidence.

In sharp contrast to other members of the local, highly conservative community, Echols was a fan of heavy metal music bands. People also associated his first name, Damien, with the anti-Christ character in *The Omen* movies. During the trial, testimony was presented regarding items found in Echols' room, such as a funeral register on which upside-down crosses, spells, and a pentagram had been inscribed. They also found a book on witchcraft and, of special note, *The Satanic Bible*. These items solidified the connection between Echols and the murders in the jury's mind, and he was convicted. The fact that there was nothing in *The Satanic Bible* even remotely resembling the murders seems to have been ignored.

It is clear that the *a priori* judgments of believers in Ritual Abuse repeatedly caused them to impute their own assumptions about Satanism to *The Satanic Bible*, whether supported by LaVey's text or not. For instance, in a 1989 case mentioned by Hicks in his *In Pursuit of Satan*, an inmate was denied access to *The Satanic Bible* and other related literature "because possession of such material constituted a security threat." The inmate then sued. At the trial, the prison warden testified that *The Satanic Bible* taught people to "murder, rape, or rob at will without regard for the moral or legal consequences." The court accepted the warden's pronouncements without bothering to actually look at LaVey's book.

One of the wilder examples of this pattern of imputing practices from popular culture stereotypes to *The Satanic Bible* is mentioned in Ellis's *Raising the Devil:*

Near Dixon, Missouri,...police investigation into a series of cattle deaths led to a panic when local police issued warnings that a cult was present. On October 19, 1978, the county's deputy sheriff told the local paper that the mutilations matched descriptions found in Anton LaVey's *Satanic Bible* and that he expected that the cult would soon abduct and sacrifice a thirteen-year-old unbaptized girl on Halloween. (Ellis 2000, p. 269)

Finally, in addition to misattributing certain ideas and practices to *The Satanic Bible*, some ritual abuse believers have gone further to attribute actually diabolical powers to LaVey's book. For instance, Hicks mentions a detective who "reports that body-snatching demons arise from the printed page." Similarly, at a 1988 "satanic-crime seminar," a priest recounted how a young man, claiming he had just seen the Devil, "slammed down *The Satanic Bible* on my desk, which I'm very afraid of; I won't touch it," as if merely touching the book might somehow ensnare him in Satan's web.

Thus LaVey's work came, largely by default, to be seriously regarded as a Satanically-inspired scripture by Ritual Abuse advocates, who attributed to it characteristics drawn from popular stereotypes of Satanism— stereotypes that are, for the most part, completely alien to the thought world of *The Satanic Bible.*

References:

Atkins, Susan, and Bob Slosser. *Child of Satan, Child of God.* Plainfield, NJ: Logos International, 1977.

Baddeley, Gavin. *Lucifer Rising: Sin, Devil Worship and Rock'n'Roll.* London: Plexus, 1999.

Brown, Rebecca. *He Came to Set the Captives Free.* Chino, CA: Chick Publications, 1986.

----------------. *Prepare for War.* Chino, CA: Chick Publications, 1987.

Bugliosi, Vincent and Curt Gentry. *Helter Skelter, The True Story of the Manson Murders.* New York: Norton, 1974.

Carlo, Philip. *The Night Stalker: The True Story of America's Most Feared Serial Killer.* NY: Kensington Books, 1996.

Carlson, Shawn, et al. *Satanism in America: How the Devil Got Much More Than His Due.* El Cerrito, CA: Gaia Press, 1989.

Cartwright, Gary. "The Word of the Devil." *Texas Monthly.* June 1989.

Ellis, Bill. *Raising the Devil: Satanism, New Religions, and the Media.* Lexington, KY: The University Press of Kentucky, 2000.

Hertenstein M. and J. Trott. *Selling Satan, The Tragic History of Mike Warnke.* Chicago: Cornerstone Press, 1993.

Hicks, Robert. *In Pursuit of Satan: The Police and the Occult.* Amherst, NY: Prometheus Books, 1991.

Katchen, Martin H. "The History of Satanic Religions." In Savid K. Sakheim and Susan E. Devine. *Out of Darkness.* New York: Lexington Books, 1992.

Kramer, Heinrich, and James Sprenger. *Malleus Maleficarum.* 1486. Transl. Montague Summers. New York: Benjamin Blom, 1970.

Lea, Henry Charles. *Materials Toward a History of Witchcraft.* New York: Thomas Yoseloff, 1957.

Los Angeles County. *Report of the Ritual Abuse Task Force.* Los Angeles Commission for Women, September 15, 1989.

Nathan, Debbie and Michael Snedeker, *Satan's Silence: Ritual Abuse and the Making of a Modern American Witch Hunt.* NY: Basic Books, 1995.

O'Sullivan, Gerry. "The Satanism Scare." *Postmodern Culture* 1:2. January 1991.

Passantino, Bob and Gretchen. "Satanic Ritual Abuse in Popular Christian Literature, Why Christians Fall for a Lie Searching for the Truth." *Journal of Psychology and Theology* 20:3. 1992.

Papworth, Mark. "Excerpts from an Interview with forensic archeologist, and faculty at the Evergreen State College, Dr. Mark Papworth." 1/3/96. http://members.aol.com/IngramOrg/papworth.htm

Raschke, Carl A. *Painted Black.* NY, NY: Harper, 1990.

Richardson, James, Joel Best and David G. Bromley. *The Satanism Scare*. NY: Aldine de Gruyter, 1991.

Robinson, Bruce A. "Satanic Ritual Abuse." In James R. Lewis. *The Encyclopedia of Cults, Sects and New Religions.* Amherst, NY: Prometheus Books, 2001.

Smith, Michelle, and Lawrence Pazder. *Michelle Remembers.* 1980; Reissued 1989. NY: Pocket Books.

St. Clair, David. *Say You Love Satan.* NY, NY: Dell, 1987.

Stratford, Lauren, and Johanna Michaelson. *Satan's Underground: The Extraordinary Story of One Woman's Escape*. NY: Pelical Publications, Reissued 1991.

Tudor, Andrew. *Monsters and Mad Scientists: A Cultural History of the Horror Movie.* Oxford, UK: Basil Blackwell, 1989.

Victor, Jeffrey. *Satanic Panic: The Creation of a Contemporary Legend.* Chicago: Open Court, 1993.

Magickal Children:
The New Teen Witchcraft[*]

By day, Barbie, Christie and Kayla are fashionable school girls, by night they turn into magical enchantresses. Each doll comes with 2 outfits, spell book, case, edible potions and potion cups. Transform Barbie from an ordinary girl to one of the Charm Girls. Just put on Barbie's enchanted Charm Girl jacket and she's ready to mix up delicious potions that you can really drink. Barbie comes with costume, dragonfly, mixing pot, stand, spoon, stirrer, three bottles, book with a secret compartment, and two packets of magic powder (sugar-based mixes you mix with water).

Promotional blurb for Secret Spells Barbie by Mattel, 10/17/03

Apparently there's a TV commercial for this new doll, one that instructs Secret Spells Barbie fans to gather "at a secret time, in a secret place" to enact these "secret spells." And then it cuts to a shot of our fair witches-in-training "secreted" away at the library mixing "potions" and "doing spells" and one rogue girl perks up and asks whether the spells actually work, and sure enough right then a hunky teen boy appears and strolls right up to the girl who has the Secret Spells "kit," and she grins all knowingly and enchantingly and giggle titter wink ooh isn't this wacky witchcraft fun?

Mark Morford, "Barbie The Hot Pagan Witch," *SF Gate* 10/29/03

The phenomenon of teen witchcraft that arose in the wake of the 1996 film *The Craft* (Pearson 2002, p. 42) has often been contemptuously dismissed by "mainstream" Pagans. However, when a toy maker like Mattel can create and market a crypto-Pagan Barbie, it means that teen witchcraft has reached a critical mass and merits closer scrutiny. I will frame my approach to this topic with the narrative of how I came to undertake this line of research, and how my ideas have developed over the past few years.

I currently teach at a relatively small regional university in central Wisconsin. I am a three-hour drive from the nearest large metropolitan area: Minneapolis to the west and Milwaukee to the southeast. The closest city of any significance is Madison, which is a two-hour-plus drive to the south. Since moving to central Wisconsin 1999, I had not been to any large bookstores because the closest was an hour-and-a-half away.

In 2002, however, a new Barnes & Noble opened in a shopping area less than a half hour north of were I live. When I finally stopped in, I was more than a little shocked. The sections designated "New Age" consisted of five bookcases, fully a third of which were devoted to Paganism/Witchcraft/Magic. My immediate reaction was, "This is the middle of nowhere! Where is the audience for these books?" Obviously there was an audience, but one that had escaped my notice except for a handful of Pagan students I had met in my classes.

This was a threshold event for me. I decided I wanted to understand what was happening with the new teen Paganism. To this end, I got together with some of the Pagan students who had previously taken classes with me and organized a couple of group independent studies on Paganism. I will to return to what I learned from this group later in this paper.

Encyclopedia

Around the time of my epiphany, I was working with Shelley Rabinovitch on *The Encyclopedia of Modern Witchcraft and Neo-Paganism* (2002). I decided that I wanted to undertake some research in an effort to try to understand what had taken place to reshape Pagan demographics so drastically. This project eventually ended up as the research reported in the encyclopedia's appendix, "Numbering Neo-Pagans."

Without going into too many details, in that report I focused on evaluating various estimates of the total Pagan population in North America. I noted that an estimate that has been circulating within scholarly circles since the early 1990s is that the total Pagan population in the US and Canada was approximately 200,000 (e.g., both Berger 1999 and Pike 2001 refer to this figure). In sharp contrast, insiders estimate 500,000-1,000,000 Pagans. Using a variety of different data items indicating Paganism has been growing explosively over the past decade or so, I concluded that 750,000 participants—which is close to the population estimated in an online survey conducted by COG around the turn of this century—is a *conservative* estimate. I was also interested in *what I perceived at the time* as the internet's central role in facilitating this expansion, and particularly in the internet's contribution to the growth in numbers of young solitaries.

As a counterpoint, I referred to Danny Jorgensen and Scott Russell's "American Neopaganism: The Participants' Social Identities." (1999) Jorgensen and Russell repeated the 200,000 practitioners estimate (though the authors also noted that "estimates of twice that number are not implausible"). This is an important statistical study which indicates that Pagans tend to be successful, educated and involved rather than the marginal individuals they had been portrayed in certain early studies.

For my present purpose, one of the most striking aspects of Jorgensen and Russell's research is that they excluded all individuals under 18, noting that "Neopagan beliefs and practice are popular among American youth, but they usually do not participate in this subculture except when their family of origin is Neopagan." This may have been an accurate observation in 1996 when Russell collected the empirical data reported in their article, but it is highly inaccurate with respect to the new crop of Pagans, many of whom become involved while in middle school and high school. The growing number of younger participants is reflected in the proportion of teenagers seeking to communicate with other Pagans on the Witches' Voice site. On March 18, 2002, for example, this website contained personal notices from 35, 261 "Witches, Wiccans, Pagans and Heathens." Out of these, 7,241—or slightly more than 20%—were teenagers. From a casual perusal of their notices, it is clear that the great majority of these young people are *not* being raised in Pagan households.

I do not think this means that Jorgensen and Russell were mistaken, but rather what I think this means is that the demographics of the Pagan movement have shifted radically since 1996. One of the most important factors responsible for this shift is the internet.

The internet did more than simply bring new people into the movement; it also dramatically altered the overall social organization of Paganism. Never a centralized movement, for well over a decade before the internet took off in 1996 Paganism had been experiencing increasing fragmentation due to the growing numbers of solitaries—individuals who, for the most part, practiced their religion alone, though they might occasionally participate in group rituals, particularly at festivals. The advent of online Paganism *dramatically* accelerated the numbers of Pagans practicing their religion by themselves. Not only did the internet make the solitary option more viable for pre-1996 Pagans, but also the great majority of new "converts" brought in via the internet tended to become solitary online Pagans.

The internet allows Pagans to participate actively in a lively online community without ever getting together in the non-internet realm. It is also no longer necessary to subscribe to print periodicals to keep up with the movement, and anything one might desire as far as books and supplies can be obtained through online stores (at this writing, Witches' Voice contained links to over 500 online stores). And it is not just specialty stores and specialty publishers like Llewellyn that have cashed in on this phenomenon. Citing a 1999 posting to a Wiccan mailing list that included a personal interview with a Barnes & Noble executive, Robinson (2001) reports that,

> A marketing executive from Barnes and Noble, the 'World's Largest Bookseller Online,' estimates a U.S. 'Pagan Buying Audience' of 10 million.... Of course, this number is only an estimate of the number of people who buy Pagan books–not the number of actual Pagans. B&N allocates more space to Pagan books than the audience would indicate, because 'Pagan book buyers' tend to buy more books per capita than those of all other faith groups.

In an email communication I received from Fritz Jung–the founder and webmaster of Witches' Voice–Fritz estimated that over 80% of all Pagans are now solitaries. This corresponds with my own informal observations.

Lewellynization

A point I mentioned but did not deal with at length in "Numbering Neo-Pagans" was that the internet would probably not have had the major impact it did had not certain changes already been taking place. I have previously mentioned the increasing numbers of solitaries.

In the original text from the 1979 edition of *The Spiral Dance*, Starhawk mentions solitaries, portraying the solitary option as a valid, but implying that it should be regarded as an intermediate or transitional state that one abandons as soon as one finds a congenial group. Almost ten years later when Scott Cunningham's *Wicca: A Guide for the Solitary Practitioner* (1990; the original edition was published in 1988) first appeared, the situation had changed significantly. By the time of the advent of the internet, the solitary option was recognized as perfectly legitimate by all but the most hidebound traditionalists. Thus what the internet facilitated was, as I have already noted, an increase in both the numbers and relative proportion of solitaries. (We should note in passing that by 2002, Cunningham's book had sold over 400,000 copies–another figure indicating that the 200,000 estimate is probably way off.) Another important development that was set in motion long before the advent of the internet was the growth of generic Wicca, commonly referred to as Eclectic Witchcraft (though I quickly want to add that I do not think every Eclectic Pagan merits the "generic" label!).

A major figure in the creation of generic Wicca was Carl Weschcke, who for many years exercised a near monopoly over Pagan publishing. Llewellyn Publications had (and has) a vested interest in turning out books with the widest possible market appeal. There was less profit in books directed to members of specific traditions; hence the emphasis on generic Witchcraft. For the same reason, Llewellyn was not interested in publishing books that turned readers off by straining their intellects too much; hence the "dumbing down" of Paganism that insiders sometimes refer to as "Llewellynization."

Even today, long after the passing of Weschcke's hegemony, most publishers of Pagan trade books adhere to the Llewellyn program–hence the hundreds, or what seems like hundreds, of "Witchcraft 101" books, including *The Complete Idiot's Guide to Wiccan and Witchcraft* (2000). This latter volume is actually not so bad, as Witchcraft 101 books go. And it must have been quite successful, because it was followed two years later by *The Complete Idiot's Guide to Paganism* (2002).

The commercialization of Paganism has even led to the creation and marketing of at least a half dozen "spell kits" which contain various items for cooking up magic spells. The most relevant kit for the theme of the present paper is Silver Ravenwolf's *Teen Witch Kit*. Furthermore, Ravenwolf's simplified introduction to Paganism for young people, *Teen Witch*, has sold over 160,000 copies. This book and other Ravenwolf titles have been translated into a dozen different languages, including Armenian and Hungarian.

ASANAS Conference and *The Craft*

To summarize, my thinking up this point was that the changes the Pagan movement was experiencing were being driven by (1) the Internet, and (2) the "dumbing down" of Paganism, especially by commercial publishers like Llewellyn. I presented a paper, "The Triumph of Generic Witchcraft," on these themes at the ASANAS conference in May of 2003. I also met three other people who were presenting papers on teen witchcraft at that gathering, Doug Ezzy, Hannah Sanders, and Peg Aloi. Their papers were:

> Hannah Sanders, "Spelling For Teens: The Pedagogies of Power and Practice in the Literature of Teenage Witchcraft"
> Peg Aloi, "A Charming Spell: The Intentional and Unintentional Influence of Popular Media Upon Teenage Witchcraft in America"
> Doug Ezzy, "New Age Witchcraft? Popular Spellbooks and the Re-enchantment of Everyday Life." (published in *Culture and Religion* 4:1. 2003).

These individuals also informed me that a number of other academicians had recognized the significance of teen witchcraft and were researching the topic.

Helen Berger and Ezzy, for example, are conducting an international study of young Witches (18 to 22yrs old) in the US, UK and Australia. They plan to interview 30 Witches in each country. They currently have completed in the vicinity of 70 of these interviews. Their research examines the processes of becoming a young Witch, including the role of books, television shows and the Internet. They are also interested in what these young Witches do, the nature of their practices and rituals. Their findings to date suggest that Witchcraft is an important part of these young people's lives and has a largely positive effect on their self-esteem and self-understandings.

For my purpose of reconstructing what had happened since the mid-nineties, Peg Aloi's paper was the most illuminating. Aloi's analysis focuses on the four year period from 1996 to 2000 in which witches became "entrenched as media darlings who could not only be benevolent, but sexy, comical and in some cases, role models for the young women who watched them." She argues that the threshold event setting this trend in motion was the 1996 film *The Craft*, which "has undeniably been the single greatest influence on the growth of teenage witchcraft in America." After surveying the influence of the witch characters in *The Craft*, *Buffy*, *Charmed* and *Practical Magic*, Aloi further notes with respect to *The Craft* that "at first it was not clear to pagan film reviewers (even myself) how many teenagers... would embark upon the path of paganism as a direct result of seeing this film."

The critical four year period form '96 to 2000 noted by Aloi also corresponds with the internet explosion that I saw as the engine driving the expansion of Paganism. Her paper led me to see that certain films and TV shows constituted a more important influence than the internet and pagan publishing driving the Teen Witch phenomenon. Aloi also noted that the teen witchcraft movement developed without the guidance of mainstream Pagans because adult Pagans backed away from opportunities to mentor them:

> It is no coincidence that, concomitant with the arrival of these media texts featuring young beautiful witches, the adult pagan community was inundated with requests from teenaged seekers wanting more information. Because the shows featured characters dealing with problems common to all adolescents, not just witches, the tendency for teenage girls to want to solve their problems with magic and spells, like their primetime role models, became a pervasive trend in schools and, most notably, on the internet where this phenomenon has mainly been documented. Because of the many sensitive issues surrounding adult mentorship of pagan teens, the majority of the pagan community very quickly dealt with the situation by more or less refusing mentorship to anyone under the age of 18, and for younger seekers this often meant a reply to their enquiry saying "Wait a few years, and here are some books you can read in the meantime."

For better or for worse, the books that adult Pagans might have recommended to adolescent Witches were quickly supplanted by a new breed of Teen Witch books.

In "A New Broom Sweeps the World of Witchery," (New York Times, Oct. 26, 1998), Doreen Carvajal reports that executives at Llewellyn Publishing "noticed a surge in sales with the popularity of *The Craft*, a B-movie about a small coven of good, bad, and moderately well-behaved teenage witches dressed in knee-highs and school uniforms by day, hip clothes by night. ... Llewellyn responded by publishing a variety of books on witchcraft for beginners, including *Teen Witch*, with a cover of bemused 15-year-old girls in jeans and short skirts posed like a movie poster for *The Craft*. 'Our typical reader had been a boomer who grew up in the '60s who had been looking for a more appealing explanation of spirituality,' said Von Braschler, Llewellyn's director of trade sales. 'Now our typical reader is becoming a very young woman in her teens. We're basing that on the letters we get for the authors.'"

In 1998 when Carvajal's article was written, the expression "Teen Witch" was state-of-the-art hip. However, the "teen" part of "Teen Witch" is already passe. As one of my students noted, the only people who want to be *Teen* Witches are pre-teens. This change is reflected in the subtitle of Ravenwolf's recent, *Solitary Witch: The Ultimate Book of Shadows for the New Generation*, which drops the "Teen Witch" phrase and returns to the "New Generation" rubric of her earlier titles.

Pagan Students: Post-Teen Witch

At this point in the discussion, I would like to return to the group of Pagan students I mentioned earlier. To facilitate my research, I recruited Pagan students for a group independent study on Paganism. Six students, all female solitaries, eventually signed up in the spring of 2003. In the subsequent term, I organized a second independent study with seven students. We met once a week for two hours and discussed assigned readings. What they got out of the class was a deeper knowledge of Paganism; what I got out of the class was a clearer sense of what might be referred to as "new generation" Pagans. In lieu of assigning a formal paper, I asked these students to help me with my research in various ways. I learned the most, however, from our in-class interactions. They not only provided me with feedback and criticism, but just coming to know them as people and observing them in the context of our discussions was enlightening.

All were, as I mentioned, self-taught solitaries. All had been involved in Paganism since at least high school, had never circled with anyone else, had never attended any Pagan event (e.g., Pagan festivals), and had never even met– at least as far as they knew–any *initiated* Witches. Furthermore, they related to me that all of the other Pagans they knew fit the same profile. I found this quite intriguing, partly because it contrasted so markedly from the profile of participants in the Pagan scene that I had observed in the early 1990s in California.

One might suppose that people who had become self-identified Witches in high school–or, in a couple of cases, even younger–would be alienated outsiders, or at least have counter-cultural tendencies. With perhaps one exception, however, this was not the case. In fact, three of these students were active members of sororities, which was certainly enough to demolish my assumptions about the kind of public school student who might become involved in Paganism.

I had also assumed, based on my familiarity with the growing body of literature directed to Teen Witches, that magic would be a major component of their practice–but it wasn't. When asked questions about "spells" and such, all of the Pagan students who participated as guest speakers in a couple of my classes noted that they hardly ever worked magic. In fact, over the course of the entire first semester together, I think the only magical work my students did was a ritual for my wife, who has been going through a life-threatening health crisis. (Congruent with Pagan ethics, they asked my wife beforehand if this would be okay.)

What seemed to be most important for my students were not the practices associated with Paganism, but rather that Paganism confirmed their personal attitudes toward life and their beliefs about the nature of reality. Thus when we read *Drawing Down the Moon*, they completely identified with Adler's notion that people who become Pagan experience a sense of "coming home" rather than a traditional conversion experience.

My students also identified with the pre-Christian peoples and religions of ancient Europe–a self-identity that provided them with the feeling that they were not simply marginal oddballs. Thus, for example, during a discussion in which we discussed the discrimination that some modern Pagans had experienced at the hands of Christians, one of my students commented that, "Well, back in the days of the Roman Empire, we persecuted them!" This was a striking remark, reflecting a strong sense of solidarity with ancient Paganism (a solidarity this student felt despite the fact that over the course of the semester we had often critiqued the notion that modern Paganism was a lineal descendant of the pre-Christian religions of Europe).

So will the current crop of young Pagans who persist in their Paganism beyond adolescence come to fit this same general profile? I tend to think so, though I don't know if spellcraft will be as insignificant for most post-adolescent Witches as it is for my Pagan students. The problem with magic, of course, is that it is incapable of magically solving all one's problems. So if manipulative magic is the only reason one becomes involved, it shouldn't take too many failed spells for Secret-Spells-Barbie types to drop out and go back to idealizing Malibu Barbie or some other incarnation of the obnoxious plastic bleach blonde.

"After the magic is gone," what remains attractive for the new Pagan is the unique identity and mystique of being a Witch. One feels connected with romanticized ancient cultures. The world is re-enchanted. The body and sensuality are valued as sacred, rather than as subjects of guilt. And, without attending church or tithing, one can claim membership in a religious movement that demands respect as a legitimate religion. Not a bad deal.

Center and Periphery

As part of their participation in my research project, I also asked these students to solicit feedback on the "new Paganism" from some of the longtime Pagans I knew. They emailed these contacts a form letter that noted the transformation of Paganism from a small movement consisting of specific traditions organized around covens to a much larger movement consisting of eclectic solitaries. This letter further noted that the original counter-cultural flavor of the movement had been diluted, to the point where Paganism seemed to be well on its way to becoming mainstream, and also that Paganism seemed to be becoming a major youth fad. What, then, did this indicate about the future of the movement?

Without going into details, a shared characteristic of most responses was to downplay the significance of the new Paganism. Instead, the tendency of the people we contacted was to emphasize the changes taking place within mainstream Paganism. I was initially surprised by this response, but with a little reflection it was easy to see what had happened: Whereas we were standing (metaphorically speaking) on the periphery of the Pagan movement, our respondents were standing in the "center," and they had unconsciously privileged their epistemological position and seemed fundamentally unable to consider the possibility that the new Paganism was a serious phenomenon.

So where does that leave us?

I fully understand that adolescent Paganism looks like a "cherry blossom" phenomenon that will burst forth in full bloom, only to drop away within a brief span of time and any serious remnants absorbed into the Pagan "mainstream." But I don't think so. Sociologists of religion who have conducted broad kinds of statistical research on contemporary religiosity have noted that, in tandem with the weaker social relationships that characterize modern society, there is an increasing tendency for people to "hand craft" their own individual spirituality (though they draw from and perhaps even participate sporadically in organized religion). It seems to me that solitary, eclectic Paganism is perfectly suited to thrive in this new environment, meaning that the future looks bright for the new Paganism.

I also wonder about the long-term influence of Harry Potter and his various imitators. I think the Teen Witch fad has already peaked, but the popularity of fantasy fiction is still waxing. And while Harry and other magical figures like Gandolf of *The Lord of the Rings* fame may not immediately inspire young people to become wizards in same the way *The Craft* inspired people to become Witches, my feeling is that they will leave a deeper cultural imprint in the long run. Specifically, I believe that the generation that is currently cutting their teeth on Harry and Gandolf will be far more open to Pagan involvement in the future, indicating that Paganism in some form will become a large, mainstream religion within the next several decades.

* An earlier version of this paper was presented at the Pagan Studies Conference, Atlanta, Georgia, 11/21/03.

References:

Berger, Helen A. *A Community of Witches: Contemporary Neo-paganism and Witchcraft in the United States*. Columbia, SC: University of South Carolina Press, 1999.

Cunningham, Scott. *Wicca: A Guide for the Solitary Practitioner*. St. Paul, MN: Llewellyn Publishing, 1990.

Curott, Phyllis. Book of Shadows: *A Modern Woman's Journey into the Wisdom of Witchcraft and the Magic of the Goddess*. New York, NY: Broadway Books, 1999.

Hobbes Internet Timeline. http://www.zakon.org/robert/internet/timeline (1993-2002)

Jorgensen, Danny and Scott Russell. "American Neopaganism: The Participants' Social Identities." *Journal for the Scientific Study of Religion*. 38:3 (1999), pp. 325-338.

Pearson, Joanne, ed. *Beyond Belief Boundaries: Wicca, Celtic Spirituality and the New Age*. Andershot, Hanes, UK: Ashgate, 2002.

Pike, Sarah M. *Earthly Bodies, Magical Selves: Contemporary Pagans and the Search for Community*. Berkeley, CA: University of California Press, 2001.

Shelley Rabinovitch and James Lewis. *The Encyclopedia of Modern Witchcraft and Neo-Paganism*. New York, NY: Citadel, 2002.

Starhawk. *The Spiral Dance*. San Francisco, CA: Harper San Francisco, 1979.

Reid, Sian Lee. Disorganized Religion: An Exploration of the Neopagan Craft in Canada. Department of Sociology and Anthropology. Carleton University, 2001.

Robinson, Bruce A. "How many Wiccans are there in the U.S.?" (2001) at the Ontario Consultants for Religious Tolerance website. www.religioustolerance.com.

Of Tolerance, Toddlers and Trailers:
An Introduction to Legitimation Strategies

> Domination [is] the probability that certain specific commands (or all commands) will be obeyed by a given group of persons. ... [C]ustom, personal advantage, purely affectual or ideal motives of solidarity, do not form a sufficiently reliable basis for a given domination. In addition there is normally a further element, the belief in *legitimacy*.
>
> — Max Weber, *Economy and Society*

When I was an undergraduate, I remember a short discussion from a philosophy class in which we analyzed our fear of standing on the edge of a precipice. The gist of the discussion was that, although we can provide a good rationale for this dread—perhaps we will slip or perhaps a wind will come up that will cause us to trip and fall—the anxiety we feel in these situations nevertheless seems to go deeper than the fear suggested by these reasonable-sounding explanations. When the instructor finally proposed that what we really fear is that some secret part of us will prompt us to jump to our deaths, I had the uncanny feeling he was right.

Controversial new religions have been the focus of my research for the better part of two decades. With a few exceptions, I have not been a critic of such movements. Rather, my scholarship has tended to debunk popular stereotypes. I have, however, come to at least one conclusion with which anti-cultists would agree, namely every one of us has a secret self that wants to submit to a higher authority, not unlike the secret self that wants to cast us into the abyss. It is this impulse that surfaces under the sway of charisma.

Whenever possible in the course of my field research with new religions, I have sought direct contact with the leadership. Even when surrounded by adoring devotees in highly-charged environments, I have never been even remotely impressed by a leader's imputed charisma. If, as Max Weber and later analysts theorized, charisma is socially constructed rather than an inherent characteristic of charismatic leaders, then this is as it should be. Because they are outsiders to the group's social world, academic observers should be completely immune to the magnetic influence of such gurus.

There was, however, one exception to the otherwise uniform uneventfulness of my encounters. Unexpectedly, I stepped into the magical atmosphere of a religious leader's charisma, and briefly experienced her as someone of more than ordinary specialness. This leader was Elizabeth Clare Prophet, the spiritual leader of Church Universal and Triumphant. What surprised me then–and what continues to unsettle me to this day–is that I never consciously regarded her as a spiritually-elevated individual, much less (as she claimed) the mouthpiece for such figures as Jesus, Buddha and others. In fact, even at the time, I felt that she was a not-particularly-sensitive individual with an exaggerated sense of self who over-identified with her guru persona.

Although I am reluctant to discuss it, this experience has come to constitute a kind of touchstone in my reflections on the role of charisma in new religious movements. I will thus lead into my analysis of the legitimation of new religions by describing Church Universal and Triumphant, relating the story of the events that led up to my epiphany, and sharing my reflections on this experience.

Church Universal and Triumphant

The Church Universal and Triumphant (C.U.T.) is a second-generation splinter of the "I AM" Religious Activity. The "I AM" Activity, founded by Guy Warren Ballard and his wife Edna W. Ballard, is a popularized form of Theosophy. Mark L. Prophet had been active in two earlier "I AM" splinter groups, the Bridge to Freedom (now the New Age Church of Truth) and the Lighthouse of Freedom. He eventually founded his own group, the Summit Lighthouse, in Washington, D.C. in 1958. In the Theosophical tradition, the spiritual evolution of the planet is conceived of as being in the hands of a group of divinely illumined beings--Jesus, Gautama Buddha, and other advanced souls. In the tradition of earlier theosophical leaders, Prophet viewed himself as serving as the mouthpiece for these Ascended Masters. Elizabeth Clare Wulf joined the group in 1961, eventually marrying Mark Prophet. Over the course of their marriage, Elizabeth Prophet also became a Messenger. After her husband's death in 1973, Elizabeth took over his roles as the primary mouthpiece for the Masters and as leader of the organization.

The headquarters of Summit Lighthouse moved to Colorado Springs in 1966. In 1974, Church Universal and Triumphant (C.U.T.) was incorporated, taking over ministerial and liturgical activities from Summit Lighthouse, which remained the publishing wing of the organization. During the seventies, the work of C.U.T. expanded tremendously. After several moves within southern California, Church headquarters was finally established on the Royal Teton Ranch, in Montana just north of Yellowstone Park in 1986. The Church also established an intentional community of several thousand people in the surrounding area.

The core beliefs of Church Universal and Triumphant are held in common with other branches of the Theosophical tradition. These include the notion of Ascended Masters guiding the spiritual evolution of the planet, and certain basic ideas from the South Asian tradition, such as the belief in reincarnation and karma. The Church views itself as part of the larger Judeo-Christian tradition, though traditional Christians would not thus classify it.

When "cults" became a public issue in the mid-1970s, Church Universal and Triumphant was not particularly prominent. The group remained a relatively minor player in the cult wars until the move to Montana. As should have been anticipated, the intrusion of a large number of exotic outsiders into a predominantly rural area evoked curiosity and antagonism.

Much of the Church's subsequent negative media coverage derived from incidents clustered around its extensive fallout shelters and its preparations for the possibility of a nuclear attack against the United States. At one point in the construction, for instance, fuel stored in several underground tanks ruptured and spilled gas and diesel oil into the water table. Also, in 1990 members from around the world gathered in Montana because of the predicted possibility of an atomic holocaust. This story made the front page of *The New York Times* on December 15, 1990, resulting in a flood of reporters from around the world eager for sensationalist stories about a "doomsday cult."

Also, in 1989 two Church members--one of whom was Elizabeth Prophet's third husband--attempted to acquire otherwise legal weapons in a non-public, illegal manner for storage in underground shelters, providing more fuel for the organization's negative public image as a survivalist group. The motivation for this ill-considered act was to avoid the negative media exposure that would have resulted if members had purchased guns in Montana. The plan, however, backfired and resulted in a public relations disaster. This and other incidents was the basis for later accusations that Church Universal and Triumphant was a potential Waco. (Lewis 1998)

Contact and First Impressions

I became involved with Church Universal and Triumphant shortly before the media storm that broke in the wake of the Branch Davidian tragedy. This came about as the indirect result of a deprogramming case. LaVerne Macchio, a church member, was kidnapped in the middle of the night on November 20, 1991, while her four small children looked on in horror. She was released after seven days. Her deprogrammers and kidnappers were eventually indicted and charged with second-degree kidnapping.

In the fall of 1992, I was contacted by Church Universal and Triumphant and asked to testify as an expert witness in the Macchio case. A number of my scholarly articles presented data which undermined the notion that non-traditional religions exercised extraordinary forms of influence over their members. Because the kidnappers were almost certain to invoke the mind control /brainwashing accusation as part of their defense, the prosecution felt it important to have a scholar present who could effectively debunk the idea. Intrigued by the case, I tentatively agreed to participate on the condition that the Church bring me and my wife to Montana for a week, put us up at their headquarters, show us everything we wished to see, and allow us to speak with anyone with whom we desired a conversation. Assured that those conditions would be met, we prepared to spend a week in the wilds of Montana.

Anti-cultists have generally regarded the many academics who criticize the cult stereotype–and who, as a consequence, have tended to defend non-traditional religions against unreasonable persecution–as naive and gullible. However, based on my own experience as well as many conversations with colleagues, I can testify that just the opposite attitude is more often case. Scholars of stigmatized religions have a secret fear that they will one day examine a controversial religious group, give it a clean bill of health, and later discover that they have defended the People's Temple, or worse. This anxiety causes them to be, if anything, *more* skeptical than the average observer and to strive even harder for methodological objectivity than they might ordinarily.

Hence, despite my decade-long involvement with alternative religions–a ten-year period in which I had found most accusations leveled against Moonies, Hare Krishnas, and so forth to be foundationless–I was still ready to entertain many of the worst charges leveled against Elizabeth Clare Prophet's Church Universal and Triumphant in the mass media. Because much of my own scholarship had been critical of the notion of "cultic mind control," I categorically rejected the idea that the Church "brainwashed" its adherents. There were, however, other accusations about which I had serious doubts, namely: Were Church members gun-toting doomsday crazies, convinced that the endtime was about to be brought about via an exchange of nuclear weapons? Was Elizabeth Prophet a power-hungry megalomaniac who lived an extravagant lifestyle by exploiting her followers? Was the Church an environmentally indifferent community that carelessly dumped fuel oil and raw sewage into the pristine Yellowstone River? In this critical frame of mind, my wife and I flew to Montana in October 1992.

Congruent with my experiences of most other new religions, I found the adult members of the community to be balanced, well-integrated individuals and the children bright and open. Over the course of the week, these impressions were continually reinforced. I had innumerable conversations with intelligent staff members during which we discussed "metaphysical" matters. Because of my status as an outsider studying the Church, my conversation partners were often careful to distinguish personal beliefs from doctrines taught by Church Universal and Triumphant. Although the intention behind making these distinctions was to prevent me from accidentally reporting an individual belief as a Church belief, these words of caution gave me an invaluable insight into the thoughtworld of members: Although all members adhered to certain basic beliefs, these beliefs were appropriated selectively, allowing room for a wide variance of interpretation and even disagreement. This internal tolerance spoke well for an organization that claimed to receive direct, authoritative revelations from the highest spiritual sources.

There are many incidents from that visit that stand out in my mind--too many to go into here. I was, however, particularly impressed by a relatively minor incident that occurred near the beginning of our visit. While my wife and I were with the two-year-olds during a tour of the Ranch's Montessori school, a young toddler walked up to me, looked me over–as if to make some kind of quick evaluation of this stranger in his classroom–turned around, backed up, and plopped himself down on my lap. While I realize that I may be reading more into this incident than it merits, I was impressed. The toddler's action indicated that he was open and trusting–not the kind of behavior one would anticipate from an abused child. He also seemed to be exercising his faculty of discrimination, as if he would not have plopped himself into the lap of just any stranger–only strangers he judged to be "okay" in some way.

The other event that stands out in my mind from the visit was my first meeting with Elizabeth Prophet. Throughout the week, my wife and I had been in many homes, particularly in the Glastonbury area where members buy land from the Church and build their own houses. Many members were quite well-off and had constructed homes reflecting their financial status. During October of 1992 when I was at the Ranch, Elizabeth, her husband, and one of her adult daughters were living in a small trailer on a tiny lot immediately adjacent to the headquarters complex, and this had apparently been her residence for several years. When my wife and I finally got together with Elizabeth, we found her to be a down-to-earth individual whom we could engage in very ordinary conversation and who, at the time, seemed to be very open to receiving advice.

Again I was very favorably impressed. Had her personal material comfort been uppermost in her mind, Elizabeth could have requested–and I am sure her request would have been honored–to live in better accommodations. However, rather than place undue strain on the Church's resources, she was apparently willing to accept humbler circumstances. (It should be noted that she eventually *did* move into a very comfortable home.) She could also have set up our meeting so as to have established and maintained an image of herself as a ruling queen receiving emissaries from the outside world. Instead, she approached us as regular people. During this initial encounter, I did not experience Elizabeth as someone of more than ordinarily specialness.

I should also emphasize that not all of my initial impressions were positive. For example, I developed a distinct distaste for macrobiotic cooking (the only kind of food served in the Ranch cafeteria) during that week. And many of the Church members I observed appeared mildly unhealthy, a characteristic I attributed to the food. I was also never entirely comfortable with either the members' habit of referring to Elizabeth as "Mother," or with the peculiar rhythmic cadence of her voice whenever she was relaying "dictations" from the Ascended Masters. I had a similar but stronger reaction to decreeing, the Church's central spiritual practice. Said to purify and transform individuals by attuning them to divine vibrations, decrees are also supposed to bring the power of the divine to bear on earthly matters. For example,

> Let the light flow into my being,
> Let the light expand in the center of my heart,
> Let the light expand in the center of the earth,
> And let the earth be transformed into the new day! (Vesta, "The New Day")

For maximum effect, these poetic invocations are repeated as rapidly as possible. My wife and I received special permission to participate in a Sunday morning decreeing session with hundreds of members. It is almost impossible to describe what this is like to anyone who has never experienced it. My impression was that the congregation was simultaneously praying, chanting, and cheering on some kind of cosmic football team. At that moment, I could easily understand how a more skeptical observer in my shoes would have been shaking his head at the bizarre ritual behavior of these "brainwashed cultists." Thus while my overall experience during the trip was positive, I also walked away with some less rosy impressions.

As it happened, the kidnapping trial that originally brought me to the Ranch was closed to the testimony of outside experts by the presiding judge. I had, however, found the group attractive enough that testifying in the trial was no longer my central reason for wanting to maintain contact with the Church. Church Universal and Triumphant was an intrinsically interesting movement. Also, without ignoring the organization's failings, my baseline evaluation was that the leadership and the community were fundamentally *trying to do good*. I thus found myself desiring to return to Montana for a more prolonged visit. In order to accomplish this, I persuaded the Church that they would benefit by having a whole group of academics study them. Church Universal and Triumphant eventually agreed to open its doors to a group of scholars who visited the Ranch in the summer of 1993 around the time of the Church's major summer conference. (Lewis and Melton 1994)

Theophany

For a number of reasons, we arrived at the conference after it had been underway for several days. During our October visit, my wife Evelyn had developed a personal connection with Elizabeth. Following the first evening program we attended they went off together, leaving me with my academic colleagues. As I would later discover, during their private conversation Evelyn mentioned that I was heavily burdened by anxieties. I eventually caught up with them at Elizabeth's trailer. I was still exhausted from the trip and it was quite late in the evening. I recall briefly sitting in the trailer's living room with Elizabeth, her husband and my wife, while watching television and talking about incidents from our trip.

It was in this decidedly *un*exotic, low-pressure atmosphere that I first noticed I was regarding Elizabeth somehow differently, though initially I dismissed my state of mind as the natural deference one might have for the head of any large religious organization. When we got up to leave, Elizabeth, in response to the information she had received from Evelyn, performed a quick ritual around me with a ceremonial sword designed to "cut" away troublesome thoughts. I recall feeling somehow honored that she would take the time to focus on my spiritual well-being–though I never subsequently perceived that this "mini-exorcism" had lightened my burden in any way. I also noticed that she seemed to be radiating a tangible "magnetism"–a field of force that marked her off from other people as someone special.

Unwittingly, I had subtly fallen under the spell of charisma. Even at the time, I remember thinking about what I had been taught regarding the social construction of charisma, and reflected that perhaps there were exceptions to this principle–that there might actually be some human beings who were *intrinsically* charismatic. It did not take long, however, for me to be disabused of this notion. Evelyn and I stayed on at the Royal Teton Ranch for the next month. During that time, we gathered a range of new impressions–some negative and some positive, but mostly the later. However, I had a few unsettling encounters with "Mother's" personal failings during our last couple of days on the Ranch that finally let the air out of whatever remained of my inflated sense of her importance.

What, I later asked myself, had allowed me to be drawn into the rarified atmosphere of Elizabeth's charisma, however briefly? Although my experience was profoundly personal and immediate, in hindsight it is not difficult to place in a broader perspective. Unlike some of my colleagues who never bother to actually meet the people they write about, I typically immerse myself in the religious groups I research, fully participating in their practices (when possible) and getting to know members as flesh-and-blood people. Methodologically, this kind of an approach, when properly carried out, constitutes the "participation" aspect of participant-observer research. The explicit goal of such an approach is to be able see the world as if one is a member of the subculture one is studying, to the extent that this is reasonably possible. With respect to Church Universal and Triumphant, I had met a host of likeable, intelligent people who honored Elizabeth Prophet as the mouthpiece for the greatest spiritual teachers in our planet's history. Although they never expressed any but the most muted devotional feelings in my presence, it was easy enough to sense that many were personally devoted to Elizabeth.

I had consciously allowed myself to be drawn into the Church's aura, but had not realized that I would thereby come under the sway of certain group attitudes–attitudes that infiltrated my subconscious and began to shape my experiences, however subtly. These forces were at work despite my critical reservations, and despite the commonplace circumstances in which I had fallen under the sway of the power of charisma. (Perhaps the mundane circumstances actually contributed to the experience; I might have raised my defenses in a more "exalted" setting.) One does not need to invoke exotic theories of mind control to explain the social influences at work in this situation, but I found, to my surprise and dismay, that there was a gap between my abstract understanding of these social processes and my concrete experience of the same processes.

In spite of the discomfort of these memories, I am nevertheless grateful for having experienced charisma in something like the manner in which movement participants experience their leader. Within the subculture of a new religion, charismatic leaders possess a luminous, magnetic quality that followers experience as a real force. And although such leaders typically legitimate their teachings in a variety of ways, their personal aura of power is frequently the crucial element that makes everything else "work," especially in the early stages of a movement.

Legitimation

In the 1950s and early 1960s, analyses of social movements tended to focus on explanations of individual participation. By the 1970s, however, attention had shifted away from a preoccupation with what might be called the "micro" level (motives of individual participants), and social scientists began to look at the "macro" level (strategies utilized by movements to accomplish their goals). One of these new perspectives gave particular attention to the human and material resources that movements attempt to tap, and hence was referred to as "resource mobilization theory."

An important ideological resource for emergent movements, particularly in hostile social environments, is legitimacy. New religious movements actively seek legitimacy. However, scholars of new religious movements have not bothered to analyze the actual notion of legitimation, perhaps because, for the purpose of understanding the groups we study, it appears to be a simple concept. Like many other taken-for-granted ideas, however, there are nuances in legitimacy that easily escape the casual observer. Though it is not difficult to point to concrete examples of legitimation, this concept becomes slippery as soon as one attempts to specify its meaning with precision.

The classic discussion is Max Weber's tripartite schema of traditional, rational-legal, and charismatic legitimations of authority. The dynamics (in the sense of upsetting rather than reinforcing established authority structures) of this schema are largely confined to the factor of charisma, a form of legitimation Weber viewed as especially–though not exclusively– characteristic of new religious movements. Weber also made it clear that he was discussing ideal types, meaning that in the empirical world one would never be able to find a pure example of charismatic authority. However, no later discussions of charisma have taken the further step of explicitly examining how the other sources of legitimacy analyzed by Weber might be deployed in modified ways by charismatic leaders.

The discussion of the strategies power elites deploy to maintain their position has consumed a small lake of scholarly ink, not to mention a small forest of trees that sacrificed their lives to the paper industry. In contrast, the analysis of the legitimation strategies deployed by new religions has not moved forward substantially since Weber. Although scholars of new religions use the term freely, no one has published a single article, much less a book, focused on this issue–despite the fact that legitimacy is a core issue for emergent religious movements. The rudimentary state of this topic means that any attempt to extend Weber's discussion in this arena must necessarily be preliminary and exploratory.

Weber's work on the legitimation of authority provides a useful starting point for understanding the legitimation strategies deployed by new religions, but it should immediately be noted that his analysis is also inadequate. For example, in contrast to what one might anticipate from the discussion of charismatic authority in Weber's *Economy and Society*, one often finds new religions appealing to tradition–though the explicit nature of such appeals means that they constitute a variation from what Weber had in mind by the traditional legitimation of authority, which he viewed as largely implicit. Also, when nascent movements attempt to justify a new idea, practice or social arrangement by attributing it to the authority of tradition, it is through a reinterpretation of the past that they are able to portray themselves as the true embodiment of tradition. Such modifications of his schema indicate that Weber did not have the last word on this issue. In fact, upon closer examination, one finds that contemporary new religions rely upon a wide range of different strategies to gain legitimacy.

One factor contributing to this diversification of strategies is the different audiences the leadership of a new religion must address. In addition to seeking legitimacy in the eyes of followers and potential converts, an emergent movement is often compelled to address the issue of how it is regarded by the larger society–particularly by governmental agencies with the power to disrupt the group. This means that a new religion has at least four different (though overlapping) areas where legitimacy is a concern: making converts, maintaining followers, shaping public opinion, and appeasing government authorities. Also, like the members of any elite, founders of new religions feel compelled to justify their leadership positions to themselves.

The present study proposes to advance the understanding of legitimacy by discussing a variety of ways in which new religions draw on the authority of charisma, tradition and rationality. This will be accomplished through the notion of *legitimation strategies*.

Legitimation Strategies

Charisma–which, in Weber's use of the term, includes direct revelations from divinity as well as the leader's ability to provide both mundane and supernatural benefits to followers–may be the keystone in a new movement's attractiveness, but charismatic leaders typically appeal to a variety of other sources of legitimacy. For instance, as has already been mentioned, founders of new religions often appeal to the authority of tradition. Many modern movements also appeal to the authority of reason and science. Yet another strategy is to appeal to an ancient wisdom or to a primordial religiosity that antedates current religions.

Despite many areas of overlap, it is useful to view these various appeals as distinct *legitimation strategies*—though it should immediately be noted that the term "strategy" in this context is *not* meant to imply that religious founders necessarily set out to design legitimation strategies in the same way business executives develop marketing strategies or generals develop military strategies. Rather, in the majority of cases, a new religion's legitimation strategies emerge more or less spontaneously out of the ongoing life of the community. Grouping strategies according to Weber's tripartite schema, *some* of the strategies by which new religions legitimate their authority are:

I. Charismatic Appeals

The "pure charisma" (in the ordinary language sense of this term) of the leadership

Evidence that the leader has superior spiritual and/or psychic gifts (miracles; prophecies)

Evidence that the leader has superior insight and/or wisdom

Evidence that, under the inspired guidance of the leader, the group has manifested an attractive, superior community that has benefited followers in various ways (more loving, healthier, and so on).

An appeal to direct revelation, in the specific sense that the leader has received a direct transmission from the Sacred, however conceived. These revelations can lead to the production of new, authoritative scriptures, to the discovery of previously unknown sacred beings and/or to the leader's self-discovery that she or he is spiritually special.

Although any sort of revelation easily leads to the claim that the leader has a unique status as a chosen emissary of the Divine, even in the absence of such revelations the leader can lay claim to a special status, from prophet to avatar.

II. Rational Appeals

A direct appeal to reason/rationality

An appeal to "common sense" or ordinary experience

An appeal to the authority of science. This particular appeal, which has been highly popular among contemporary new religions, can take a number of different forms, as will be demonstrated in later chapters.

III. Traditional Appeals

An appeal to tradition, often reinterpreted to legitimate innovation. Especially in Protestantism, this takes the form of an appeal to the Bible, frequently finding new meanings or new emphases that previous Christians somehow overlooked (for example, Martin Luther).

One can also appeal to the authority of traditional religious figures, attributing new teachings to them that differ from traditional doctrines.

A more ambiguous variation on this strategy is the appeal to an ancient wisdom or a primordial religiosity that antedates current religions. In certain ways this is an appeal to "tradition"; in other ways it represents a different kind of an appeal.

This is not meant to be an exhaustive overview. Rather, this list is simply intended to indicate the variety of possibilities.

The lines of division between these legitimation strategies are often hazy and overlapping. A new age channeler relaying teachings from "Master Jesus", for example, is simultaneously appealing to the authority of direct revelation and to the authority of a traditional religious figure. Though here merged into a single appeal, it is nevertheless analytically useful to separate them. In this specific case, it is easy to see that the channeler could claim, alternately, that he or she is receiving transmissions from, let us say, a Venusian starship captain. In this case the message would still be authoritative because of its status as a direct revelation, but not because it is coming from a traditional religious figure.

The strategies listed above are directed primarily toward a new religion's immediate audience, namely followers and potential converts. As long as the movement remains small and non-controversial, efforts to legitimate the group rarely extend beyond this audience. When, however, a conflict arises that attracts enough outside attention to potentially disrupt the ongoing life of a religious community, new kinds of legitimation concerns come into play.

In the context of the contemporary world, such controversies can lead to news media stories that call a non-traditional group's legitimacy into question, especially when reporters begin to describe the group as a "cult". Legal actions such as lawsuits leveled by disgruntled ex-members present both a financial challenge and, at least potentially, a challenge to a movement's legitimacy. Further, highly controversial religions are sometimes subjected to police actions for real or imagined breaches of the law. In such situations, a group can find itself placed in the position of having to defend its status as a legitimate religion. This is especially the case when the other parties in a controversy–angry former members, anti-cultists, hostile governments and so forth–seek to tip the scales of power in their favor by attempting to *de*-legitimate the movement.

When this happens, the religious group finds itself compelled to address the issue of legitimacy to new audiences–public opinion, law enforcement, judges and other government officials. In both the law court and the "court of public opinion", the group tries to prove that it is a legitimate religion. Beyond trying to manage its public image and taking certain legal counter-measures, few other options are open to small religious movements.

Though closely related, the notion of a religion's societal legitimacy is somewhat different from Weber's notion of legitimacy. Weber focused on the legitimation of authority in situations where power is exercised over other people. In contrast, the legitimacy new religions seek in the public eye has more to do with social acceptance—rather like the acceptance accorded to a legitimate child (as opposed to an illegitimate child). Relations of power are still involved, of course, but the larger society's recognition of a religion as legitimate means recognizing a religion's status as a genuine religion and thus recognizing its right to exist within the society, rather than recognizing a religion's right to exercise authority over its members.

Critics of new religions seek to persuade society that such religions are illegitimate, meaning they should not be accorded the status of a religion. Many critics would also argue that certain non-traditional or unusual religions should be abolished altogether. In other words, they seek to legitimate the repression of such groups. This represents another variation on Weber's notion: The repressive authority of the government is already recognized as legitimate. So the goal of critics is not to strengthen the legitimacy of the government's police powers, but rather to prompt the government to exercise this power against new religions by convincing the public and the authorities to *reclassify* the religion in question as a pseudo-religion, or even as a criminal organization.

True Lies:
Forging and Re-Forging the Jesus in India Tradition

Appealing to the authority of traditional religious figures while simultaneously attributing teachings to them that make one's own views appear the true embodiment of tradition is a legitimation strategy one often finds in new religions. Creating new documents and then claiming either that they were received by direct revelation or that they represent previously unknown but ancient texts is also common. The present chapter will examine these complementary legitimation strategies via an analysis of the Jesus-in-India tradition. This particular tradition was chosen because the legend of Jesus' trip to India is *not* an essential or core component of any existing religion, past or present. The analysis can thus be completely blunt while at the same time avoiding the impression that the aim is to undermine the legitimacy of a specific religious group. Also, the processes at work in the generation and perpetuation of the Jesus-in-India tradition are exceptionally lucid, making this particular legend an excellent case study.

The legend that Jesus studied in India prior to his ministry in Palestine can be traced back to a manuscript found in Hemis Monastery that was said to have recorded this visit. The last person claiming to have seen this manuscript was Elizabeth Caspari. An account of this event can be found in Elizabeth Clare Prophet's *The Lost Years of Jesus*:

> [T]he librarian and two other monks approached the ladies carrying three objects. Madame Caspari recognized them as Buddhist books made of sheets of parchment sandwiched between two pieces of wood and wrapped in brocades–green and red and blue seeded with gold.
>
> With great reverence, the librarian unwrapped one of the books and presented the parchments to Mrs Gasque, "These books say your Jesus was here!"....
>
> She pondered the implications of the find. Her mind whirled, reeled as she thought of Jesus travelling, perhaps all over the world. She realized that up until that hour, Jesus had been to her, as to most Christians, a product of Palestine. He was born there; he lived and died there. Any religious training he received was a part of the Jewish tradition. To place Jesus in Tibet or in India would mean that he had studied their customs, their languages, *their religion!*
>
> Why did Jesus feel compelled to undertake this journey, just as she had, prior to his Palestinian mission? And to what manifold purposes did our Father send him? Indeed, this casual encounter atop the world had far-reaching theological implications. Maybe the teachings of Jesus told to John substantiated in turn the teachings of Gautama or the Vedas (Prophet 1984, 317-320).

What Elizabeth Caspari did not realize on that day in 1939 was that she and the other members of her party would be the last persons to claim they had actually seen this quasi-legendary manuscript. The openness of the monks to Caspari's group stands in marked contrast to their response to earlier visits by Westerners, during which the very existence of such texts had been denied. Though Caspari took innumerable photos of her journey, unfortunately her photograph of this encounter does not show the single open page clearly enough for anyone to be able to distinguish the delicate Tibetan characters in the book. And contrary to the rather dramatic retelling of the event in Prophet's book, Caspari was apparently not cognizant of the importance of her find. Not only did she not bother to take more pictures of the manuscript, but she also failed to make further enquiries.

Caspari's story is part of a century-old tradition, which asserts that Jesus journeyed to India to undertake a course in esoteric training. This tradition has been enthusiastically embraced by many contemporary Hindu religious teachers and certain Western esoteric groups Ancient texts discovered in India in the past few centuries, as well as certain traditional Indian legends, supposedly provide evidence for this exotic view of Jesus' early education. For a large percentage of participants in the contemporary occult/metaphysical/"New Age" subculture, Jesus' Indian visit is an historical fact, as well established as–if not actually more real than–the events recorded in the canonical gospels. Although no mainstream religious scholar has taken this thesis seriously, this tale has been especially popular among Indian religious teachers with Western followers, from Swami Rama to Bhaktivedanta Prabhupada to Osho (Bhagwan Rajneesh).

The present chapter will examine the legend of the Hemis manuscript. Although its existence was attested to by a number of different authors, it was clearly a forged document. As will be demonstrated, the story of Jesus in India is rather like the inkblot tests utilized by psychologists, in that each successive promoter of the tale anticipated discovering his own religious beliefs reflected in Jesus' teachings. When they failed to do so, they either supplied the missing components, or edited pre-existing texts to fit their preconceptions of what Jesus must have said and done. Each successive person who perpetuated this legend was attracted to it for the same reason–the Indian Jesus could be deployed to legitimate their own brand of spirituality as well as to undermine the legitimacy of the orthodox interpretation of Christian tradition.

The "Discovery" of Jesus in India

There are two distinct classes of narratives about Jesus' travels in India. The first set of tales involves an early sojourn between the age of 12, corresponding with the last canonical mention of the young Nazarene's life before his ministry in Palestine, and 30, when his ministry began. The purpose of this visit was to acquire esoteric knowledge. The second set of tales has Jesus survive the crucifixion and then journey to India where he lives until he passes on at a ripe old age. These two kinds of narratives are not normally presented in combination. The present discussion will focus on the first tradition, which is more developed as well as more widely accepted. The second tradition will be dealt with briefly because of its connection with the first.

The idea that Jesus studied in India began–or, at least, first received widespread attention–in 1894 when the Russian Nicolas Notovitch published *La vie inconnue du Jesus Christ* (later translated as *The Unknown Life of Jesus Christ*). The bulk of this work recounts a trip Notovitch made to Kashmir in 1887. While there, he hears of a Buddhist monastery possessing ancient texts that include an account of Jesus' visit to India as a young man. He subsequently travels to Leh in Ladakh where he visits Hemis monastery at which, through an interpreter, he transcribes the most significant sections of two large books containing the story of Issa (as Jesus is called in India). This translated text is subsequently incorporated into his *Unknown Life*, under the title *The Life of Saint Issa*.

After telling the story of Israel leading up to Jesus' childhood, Notovich's transcription relates how Jesus left home at the age of 13 because he did not wish to marry. He first journeys to northwest India, where he encounters Jains. He then moves to the east coast of India at Juggernath, where,

> [Brahmin priests] taught him to read and understand the Vedas, to cure by aid of prayer, to teach, to explain the holy scriptures to the people, and to drive out evil spirits from the bodies of men, restoring unto them their sanity (*The Life of Saint Issa* 5:4).

He remains in eastern India for six years, visiting holy places like Benares, preaching the doctrine of the one true God against local superstitions, and the doctrine of equality against the caste system. Despite the fact that he is supposedly learning much from his Hindu mentors, in his sermons he emphatically denies the authority of the Vedas and the reality of the chief divinities of the classical Hindu pantheon. Making enemies of the Hindu priests who decide to have him murdered, he escapes to the Himalayas, where he studies the Pali sutras with Buddhists for another six years. Not one to give up old habits, however, he spends his spare time preaching against superstition, once again angering his mentors. Beyond condemning idolatry, Jesus preaches against the doctrine of reincarnation and condemns the practice of miracle working. Afterwards he visits Persia, where he enters into conflict with Zoroastrians. Finally he leaves and he returns to Palestine. The story then continues on to relate the familiar events of Jesus' Biblical ministry and the Passion, although retold so as to present a story strikingly at odds with the canonical narrative.

Notovitch's book was an instant hit in Europe. Despite immediately being attacked as a forgery, *The Unknown Life of Jesus Christ* prompted other writers to seek, and even to claim they had found, the same document at Hemis Monastery. The earliest of these supporting claims was made by Swami Abhedananda, a member of the Ramakrishna movement who knew the prominent scholar Max Müller. In 1922, he went to Hemis monastery, where he is said to have read the same book Notovtich transcribed in 1887.

Abhedananda subsequently published certain sections of it in his Bengali book, *Kashmir O Tibbate (In Kashmir and Tibet,* 1929). In 1984, these sections, along with certain parts of Abhedananda's Bengali work, were translated and appeared in Elizabeth Clare Prophet's, *The Lost Years of Jesus.* The relevant passages reflect the same basic document, with the exception that Abhedananda deleted the anti-Hindu tone found in *The Unknown Life of Jesus Christ,* and made Issa's theology more congruent with Advaita Vedanta philosophy.

Later another Russian, Nicholas Roerich, also sought out the text at Hemis, but did not find the Notovitch manuscript. Nevertheless, he eventually authored and co-authored a number of books in which he cited passages he claimed were taken from other, unnamed sources dealing with Issa's trip to India. Many of these, however, appear to have been taken directly from Notovitch. He also made reference to a number of legends about Jesus that were widespread in that part of India.

In addition to *The Unknown Life of Jesus Christ,* Roerich also appears to have been influenced by Levi Dowling's *The Aquarian Gospel of Jesus Christ,* an early twentieth-century "esoteric gospel" in which Jesus is portrayed as studying in Asia as well as in a number of Western mystery schools. Though the latter author's account of Jesus' India visit was clearly indebted to Notovitch, Dowling, unlike the others, claimed to have copied the *Aquarian Gospel* directly from the Akashic Records (a familiar concept in occult lore)—a purely spiritual record of events on earth that, according to Dowling, he accessed via clairvoyance–rather than from physical manuscripts secreted away in isolated monasteries.

Beyond Elisabeth Caspari's account mentioned at the beginning of the present chapter, these are the principal sources of what we might call the younger Jesus-in-India tradition. How plausible is this tradition? The central difficulty with this story is, of course, that the manuscript, if it ever existed, was never accessible to more than a few outsiders. Furthermore, the current status of these hypothetical texts is that they were supposedly moved to another monastery further into Tibet, where they were apparently seized and presumably destroyed by the Chinese.

With respect to the actual story related in the text, there are simply too many improbabilities for Notovitch's original narrative to be literally true. However, even if we allow for the possibility that Notovitch embellished his narrative to make it more engaging, the manuscript cannot fail to strike even sympathetic readers as spurious. Many items of historical information are anachronistic; others are simply false. For example, the Juggernath temple in eastern India, which appears to have been Jesus' destination after he left the Jains, was built over a thousand years following Jesus' death. One should also note that the designation "Issa" for Jesus comes from the Qu'ran, composed some six centuries after Jesus' time. Other incorrect items of data include the assertion that the Buddhists are monotheists, "worshiping the one and sublime Brahma" (VI:2).

More importantly, the narrative fails to support the very thesis it sets out to demonstrate, namely that Jesus received his training among the masters of the East. Particularly in Notovitch's version of the story, Jesus does little but attack Indian beliefs and practices, denouncing Hinduism and Buddhism as false and idolatrous. In short, we are forced to conclude not only that the hypothetical manuscript supposedly examined by Notovitch does not tell us anything about the historical Jesus, but, further, that *The Life of Saint Issa* must have been written by someone from the West, almost certainly by the author of *The Unknown Life of Jesus Christ* himself. Before attempting to understand Notovitch's forgery and the motives of subsequent, unconnected individuals who bore false witness to the existence of *The Life of Saint Issa*, we should briefly examine what might be called the older Jesus-in-India tradition.

Around the end of the 19th century, a somewhat different narrative about Jesus in India emerged. Although there are different versions, they all tell the story of how Jesus survived the crucifixion and subsequently moved to India. In one version, Jesus becomes famous in India under the name Yuz-assaf. Eventually, Jesus settles in Srinagar in Kashmir and dies at 120 years of age. This story of Jesus apparently originated in an 1899 book by Mirza Ghulam Ahmad, *Masih Hindustan Mein* (later published in English under the title *Jesus in India)*. Ahmad relates how he came across a grave on Khan Yar Street in Srinagar described as a prophet's grave. When he finds that this prophet was named Yuz-Assaf, Ahmad leaps to the conclusion that this must be Jesus' grave. Following his discovery, he infers a number of other things, such as that the Kashmiri people are part of the ten lost tribes who Jesus sought out in his old age. He also discovers Mary's grave not far away. Ahmad seems to have been the first person to claim to have found Jesus' grave in Srinagar.

What is relevant in these claims for the younger Jesus-in-India tradition is that Notovitch, who passed through Srinagar during his 1887 trip, never mentions anything about the later Jesus-in-India tradition. This indicates that, far from being an ancient legend, the story of Jesus' life and burial in Kashmir originated after Notovitch's time. And in the same way that narratives about Jesus' old age and death in India started with Ahmad, narratives about Jesus travelling to India as a young man began with Notovitch. Not only is there no hint of such a trip in any of the documents that have survived from the early Christian era, but, down through the centuries, no one ever seriously proposed a connection between India and Jesus prior to Notovitch.

The Original Forgery

Though we can safely conclude that *The Life of Saint Issa* is a forgery, we should remember that the history of religion contains innumerable examples of such forged documents–including examples from such "mainstream" religions as Christianity and Buddhism–before we judge Notovitch too harshly. Many of the principal scriptures of Mahayana Buddhism, for instance, claim to have been authored by the historical Buddha, despite the fact that they did not appear until many centuries after his death.

It is also generally accepted that some of the epistles supposedly authored by Paul were simply forged. In both of these cases, the respective authors' strategy was to draw on the prestige of a great religious figure to legitimate particular doctrines and associated practices. In *The Gnostic Gospels,* for example, Elaine Pagels notes that a number of the pseudo-Pauline letters pick up on and amplify the antifeminist tenor of the Paul's own views, presumably to legitimate the repression of uppity women in their congregations; for example, I Timothy 2:11-12,

> Let a woman learn in silence with all submissiveness. I permit no woman to teach or to have authority over men; she is to keep silent (cited in Pagels 1989, 630).

An extension of this strategy is to forge a narrative in which an authoritative figure is reported as advocating a particular ideology.

In addition to associating documents with important people–either as authors or as spokespersons–texts are also forged that claim to be very ancient. The goal of both approaches is to legitimate whatever ideas are being propagated by the document. Appealing to a pure, uncorrupted, original truth that antedates current religions is frequently employed by founders of new religions. The attractiveness of this strategy is based on a deep pattern in the human psyche that tends to regard ancient origins as particularly sacred. This pattern and its implications for religion have been exhaustively explored by historians of religion like Mircea Eliade.

Gerald Gardner, the founder of the relatively recent (mid-twentieth century) religion of Neopagan Witchcraft (commonly referred to as the "Craft" by insiders), is a useful example of someone who forged a number of important documents he later claimed to be very old. For example, in the context of an argument over how a Witch "coven" should be run and how Witches should comport themselves in public, Gardner devised a set of "Craft Laws" that legitimated his personal ideas on these matters. Rather than crediting authorship to himself, he composed the document in archaic, King James-style English and claimed that the laws were very ancient. These Craft Laws became one of the founding documents of the Neopagan movement. For our present discussion, what is significant about this incident is that Gardner felt no need to name a particular person as the author of his forgery; merely ascribing ancient origins was enough to legitimate it (Lewis 1999, 345-352). In both of these cases, we are probably safe in inferring that the unknown author of First Timothy as well as Gerald Gardner believed in the truth of most if not all of the ideas they were expressing, but felt a need to support their position with an appeal to a greater authority.

Notovitch drew on both of these sources of legitimacy--an authoritative historical figure (Jesus) and ancient origins. Assuming Notovitch put his own views in the mouth of Jesus, it appears that he accepted some form of Deism. From Jesus' non-virgin birth to his non-resurrection to his message of moralism, anti-priestcraft, and anti-miracle-working, *The Life of Saint Issa* expresses a thoroughly Deist theology. There are, however, a few unique twists. The majority of Chapter Twelve (12:9-21), for example, is devoted to extolling the nobility of women in their roles as wives and mothers, and encouraging men to support and protect the opposite sex; for example,

> Respect woman, for she is the mother of the universe, and all the truth of divine creation lies in her. She is the basis of all that is good and beautiful, as she is also the germ of life and death. On her depends the whole existence of man, for she is his natural and moral support (12:10-11).

Also, in a complete reversal from the canonical story, Pilate is intent on executing Jesus, while the priests and elders of Israel defend him. When Jesus is finally brought before Pilate and tried, the priests and elders–changing places with the canonical Pilate–even wash their hands of the matter, saying, "We are innocent of the death of this just man" (13:25). This reassignment of guilt is interesting because it corresponds with the consensus of modern scholarship, which is that Roman authorities, not Jewish authorities, were responsible for the execution of Jesus.

Though we know too little about Notovitch's life to be able to say what motivated him to devote so much space (relatively speaking) to a discourse in praise of women, we do know enough about his background to be able to surmise why he rewrote the trial of Jesus. Though at least nominally a member of the Russian Orthodox Church, Notovitch's background was Jewish, strongly suggesting a very personal motive for turning the ancient Romans into "Christ killers," rather than blaming the Jewish people. Also, given the passion with which Notovitch's Jesus expresses himself, we are probably justified in inferring that, for the most part at least, Notovitch truly believed in the ideas contained in the text of his fabrication–true lies, if you will.

That being said, however, we should not completely factor out the role played by pecuniary motives. Notovitch was a professional writer. He undoubtedly expected that *The Unknown Life of Jesus Christ* would sell well, if not become an international bestseller:

> At least eight editions were published in France in 1894 [the year it first appeared], and three separate English translations appeared in the United States. Another English translation was published in London the following year. It was also translated into German, Spanish, Swedish, and Italian (Prophet 1984, 20).

Thus although Notovitch probably hoped to popularise the views expressed in *The Unknown Life of Jesus Christ,* he was also consciously engaged in the construction of a forgery from which he anticipated financial rewards.

Re-forging the Story

The strongest objection that can be raised against the charge that *The Life of Saint Issa* was a forgery is that other witnesses claimed either to have seen the manuscript or to have recovered similar documents that resembled *The Life of Saint Issa*. Swami Abhedanada made the former claim; Nicolas Roerich made the latter. These men, otherwise viewed as 'honourable', however, had their own reasons for perpetuating Notovitch's bogus story. Their motives can best be inferred from the modifications and additions they made to Notovitch's text.

As noted earlier, Abhedananda reproduced somewhat modified passages from *The Life of Saint Issa* in his 1929 Bengali work, *In Kashmir and Tibet*. The differences are revealing: Notovitch's Issa is "taught" by the Brahmins (5:4), and, some time later, he warns the people that they should "Listen not to the Vedas, for their truth is counterfeit" (5:26). In sharp contrast, Abhedananda's Issa becomes a "disciple" of the Brahmins, eventually "reading, learning and expounding the Vedas" (5:4). The Swami is also more charitable toward the Jains. Notovitch's Issa rejects their invitation to stay with them because they represent a false religion,

[T]he devotees of the god Jaine prayed him to dwell among them. But he left the erring worshippers of Jaine and went to Juggernaut...(5:2-3).

Abhedananda's Issa, however, turns down their invitation from a desire to remain out of the public spotlight,

And they asked him to stay in their temples. But he did not accept their invitation, because he did not want any attention from others at that time (5:3).

These are not minor differences that can be summarily dismissed. Abhedananda's Jesus is simply not Notovitch's iconoclastic prophet, railing against the perversities of the heathen. Rather, as Ramakrishna (the founder of the Swami's movement) taught, Abhedananda's Jesus was a Hindu avatar.

There are three principal ways of accounting for this discrepancy. First, there was a text at Hemis Monastery that Notovitch recorded correctly but which Abhedananda changed to suit his own views. Second, there was a text that Abhedananda recorded correctly but which Notovitch changed to suit his own views. Or third, there never was a real book at Hemis, but Abhedananda played along with forgery–albeit with some profound modifications of Notovitch's text–for his own purposes. If we take the third option as the most likely one, what might the Swami's motives have been?

For all of Abhedananda's life, the British ruled South Asia and treated Indians as second-class citizens. Furthermore, though English administrators were ambivalent about Western missionary activity in the subcontinent, few regarded indigenous religious traditions as anything more than barbaric superstitions. But what if the founder of the conquerors' own faith had spent the larger part of his life in the Indian subcontinent, studying at the feet of Hindu and Buddhist sages? Perhaps Jesus himself even preached some form of Indian wisdom after his return to Palestine, though most traces of such teachings disappeared or were destroyed by the early church. The appeal of this idea to a subject people would be tremendous. If true, it would imply that Indian civilization is the foundation for western civilization–or, at least, the foundation of the western religious tradition.

Abhedananda's initial interest in the story of Jesus' Indian sojourn probably derived from this attraction. After examining a copy of *The Unknown Life of Jesus Christ*, however, the Swami would have been appalled by many of the teachings of Notovitch's Jesus. At that point (to grant him the benefit of the doubt), maybe Abhedananda concluded the story was real, but that Notovitch had re-interpreted it according to western prejudices. The Swami would then have gone to Hemis in search of the original manuscript, only to find that it was missing or to encounter monks denying it was ever there. Disappointed, perhaps Abhedananda then decided to go back over *The Life of Saint Issa* and rewrite it to conform with his preconception of what the original manuscript must have said, according his notion of Jesus as a Hindu-style avatar. (It should be noted that the section of the Swami's travelogue translated for Prophet's *The Lost Years of Jesus* relates that he **did** see the original from which Notovitch's book was transcribed. This particular section was, however, written in the third person, indicating that it had been added to the 1954 second edition by a later editor over a decade after Abhedananda's death.)

Being aware of the standards of Western scholarship, however, the Swami would have been reluctant to present his discovery in English to a Western audience. Knowing that there was no real text on the shelves of the Hemis monastery library (or doubting that such a text existed), and knowing further that the monks themselves would deny the manuscript's existence, Abhedananda would have been aware that any claim of discovering the original Notovitch text would embroil him in the same controversies that greeted the initial publication of *The Unknown Life of Jesus Christ* in 1894. (The Swami was, as noted earlier, an acquaintance of the noted scholar Max Muller who wrote an article (Muller, 1894) condemning *The Life of Saint Issa* as a fraud.) He therefore, with regret, decided to restrict the publication of his rewritten passages from *The Life of Saint Issa* to a Bengali book that would be unlikely to attract the attention of Western critics.

Had Abhedananda found a real text at Hemis containing the ideas expressed in his *In Kashmir and Tibet*, he would certainly have broadcast his findings to the widest possible audience, both scholarly and popular, for the reasons mentioned above. That he did not is strong evidence that the Swami never, in fact, laid eyes on such a manuscript. At the same time, Abhedananda's "re-forging" of *The Life of Saint Issa* falls into the category of a "true lie"–a falsified document expressing what the author felt were profound truths.

"Other Sources"

Nicholas Roerich, another man viewed as 'honourable', also entered into complicity with the Notovitch legend, but stopped short of claiming to have seen the original manuscript at Hemis monastery. Instead, he first, mentions the story of the earlier Russian traveller who transcribed the story of Jesus, second, recounts local legends about Issa's visit, third, implies that the monks know the details of Issa's Indian travels, but keep them secret, and fourth, provides quotations from other (unnamed) "sources" and "documents" that repeat–and often paraphrase–*The Life of Saint Issa*. This set of strategies allowed Roerich to confirm Notovitch's basic story while simultaneously avoiding the criticism that might have been evoked had he claimed to have actually seen texts on Jesus' Indian sojourn in the library at Hemis.

Like Abhedananda's Issa, Roerich's Issa is less antagonistic to Hindu and Buddhist religiosity than Notovitch's Issa. Specifically, although Roerich's Jesus attacks idolatry and the caste system, he does not condemn Jains, Hindus or Buddhists as following "counterfeit" traditions. Unsurprisingly, the Jesus one encounters in Roerich's writings is closer to the Theosophical view of Jesus (Roerich's own religious persuasion) than to either Notovitch's Deist or Abhedananda's Vedantist Jesus.

Interestingly, in the book *Himalaya* (1929), Roerich also paraphrases passages from *The Aquarian Gospel of Jesus Christ* which, he claims, were taken from "Another source–historically less established–[that] speaks also about the life in Jesus in Tibet." This other source is never named, for obvious reasons. *The Aquarian Gospel* is a broad-ranging work, only a portion of which is devoted to Jesus' alleged studies in South Asia. The India and Tibet sections of *The Aquarian Gospel* are, however, directly inspired by *The Unknown Life of Jesus Christ,* although, as I have already noted, Levi Cowling was not guilty of actual plagiarism. Like Notovitch's Issa, Cowling's Jesus travels to eastern India, preaches against the caste system and Idolatry, and then moves on to the Himalayas. To cite a few relevant passages from *The Aquarian Gospel,*

> And Jesus was accepted as a pupil in the temple Jagannath; and here learned the Vedas and the Manic laws. The Brahmic masters wondered at the clear conceptions of the child, and often were amazed when he explained to them the meaning of the laws (Dowling 1916; 21:19-20).

Here one can see the direct influence of Notovitch's story, but not his wording. In only a very few short lines does one find Notovitch's language reflected in Cowling's text. Notovitch, for instance, has Jesus say, "Worship not the idols, for they hear you not." (5:26) Cowling is obviously working from this same passage when his Aquarian Jesus similarly asserts, "Tear down your idols; they can hear you not..." (26:21).

Roerich's use of Cowling is less sophisticated than Cowling's use of Notovitch. For example, the Aquarian Jesus becomes interested in travelling to Buddhist Lhasa (an anachronism, as Buddhism did not become established in Tibet until the seventh century) where he meets the Chinese sage, Ming-tse,

> In Lassa of Tibet there was a master's temple, rich in manuscripts of ancient lore. The Indian sage had read these manuscripts, and he revealed to Jesus many of the secret lessons they contained; but Jesus wished to read them for himself. Now, Meng-ste, greatest sage of all the farther East, was in this temple of Tibet (36:1-3).

Roerich's clumsy paraphrase is lifted directly from *The Aquarian Gospel,*

> Near Lhassa was a temple of teaching, with a wealth of manuscripts. Jesus wanted to acquaint himself with them. Ming-ste, a great sage of all the East, was in this temple (*Himalaya* 1929, 153).

In addition to supplying his narrative with details taken from a source other than Notovitch, Roerich was likely attracted to Cowling's work because the Aquarian Jesus was far more compatible with his own Theosophical beliefs. Reincarnation, for instance, is one of the core tenets of Theosophy. For this reason, Roerich neglects to cite *The Life of Saint Issa* where Notovitch's Issa says, "Never would [God] so humiliate his child as to transmigrate his soul..." (6:11). Instead, he is more attracted to Jesus' discourse on reincarnation in *The Aquarian Gospel of Jesus Christ*, where he comments on the source of singing talent,

> From whence this talent and this power? In one short life they could not gain such grace of voice, such knowledge of the laws of harmony and tone. Men call them prodigies. There are no prodigies. All things result from natural law. These people are not young. A thousand years would not suffice to give them such divine expressiveness, and such purity of voice and touch. Ten thousand years ago these people mastered harmony. In days of old they trod the busy thoroughfares of life, and caught the melody of birds, and played on harps of perfect form. And they have come again to learn still other lessons from the varied notes of manifests (37:11-15).

Once again, Roerich simply paraphrases Cowling's passage, attributing it to the same unnamed source as the story of Jesus' trip to Tibet,

> Said Jesus of skilled singers: "Whence is their talent and their power? For in one short life they could not possibly accumulate a quality of voice and the knowledge of harmony and of tone. Are these miracles? No, because all things take place as a result of natural law. Many thousands of years ago these people already moulded their harmonies and their harmonies. And they come again to learn still more from varied manifestations" (*Himalaya* 1929, 156).

While it is easy to see what Roerich did, it is less clear why he did it. Perhaps, to extend him the same benefit of the doubt we gave Abhedananda, Roerich travelled to South Asia sincerely expecting to find ancient manuscripts confirming not only Jesus' Indian sojourn, but also containing a record of Jesus' "real" teachings–teachings which would confirm Roerich's own Theosophical views. Instead, all he encountered were a few legends scattered about here and there.

Disappointed in his quest, perhaps he became convinced that the documents he sought really existed, but that the Buddhist monks had misplaced them or were hiding them from outsiders. He suggests that he believes the latter when he describes how each "silent" lama at Leh "knows much" about the stories he "secretly and cautiously" guards. (*Altai-Himalaya*, p. 120) He may also have convinced himself of the ultimate reality of the Hemis manuscript because of the prevalence of the legend among the ordinary people ("In what possible way could a recent forgery penetrate into the consciousness of the whole East?" Ibid., p. 119). In any event, we can infer that Roerich eventually decided to work up a story about the Jesus who he is certain must have visited India, and who must have taught esoteric truths.

Rather than rewrite the tale from scratch, however, Roerich made liberal use of *The Life of Saint Issa* and *The Aquarian Gospel of Jesus Christ*. Perhaps he felt that these two narratives were both somehow real, or at least based on real documents. After reading Roerich, one gets the impression that he believed Notovitch had actually seen a real manuscript, but inferred that his fellow Russian inserted his own prejudices into *The Life of Saint Issa*. Thus, like Swami Abhedananda, Roerich would have felt comfortable editing Notovitch's work so as to present only the passages free of Notovitch's "additions." Roerich also apparently believed that Cowling, another esotericist like himself, had really accessed the Akashic Records and had presented an accurate account of Jesus' life. He thus felt he could paraphrase details of Jesus' Indian travels from the *Aquarian Gospel* because he "knew" Cowling's narrative was true. Thus while Roerich's sense of honour prevented him from actually forging new documents from scratch, he gave in to the temptation to fudge the facts in order to spread the truth.

But why, we might ask at this point, was confirming Jesus' India trip so important that a man of Roerich's stature would fall victim to the "true lies" syndrome? In terms of our earlier discussion, it appears that Roerich was attracted to the possibility of legitimating his occult beliefs at the expense of traditional Christianity:

> But who can fail to recognize that many of the so-called "Apocrypha" are far more basically true than many official documents? (ibid., 126).

In this passage, it is not hard to realize that the "official documents" being referred to are Christian scriptures. Roerich, in other words, is asserting that the Jesus he found in India is the real Jesus, and that the Biblical account of Jesus' life and teachings is flawed. Although understated, the above statement captures the central premise of Roerich's entire edifice, and provides the key to understanding his motive.

Concluding Remarks

As we have seen, the story of Jesus in India is rather like a psychologist's ink blot test, in that each successive promoter of the tale anticipated discovering his own religious beliefs reflected in Jesus' teachings. When he failed to do so, he either supplied the missing components or edited pre-existing texts to fit his preconception of what Jesus must have said and done. Each successive person who perpetuated the Issa tradition was attracted to the legend for the same reason--the Indian Jesus could be deployed to legitimate their own brand of spirituality as well as to undermine the legitimacy of the dominant Christian tradition.

This same attraction explains why so many Indian gurus, New Age teachers, and the like have adopted and propagated the legend, though sometimes they modify it further. In the final section of Elizabeth Clare Prophet's *The Lost Teachings of Jesus*, for instance, Prophet asserts that the "texts and legends" (e.g., Notovitch, Abhedananda, Roerich, and others) examined in her book indicate that Jesus "prayed, meditated, practiced yoga, studied and taught" (1984, 353). None of these texts, however, mention either meditation or yoga. Rather, it seems Prophet has simply inferred that Jesus "must" have practiced these spiritual techniques, based on her own preconception of what Jesus was like.

Through the case study of the legend of Jesus' journey to India, the present chapter analysed the phenomenon of the fabrication of a pseudo-tradition as a legitimation strategy. The larger significance of this particular discussion for religious studies is that the history of religions contains innumerable examples of forged scriptures–including documents in the scriptural canons of major world religions like Christianity and Buddhism. This legitimation strategy is thus a concrete example of how the study of contemporary new religions potentially sheds light on our understanding of traditional religions, if only because such an approach compels us to view familiar phenomena against the backdrop of unfamiliar comparisons.

References:

Abhedananda, Swami. *Parivrajaka Swami Abhedananda*. 1929. Revised Second Edition under the Editorship of Swami Prajnananda. *Kashmir O Tibbate (In Kashmir and Tibet)*. 1954.

Bock, Janet. *The Jesus Mystery: Of Lost Years and Unknown Travels*. Los Angeles: Aura Books, 1980.

Brown, Leslie. *The Indian Christians of St. Thomas: an Account of the Ancient Syrian Church of Malabar*. Cambridge, UK: Cambridge University Press, 1982.

Douglas, J. Archibald. "The Chief Lama of Himis on the Alleged 'Unknown Life of Christ.'"*Nineteenth Century*. April 1896, pp. 667-78.

Dowling, Levi H. *The Aquarian Gospel of Jesus the Christ: The Philosophic and Practical Basis of the Religion of the Aquarian Age of the World and of the Church Universal, Transcribed from the Book of God's Remembrances, Known as the Akashic Records*. London: L.N. Fowler, 1916, 4th ed. c1911.

Goodspeed, Edgar J. *Strange New Gospels*. Chicago, IL: University of Chicago Press, 1931.

Grant, Francis R., Mary Siegrist, George Grebenstchikoff, Ivan Narodny, and Nicholas Roerich. *Himalaya: A Monograph*. New York: Brentanos, 1926.

Grönbold, G. *Jesus in Indien. Das Ende einer Legende*. München, Germany, 1985.

Hale, Edward Everett. "The Unknown Life of Christ." *North American Review*. 159. 1894, pp 594-601.

"Hamis Knows Not 'Issa': Clear Proof That Notovitch Is a Romancer." *New York Times* 19. April 1896, p. 28.

Kersten, Holger. *Jesus Lived in India*. Shaftesbury, Dorset: Longmead, 1986. (Originally published as, *Jesus lebte in Indien*, 1983.

Klatt, N. *Jesus in Indien* EZW-Texte nr.13, XII/1986, Stuttgart, Germany.

Kranenborg, Reender. "Jesus' Stay in India." *Syzygy: Journal of Alternative Religion and Culture* 6:2. 1997, pp. 169-183.

Lewis, James R. *Witchcraft Today*. Santa Barbara: ABC-Clio, 1999.

Müller. F. Max. "The Alleged Sojourn of Christ in India." *Nineteenth Century*. October 1894, pp. 515-21.

Notovitch, Nicolas. *The Unknown Life of Jesus Christ*, trans. Virchand R. Gandhi. Chicago: Progressive Thinker Publishing House, 1907. (Originally Publ. as, *La vie inconnue du Jesus Christ*, 1894.)

Paelian, Garabed. *Nicholas Roerich*. Agoura, CA: Aquarian Education Group, 1974.

Pagels, Elaine. *The Gnostic Gospels*. 1979; New York: Vintage, 1989.

Prophet, Elizabeth Clare. *The Lost Years of Jesus: On the Discoveries of Notovitch, Abhedananda, Roerich, and Caspari*. Livingston, MT: Summit University Press, 1984.

Roerich, Nicholas. *Altai-Himalaya: A Travel Diary*. New York: Frederick A. Stokes Co., 1929.

_____. *Heart of Asia*. New York: Roerich Museum Press, 1929.

Shivani, Sister (Mary LePage). *An Apostle of Monism: An Authentic Account of the Activities of Swami Abhedananda in America*. Calcutta, India: Ramakrishna Vedanta Math, 1947.

The Other Side:
The Science of Life After Death

Speculation about past lifetimes, near-death experiences, receiving messages from the dead and so forth constitute a significant component of New Age spirituality. This speculation is often grounded in scientific and quasi-scientific research that provide–or at least appear to provide–empirical evidence of post-mortem survival. Because interest in the fate of the individual after death is a universal concern, much of this research is attractive to people who are not otherwise involved in the New Age subculture. Similarly, some of the research that interests people within the New Age is not being carried out by researchers who are themselves participants in alternative spirituality. Thus, while the boundaries of the New Age movement are often vague and highly permeable, the nature of the afterlife topic is such that it violates these boundaries in a more profound way than any other topic of New Age concern except holistic health.

Until recently, the idea of an afterlife was one of the constants of human thought. Even prehistoric sites contain graves in which one finds utensils, weapons, and other artifacts indicating some sort of belief in a continuation of life beyond the dissolution of the physical body. Contemporary science has, however, called this universal belief into question. By demonstrating that the day-to-day operations of the human organism can be explained in terms of physics and chemistry, science has introduced doubts about the existence of a spiritual self or soul existing independently of the physical body.

The notion of the continuity of human life is, however, a stubborn belief. Though the authority of traditional religion may no longer be enough to assure us of life after death, this belief has been resurrected on the authority of the very institution that seemed to call it into question–science. New forms of "scientific religion" emerged in the nineteenth century that claimed to establish religion, including afterlife beliefs, on a new, empirical footing. These new religions, particularly Spiritualism and the New Thought movement, were major contributors to the contemporary occult/metaphysical/New Age subculture.

The Spiritualist Movement

Spiritualism is a religious movement emphasizing belief in survival after death, a belief Spiritualists claim is based upon scientific proof. This proof is provided by communication with the surviving personalities of deceased human beings by means of mediumship–the supernormal ability to receive messages from disembodied spirits. Nineteenth century Spiritualism provided a significant impetus for what became known as psychical research and, later, as parapsychology.

The continuity of the personality after death through a new birth into a spiritual body (not a new physical body) represents a central important tenet of Spiritualism. According to Spiritualists, at death the soul, which is composed of a sort of subtle matter, withdraws itself and remains near the earth plane for a longer or shorter period of time. After this, it advances in knowledge and moral qualities and proceeds to higher planes, until it eventually reaches the sphere of pure spirit. The rapidity at which the soul advances is in direct proportion to the mental and moral faculties acquired during earth life. Spiritualists originally conceived of the spiritual planes as spheres encircling the earth, one above the other, whereas now they are more commonly supposed to interpenetrate each other and to co-exist at different rates of vibration.

Bliss, hell, and eternal damnation are not part of Spiritualist belief; nor are notions of final judgement and the resurrection of the physical body. Communication with the dead, through the agency of mediums, represents the other central belief of Spiritualism. Spirits contacted by mediums are traditionally asked first of all to prove their identities by giving correct information about their earthly lives and concerns. This and related practices is the basis for Spiritualist claims that their religion is based on a science.

The phenomena of traditional Spiritualism fall into three main groups, which include physical mediumship, spiritual healing, and mental mediumship. Among the physical phenomena are acoustic phenomena, such as raps and blows; apports, passing of matter through matter, transportation of the human body; chemical phenomena, such as psychic photography; electric and magnetic phenomena; fire immunity; levitation of the human body and materialization; telekinesis, that is the movement of objects without contact; psycho-physiological phenomena, elongation, transfiguration, trance, ectoplasm, aura and emanations; thermodynamic effects, such as psychic winds.

Spiritual healing includes contact healing, which is a laying on of hands, and absent healing, in which the medium, working with disembodied "spirit doctors," has no direct contact with the patient and effects healing at a distance. Mental phenomena include clairvoyance, clairaudience, crystal gazing, divination, premonition, dowsing, healing, psychometry, trance speaking, telepathy and xenoglossis. Many of these phenomena have been explained as the result of the unknown mental processes of the medium, although the more common interpretation involves the role of an extraneous factor–the will of someone other, living person, a disembodied human consciousness (a spirit), or something unknown of non-human origin.

Seemingly the most obvious explanation and the one with the greatest appeal is the spirit hypothesis. This theory was adopted by many non-Spiritualist psychical researchers, according to whom a human spirit which has survived death is able to cause such phenomena. Both Spiritualist and alternative explanations must deal with the validation of paranormal phenomena, because the history of mediumship has often been plagued by fraud and tricks by fake mediums.

The belief in the possibility of communication with the spirit world has been held in most of the societies of which we have records. Spiritualism has many parallels and predecessors among so-called "primitive" people, in the miracles of world religions, and in the phenomena associated with witchcraft, poltergeist activity, possession and the like. These manifestations were not always associated with the spirits of deceased people; traditionally, they were associated with angelic or diabolic possession, most frequently with the latter.

The significance of the doctrine of Animal Magnetism, described in Franz Antoine Mesmer's *De Planetarum Influxu* in 1766, was very considerable from the Spiritualist point of view. Mesmerism (the precursor to both hypnotism and psychic healing), along with Swedenborgianism, began in Europe in the late eighteenth century, and was later exported to the United States. Its transition to Spiritualism was effected by Andrew Jackson Davis, a student of Swedenborg who practiced the psychic diagnosis of illness. Davis wrote a number of books on what he termed the Harmonial Philosophy, dealing with the origins and nature of the universe, and with the afterlife. Swedenborg was a Swedish mystic who became famous for his visions of higher spiritual realms, and for his travels to these realms. His voluminous writings record, among other topics, the state of spirits in the afterlife. Directly through his own writings and indirectly through Davis, Swedenborg provided a theological schema for the phenomena of spiritualism.

Swedenborg pictured the human being as existing simultaneously in the spiritual realm and in the realm of everyday experience. The spiritual realm exerts a powerful influence over human life, though people are, for the most part, unaware of the spirit. After dropping the physical body at death, souls transit into an intermediate, earth-like realm where they meet deceased friends and relatives. These aspects of Swedenborg's schema, but not others, were incorporated into the ideology of the Spiritualist movement.

The events generally regarded as the origin of modern Spiritualism began in 1848, when the Fox sisters started communicating with spirits through rappings in their house at Hydesville, New York. Margareta and Kate Fox, then aged fifteen and twelve, lived with their parents, John, a Methodist farmer, and Margaret, in Hydesville, near Rochester, New York. From the time the family moved there near the end of 1847, the Foxes were disturbed and kept awake at night by unexplainable sounds, such as raps and bangs, which were imputed to the presence of spirits in the house.

The Foxes belief that they were communicating with a discarnate spirit received support when, on the night of March 31, 1848, Maggie and Katie began to clap their hands and the raps answered them back by imitating the pattern of the hand-claps. Maggie and Kate Fox then requested "Mr. Splitfoot" (a reference to the cloven feet of the devil) to respond to questions with his raps. While such phenomena are, as we have seen, not especially unusual, the Foxes attracted a great deal of public attention, and people from miles around would stop by to observe the phenomenon of spirit communication. Initially, the spirit knocked two times for "yes" and made no noise for "no." After a while, however, David Fox, an older brother, developed a complex codes of knocks for the alphabet, in which the ghost was able to communicate more complex messages. The rappings, later witnessed by the neighbors, resolved into alphabetical messages which allegedly came from Charles Rosa, a peddler who claimed to have been murdered for his money by a former occupant of the house, and to have been buried in the cellar. Some human remains were, in fact, found in the cellar, as John Fox subsequently maintained.

Not long afterwards, Leah Fish, the two girls' older sister, brought her mother and Kate to Rochester. However, the phenomenon followed Kate. Around the time of the move, news of the rappings was beginning to create national interest, and a variety of different people in the Rochester area discovered that they had mediumistic abilities as well. Spirit knockings were everywhere, and the "Rochester knockings" attracted tremendous press coverage.

The phenomenon became very popular, and the two sisters began to give public demonstrations of their ability to communicate with the spirit world. Leah became the manager of Maggie and Kate, who toured many cities and held seances in parlors, charging fees. During their elaborate performances, tables moved and objects materialized. They were soon followed by other mediums, and provided a fertile ground for a new way of looking at life and, eventually, a new religious movement.

Among the most common physical phenomena were cases of telekinesis, such as those that occurred in the presence of the famous medium D.D. Home. The most common mental phenomena, which had already attained some prominence in the mesmeric movement of the preceding half-century, included clairvoyance. Trance mediums, such as Mrs Gladys Osborne Leonard and Mrs Leonora E. Piper, would sometimes assert that they had been in the other world and had spoken with its inhabitants. In other cases the medium's body was purportedly controlled by spirits who, through automatic writing and automatic speaking, gave information about their earthly lives and transmitted detailed and often lengthy accounts of the next world and its inhabitants. Sometimes they communicated ethical and theological teachings, like those of the British clergyman Reverend W. Stainton Moses, whose *Spirit Teachings* (1883) was at one time considered a kind of "bible" within Anglo-American Spiritualism.

Spiritualism became a widespread movement through informal seances (termed *home circles* or *sittings*) held in private homes with the aim of communicating with the dead. Such circles where highly popular in the late nineteenth and early twentieth centuries when Spiritualism was faddish. Home circles were not infrequently held without the assistance of professional mediums. In the wake of the frenzied publicity surrounding the Fox sisters, many ordinary people organized circles with their family and friends in an effort to manifest spiritualistic phenomena. In England in the 1870s, the weekly magazine *The Spiritualist* went so far as to provide guidelines for such grassroots activity. It was usually possible to find at least one individual in every such gathering with the necessary mediumistic abilities. The home circle, which had made Spiritualism a popular movement extending well beyond Spiritualist denominational boundaries, faded into relative obscurity by early in the twentieth century.

Perhaps the most popular form of mediumship was so-called automatic writing. In automatic writing, writers (or, sometimes, typists) record information from sources other than their own conscious mind. Automatic writing was very popular during spiritualism's heyday in the nineteenth century, a popularity that has continued into the present. Most practitioners assert that automatic writing represents communications from the souls of the dead. When not dismissed as outright fakery, critics have postulated that the writer-medium is simply channeling her or his own subconscious. Alternately, some psychical researchers have hypothesized that the writer is unconsciously tapping information via ESP (extrasensory perception).

Automatic writing came into vogue in the 1850s as a result of the experiences of Judge John Worth Edmonds, who claimed to have recorded communications from Francis Bacon and Emanuel Swedenborg. As one might anticipate, the fashion of automatic writing resulted in the production of numerous book manuscripts, of widely varying merit. The bulk of such productions are not particularly remarkable. There have, however, been some exceptions. The 19th century researcher Frederic W. H. Myers, for example, discovered an individual who could record two different communications simultaneously, a task Myers thought to be almost impossible to fake.

Although a considerable number of people began to discover and practice mediumistic powers, the Spiritualist movement soon began to come under attack. It was condemned by official religions, and suffered negative publicity as a result of the many investigations of mediums that exposed frauds.

After enjoying a resurgence of popularity during and after World War I, the heyday of mediumship was over by 1920, though interest in Spiritualism continued throughtout the world.

In Britain Spiritualism enjoys a larger following than in the United States, even though its growth was difficult because habit and tradition were more firmly settled, due especially to the influence of the Church of England. Efforts to organize Spiritualist groups in that country began in 1865. One of the key figures in British Spiritualism was the medium Maurice Barbanell, who founded *Psychic News,* a leading Spiritualist newspaper. The British National Association of Spiritualists was founded in 1884, and in 1890 Emma Hardinge Britten, founder of the Spiritualist journal *Two Worlds,* established the National Federation of Spiritualist Churches. This group reorganized in 1901 as the Spiritualist National Union in order to unite Spiritualist churches and promote research on mediumship and healing.

In the United Stated, in response to fraud and other issues within the movement, the National Spiritualist Association of Churches (NSAC) was established in Chicago in 1893. A presbyterial structure was established, with state associations of member congregations and an annual national convention. The NSAC immediately set about establishing standards for Spiritualist ministry and investigating reports of fraud. Even today, with a number of other Spiritualist organizations in existence, the NSAC maintains the highest standards for ordination. The NSAC has also spent a great deal of time and energy on establishing a common statement of Spiritualist beliefs. In 1899 it adopted a "Declaration of Principles" with six articles. The full nine articles are as follows:

1) We believe in Infinite Intelligence.
2) We believe that the phenomena of Nature, both physical and spiritual, are the expression of Infinite Intelligence.
3) We affirm that a correct understanding of such expression and living in accordance therewith constitute true religion.
4) We affirm that the existence and personal identity of the individual continue after the change called death.
5) We affirm that communication with the so-called dead is a fact, scientifically proven by the phenomena of Spiritualism.
6) We believe that the highest morality is contained in the Golden Rule: "Whatsoever ye would that others should do unto you, do ye also unto them."
7) We affirm the moral responsibility of the individual, and that he makes his own happiness or unhappiness as he obeys or disobeys Nature's physical and spiritual laws.
8) We affirm that the doorway to reformation is never closed against any human soul here or hereafter.
9) We affirm that the precept of Prophecy and Healing contained in the Bible is a divine attribute proven through Mediumship.

The last three articles, added later, reflect a move away from an emphasis on remarkable phenomena and toward an emphasis on philosophical development. Besides these nine articles, the NSAC also established common definitions of spiritualist terms and practices. The two major controversies of the twentieth century centered on the questions of whether spiritualists are also Christians and whether spiritualists believe in reincarnation. In 1930 the NSAC explicitly specifically condemned belief in reincarnation, which had repercussions in the form of lost memberships.

The controversy over Christian identity has been less clear-cut. Spiritualism in general has historically drawn most of its membership from Christian denominations, and most Spiritualists identify with some form of Christian practice in the sense that they might say that Jesus was a master medium and Spiritualist healer. If, however, they are asked to identify as a Christian in a more traditional sense–in the context of denominations and historic creeds–most are reluctant to do so. The NSAC has generally taken the position that spiritualists are not also Christians. Those who wish to identify as Christians have tended to gravitate to other Spiritualist organizations.

As for reincarnation, an early form of reincarnationist-oriented Spiritualism was Spiritism, whose doctrine goes beyond proof of survival after death to include the notion of rebirth. Their origins lie in the philosophy of the French doctor Hippolyte Leon Denizard Rivail (1804-1869). His pseudonym, Allan Kardec, was adopted on the basis of information he received about past lives during which his name was Allan and Kardec. This information was received through Celina Japhet, a professional somnambulist in whose seances he participated. Many messages, produced while in trance, developed the notion of reincarnation. Spiritist belief in reincarnation is related to the reincarnation theories of Theosophy, which ultimately derived its understanding of reincarnation from Asian religions.

According to Kardec, reincarnation through many lives is necessary for achieving spiritual progress. Also, the interference of past incarnations may be the cause of such problems as epilepsy, schizophrenia, and multiple personality disorders, so that understanding past lives may heal these disorders. This, it should be noted, is the basic premise of past-lives therapy, which Kardec anticipated by a century. Kardec encouraged the practice of healing/therapy through the acceptance of spirit communications. He also criticized contemporaneous psychical research through the monthly magazine *La Revue Spirite,* and through the Society of Psychologic Studies, of which he was president. Although it enjoyed brief popularity in Europe, Kardec's Spiritism, also known as Kardecism, is today well established in South America, especially Brazil.

Spiritualism and Parapsychology

Spiritualist and Spiritist investigations formed the basis of psychical research, which later became known as parapsychology. The term parapsychology, coined in 1889 by German psychologist Max Dessoir, refers to the scientific study of paranormal and mediumistic phenomena. These phenomena include practically everything beyond those normally understood in terms of physical cause and effect, such as telepathy, clairvoyance, precognition, psychokinesis, etc. Among its subjects of investigation is the problem of survival–the continued possession of personality after death–which reflects parapsychology's origins in Spiritualism. Major efforts have been made in this area which, during the first phase of parapsychology's history, was given more attention by investigators than any other issue.

Interest in spirit communication has always been part of popular culture. In the nineteenth century, the practice of mesmerism had popularized the trance state, encouraging the idea of a psychical ability to communicate with the deceased spirits during such altered states. This interest in spirit communication formed the basis of later interest in the more general phenomenon of telepathy. Experiments in telepathy, in turn, provided scientific support for the contention that mind can exist independently of brain.

Most of the early researchers of survival after death, such as William James, Oliver Lodge, and F.W.H. Myers, belonged to the Society of Psychical Research (SPR), founded in Britain to investigate mesmerist, psychical and Spiritualist claims. They were convinced that the statements of many mediums were accurate, and that mediums gave correct information which could not be obtained in any normal way. Trance communications, such as those received by one Mrs. Piper, and cross-correspondences were often regarded as proof that the communicators survived death. However, SPR investigators were never able to establish whether the information was definitely coming from the world of the dead, or whether it was obtained by the medium's abilities to pick up relevant facts through telepathy or clairvoyance.

Other important experimental researches on mediumship and telepathy were undertaken during the first quarter of the 20th century in university departments of psychology, particularly at the Universities of Harvard and Stanford in the United States, and the University of Groningen in Holland. Laboratory researches on parapsychology were launched in 1927 at Duke University and parapsychology was established as a reputable field–or, perhaps more accurately, as a quasi-reputable field–for scientific studies with the publication of J.B. Rhine's report, *Extra-sensory Perception* (1934). The emphasis on mediumistic studies decreased after William McDougall, professor of psychology at Harvard and member of the SPR, concluded that the mediumistic approach to the problem of survival after death could never result in a definitive solution.

The subject of apparitions and hallucinations, considered an alternative proof of survival after death, has also been extensively investigated over the years. None of these investigations brought scientific recognition to the idea of the immortality of the soul or of the possibility of communication between the living and the dead. Newer developments in survival research, such as investigations of poltergeists, out-of-the-body experiences, psychokinesis, and reincarnation have as yet not provided unassailable proof of life after death. Nevertheless, research on survival continues.

One interesting example of contemporary survival research is electronic voice phenomena (EVP). Electronic voice phenomena refers to what appear to be voices of departed spirits recorded on audio tape. EVP is also sometimes referred to as Raudive Voices, a designation derived from the name of Konstantin Raudive, an EVP researcher. Like everything else in the field of afterlife investigations, electronic voice phenomenon has generated controversy. EVP researchers believe they record communications from the deceased and, sometimes, from extraterrestrials. Skeptics predictably respond that the "spirit voices" either represent the intrusion of broadcasts from radio, television and CBs, or are imagined from static.

EVP is an interesting innovation in the arena of efforts to communicate with discarnate entities. Such early figures in electrical design as Thomas Edison asserted that it would probably be possible to construct an electronic machine through which one could communicate with the dead. Edison actually worked on such a device, as mentioned in the *Scientific American* of October 1920. He failed, however, to complete his EVP machine before his death a decade later. The subject languished for decades until, in 1956, Attila von Sealay, a psychic, cooperated with researchers in an attempt to record spirit voices on tape. Von Sealay asserted that in 1938 he began to sense a "tiny voice" near him. He thought the voice was that of his deceased son, Edson. The experiments resulted in what sounded like voices, whistles and rappings.

Despite this prior history, Friedrich Jurgenson, a Swedish opera singer, painter, and producer, is usually credited with the discovery of EVP, perhaps because his work became so widely known and influenced so many other investigators. Jurgenson's EVP work began innocently enough when he was tape recording birds near his Swedish villa. Listening to his recording, he heard a Norwegian voice talking about "nocturnal bird songs." Initially, he thought a radio broadcast had somehow been recorded. He decided to experiment with other recording sessions to see if the same phenomenon would recur. He heard no voices while recording, but many when he played back the tape. These voices provided personal information about Jurgenson, as well as instructions on how to record yet more such communications.

In 1964, Jurgenson discussed his experiences in *Voices from the Universe*, which was published along with a recording of EVP sounds. The next year, he encountered Konstantin Raudive, a philosopher and psychologist who became interested in researching electronic voice phenomena. Raudive made over 100,000 recordings. His research, published in German as *The Inaudible Made Audible,* was translated and published in English as *Breakthrough* (1971). His work was so widely studied that EVP voices became known as "Raudive voices."

The greatest contemporary interest in EVP investigation is in the United States and Germany. In Germany, there are two EVP organizations: the Association for Voice Taping Research (VTF), founded in the 1970s, and the Research Association for Voice Taping (FGT). The American Association, Electronic Voice Phenomena, was started in the United States in 1982 by Sarah Estep. EVP seminars and conferences are held worldwide. Many of these enthusiasts are electronics experts and engineers who design sensitive and sophisticated equipment for taping the communications.

Estep classifies such communications into three different categories: Class C are faint voices that are often difficult to decipher. Class A are clear voices that can be discerned without headphones, and can even be copied onto other tapes. Class B communications are intermediate in clarity and volume. Beyond the tendency to speak in brief and sometimes cryptic and ungrammatical phrases, EVP's exhibit no particular pattern. The communications come through in different languages, sometimes disregarding the languages of the researchers. At times, the voices will sing in indistinct lyrics. At other times, several or even numerous voices come through simultaneously. Animal sounds have also been taped.

Many otherwise non-skeptical researchers feel that the electronic voice phenomenon can be adequately explained without resort to the idea that the communications come from departed spirits. Other critics have hypothesized that EVP voices result from psychokinesis. In other words, according to this line of interpretation, EVP researchers are so intent on recording spirit voices that they unconsciously imprint sounds on the recording with their own psychokinetic powers. Raudive, who passed away on September 2, 1974, had no particular theory about the source of EVP. Despite the ambiguity of EVP communications, investigators continue to work on producing recordings that will satisfactorily demonstrate survival after death. Similar research using film, video, and even computers has also been pursued.

The Near Death Experience

More recently, the quest for a scientific basis for belief in life after death has shifted to an interest in near death experiences. The term near death experience (NDE) refers to the seemingly supernatural experiences of individuals who have suffered apparent death and then restored to life. George Gallup's *Adventures in Immortality* reported the results of a national survey in which the incidence of NDEs was documented in about five percent of the adult population, or eight million Americans. More generally, Gallup also found belief in life after death to be quite widespread–over two-thirds of the nation hold some kind of belief in an afterlife.

While the near death experience has attracted the most interest from participants in the New Age subculture, NDE research has its roots in older parapsychological interest in the out-of-body experience, traditionally referred to as astral projection. Out-of-body, or ecsomatic, experiences (OOBEs or OBEs) are characterized by perceiving the world from a position different from the one occupied by one's physical body. During OBEs, people often have the experience of quitting their bodies and then viewing them as if from outside.

OBEs usually occur to dying or injured persons, when the subject is asleep or apparently unconscious under anaesthetics, though they can also appear in ordinary circumstances. Some people claim to have experienced OBEs since adolescence or early childhood. The similarity among reports of OBEs–often widely separated by geography and even history–is sometimes proffered as a proof of the reality of travel of consciousness out of the body. OBEs can manifest in a variety of forms. In the most elaborate, people experience their consciousness as escaping from their body, which is then perceived as a lifeless object. Usually a mist or ball of light or ethereal body seems to surround the escaping consciousness, and to be attached to it by a silvery or white cord.

It has been asserted that, if consciousness really can leave the body before death, then OBEs can be regarded as proof of survival after death. However, the possibility that these experiences may actually be departures of one's mind or imagination from one's body is not currently supported by mainstream science. The tales found in popular and Spiritualistic literature lack corroboration and documentation. Some considerable studies of these phenomena are reported in parapsychological literature, and may be found in the works of H. Hart, R. Crookall, S. Smith, R. Monroe, C.E. Green and C. McCreery, and of a team of researchers headed by R.L. Morriss. Some of the cases reported in these studies have been published by the Society for Psychical Research.

Among the most interesting phenomena are those collected by Celia Green, in particular the case of a person who was sitting peacefully on a double-decker bus and found himself looking at himself from the stairs of the bus. All of his senses seemed to be on the stairs, whereas only his physical body remained at the seat. Green distinguishes between parasomatic experiences, in which the subject finds himself in an alternative body that resembles his physical one, and asomatic experiences, in which the subject is not associated with any spatial entity at all. In his highly popular book *Journeys Out of the Body*, Robert Monroe gives instructions on how to produce one's own OBEs. He also discusses the history of his OBEs, which began with intentional repeated inhalations of the fumes of contact cement and Trilene, and continued through self-hypnosis.

An experiment performed by Professor Charles Tart with a subject who had a reportedly high ability for OBEs was considered very promising. The subject, presumably informed by out-of-body vision, reported correctly a five-digit number thought to be hidden from her view. However, the experiment was not conclusive because Tart discovered that there were other ways in which the subject might have determined the number.

The near death experience, sometimes also called the "pseudo-death" experience, refers to the OBE experiences of individuals who have suffered apparent death and have been restored to life. The systematic scientific study of near-death experiences is recent, though accounts can be found in literature and historical documents dating back hundreds of years, such as those of ancient philosophers, like Plato, and of modern writers, like Melville and Tolstoy.

A small number of cases were collected by interested investigators beginning in the late nineteenth century, especially by the pioneers of psychical research, such as Edmund Gurney, Sir William Barrett and James H. Hyslop, who also studied the deathbed visions that constitute a common element of NDEs. However, it was only after the advent of medical techniques of resuscitation, like modern cardiopulmonary resuscitation measures, that near death experiences became a widespread phenomenon.

The main impetus for modern studies on NDEs was the work of Raymond A. Moody. During his training as a doctor, Moody found that there were many patients who claimed to have had near-death experiences. Without attempting to be particularly systematic, he put together the stories of about fifty cases in the book *Life After Life* (1975), which became a best-seller in the United States and throughout the world. This successful book was followed by *Reflections on Life After Life* (1977).

He gathered the reports of people who were resuscitated after having been pronounced clinically dead, people who came very close to death because of accidents or severe injury, and persons who, as they died, told their experiences to other people who were present. Moody found great similarities among the reports of near-death experiences, and was able to identify many recurrent motifs, such as a feeling of ineffability, hearing the news of one's own death, feelings of floating out of the body, seeing the resuscitation team working, feelings of peace, hearing ringing noises, entering a dark tunnel, and encountering other spirits, including a being of light who helps one evaluate one's life.

His findings, which were dependent on the memories of people who came to him with their reports, were very similar to the findings of other researchers, such as Elisabeth Kubler-Ross, and appeared to offer evidence of life after death. Moody himself has indicated some plausible, alternative explanations of the recurrent elements of the near-death experience, referring, for instance, to the results of isolation studies, to hallucinations produced by drugs, and cerebral anoxia. He was, however, not satisfied with those explanations, and has asserted that the key elements were the uniformity of the descriptions, and the reported vividness of near-death experiences.

Moody has left many issues unexplained, including the relationship between the core experience and the condition that brings it about, and the role of an individual's religious belief system in shaping the near-death experience. Nevertheless, he stimulated a number of scientific studies by other clinical, psychological and parapsychological researchers, for whom near-death experiences became a major subject.

Moody outlined nine elements that seemed to occur generally but not universally in the NDE experiencers:

1. Hearing a buzzing or ringing noise, while having a sense of being dead. At this initial stage of the NDE, the experiencers are confused and try, unsuccessfully, to communicate with other people at the scene of their death.

2. Peace and painlessness. While people are dying they may be in intense pain, but, as soon as they leave the body, the pain vanishes and they experience peace.

3. Out-of-body experience. NDEers often have the experience of rising up and floating above their own body surrounded by a medical team, and watching it down below, while feeling very detached and comfortable. They experience the feeling of being in a spiritual body that looks like a sort of living energy field.

4. The tunnel experience. The NDEers then experience being drawn into darkness through a tunnel, at an extremely high speed, or going up a stairway (or some other symbol of crossing a threshold) until they achieve a realm of radiant golden-white light.

5. Rising rapidly into the heavens. Instead of a tunnel, some NDEers report an experience of rising suddenly into the heavens, and seeing the earth and the celestial sphere as if they were astronauts in space.

6. People of light. Once on the other side of the tunnel, or after they have risen into the heavens, NDEers meet people who glow with an inner light. Often they find that friends and relatives who have already died are there to greet them.

7. The Being of light. After connecting with these beings, NDEers meet a powerful, spiritual Being who some have called an angel, God, or Jesus. Also, although NDEers sometimes report feeling scared, none feels that they either were on the way to hell or that they fell into it.

8. The life review. This higher Being presents NDEers with a panoramic review of everything they have done. In particular, they experience the effects of every act they have ever done to other people, and come away feeling that love is the most important thing in life.

9. Reluctance to return. The higher Being sometimes says that the NDEer must return to life. In other experiences, the NDEer is given a choice of staying or returning. In either case, NDEers experience a reluctance to return. The people who choose to return do so only because of loved ones they do not wish to leave behind.

Moody's work was anecdotal and he was careful to point out that it should not be regarded as a scientific study, since the case history material presented was highly selective and the data were not subjected to statistical analysis. The first book to report an investigation of NDEs from a systematic scientific point of view was published in 1980 by psychologist Kenneth Ring. His *Life at Death* was based on interviews with 102 near-death survivors. The statistical analysis of the data presented was supplemented by extensive qualitative materials, in order to evaluate Moody's prior findings. Ring was concerned with comparing NDEs of illness victims, accident victims, and people who had attempted suicide. His book showed that NDEs were largely invariant over different conditions of near-death onset and that they had a high incidence of occurrence in all categories studied.

One of the results of the increasing interest in near-death studies was the establishment of the International Association for Near-Death Studies in 1981. Early in the following year two major scientific studies on NDEs were published. Cardiologist Michael B. Sabom's *Recollections of Death* reported the results of interviews with 116 near-death survivors. George Gallup's *Adventures in Immortality* reported the results of a national survey, in which the incidence of NDEs was documented in about five percent of the adult population, or eight million Americans.

NDEs have frequently been regarded as evidence for immortality of the soul or, at the least, for life after death. Such experiences can be seen as a powerful proof of the belief in a soul as a separate entity from the body in which it lives and develops throughout life, but which survives the death of the physical body.

However, a number of skeptics have been quick to dismiss NDE research as subjective and as inadequate proof of life after death, and the significance of the near death experience has been hotly debated. It has been argued that it is not reasonable to consider NDEs as survival evidence unless other naturalistic causes for these experiences can be excluded. It is possible that all NDEs can be explained by naturalistic causes, such as psychological, physiological, neurological or pharmacological causes. Religious beliefs, wishful thinking, or medications such as morphine may facilitate the experience. Also, disturbance of brain functions and cerebral anoxia are known causes of hallucinations, and these may occur in nearly all dying patients.

In response to critics who have considered NDEs mere hallucinations, supporters of the out-of-body thesis have pointed out that NDEs have regularly been experienced while NDEers were registering flat EEGs (electroenephalograms), meaning that all brain activity had stopped. Supporters of the out-of-body thesis argue that, because even hallucinations produce brain wave activity, NDEers must be out-of-the-body at the time of their near death experience.

Other critics have asserted that the tunnel experience is a memory of our experiences traveling down the birth canal and being drawn into the bright light of the delivery room. During the stress connected with being near death we regress to these memories, which are given a religious interpretation in order to escape the fear associated with death. Such explanations are convincing to those intent dismissing the "metaphysical" implications of NDEs, and unconvincing to those who view NDEs as "proof" of life after death. This mixed evaluation can be generalized to cover the entire NDE phenomenon–convincing to those who are already inclined to accept a spiritual dimension as real, and unconvincing to those who are predisposed to reject spiritual explanations.

Whatever the metaphysical status of NDEs, studies have unequivocally shown that NDEs have substantial social, moral, cultural and even political implications. Most of the research that has dealt with near-death experiences has suggested that profound transformations occur in the patients, particularly with regard to the loss of the fear of death. In Kenneth Ring's investigation, for instance, considerable evidence was given to support the thesis that surviving a near-death episode does indeed lead to profound personal changes. Usually these changes are mediated by the individual's interpretation of the near-death experience, which often acquires definite spiritual or religious overtones, and is interpreted as a proof of the existence of joyous and pain-free life after death.

A person who has survived a death experience has been given a second chance to live, and his or her life represents a continuing testimony to the profundity of that event. Although the existing literature contains relatively little research on such transformations, it has been observed that substantial value transformations usually occur, especially if a life-review was experienced as part of the NDE. NDEers generally live life more fully and love more openly; they de-emphasize the values related to conventional definitions of success such as money and outer accomplishment, whereas values such as kindness, compassion, and unconditional love for others are stressed.

Another important transformation is represented by a greater willingness to accept others by removing social boundaries and recognizing the equality of all people, and by having a less judgmental approach to others. Closely related to concern for others are what are usually considered the three major changes associated to near-death experiences:

1. The increase in conviction of belief in life after death.
2. The loss of fear of death.
3. The increase in religiousness.

Other effects include the increased feelings of self-worth, the decreased need to impress others, and an awakening or enhancement of psychic sensitivities. NDEs provide the basis for a significant development of moral consciousness, and their long-term effects often prove to be very salutary. The transformative impact of the near-death experience may explain traditional initiatory rites that sometimes seem to actually bring the initiate to the point of death. Given the profundity of near-death experiences and the social implications of such experiences, awareness of NDEs may actually have been a factor in the institution of such "death/rebirth" rites.

Channeling

In addition to contemporary interest in NDEs, the current period is characterized by the popularity of new forms of mediumship under the label "channeling": The term channeling was popularized in UFO circles as the name for psychic communications from "space brothers," and was only later applied to New Age mediums. While some channels retain full consciousness during their transmissions, most of the prominent New Age channels are what traditional Spiritualists would refer to as trance mediums–mediums who lose consciousness while a disembodied spirit takes over the channel's body and communicates through it. These spirits frequently claim to be spiritually advanced souls whose communications convey metaphysical teachings. The teaching function of this communication contrasts with traditional, nineteenth century mediums who were more concerned with transmitting messages from departed relatives and with demonstrating the reality of life after death.

As vehicles for communications from the other world, channels are merely the most recent manifestations of a phenomenon that can be traced back at least as far as archaic shamanism. Ancient shamans mediated the relationship between their communities and the other world, often transmitting messages from the deceased. Modern channels also sometimes view themselves as being in the tradition of ancient prophets, transmitting messages from more elevated sources. Unlike the prophets, however, New Age channels rarely claim to be delivering messages directly from God, nor do they usually rail against the sins of society as did the Hebrew prophets. Most often their communications consist of some form of New Age philosophy, which they explain to their listeners. With respect to this teaching function, contemporary channels can be placed in the tradition of Western theosophy.

Although neither movement would claim them, New Age channels can be understood as representing a blend of Spiritualism and theosophy.

Important precursors to modern channeling were Edgar Cayce, Janes Roberts, and Ruth Montgomery. Cayce was a trance medium (although he identified no spirit guide) who passed away in 1945 but–through the promotional activities of his son–achieved the peak of his fame in the 1960s. He began his psychic career giving health readings, and only later began "channeling" information about past lifetimes. Upon occasion, he would relay messages from departed relatives. In the early 1970s, a series of books began appearing through the author Jane Roberts whom Roberts claimed contained information from Seth, a discarnate spirit entity. A number of the Seth books, which contained metaphysical information related to New Age philosophy, became best-sellers. Ruth Montgomery was a newspaper reporter who became a popular New Age author after she became interested in psychic phenomena. In her writings, Montgomery described her meetings with the Guides (spirits from the other world) who communicated with her via automatic writing (or, in Montgomery's case, through what might be called "automatic typing") Her contact with the Guides was focused on the reception of information about the other realm, reincarnation, and a variety of occult topics which appeared in a series of popular books.

At the time the New Age became a popular topic in 1987, the most publicized channel was J.Z. Knight. She made frequent media appearances, even channeling for TV audiences, before the general public's interest waned. Knight channeled an entity named Ramtha, who claimed to be the spirit of an ancient Atlantean warlord. When channeling Ramtha, Knight appeared to take on a more masculine demeanor, and spoke in an indecipherable accent that many less famous channels imitated. Ramtha taught a variation on New Age philosophy build around standard metaphysical teachings. Channeling began a gradual but steady decline in popularity following the media blitz of the late eighties.

The entities speaking through channels have sometimes described themselves in standard Spiritualist terminology as "spirit guides," while others, relying on theosophical language, have claimed to be "ascended masters." Some claim to be a spirits of a wide variety of historical personalities, nature spirits, angels, gods, goddesses, extraterrestrials, or even the spirits of discarnate animals. Yet others tune into higher levels of their own consciousness (e.g., their "higher self"), or into the cosmic library, sometimes referred to as the Akashic Records.

A number of popular New Age books have been produced by automatic writing. Other than Montgomery's books, the most well-known channeled book is probably *A Course in Miracles*, which claims to be the New Age teachings of the historical Jesus. Some channelers are primarily psychics who give private readings to individual clients. Others conduct workshops and lectures for large groups, and have become quite well-known in new age circles–e.g., Jach Pursel (Lazaris) and Penny Torres (Mafu).

Large numbers of people have learned to channel, and there are many publications, tapes, and videos available that contain channeled material. Despite the number of people involved in this phenomenon, the range of ideas presented by channels is rather limited. For critics, this is a sign that the teachings are derivative, being picked up–consciously or unconsciously–by the channel from the ideas present in the surrounding New Age subculture. For believers, the convergence of viewpoint of diverse channels indicates that they are all drawing upon the same universal truths.

Because so many of the entities that speak through the channels identify themselves as the souls of departed persons, channeling is difficult to accept for those who do not believe in life after death. However, unlike Spiritualist mediums, their nineteenth century counterparts, the great majority of New Age channels are disinterested in proving to the skeptics that consciousness survives the transition we call death. The existence of an afterlife is simply assumed. In the late twentieth century, the debate over the reality of life after death has shifted from the investigation of mediumship and channeling to the investigation of near death experiences.

Past Lives

The assumption of the doctrine of reincarnation in New Age circles has led, among other things, to the emergence of so-called past-life therapy. One source of this new subdiscipline was the work of Edgar Cayce. In response to a health crisis, according to some accounts, an acquaintance hypnotized Cayce (in other accounts, the trance was self-induced). During the trance, Cayce diagnosed his own health problem and prescribed a cure. Soon after this experience, he began to perform the same trance prescriptions for others, and his reputation gradually grew.

A turning point in his readings began in 1923 when Cayce met Arthur Lammers, a wealthy printer and student of theosophy and Eastern religions. Cayce traveled to Dayton, Ohio, to conduct a series of private readings. One of Lammers' central articles of faith was belief in reincarnation, and Cayce mentioned Lammers' past lives in one of the private readings. Cayce subsequently began to explore the past lives of his other clients, including past lives in such exotic lands as Atlantis. He soon added past-life readings to his health readings. Cayce gave readings for the rest of his life, until shortly before his death.

Because stenographic records of readings were kept for most of his life, a tremendous body of material was accumulated, and formed the basis for later books. More than any other single factor, the promotion of the Cayce material popularized the notion of "past-life" readings to the general public. Cayce books also feed the widespread interest about—and helped to spread belief in—reincarnation. Another source for the contemporary practice of past-life therapy was the Dianetics movement.

Dianetics is a form of popular psychotherapy–synthesis of modern psychology and Oriental philosophy–devised and propagated by L. Ron Hubbard, popular fiction writer and founder of the Church of Scientology. In 1948 Hubbard circulated a document entitled *Dianetics: The Original Thesis*, the first statement of a theory that would make him famous as well as controversial. In 1950 he published his most famous book, *Dianetics: The Modern Science of Mental Health*. This work became an instant bestseller, generating numerous articles and discussion groups. It was somewhat of a fad, becoming particularly popular on college campuses and within the movie industry. A brief account of Dianetics therapy can be found near the beginning of Aldous Huxley's novel *Island*, when a young resident of the island helps the protagonist come to grips with a traumatic encounter with snakes.

The basic concept in *Dianetics* is that the mind has two very distinct parts. Hubbard called the conscious part the "analytical mind." The second, termed the "reactive mind," comes into play when the individual is "unconscious"–in full or in part. "Unconsciousness" could be caused by the shock of an accident, the anesthetic used for an operation, the pain of an injury or the deliriums of illness. According to Hubbard, the reactive mind stores particular types of mental image pictures he called "engrams." Engrams are a complete recording of every perception present in a moment of partial or full "unconsciousness." This part of the mind can cause unevaluated, unknowing and unwanted fears, emotions, pains and psychosomatic illnesses. The goal of "auditing"–the therapeutic application of Dianetics and Scientology processes and procedures–is to rid oneself of the power of the reactive mind.

Hubbard taught that some engrams are recorded before the individual is born and even during conception. Dianetics theory eventually expanded to include the notion of engrams carrying information from past lifetimes. As Hubbard developed his work, he added "exteriorization" (a notion similar to out-of-body experiences) and reincarnation memories to his ideas. The expanded system he termed Scientology. The practice of past-life therapy, as performed by contemporary psychologists and psychiatrists, is clearly reminiscent of Hubbard's notion that the sources of some engrams can be found in previous existences.

Though current past-life therapists tend to deny the link because of Scientology's negative public image, Winafred Blake Lucas, in her definitive *Regression Therapy: A Handbook for Professionals*, acknowledges that Dianetics "has covertly impacted much of the past-life work we know today." (p. 5) While highly critical of Scientology, Lucas credits Dianetics with originating

> ...the proposal, startling at the time, that past lives existed and could be contacted by traveling backwards on an emotional-physical bridge searching for an engram (an original traumatic situation still influencing behavior). The past lives recovered by this technique that L. Ron Hubbard reported in *Have You Lived Before this Life?* (1958) were in part similar to those found in contemporary regressions....(p. 6)

She further notes that even Dianetics' regression technique, namely "flowing backward on a feeling or physical sensing," (p. 6) is utilized by many current practitioners.

Past-life therapy consists of treating patients affected by various emotional and physical symptoms by guiding them through memories about their previous lives. The most common symptoms treated through past-life therapy include phobias, anxieties, fears, panic attacks, as well as obesity, insomnia, acrophobia, allergies, and the like. Past-life therapists assert that most of these symptoms are carry overs from other lifetimes, and that even certain physical disorders represent the manifestations of wounds or other accidents from previous lifetimes.

Past-life therapy differs from conventional therapies in that it is typically conducted in an altered state of consciousness, that is, a state of mind resulting from process of restricting and intensifying the focus of attention through particular techniques of induction. Among the most common techniques are hypnosis, relaxation, breathing exercises and visualizations. Visualizations usually suggest the transition from one level or state of consciousness to another state where the earlier experience can be contacted. The transition is visualized by imagining a stairway, an elevator, a tunnel, or some other passageway that finally leads to a past lifetime, or to a prenatal or birth state

The retrieval of memories of past-lives involves a three-step process: (1) the identification of a figure perceived as a personal projection or subpersonality; (2) disidentification, through which one realizes one's true nature as being distinct from that of the perceived figure; and (3) transformation, by which the individual begins to change attitudes and perceptions regarding past traumas and events, psychological patterns, particular individuals.

It has been argued that simply living out a regression with its physical and emotional aspects leads to remission of the troubling symptom. The remission of symptoms by such processes as cathartic abreaction of a related traumatic situation represented the principal focus of past-life therapy through the 1970's. This focus was continued through the 1980's, though increasing emphasis was placed on the concept of the soul's journey and on the meaning of life.

Part of the basis of past-life therapy can be found in Sigmund Freud's idea that what individuals experienced earlier determines their current behavior, and that making the unconscious conscious would induce healing. Carl Jung's use of active imagination, on the other hand, influenced the emergence of imagery techniques in the 1970's, which were considered particularly useful for reporting past-life memories.

There were few reports of people remembering their own past lives except under hypnosis prior to the 1960's, and it was not until the 1970's that the concepts of prenatal memories and past-life recall were seriously explored. However, some authors, such as Stanislav Grof, found that deep breathing and imaging could facilitate the recall of birth memories. Paul Brunton, in his *Hermit in the Himalayas* (1927), had explored the techniques used by the yogis to access past lives.

During the 1960's, the improvement of hypnotic techniques and applications led to attempts to retrieve past lives, as suggested by the famous Bridey Murphey case, and by the early 1970's the use of age regression–that is, the process of moving chronologically backwards under hypnosis to access early childhood memories–became generally acceptable. Past-life therapy began to gain approval when the British psychiatrist Denys Kelsey postulated the existence of an element in human beings that is capable of recording events even in the absence of a physical body. This hypothesis was strengthened by the reports of Joan Grant, who recorded her own past-life memories in the book *Far Memory and Pharaoh*. Kelsey and Grant's joint book *Many Lifetimes* (1967) represents one of the first accounts of responsible regression therapy.

Many experiments in the retrieval of past-life memories were conducted during the 1970's, such as those reported in G.M. Glaskin's *Windows of the Mind* (1974), and Marcia Moore's *Hypersentience* (1976). Especially important were four innovative books published in 1978, in which symptom remission was considered the principal goal of past-life therapy. The best known is Helen Wambach's *Reliving Past Lives*, in which the author summarized the results of various hypnosis workshops, during which participants were asked about their previous lives during one of ten specified past time periods. Data about artifacts, customs, and clothing of various time periods, as well as material on future lifetimes were gathered by the author.

Another popular book was Edith Fiore's *You Have Been Here Before*, an account of past life memories through the process of age regression. Morris Netherton's book *Past Lives Therapy* was released in the same year, as well as Thorwald Dethlefsen's *Voices from Other Lives*, which had a strong impact on European psychologists. In the next decade the emphasis shifted from symptoms to spiritual implications and the meaning of life. This shift was facilitated by the increasing interest in ancient Eastern philosophical theories, encouraged by authors such as Paul Brunton and L. Adams Beck.

New theorizing in modern physics and biology that referred to consciousness as a fundamental aspect of existence had a considerable impact on this emergent paradigm. Also important was the psychedelic experimentation of the 1960's, when the possibility of reaching other levels of consciousness through LSD therapy helped to open the way to the recall of past-life memories. Larry Dossey's *Recovery of the Soul* (1989), with the concept of nonlocal mind, Bernie Siegel's *Love, Medicine, and Miracles* (1988), and Deepak Chopra's *Quantum Healing* (1989) contributed to the revision of the medical model in the late 1980's, when modern medicine started to refer to the physical body as an energy field, and to healing as a transformation of energy. These changes helped to provide a theoretical grounding for therapy involving past-life memories, as Marilyn Ferguson's *The Aquarian Conspiracy* (1980) documents.

The Association for Past-Life Research and Therapy was established in 1980 for the purposes of organizing seminars and establishing criteria for the practice of past-life therapy. Its *Journal of Regression Therapy* was founded in 1986, in order to provide an opportunity to share therapeutic procedures, experiences, and research. Among the contributions to the field are Joel Whitton's *Life Between Life* (1986), and Brian Weiss's *Many Lives, Many Masters* (1989), both dealing with the experience between lives; Roger Woolger's *Other Lives, Other Selves* (1987); Raymond Moody's *Coming Back: A Psychiatrist Explores Past-Life Journeys* (1990); and Garret Oppenheim's *Who Were You Before You Were You?* (1990).

Soul Mates and Walk-ins

The interest in past lives within the New Age subculture has also given birth to some unique conceptions of the nature of spiritual reality, such as the idea of soul mates which is the notion that two individuals are "made for each other," and seek union with the other across the course of many lifetimes. The notion of a soul mate, of another person who is one's ideal partner and with whom one has a pre-existing spiritual bond, is a distinctly contemporary, Western notion, shaped by Western romanticism. The soul mate idea, in other words, is part of no traditional religion, but is a new idea that was birthed in the West's metaphysical-occult subculture. The soul mate idea became particularly popular in the Seventies and Eighties. Part of the notion is the idea that one usually seeks one's soul mate across many reincarnations. Beyond these basics, there are many variations in the soul mate idea.

Some conceptualizations of soul mates postulate that are that they are two halves of one soul who have been split apart to be able to speed up the process of spiritual evolution by taking in earth-plane experiences twice as fast. From this perspective, finding one's soul mate is quite literally finding one's other half. While in some ways a significantly different idea, a notion is advanced in the Platonic dialogue *Symposium* which resembles this particular theory of soul mates. In the distant past, humanity was composed of self-sufficient beings, who had two heads, four arms, and four legs.

Humanity, however, had the audacity to challenge the gods, and as punishment were severed in half. Henceforth, rather than seeking to overthrow the gods, humanity has been preoccupied with the pursuits of love and sex, which is based on the craving to reunite with one's other half. This story may have shaped the notion of soul mates.

Another, more modest theory is that a soul mate is not one's missing half, but, rather, someone whom one has been involved with for many different lifetimes, and for with whom one thus has an exceptionally strong link. These pairs of soul mates are reunited in lifetime after lifetime to continue their relationship and to help each other out. Over the course of many lifetimes, they sometimes exchange sex roles. (The possibility of a homosexual romance is rarely considered in existing literature on soul mates.) Yet another, less popular, conceptualization postulates that a wide variety of different people are our soul mates, with whom we are reunited in a wide diversity of roles, as lovers, spouses, siblings, parents/children, and so forth.

Some people have taken this notion quite seriously, devoting a good deal of time and effort to the task of finding their soul mate. Richard Bach, author of the popular book *Jonathan Livingston Seagull*, described his three-year search in *The Bridge Across Forever*. He found that his soul mate was actress Leslie Parrish. Others seek out astrologers, psychics, and past-life regressions in the quest for their perfect partner. There are even visualization and "dream programming" methods which supposedly allow one to find or to attract a soul mate.

A distinctly New Age notion related to the afterlife–or, at least, to relationships with discarnate entities–is the idea of walk-ins. A walk-in is an entity who occupies a body that has been vacated by its original soul. The situation is somewhat similar to possession, although in possession the original soul is merely overshadowed–rather than completely supplanted–by the possessing entity. The walk-in concept seems to be related to certain traditional Indian tales about aging yoga masters taking over the bodies of young people who died prematurely.

Another possible source for the contemporary walk-in notion is the well-known (in theosophical circles) teaching that Jesus and Christ were separate souls. According to this teaching, Jesus prepared his physical body to receive Christ and, at a certain point in his career, vacated his body so as to allow Christ to take it over and preach to the world. An underlying notion here is that Christ was such a highly evolved soul that it would have been difficult if not impossible for him to have incarnated as a baby, and that even if he could have done so, it would have been a waste of precious time for such a highly developed soul to have to go through childhood.

The contemporary notion of walk-ins was popularized by Ruth Montgomery, who developed the notion in her 1979 book, *Strangers Among Us*. In 1983 Montgomery published another book, *Threshold to Tomorrow*, containing case histories of seventeen walk-ins. According to Montgomery, history is full of walk-ins, including such famous historical figures as Moses, Jesus, Muhammad, Christopher Columbus, Abraham Lincoln, Mary Baker Eddy, Gandhi, George Washington, Benjamin Franklin, Thomas Jefferson, Alexander Hamilton, and James Madison. In fact, it seems that almost everyone manifesting exceptional creativity and leadership would be identified by Montgomery as a walk-in. In her words, "Some of the world's greatest spiritual and political leaders, scientists, and philosophers in ages past are said to have been Walk-ins." (p. 12)

In a later book, *Aliens Among Us* (1985), Montgomery developed the notion of extra-terrestrial walk-ins: The idea that souls from other planets have come to earth to take over the bodies of human beings. These ideas became extremely popular in New Age circles, and for a while it seemed that almost every hard core New Ager was claiming to be some kind of walk-in. Some New Age magazines even carried articles that asked the question, "Are you a Walk-in?" Such articles utterly trivialized the notion by presenting criteria for determining whether or not one had "walked-in"– criteria that were often so general that almost anyone could imagine her or himself to be an exotic walk-in.

According to Montgomery, walk-ins are frequently people who have gone through an exceptionally traumatic–most often a life-threatening–experience, after which they feel they are different individuals. Sometimes this event is an actual death/revival (near death) experience. At other times it is an emotional trauma that leads one to question the value of living itself (a condition that enables the disembodied entity to convince the original soul to abandon its body). In most cases, the walk-in inherits the memory patterns of the former inhabitant of its new body.

The prominent near-death researcher Kenneth Ring has compared the walk-in experience with the near-death experience, noting that parallel transformations occur in individual's lives after both such experiences. The walk-in notion has been enthusiastically accepted by some, and severely criticized by others. In any event, the walk-in idea represents yet another contemporary effort to apprehend the reality of the Other Side. Thus, far from being "deceased," the afterlife continues to inspire creative reflection in the New Age subculture, and will undoubtedly continue to do so.

Sources:

Alcock, James E. *Parapsychology. Science or Magic? A Psychological Perspective.* Oxford, England: Pergamon Press, 1981.

Almeder, Robert. *Beyond Death. Evidence for Life After Death.* Springfield, IL: Charles C Thomas, 1987.

Barrett, H. D. *Life Work of Cora L. V. Richmond.* Chicago: Hack & Anderson, 1895.

Berger, Arthur S., and Berger, Joice. *The Encyclopedia of Parapsychology and Psychical Research.* New York: Paragon House, 1991.

Bletzer, June. *The Donning International Encyclopedic Psychic Dictionary.* Norfolk, VA: Donning, 1986.

Brandon, Ruth. *The Spiritualists,* New York: Alfred A. Knopf Inc., 1983.

Brown, Slater, *The Heyday of Spiritualism.* New York: Hawthorn Books, 1970.

Burkhardt, Frederic, and Fredson Bowers, eds. *The Works of William James: Essays in Psychical Research.* Cambridge Mass.: Harvard University Press, 1986.

Cavendish, Richard, ed. *Encyclopedia of the Unexplained. Magic, Occultism and Parapsychology.* London: Arkana Penguin Books, 1989.

Cayce, Edgar. *What I Believe.* Virginia Beach, VA: Edgar Cayce Publishing Company, 1946.

Cayce, Hugh Lynn. *Venture Inward.* New York: Harper & Row, 1964. Reprint. New York: Paperback Library, 1966.

Chaney, Rev. Robert G. *Mediums and the Development of Mediumship.* Freeport, N.Y.: Books for Libraries Press, 1972.

Grattan-Guinness, Ivor. *Psychical Research: A Guide to Its History, Principles and Practices.* Wellingborough, Northamptonshire, England: The Aquarian Press, 1982.

Darnton, Robert. *Mesmerism and the End of the Enlightenment in France.* NY: Schocken Books, 1970.

Douglas, Alfred. *Extrasensory Powers: A Century of Psychical Research.* London: Victor Gollancz Ltd., 1976.

Doyle, Sir Arthur Conan. *The Coming of the Fairies.* London: Hodder & Stoughton, 1922.

_____. *The Edge of the Unknown.* New York: Berkley Medallion Books, 1968. First published by G. P. Putnam's Sons, 1930.

_____. *The History of Spiritualism.* New York: Arno Press, 1975.

Estep, Sarah. *Voices of Eternity.* New York: Fawcett Gold Medal, 1988.

Fodor, Nandor. *An Encyclopaedia of Psychic Science.* Secaucus, N.J.: The Citadel Press, 1966. First published 1933.

Gallup, George. *Adventures in Immortality.* New York: MacGraw-Hill, 1982.

Gauld, Alan. *The Founders of Psychical Research.* London: Routledge & Kegan Paul, 1968.

Green, Celia, and Charles McCreery. *Apparitions.* London: Hamish Hamilton, 1975.

Greyson, Bruce, and Flynn, Charles P., eds. *The Near-Death Experience. Problems, Prospects, Perspectives.* Springfield, Illinois: Charles C Thomas, 1984.

Guiley, Rosemary Ellen. *The Encyclopedia of Ghosts and Spirits.* New York: Facts on File, 1992.

_____. *Harper's Encyclopedia of Mystical & Paranormal Experience.* San Francisco: Harper Collins, 1991.

Gurney, Edmund, F. W. H. Myers, and Frank Podmore. *Phantasms of the Living.* 1886. London: Kegan Paul, Trench, Trubner & Co., Ltd., 1918.

Harlow, Ralph, S. *A Life after Death.* Garden City, NY: Doubleday, 1961.

Haynes, Renee. *The Society for Psychical Research, 1882-1892: A History.* London: Heinemann, 1982.

Head, Joseph, and S. L. Cranston. *Reincarnation: The Phoenix Fire Mystery.* New York: Julian Press/Crown, 1977.

Hubbard, L. Ron. *Dianetics: The Modern Science of Mental Health.* NY: Hermitage House, 1950.

_____. *Have You Lived Before This Life?* Los Angeles, CA: Church of Scientology of California, 1977.

James, William. *The Will to Believe and Other Essays in Popular Philosophy* and *Human Immortality.* 1897 & 1898; NY: Dover, 1956.

The Journal of Regression Therapy. Riverside, CA: APRT, 1986-present.

Klimo, Jon. *Channeling.* Los Angeles: Jeremy P. Tarcher, Inc., 1987.

Kubler-Ross, Elisabeth. *Questions and Answers on Death and Dying.* New York: Macmillan, 1974.

_____. *Living with Death and Dying.* New York: Macmillan, 1981.

Lucas, Winafred Blake. *Regression Therapy: A Handbook for Professionals, Vol. I.* Crest Park, CA: Deep Forest Press, 1993.

McAdams, Elizabeth, and Raymond Bayless. *The Case for Life after Death.* Chicago: Nelson-Hall, 1981.

Melton, J. Gordon. *The Encyclopedia of American Religions.* 4th ed. Detroit: Gale Research, 1993.

Mitchell, Edgar D. *Psychic Exploration. A Challenge for Science.* New York: G.P. Putnam's Sons, 1974.

Montgomery, Ruth. *Aliens Among Us.* New York: Putnam's, 1985.

_____. *Companions Along the Way.* New York: Coward, McCann & Geoghegan Inc., 1974.

_____. *Strangers Among Us: Enlightened Beings from a World to Come.* New York: Coward, McCann & Geoghegan, 1979.

_____. *Threshold to Tomorrow.* New York: G. P. Putnam's Sons, 1983.

Moody, Raymond A. *Life After Life.* New York: Bantam, 1976.

_____. *The Light Beyond.* New York: Bantam, 1989.

Moore, Brooke Noel. *The Philosophical Possibilities Beyond Death.* Springfield, Ill.: Charles C Thomas Publisher, 1981.

Muhl, Anita. *Automatic Writing.* New York: Helix Press, 1963.

Murphy, Gardner, and Robert O. Ballou, eds. *William James on Psychical Research.* New York: Viking Press, 1960.

Myers, Frederic W. H. *Human Personality and Its Survival of Bodily Death.* Vols. 1 and 2. 1903. New ed. New York: Longmans, Green & Co., 1954.

National Spiritualist Association. *One Hundredth Anniversary of Modern American Spiritualism.* Chicago: National Spiritualist Association of Churches, 1948.

Oppenheim, Janet. *The Other World: Spiritualism and Psychical Research in England, 1850-1914.* Cambridge: Cambridge University Press, 1985.

Ostrander, Sheila, and Lynn Schroeder. *Handbook of Psi Discoveries.* New York: Berkley, 1974.

Parrish-Harra, Carol W. *The New Age Handbook on Death and Dying.* Santa Monica: IBS Press, 1989.

_____. *Messengers of Hope.* Marina Del Ray, CA: DeVorss & Co., 1983.

Pratt, J. Gaither. *ESP Research Today: A Study of Developments in Parapsychology Since 1960.* Metuchen, N.J.: The Scarecrow Press, 1973.

Raudive, Konstantin. *Breakthrough: An Amazing Experiment in Electronic Communication with the Dead.* New York: Taplinger, 1971.

Ring, Kenneth. *Heading Toward Omega.* New York: William Morrow and Company, 1984.

_____. *Life at Death. A Scientific Investigation of the Near-Death Experience.* NY: Quill, 1982.

Roberts, Jane. *The Seth Material.* Englewood Cliffs, NJ: Prentice Hall, 1970.

Rogo, D. Scott, and Raymond Bayless. *Phone Calls from the Dead.* Englewood Cliffs, NJ: Prentice-Hall, 1979.

Ryerson, Kevin, and Stephanie Harolde. *Spirit Communication: The Soul's Path.* New York: Bantam Books, 1989.

Shepard, Leslie A., ed. *Encyclopedia of Occultism & Parapsychology.* Detroit: Gale Research Inc., 1991.

Sugrue, Thomas. *There is a River.* New York: Henry Holt & Co., 1945.

Swedenborg, Emanuel. *Divine Providence.* New York: The Swedenborg Foundation, 1972. First published 1764.

_____. *Divine Love and Wisdom.* New York: American Swedenborg Printing and Publishing Society, 1904. First published 1763.

Tyrrell, G. N. M. *Apparitions.* 1943. Rev. 1953. London: The Society for Psychical Research, 1973.

Vasiliev, Leonid L. *Mysterious Phenomena of the Human Psyche.* New York: University Books, 1965.

Ward, Gary L., ed. *Spiritualism I: Spiritualist Thought.* New York: Garland Publishing Co., 1990.

Wilson, Colin. *Afterlife.* London: Harrap, 1985.

Wilson, Ian. *The After Death Experience. The Physics of the Non-Physical.* New York: William Morrow & Co., 1987.